'The mark of a great book is that it produces both a sense of discovery and a guide towards specific challenges and actions. *The Seven Cultures of Capitalism* is rich in both.'

> Leslie Dighton
> Managing Director and Founding Partner, Corporate Renewal Associates Ltd

'Appreciation of the diversity of national opportunities expands the global economic pie.'

> Robert W. Galvin
> Chairman of the Executive Committee, Motorola Inc

'An individual's value judgement is based on and embedded in a set of basic assumptions which he or she has inherited through a cultural process. Value/price and value/cost relationships are resultant therefore not only from the 'market process', but also culturally determined. This cultural dimension has been admirably researched and put in a framework by Trompenaars and Hampden-Turner in their book *The Seven Cultures of Capitalism*. The book is a joy to read and should be on the bookshelf of any manager engaged in global business activities.'

> J. P. Leemhuis
> Shell Internationale Petroleum Strategy Manager, Far East and Australasia MFRC

'An invaluable book which should be read by politicians as well as businesspeople who want to understand the new world economy.'

> Patricia Hewitt
> Deputy Director, Institute for Public Policy Research

'Path-breaking. Iconoclastic. Courageous. This book will light fires under your imagination.'

> Robert B. Textor
> Professor of Anthropology, Emeritus, Stanford University

'The different "cultures of capitalism" have coexisted for a long time, but until the fall of the iron curtain they were the "ships that pass in the night" unified under the threat of their common enemy. This time is over. The immense merit of Charles Hampden-Turner's book is to shed light – in the form of original statistics, of in-depth analysis as well as of insights, symbols and concepts – on the Seven "Knowledge Carriers" now searching for new beacons on the global sea ...'

> Albert Bressand
> Managing Director, Promethee, Paris

THE SEVEN
CULTURES
—OF—
CAPITALISM

THE SEVEN CULTURES

OF

CAPITALISM

VALUE SYSTEMS FOR CREATING WEALTH IN THE UNITED

STATES, BRITAIN, JAPAN, GERMANY, FRANCE, SWEDEN,

AND THE NETHERLANDS

CHARLES HAMPDEN-TURNER
and FONS TROMPENAARS

PIATKUS

ACKNOWLEDGMENTS

"When You're Racing With the Clock" is from *The Pajama Game*, music and lyrics by Richard Adler and Jerry Ross.

Kagemusha is a film by Akira Kurosawa.

"You'll Never Walk Alone" is from *Carousel*, music by Richard Rogers; lyrics by Oscar Hammerstein II.

The dialogue is from *My Fair Lady*, music by Frederick Loewe, lyrics by Alan Jay Lerner.

"Do You Hear the People Sing?" is from *Les Miserables*, music by Claude-Michel Schonberg, English lyrics by Herbert Kretzmer.

Cartoons by Shotaro Ishinomori, from *Japan Inc: Introduction to Japanese Economics* and used by permission of the University of California Press.

First published in 1993 by Doubleday, New York

This edition published in 1994 by
Judy Piatkus (Publishers) Ltd
5 Windmill Street, London W1P 1HF

First paperback edition 1995

**The moral right of the authors
has been asserted**

*A catalogue record for this book is available
from the British Library*

ISBN 0 7499 1330 4 hbk
ISBN 0 7499 1386 X pbk

Printed and bound in Great Britain by
Bookcraft Ltd, Midsomer Norton, Avon

Contents

Contents

Acknowledgments

IT TOOK SO MUCH LONGER than intended to write this book that those who helped us on the way are almost too numerous to remember. Napier Collyns of the Global Business Network took up the cause of this book early on and helped us to find a publisher. Harriet Rubin of Doubleday must have been prescient to have seen some merit in our early drafts. Since then Janet Coleman has struggled through many revisions. In the meantime Joe Spieler, our agent, has been very, very patient.

Several persons read one or several chapters and encouraged and/or warned us. André Laurent and Susan Schneider of INSEAD, Ronnie Lessem of City University, Martin Gillo of Advanced Micro Devices in Geneva, Doug Ure and Linda Bramble of the Niagara Institute, Philippe Alloing then of B.P. Nutrition, Oscar van Weerdenburg and Eveline Vermeulen of CIBS, Magorah Maruyama of Aoyama Gakuin University, Steve Barnett, then with Nissan North America, Göran Carstedt of IKEA North America, Bill Clover of Amoco Corporation, Keisuke Yoshitomi of the Fuji Bank, Kevan Hall of Information Services International, and Fritz Haselhoff of Groningen University. We were also helped and sustained by Michael Alexander of the International Executive Forum at the Wharton School, by Gunnar Hedlund of the Stockholm School of Economics, and Solveig Wickstom of FA Radet in Stockholm. Support has also come from Anders Hovemyr of SAS, Harry Kiwitz of Suiker Unie, Peter Lorange of the Norwegian School of Management, Peter Senge of the Systems Dynamics Group at MIT, and from Max Boisot, here at the Judge Institute. Dan Simpson of the Clorox company was an early supporter, while Ronny Vansteenkiste of the Management Centre in Brussels helped expose us to key audiences.

Rosemarie Epaminondas did wonders at the word processor and informed us about Germany. The MSS was finished thanks to her partner Maria Empira. Finally, thanks should go to the MBA students of Erasmus University upon whom much that is written here was rehearsed.

FONS TROMPENAARS
Intercultural Management
   Publishers,
Laan van Kronenburg 14,
1183 AS Amstelveen,
The Netherlands.
Tel. 010 31 20 6403 311

CHARLES HAMPDEN-TURNER
Cambridge University
Judge Institute of Management
   Studies
32 Trumpington Street
Cambridge CB2 1QY
Tel. 0223 337052

A Note on Methodology

THIS BOOK is in large part based on a questionnaire administered to 15,000 managers from around the world by the Centre for International Business Studies in Amstelveen, The Netherlands.

Managers surveyed were those who presented themselves to over 500 seminars from 1986 to 1993, conducted by CIBS and its affiliates. Most were from the "upper-middle" ranks of management who had some international responsibilities and were chosen by their organizations for further development. Questionnaires were in all cases distributed before the seminar and so were uninfluenced by its content.

While there is no unanimity on the issue, current cross-cultural research shows no evidence that those with international responsibilities are less national in their outlooks. If anything, there is a slight hardening of national attitudes among those who deal with foreigners habitually. We therefore believe the scores registered here are broadly representative.

Within America we found only one regional variation that was significant. Questions administered in the Bay Area—particularly in Marin County, where several seminars were held—had a "counter-cultural" flavor, which sharply reduced the strong contrasts between the United States and other cultures that had held true up to 1990, when the Marin seminars began. We accordingly weighted the Bay Area results to reflect greater regional balance. Samples from the Northeast, Middle West, West, Mountain region, and Texas are roughly equal. The Deep South and Pacific Northwest are somewhat underrepresented.

1

Seven Ways of Wealth Creation

The Emerging Source of National Strength

BECAUSE of their current and historical economic success, seven nations have much to teach us about the best practices of capitalism: the United States, the United Kingdom, Sweden, France, Japan, the Netherlands, and Germany. All call themselves capitalist and free enterprise nations and subscribe generally to the same philosophy, but there the resemblance ends. When we look at the day-to-day details, the meaning found in work, the attitude toward stakeholders, the styles of managing employees, the various negotiation tactics, the differences are wide, as any American who has negotiated a contract with a Japanese will tell you. And, although all of these countries have enjoyed economic success, not all of them engage their current economic tasks equally well—far from it.[1]

Something is out of kilter in the Anglo-American business community, which has for the past forty-five years been the world's chief advocate of capitalist ideology. American capitalism became the negation of communism, standing for freedom not coercion, individualism not collectivism, private not public ownership, pragmatism not theory. These arguments, a rhetorical defense of capitalism, taken together with the crumbling of communism have lulled us into a false sense of security. We have believed our own propaganda, and this has prevented us from considering that our wealth creation system could be vulnerable. We have confused media victories, "what plays in Peoria—or Moscow," with what really

1

works in factories and offices. Above all, we have confused the polarized structure of debate—at which we excelled—with the reconciled structures of organizations that create actual products and services. Adversarial arguments that defend capitalism may not augment it. While we were busy arguing with the Communists, the true economic threat was coming from an entirely different direction.

Until the mid-1970s the huge American economy did not have to cope with foreign competition. But between 1972 and 1982 the proportion of American-made goods subject to international competition jumped from 20 to 80 percent. The result was massive import penetration in the U.S. market. Before the early 1970s there had been plenty of competition, but it was all domestic. What has changed in the last decade and a half is the advent of intercultural economic competition. We now face world competition between rival cultures of capitalism.

Indeed, economic trade increasingly preempts war. Who can imagine the members of the European Community fighting each other today as they did twice in this century? Even the much publicized trade war between America and the EC is likely to remain more rhetorical than real. Why? Because you do not fight with people on whom you depend to sustain your living standards. You cannot afford to. So much of the American economy now uses EC manufacturing, research, supplies, and investment capital that even a succession of retaliatory moves would swiftly become unaffordable. International trade locks us in mutual embrace and interdependence. We are stuck with each other.

Our future economic success depends on how well we understand the deepest motivations of our trading partners. It takes more than language skills and etiquette lessons to plumb the complexity of desires and actions we can barely recognize in ourselves. There is in every culture a tacit dimension, a set of beliefs that are subconscious because the members of that culture take these so for granted that they fall below the threshold of awareness. If and when these beliefs are challenged, we may face "culture shock," a sense of being subverted by foreigners. What is truly "shocking" is that cultures are often mirror images of each other, left and right reversed or the other side of the coin exposed. We feel reproached by others expressing what we are accustomed to hiding, or hiding what we express. Above all, we are alarmed that something so different succeeds. But different traits are not so different at all. Within them are lessons or signs of our hidden character. Revealing such subconscious beliefs enables us to understand ourselves, our strengths and weaknesses, and those of our competitors. If we don't make the effort to overcome our discomfort, if we don't see the "hidden side" of our capitalist ways, we will be forever trapped by our own prejudices and unable to learn the important lessons available through calm observation of our competition.

For example, most Americans believe the nostrum "time is money." This shared belief has had great impact on the American system of wealth creation. Without this particular idea, there would have been no mass manufacturing, no Taylorism, no time-and-motion studies—all of which, in their day, contributed greatly to America's ability to create wealth. Nor would there be the current obsession with short-term performance, widely believed to be one of America's greatest economic weaknesses. It will surprise Americans to know that the workers of many other cultures do not rush through their days on tight schedules. Many economically successful cultures are happy to postpone short-term financial advantage in the hope that significant long-term benefits will accrue. Shortcuts to quick money are not admired in all cultures.

Wealth Creation Is a Moral Act

When we began this book, our goal was simply to define the seven preeminent cultures of capitalism. We wanted to know who did what well and why. Myth told us that Germans were particularly good at building infrastructure and that Americans excelled at invention (dreaming up new products), whereas the Japanese excelled at innovation (getting those new products to market). Why should such skills correspond to nationality? Wasn't wealth creation the dry stuff of science not the mysterious province of culture?

In a word, no. Wealth or values creation is in essence a moral act. The individual entrepreneurs who first organized production systematically were steeped in largely nonconformist religious convictions that blocked most customary routes to advancement in British society of the eighteenth and early nineteenth centuries. Quakers, Methodists, Presbyterians, Wesleyans, and similar sects were greatly overrepresented among the one hundred or so major entrepreneurs cited in Ashton's *History of the Industrial Revolution*. Much has been written since about the Puritan ethic and the capitalist spirit it supposedly engendered. Members of Protestant sects shared a belief that their works on this earth would justify them, that the Kingdom of Heaven was to be built by them, here and now.[2]

While controversy rages around the issue of whether Puritans were exclusively benefited by their beliefs, the central insight is surely obvious. Entrepreneurs of whatever religion must create "valuable" objects or services for intended customers before discovering whether buyers agree with these embodiments of value. The supplier says, in effect, "I so value this product, I have gone to the trouble of making it as my life's work. Do you share my enthusiasm?" To survive economically and to prosper, the answer has to be yes. A product or service then is fashioned first and foremost in the image of its maker, and of his or her maker. If customers applaud and grow in number, the faith is redeemed, economically and ethically.

But where do the moral values that drive wealth creation come from? They originate in *culture*—the word actually means "to work upon," as in *agriculture*, which means "to work upon soil or ground." Cultures that work upon products originate within nations, within sects or groups therein, and increasingly within organizations deliberately incorporated by industry.[3] The qualities of work performed by these corporations depend as much on the durable values of their work cultures as they once depended on the values of their founders. In our survey of 15,000 executives we found that culture of origin is the most important determinant of values. In any culture, a deep structure of beliefs is the invisible hand that regulates economic activity. These cultural preferences, or values, are the bedrock of national identity and the source of economic strengths—and weaknesses.

Self-evident as this determinant might appear to be, we have recently lost sight of it, especially in the English-speaking developed economies of America, Great Britain, and Australia. Reasons for our amnesia include the prominence of the value-empty discipline of Economics and the more than forty years of Cold War polarization which has persuaded us that capitalism is monolithic, a way of choosing, not a set of choices.

Economics: The Value-Empty Discipline

The English-speaking Commonwealth set considerable store by the discipline of Economics. As first Great Britain and then North America took off economically, many people and many nations clamored to know how it had been done. It fell to a Scottish schoolmaster, Adam Smith, to explain the development of wealth by nation states. That the world's major economists have since come largely from Britain and the United

States owes much to the fact that both these nations pioneered capitalism.

Yet Economics has, from its inception, been an academic discipline, describing the creation of wealth after such creation has been accomplished by persons not employing the discipline. Entrepreneur-economists, i.e., persons who actually used the discipline of economics to create value, are virtually unknown. Economics is a theory reconstructed in the academic cloister from achievements wrought elsewhere.[4] It is not a theory-in-use save for a limited amount of microeconomics taught to managers, a very small part of the business education curriculum.

Another problem in a person's reconstructing what he has not himself accomplished is that a political subtext creeps into the equation. Instead of accurate portrayals of how wealth was originally created, we get contentious views on how much of their money the rich should be allowed to keep. The logic of wealth creation becomes swamped in the politics of wealth retention, as we celebrate a greed the wealth creators never had.

One reason that Economics has not inspired wealth creators is that it remains value empty.[5] In pursuit of the ideal of science it has confined itself to a study of transactions—how people utilize money, not why they do this or what their motives might be. Even "the how" avoids discussion of technology or manufacturing in favor of a logic of money, applicable to all technologies of manufacture or distribution. We do not criticize the discipline as wrong. We are not qualified to do so. But it seems to us to leave out the very heart of the enterprise.

The Search for an Integrity of Values

Economics has traditionally dealt with the bits and pieces of the productive mix—land, labor, capital, raw materials, equipment, and information—while ignoring the integrity of the enterprise, how these constituents are organized and constructed into products and services more valuable than the separate ingredients. Value is said to be added, but how this differs from some dirty great heap of resources piled upon each other is not revealed. Economics is so concerned with counting and itemizing that it has lost sight of the one component, almost unmeasurable, that makes all economic activity possible: human relationships. Behind every economic transaction are people making choices, acting on their values, giving one thing high priority, another one low. A recent gesture from economists in this direction is the idea that when managers stop playing "liar's poker"—i.e., behave ethically—transaction costs decline.[6]

Is there nothing else then, that can be said about how the people in organizations put valued products and services together? Are there no principles of construction necessary to systems of wealth creation in general?

Wealth creation requires, at a minimum, that an organization successfully originate and bring to market products and services and that all groups who share these processes work together energetically and effectively. As we mentioned earlier, the specific way that any group accomplishes this has everything to do with the values they bring to their work. Each of the seven cultures investigated here—the United States, Japan, Germany, France, Sweden, the Netherlands, and the United Kingdom—brings a unique set of values to bear upon the act of wealth creation. These values characterize both the organization that practices them and the products and services the enterprise creates. Indeed, products and services personify the corporation that supplies them. They are its reason for being. Products can be no better than the human valuing process that goes into their making. The search for meaning, which involves integrating values into coherent forms, is one of mankind's most fundamental yearnings.[7] Our minds and value systems can absorb more information and more satisfactions, *provided* we can organize, integrate, and store what we experience. So, far from regarding enterprises and their products as being, as Economics tells us, mere accretions of resources, it would be truer to say that an enterprise is the fine-tuning and harmonizing of values often in tension with one another, the reconciliation of the dilemmas caused by conflicting values.[8] Industries create new products by joining together satisfactions, many of which have previously resisted combination, i.e., "slimming meals," "friendly computers," "safe automobiles."

To understand how cultural values influence economic choices, we must first look more closely at the processes by which value systems are constructed. How do organizations make the judgments necessary to create the systems that create the products and services that are the basis of economic activity? We have identified seven fundamental valuing processes without which wealth-creating organizations could not exist.

1. Making Rules and Discovering Exceptions

Business organizations in all fields of enterprise need to create rules, codes, procedures, and routines, everything from highly codified safety procedures to the broad guidelines in an employee handbook. Only thus can operations become systematic enough to add value. But this alone is inadequate. Organizations must also discover swiftly any case that is exceptional, that reveals a rule's limitations and hence merits particular attention. Unless they do this their rules and procedures will progressively lose touch with customers' desires and with changing environments. A business enterprise first becomes aware of such changes as exceptions to established standards and procedures. For example, suppose Hewlett Packard asks one of its suppliers of tools and dies to reduce defects to below .05 percent. Although an exception when first asked for, this standard spreads within weeks to other suppliers and becomes the rule. Soon it is universal to the industry. Unless an enterprise continually rejuvenates its rules, methods, and standards, it will find itself making products surpassed by its competitors and outmoded by the expectations of customers. The "integrity" of the enterprise, its value to stakeholders, must depend in part on how well *universalism* (rules of wide generality) is reconciled with *particularism* (special exceptions). Only thus can rules develop to cover more exceptions, vital to the success of any enterprise.

2. Constructing and Deconstructing

It is also necessary for all enterprises everywhere, to deconstruct whole products and operations so that each part can be examined for possible defects and improvements. It is equally vital then to reconstruct the whole so that the entire system is better configured, designed, and organized than it was before. Periodic upgrading and reimagining every aspect of the product is key to competitive advantage. The process of deconstruction and reconstruction—fundamental to all learning—never ends and is full of peril because the whole product or service which is in many subtle ways more than its parts, needs to join itself to customers and their purposes; yet a tiny, defective part can wreck the whole system of satisfaction. For example, an automobile may be beautifully designed overall and fit as hand to glove drivers and passengers alike, yet a single defective part, say a poorly insulated gas tank, could incinerate everyone. Only an alternating mental and physical process of analysis (breaking down) and integration (putting together) can keep the enterprise and its products in a constant state of renewal and refinement.

3. Managing Communities of Individuals

Another vital requirement of all work organizations is the provision of care, attention, information, and support to each of its individual members, while assuring that the needs of the community and the organization are well served by these individuals. It is an underlying condition of the success of an enterprise that the individual's initiative, drive, and energy be harnessed to the purposes of the organization. Here the "integrity" of the organization depends in part on how well the *individualism* of employees, shareholders, and customers is reconciled with the *communitarianism* of the larger system. Is there a balance of rights and obligations? Are benefits reciprocated between the society and the individual?[9]

4. Internalizing the Outside World

Similar yet crucially different from the tension between individuals and communities is the issue of where directions, decisions, and purposes originate. Are they generated "in here," i.e., within the enterprise and within its members, or are they generated "out there" in the wider environment? An organization that rejects any idea "not invented here" will not long trade profitably. Equally, an organization that finds little virtue in the leadership and inspiration that comes from its own members ignores a sustaining source of intelligence. Can the enterprise somehow reconcile *inner-direction* with *outer-direction*, those things invented here with those not invented here? Can it internalize the outer world so as to act decisively and competently?

5. Synchronizing Fast Processes

Yet another valuing process concerns time and how the enterprise makes use of it. A company must do its tasks swiftly, in the shortest possible intervals of passing time. In addition, many of these swiftly completed tasks need to be synchronized with each other. To have one sequence dovetail with another just in time is not difficult if these sequences move slowly, but it is very difficult if each moves fast. To get first to market with just what customers demand requires the enterprise to create an integrity of *sequential time* with *synchronized time*. The capacity to create wealth depends on reconciling both considerations, or synchronizing ever-faster processes.

6. Choosing Among Achievers

All business organizations require for their effective operation that status, position, and respect be given to those persons who have succeeded on behalf of the enterprise. It is obviously in the interests of any corporation that those who have performed best rise to positions of greater influence, there to surpass their former achievements and set an example to others. Rewards should be commensurate with contributions. But definitions of what is worth achieving in the first place must be set by the organization. Goals must be considered worthy before we achieve them, and so must the persons who set those goals. The capacity to create value must depend upon the integrity of *achieved status* with *ascribed status*.

7. Sponsoring Equal Opportunities to Excel

Finally, every enterprise needs to give its employees an equality of opportunity to make valuable contributions. If this is not done, suggestions and ideas may never be admitted to corporate awareness or mobilized on its behalf. Equality of opportunity is impossible unless everyone is heard out. Yet pushing every point made by every employee on every issue could result in corporate gridlock and chronically delayed decisions. For this reason employee contributions must be subjected to an hierarchy of expert judgment that combines and coordinates their use. A fair contest demands judges and sponsors—executives and managers at different levels in the hierarchy—who are not themselves competing with those they evaluate. The "integrity" of the organization depends on striking a balance between the need for an *equality* of input and a *hierarchy* for judging the merits of the input.

It can be legitimately asked why we choose these seven processes to measure the creation of wealth and not others. We choose them because there is substantial agreement among leading anthropologists and sociologists that these were fundamental to organized activity per se and because there are ways to measure them. Additional dimensions to the creative process can be elaborated almost indefinitely, with increasing overlaps. Our point here is that any nation or organization growing in the capacity to create wealth must manage all of these seven valuing processes.

Understanding Values in Tension

Each of the seven valuing processes crucial to creating wealth has within it a tension. This tension arises because values are really contrasts or differences; for example, courage and caution, loyalty and dissent. To put human values together, i.e., persuade your group that your dissent is loyally intended, is vital to human society, to an individualism responsive to the community. That one value in a pair is more extolled than the other is a fact of culture. Our thesis of economic development is, however, that each value in the pair is crucial to economic success. The capitalist cultures that succeed in the next century will be those that overcome their cultural predispositions to favor, for example, individualism at the expense of community, and bring seemingly opposed values into balance. Each culture in our study starts in a different place. For example, in the United States, the scale is weighted heavily on the side of individualism. In Japan, the scale tips in the opposite direction, favoring communitarianism. Economic success will accrue to the cultures which do the best job *balancing* the scale. To create a value system is to manage contrasts, i.e., between rules and exceptions, parts and wholes. We refer here to such tensions as dilemmas, although cultures vary considerably as to whether they consider these to be complementary (as does Japan) or fiercely contradictory (as does France). We take dilemmas to mean that the conflicts or tensions are resolvable, but *not* easily. The seven dilemmas below underlie the valuing processes above.

1. Universalism vs. Particularism

When no code, rule, or law seems to quite cover an exceptional case, should the most relevant rule be imposed, however imperfectly, on that case, or should the case be considered on its unique merits, regardless of the rule?[10]

2. Analyzing vs. Integrating

Are we more effective as managers when we analyze phenomena into parts, i.e., facts, items, tasks, numbers, units, points, specifics, or when we integrate and configure such details into whole patterns, relationships, and wider contexts?[11]

3. Individualism vs. Communitarianism

Is it more important to focus upon the enhancement of each individual, his or her rights, motivations, rewards, capacities, attitudes, or should more attention be paid to the advancement of the corporation as a community, which all its members are pledged to serve?[12]

4. Inner-directed vs. Outer-directed Orientation

Which are the more important guides to action, our inner-directed judgments, decisions, and commitments, or the signals, demands, and trends in the outside world to which we must adjust?[13]

5. Time as Sequence vs. Time as Synchronization

Is it more important to do things fast, in the shortest possible sequence of passing time, or to synchronize efforts so that completion is coordinated?[14]

6. Achieved Status vs. Ascribed Status

Should the status of employees depend on what they have achieved and how they have performed, or on some other characteristic important to the corporation, i.e., age, seniority, gender, education, potential, strategic role?[15]

7. Equality vs. Hierarchy

Is it more important that we treat employees as equals so as to elicit from them the best they have to give, or to emphasize the judgment and authority of the hierarchy that is coaching and evaluating them?[16]

To say that the cultures of various nations "differ" on the relative importance of those values necessary to wealth creation is an understatement. Typically, these issues are loaded with ideological fervor. How often have we heard colleagues call for "law and order" (universalism) and less personal indulgence for those suspected of wrongdoing (particularism)? Some managers demand "the facts" and "the bottom line" (analysis) and regard all attempts to put these in context (integration) as mere window dressing. If there are problems in the organization, they may look for specific persons or "troublemakers" to blame (individualism), for a "rotten apple in the barrel." In their view, there is nothing wrong with the organization (communitarianism) that cannot be cured by "kicking ass and taking names."

Everyone should be a "self-starter" (inner-directed) and must beware of "groupthink" and "running with the herd" (outer-directed). Employees must realize that "time is money" and efficiency the key (sequential time). Workers should get on with the job and not talk all the time (synchronize their efforts). For ten years our manager has been "busting his gut" to succeed in the job he was given (status by achievement), but now some wise guy has "moved the goal posts" (altered the kinds of work to which status is ascribed). All he ever wanted was an "even break" (equality) but the people "up there" (the hierarchy) weren't interested.

We can see from these examples that values clash and that getting them to work together in wealth-generating harmonies is no easy task! To break down the seven wealth-creating processes into opposing values has advantages and perils. The advantages include far greater clarity of meaning, more precise definitions, and easier slogans to remember. The perils include a sharpening of adversarialism and the possibility that wholeness may never be regained if positions harden. A common cultural trait, as we shall see, is championing one value necessary for the effectiveness of the enterprise *against* its reciprocal (and equally necessary) value. Frequently, foreign cultures are seen as representing that other value, as subverting "what we believe in." This narrow view turns other cultures from commercial rivals into ideological adversaries with no concept of "fair competition."

Our Dilemma Methodology

The methodology of our research involves posing to managers from many different countries dilemmas which oblige them to take sides. For example, we investigated dilemma #3 by asking whether in hiring a new employee it matters more that he or she "fit into the group" or has the exact "skills, knowledge, and record of success necessary for the job." This obliges the respondent to choose the communitarian answer (fit into the group) *or* the individualist answer (personal record of success).[17]

Our method forces the manager to state a preference and reveal which of the two values he regards as most fundamental. Through such questions we uncover the foundation stone upon which the respondents' value systems are based. We should be careful of our metaphors here. For most Westerners, value systems have "foundation stones," rocks of moral certainty, but for many Asians, integrity itself is the starting point. No break in harmony among values is tolerable. The connectivity is more important than what is connected. Yin must be everywhere harmonized to yang, and exactly what either of these terms mean is less important!

Some managers, especially Japanese, Germans, and the French, will found their value system first on the welfare of their group and then, only after the needs of the group are met, will attention be paid to individual needs. Other managers, especially Americans, the British, Dutch, and Swedes, will found their value systems on the welfare of the individual and then, later, form these persons into effective groups. We have plenty of evidence that those who put individualism first also care about groups and organizations, and that those who put the organization first also care about its individual members. Our methodology examines where people start when forming a values integrity. Each manager from each country is struggling to resolve the dilemmas we have posed. They simply tackle the values concerned in different orders of priority.

People from the same country tend to resolve dilemmas in the same way; thus Americans will try to do jobs faster, and the Japanese and Germans will be more concerned with the overall synchronization of separate tasks. Americans will analyze before they integrate. Germans will integrate before they analyze, and always consider the part in the context of the whole.

Cultural cohesion in these matters is not surprising. If members of a culture thought in opposite ways, chaos would ensue. Members of a culture are likely to share common attitudes because they share a common history. Cultures are indelibly marked by what worked well for them in the past. Of course, this is no guarantee that any given wealth-creating system will continue to work in the future, a realization that has caused not a little consternation on both sides of the Atlantic recently.[18]

During the course of the research we found that the responses to our seven dilemmas, explained and predicted how managers from different countries would react to conflict, why they excelled at certain jobs rather than others, and the managerial philosophies and concepts they favored.

The Circular Nature of Value Resolution

To say that managers in different countries start with one of two values-in-tension and try to reconnect the first to the second is another way of saying that value systems are circular. All our seven dilemmas can be visualized as points on virtuous circles (see below).

We can use Adam Smith's classic metaphor to show how the impulse to individualism and the impulse to communitarianism are connected. Smith's argument goes as follows: If each individual pursues his own self-interest, an invisible hand will automatically serve the common intersts of the larger society. So, social goals are a by-product of self-interest:

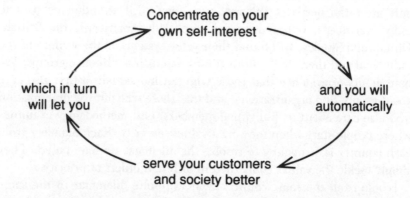

Americans and the British assume that this logic has the force of physical law. Other cultures do not. The French, Germans, and Japanese, for example, stand Smith on his head. They would say that if the needs of the group are considered first, then the invisible hand will, as we see below, reach down and automatically take care of the desires of the individual.

Expressed in this way, it might seem that the tension between individualism and communitarianism is easily resolved. But in real life it does not work out so neatly. In a dilemma in which individual and group needs seem to diverge irreconcilably, managers from different countries will begin to repair the split in precisely opposite ways. Because of this, a multicultural group working on a minor crisis can be overwhelmed with bafflement and suspicion as managers from different cultures each wonder what the foreigners are up to. American and Japanese cultures are, as we see in the following diagram, like ships that pass in the night:

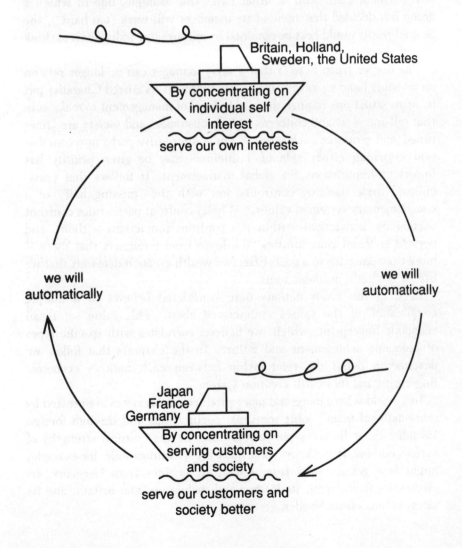

Britain, Holland,
Sweden, the United States

By concentrating on
individual self
interest

serve our own interests

we will
automatically

we will
automatically

Japan
France
Germany

By concentrating on
serving customers
and society

serve our customers and
society better

In the ship diagram, Britain, Holland, Sweden, and the United States steam from left to right, while France, Germany, and Japan steam from right to left. Inscribed on the hull of each ship is the dominant cultural value. Repressed in the water beneath each opposite ship is the subordinate cultural consequence. No sooner do relationships break down than each steams off in the opposite direction—obviously mad!

Both views are valid, but the actual result one achieves depends very much upon where one begins. In some cases it may indeed be more generative of valuable products to have employees think preponderantly about customers—the welfare of the group—than mainly about their own personal gain. And in other cases (for example, one in which a group has decided that none of its members will work "too hard"), the desired result would best be obtained by encouraging individuals to think first of themselves.

The deeper truth here is that a savvy manager can no longer rely on an invisible hand to solve half of every problem. As Alfred Chandler put it, many situations require the visible hand of management to make sure that self-interests and concerns to help customers and society are "fine-tuned' and reinforce each other.[19] These alternative paths to reconciliation in which either side of a dilemma may be given priority has important implications for global management. It follows that cross-cultural understanding confronts you with the "missing half" of a complementary system of values.[20] Wholes confront parts, rules confront particulars, convictions within you confront convictions without, and persons confront communities. You learn from foreigners that there is more than one path to a goal. Effective wealth creation demands that we use all the paths available to us.

Each of the seven nations here considered believes in a unique combination of the values enumerated above. This value set is an economic fingerprint, which, we believe, correlates with specific types of economic achievement and failure. In the chapters that follow we describe in detail the relationship between each nation's economic fingerprint and its wealth-creation system.

In a world where more and more products and services are created by cross-national teams, joint ventures, partnerships and through foreign subsidiaries, it becomes possible to combine the cultural strengths of various nations, if you know what these are. An automobile, for example, might best get its steel from Korea, its engines from Germany, its electronics from Japan, its leather and mahogany from Britain, and its safety systems from Sweden.

You can combine the traditions of excellence from many nations, provided you can manage cultural diversity and not allow it to descend into a Tower of Babel. In the same way you can also learn, and make your own, the strategies and thought processes behind these traditions of excellence. These are the twin purposes of this book. The reader should be warned, however, that this will happen only when she or he genuinely sees the world through other eyes. Many will find this book radical, in the sense of its going to the roots of entrenched beliefs and supplying alternatives. Seeing from multiple perspectives can be deeply disturbing.

2

Codifiers-in-Chief, Analyzers Extraordinary

MORE THAN ANY OTHER NATION in the modern world, the United States may be said to be the prototype of advanced capitalism. Britain's was the first industrial revolution, but America's huge domestic economy has largely set world standards for the last seventy years. The United States is surely the pathfinder in the process of world development, the nation that has most consistently eschewed socialism, championed capitalism, frowned on aristocracy and organized working class alike, and symbolizes the triumph of the middle class. No other nation has so tirelessly defended capitalism with arms and words throughout the world.

One might be pardoned for believing that capitalism as a world competitive system, if not invented and patented by Parker Brothers, is at least guaranteed and refereed worldwide by American political influence. It is the United States which, through its business schools, has gone further than any other nation in proclaiming the "mastery" of business administration and has set itself the task of making a science of management, producing an endless stream of the latest management techniques and formulas. Capitalism is, at its best, "the level playing field," which Americans rightly insist upon. To the extent that some nations use their governments to intervene in their favor, restrict foreign investment, or seek unfair advantage, it is the American "referee" who blows the whistle, who knows what is fair and unfair.[1] Those who sneer at the referee must explain why much of the world is now seeking admittance to the game; why, historically, millions have passed beneath the Statue of Liberty on their journey to economic opportunity.

The Universal Product

As we saw in the previous chapter, there are seven valuing processes without which wealth creation is impossible. In this chapter we explore the American attitude toward two of those processes and the pairs of value tensions behind them: #1. Making Rules and Discovering Exceptions (universalism vs. particularism) and #2. Constructing and Deconstructing (analyzing vs. integrating). Many of America's most extraordinary economic successes can be attributed to the high value she places on both universalism and analysis.

Examples of America's skillful application of universalist principles to business stretch from Henry Ford's "you can have any color you like as long as its black" to McDonald's and its near-identical foods available from Miami to Moscow. Even the fantasies of Walt Disney as featured in theme parks come in identical mechanized formats from Paris to Los Angeles. "It's a small world, after all . . ."

The American ideal is of the Universal Product, reducible to parts (analysis) and infinitely replicable. We can see this in products as different as microprocessors and M&Ms, Coca-Cola and superconductors. What is aspired to is the widest possible product appeal (universalism) combined with a manufacturing process that is reduced to simple steps (analysis) so the parent company can manufacture wherever costs are lowest and sell to as many people as possible. It is the vision of the world's Cookie Cutter, or breakfast-food-for-everyone.

The sheer extent of codification and preformulation in all aspects of American business sets her apart from the other cultures of capitalism. It is at once her towering strength and her Achilles' heel. The headlong pursuit of the Universal Product, the Automated Factory, the Ultra-Efficient Office tends to eclipse particular persons, unique relationships, special circumstances, and exceptional requests (particularism). Similarly, the urge to analyze and reduce everything to basics neglects the appreciation of wholes, harmonies, designs, aesthetics, and superordinate bonds (integration). It is as natural for Americans to make Levi's as it is for the French to fashion one exceptional gown for one unique customer for a very special occasion. Considerable economic success can—and has—come from both ventures. But it is important to keep in mind that, as we said in Chapter 1, the companies who are best equipped to take advantage of new economic opportunities are those that learn to achieve equilibrium between these opposed values.

The United States is by far the most universalist culture in our group. No other culture is so keen to make rules for everyone to live by.[2] No other culture has had so many foreign adults to teach its ways to.[3] No wonder, then, that the United States excelled early at mass manufacture and mass marketing. And should we be surprised that as markets became more customized, more fragmented, more oriented to unique requests, America's difficulties have mounted? This is especially true of competition with nations such as Japan and France which are culturally oriented to heterogeneity, variety, and particularities—customized goods, haute cuisine, and haute couture.

The Melting Pot

What are the origins of America's very strong allegiance to universalism? An early historical episode was the Declaration of Independence, the severance from Great Britain and the self-conscious articulation of a code guaranteeing freedom. In contrast to those of other countries, America's written Constitution was thought through and deliberated. "We hold these truths to be self-evident, that all men are created equal . . ." When faced with tyrannies of government, "it becomes the right of the people to alter or to abolish it, and to institute new Government, laying its foundations on such principles and organizing its power in such form as to them shall seem most likely to effect their Safety and Happiness." In these words of the Declaration, America originated itself in a set of principles regarded as applying to all people everywhere for all time. Or, as Henry David Thoreau put it, "the government of the world I live in was not framed, like that of Britain, in after-dinner conversations over wine."[4] America's written Constitution, its universal Bill of Rights, and the Declaration of Independence are all addressed beyond even Americans to mankind. They are monuments to universalism—and very successful they proved, allowing a nation of more than two hundred million to maintain civil order for the last 130 years.

The new nation having been established, its universal codes now constituted an invitation to immigrants to join it. Since they came from far away, they had a right to know and to know plainly the codes of the nation they had left home and friends to join. It must offer them guarantees that justified their journey. Indeed, it is hard to see how a nation could play host to people from so many lands without substituting a universal code for many particular customs. The melting pot became a powerful metaphor for the immigration process. "The huddled masses yearning to breathe free" could be reminted, like coins of the realm, stamped with the imprimatur of citizenship.[5] You socialize children to a large extent by showing them particular affection within families. But you cannot resocialize adults in this way after they have arrived in a strange land. And you must teach their children American habits of mind of which their foreign parents may be ignorant. For this reason "the American way" is codified to an extent that other nations regard as strange. One can be un-American, as we saw during the McCarthy era, but not un-Dutch.[6]

Using the Dilemmas Methodology

The cultural drive to universalize has many good effects on a nation's capacity to create wealth. There tends to be an idealization of the hard sciences and an eagerness to apply these to industry. Many aspects of wealth creation benefit from codification: engineering, safety, finance, accountancy, and law. Universalist cultures lead the world in these disciplines. The early dominance of the City of London and, later, Wall Street in worldwide money markets is another testimony to universalism.

In a very real sense, universalists want the world—the entire world—to be uniform, generalizable, lawlike, and explainable, while particularists want the world to be unique, exceptional, and mysterious. To measure this value pair with our questionnaire, we created dilemma situations, like the following one, which put the claims of a universal code in conflict with the claims of a particular friendship.

While you are talking and sharing a bottle of beer with a friend who was officially on duty as a safety controller in the company you both work for, an accident occurs, injuring a shift worker. An investigation is launched by the national safety commission and you are asked for your evidence. There are no other witnesses. What right has your friend to expect you to protect him?

    (a) A definite right?   **(b)** Some right?   **(c)** No right?

The scores of twelve different countries were as follows:

Table 2-1

	USA	NL	AUS	CAN	GER	SWE	UK	BEL	JAP	SIN	IT	FR
No right	94%	92	91	91	90	89	82	67	66	59	56	53

If you chose **(c),** you are saying that upholding the universal rule is more important than helping a friend. Note—and this is important—that all managers from all twelve nations would probably prefer to serve safety and their friends if they possibly could. It is the dilemma, not their own dispositions, that have made these loyalties incompatible. The real difference between nations, as we explained in Chapter 1, is not whether they would rather ditch safety or a good friend, but on which foundation stone they would try to resolve the dilemma.

A universalist might say, "The principle of safety at work comes first. I would expect my friend, as a friend, to understand this." A particularist might say, "My friendship with you comes first and I will testify as you wish me to, but I beg you to accept responsibility for what occurred." This latter point was made by the senior member of a Japanese group to whom the dilemma was posed. He wanted safety, he explained, but it would come only if personal friends asked it of each other. Safety was founded on friendship, an extension of it.

We posed a second dilemma, again pitting the claims of friendship against universal principle:

You run a department of a division of a large company. One of your subordinates, whom you know has trouble at home, is frequently coming in significantly late. What right has this colleague to be protected by you from others in the department?

(a) A definite right? **(b)** Some right? **(c)** No right?

Table 2-2

No right	USA	GER	SWE	UK	NL	AUS	CAN	SIN	BEL	JAP	IT	FR
	95%	94	91	84	82	82	81	61	57	56	47	43

If you selected **(a)** or **(b),** you are saying that supporting a specific friend is more important to you than supporting a general principle. As in the answers given to the question in Table 2-1, there is a sharp break between Protestant countries of North America and northwest Europe, and Catholic countries of Europe plus Asia.

Are There Limits to Universalism?

Cultures that are less extreme on the subject of universalism do not reject it entirely. On the issue of safety, the Germans, Swedes, and Netherlanders are not far behind American managers, any more than they lag far behind in holding to the rule that people show up for work on time. But there *are* subjects that only the English-speaking world, led by America, universalizes and codifies. Perhaps the most salient example is business administration. American scholarship dominates the field because it has been largely Americans who believe that any universal code of management is possible. Japan and Germany do not lack business schools because they do not know how to manage well; rather, they lack such schools because they do not believe that anything, from the running of a funeral parlor to the production of low-frequency transducers, can be covered by a coherent set of universally valid laws. It is by no means self-evident that such laws are discoverable or, even, that they exist. It is a matter of cultural assertion. Only a nation with a history of codifying successfully would believe it possible.

If we look more closely, we notice that American attempts to universalize have been quite extraordinarily ambitious: Christian Science, mental hygiene, the objectivism of Ayn Rand, Taylorism or "Scientific" Management, Douglas McGregor's "Theory Y," and many others. Americans attempt to universalize areas of life that most cultures would not regard as amenable to codification. Consider, for example, *How to Win Friends and Influence People, The Power of Positive Thinking* and a large number of best sellers, well satirized in the musical *How to Succeed in Business Without Really Trying*. "Parenting" and "wellness" are among the latest subjects for which formulas are on sale, while the trend toward "political correctness" on the nation's campuses is but the latest in a long line of moral preformulations. You must not, we are told, refer to disabled persons, but to the differently abled. A person is not short, but "vertically challenged." The prehistoric world was peopled by "cave-persons." We are not so much alarmed that this tendency will oppress us, as intrigued by the assumption behind political correctness, that altering the language will reform the speakers, that the word comes before the deed. The whole American trend of what has been called "spiritual technology" represents an attempt to universalize the unique occurrences of art, life, love, friendship, sociability, trust, and parenthood. But even if we agree that some of these antics are comic or sad, do they harm business? Don't the advantages of universalizing easily outweigh the disadvantages?

Historically, there may have been more advantages to ultra-universalism than there are in the modern economy. Taylorism, or Scientific Management, which tried to subsume the entire life of the workplace within the principles of engineering, is now seen as overambitious. It tried, via time and motion studies and machine-timed movements, to demonstrate "scientifically" the one best way of operating. In so doing, it seriously deskilled workers. As the villainous novelist in *The Caine Mutiny* put it, they were "designed by geniuses to be run by idiots." Any system of management that identifies with science risks turning people into the universalistic objects of science.

The directions in the modern world economy are away from the simple toward the complex, away from mere things toward knowledge, away from mass markets to greater and greater customization. Much of the calculations of classical economists depend upon products being the same, commodities. But increasingly products are different in terms of quality and customization. The maker of complex, customized products must communicate person to person in deep relationships over time with clients. You do not switch customers or suppliers day by day on the basis of price calculations, you stay with particular partners in joint ventures for much of your working life. When a few years ago the value of the Japanese yen doubled against the U.S. dollar, we were confidently told by economists and universalists that the balance of international payments would now right itself. Orders would rush in for cheaper U.S. goods. It did not happen, because the quality revolution makes demand inelastic—people were willing to pay higher prices for products they had judged to be superior in quality. People are increasingly reluctant to break relationships with those particular partners who keep them supplied and informed. It is mostly the bottom end of the economy that still behaves "scientifically," and the danger for Anglo-Saxons is that their love affair with scientism will consign them to the world of widgets and pork bellies.

America's great successes are those of preprepared codes, and her failures occur when these reach their limits. Coca Cola and Pepsi Cola, for example, are formulas prepared as condensed essences and then distributed to bottlers who dilute them. McDonald's, and fast food generally, appeals to highly standardized tastes for simple foods. Hotel and motel chains are often replicas of each other. Behind the fantasy of Disneyland lies standard, machine-controlled formats in which human beings, if present at all, have carefully scripted presentations. Prepared formulas can usually satisfy mundane needs for milk shakes, frankfurters, and cheap lodgings. But if America makes Coke and Japan makes FAX machines, the balance of payments deficit can only worsen. It is in the supply of complex and knowledge-intensive products that it becomes impossible to know in advance what customers will buy, unless information flows back and forth between the maker and the buyer. What is needed is nothing less than a dialogue with a particular person, as opposed to a demonstration by the salesperson of the universal validity of a technique, such as "think-and-grow-rich" or "dress-for-success."

Signs of Excessive Universalism

The McCarthy era was an interesting example of the excesses of universalism. The Un-American Activities Committee obliged witnesses to inform on particular American friends in order to establish their own "Americanism," a universal set of correct ideas. Our point is not that Americans are less tolerant than other nations; on the contrary, they are probably more so. But in no other Western country, surely, could aberration have taken this form of failing to understand that "Americanism" is meaningless if you must betray (American) friends to prove it. Loyalty oath controversies, prayer amendments, and the Prohibition era all show similar confusions. They never stood much chance of stemming disloyalty, combatting disbelief, or preventing Americans from drinking in particular instances, any more than a ban on abortions would stop coat-hanger terminations. But this does not seem to be the main concern of their advocates, who appear to seek an elevated moral code to which particulars are sinful exceptions. The universal as a beautiful ideal is its own justification.

There is another hazard. The insistence that knowledge counts only if it can be successfully systematized means that the most easily codifiable—not the most important or the most useful—aspects of management culture will dominate over the least easily codifiable. Finance, law, and economics will be far more influential than human resources, creativity, employee relations, and product quality. If these remain as particulars, they are subordinated to the more universal disciplines. How much it costs the American economy to have twenty-five times the number of lawyers that Japan employs to sue and be sued, to have urgent decisions delayed by litigation, and to pay out astronomical sums in damages and in insurance premiums is impossible to estimate, but universalizing personal conflicts into federal cases is exorbitantly expensive. The fact that Sid looked cross-eyed at Sadie near the coffee percolator can be dealt with in thirty seconds as a particular incident of bad behavior that need not occur again. Or it can go to the Supreme Court as a landmark case of corporate responsibility for sexual harassment. The universalist solution is considerably more labor-intensive than the particularist one.

Now it happens that cultures like Britain and the United States give considerably greater status to finance, accountancy, and law than do other economies. They have conglomerate-style organizations consisting of businesses in many different technologies, coordinated by the only disciplines these have in common: finance and law.[7] In this way some universals rule over all particulars, many of which, including technology, design, marketing, and human resources, have too few representatives at the top and suffer by default. The problem with universals is that they can progressively lose touch with the real clay of industrial experience, especially with the particulars being bought and sold. You mistake the shadows for the substance, the profit figures for the genuine satisfactions. When we distill all the mess of the factory into clean figures on crisp white paper that a manager can manipulate, much may be lost in the cleansing.[8]

An interesting example of excessive universalism is the traditional style of business strategy as taught at the Harvard Business School and persistently attacked by Henry Mintzberg from across the Canadian border. He points out that students are trained to design strategy, literally on paper, after reading cases interspersed with written concepts. It all occurs at a high level of abstraction, after which the design will supposedly be implemented by subordinates. But here is where the trouble starts. Neither at business school nor in subsequent jobs in consulting, financial analysis, and, before long, top management do these "designers-on-paper" encounter the kinds of work their subordinates must do. Indeed, their first encounter with subordinates is likely to reveal a curious reluctance to enact strategies encoded from on high. It is possible, Mintzberg claims, to reach the top of an organization "without ever getting your hands on the clay of industrial experience." To have mastered an idea conceptually is thought to be equivalent to having done the job it stands for. Such students know all the universals but few of the particulars that these codes are supposed to organize.[9]

A business school graduate with his head stuffed full of nostrums about situations he has yet to encounter is likely to spend much of his working life trying to cram these ideas into the heads of recalcitrant subordinates. He will talk more than he listens and "see" mostly those phenomena for which he already has constructs.

Strategy, Mintzberg argues, can be viable only if it is first seen to emerge from what the corporation is already doing, its embryonic, particular achievements and distinctive competencies. Otherwise a plan of action of immaculate logic may fail for lack of those willing, able, or situated to carry it through. The "perfect plan" designed miles from the front lines may resemble the battle of Passchendaele in World War I, when troops were ordered to advance through a sea of mud, freshly churned by artillery barrages, by top brass entirely ignorant of these conditions. Twenty thousand Allied soldiers died in a matter of minutes while generals bewailed the "lack of military ardor"[10] The teaching of supposed universals is an invitation to "management by remote control," a board game of numbers and abstractions. In contrast, Japanese recruits, even those from elite schools such as Tokyo University, work in the factory, help represent the blue-collar union, and are rotated through scores of humble jobs to discover what abstractions stand for.

The Potential of Particularism

For all such reasons a culture will not necessarily achieve success in world trade in proportion to its universalism. Competitive advantages such as worker participation, quality circles, and personal service to customers tend to be nonrecurring, particularistic connections. "He who would do good . . . must do it in minute particulars," wrote William Blake. Participation, for example, is a particular act of assistance to the organization or it is nothing. If the answer is already encoded in the manager's head, then he does not need participants, only operatives. Participation is not "a technique" designed to get workers to do what their manager wanted in the first place, but a willingness to be surprised by an unforeseen initiative or suggestion.

We participate, in the true sense of the word, only if our supervisor does not know it already, and if he stands prepared to change his mind as a result. You cannot have "good human relations" if either party believes that he or she has a universal explanation for that relationship, controllable unilaterally. Hence, when Tom Peters, in *Passion for Excellence*, describes enthusiasm as "a good technique"[11] and Richard Pascale and Tony Athos in *The Art of Japanese Management* describe ambiguity as a "technique,"[12] they are still trapped in American cultural paradigms. Enthusiasm employed as a technique will fail no sooner than its targets recognize it as such. They want not all-purpose glad-handing, but pleasure in their particular contributions. As for ambiguity, it stems from the myriad variations within human conduct, so that you never really know the result until the dialogue is complete.

The authors were recently consultants to an American electronics company concerned that it was not succeeding in forging a sufficient number of partnerships and joint ventures with original equipment manufacturers in Europe to whom it sold its chips. It was not for want of propositioning would-be partners. On many occasions the company had proposed contracts under which it would share the costs and profits of new projects. Our inquiry elicited the fact that for Americans, proposing the contract or codification of a partnership was meant as a declaration of its serious commitment to a European customer. But for those customers such propositions were premature; they first wished to see a particular friendship formed, after which a more formal contract could follow. Yet the U.S. company felt rejected. It believed that its sincere efforts to forge closer links had been scorned. Whether a contract, or a "covenant," as Bill Clinton called it during his U.S. presidential campaign, precedes a particular relationship or follows it, is a matter that confuses dealings between America and much of Europe and Japan. Some European nations believe that in the absence of friendly and particular contacts, an attempt to "sign up" the partner is coercive.

Hard and Soft Universalism

There are two general styles of universalism, which we may call "hard" and "soft." Examples of hard universalism include Scientific Management, Operations Research, Linear Programming, the Hays Evaluation method, Shareholder Value Analysis, Management by Objectives, Market Segmentation, PIMS (Profit Impact of Market Strategy), and Value Chain Analysis. These share a simplified, purified, if possible numerical, ideal, considered somehow better than the mess from which it is abstracted. All tend to ignore the particularities of product or technology. For example, the well-known portfolio management matrix of "Cash Cows," "Dogs," and "Stars" evinces no concern—and probably lacks knowledge of any particular technological potentials that lie behind these stereotypes.[13] When is Dog not a Dog?

Soft universalism typically appeals to the "hands on" manager and questions the value of academic tools.[14] But any examination of soft universalism reveals that only the style is different, not the substance. "Sticking to your knitting" and "managing by walking about" while keeping "close to your customers" and also prescriptions for excellence, formulas prepared in advance and intended as advertisements for consulting practices. The appeal of soft universalism was never so clear as in Douglas McGregor's classic *The Human Side of the Enterprise*.[15] There are two "theories of motivation," this book argued, Theory X and Theory Y. In Theory X the manager assumes his subordinates to be lazy, unmotivated, security seeking, passive, and exploitive. In Theory Y the manager assumes his subordinates to be energetic, resourceful, risk taking, active, and responsible. This second theory, or belief, is seen as a self-fulfilling prophecy. By espousing this view you help to make it happen.

Unfortunately, "good attitudes" do not necessarily fulfill themselves, especially when that is the conscious purpose of those who hold them. If a subordinate believes a superior is trying to control him by self-fulfilling optimism, he will typically prepare a nasty surprise. What people want from human relationships are responses to their particular needs, not the "Zip, Zoom, Zowie, and Zenith!" chorused by the Boosters Club in Sinclair Lewis's *Babbitt*.[16] A universalized belief that you can elicit good motivation from your workers by the instrumentality of glad thoughts is questionable.

Behaviorism, America's only home-grown psychology, is a product of American culture. It has long aspired to develop a universal code of principles unilaterally applied, which allow E, the Experimenter, to condition the responses of S, the Subject, by a prepared schedule of reinforcements designed to reward and punish. Such a "science" regards any particular motives or wants of S as irrelevant and any relationship between E and S as likely to contaminate the results. Particularism becomes an "unexplained variance" to be minimized where possible. Behaviorism has been highly influential in providing the "rewards" of external wage incentives, stock options, and bonuses for behaviors sought by management.

Although pay-for-performance has been widely copied, the "science" of behaviorism remains largely American. To the best of our knowledge, only Americans in any significant numbers believe that such a psychology is either possible or desirable. The cultural urge to codify in advance of human encounters, to know before exchanging views with another person, is quite unusually strong in Americans. It is less a reality than a persisting dream. Thus, *The Hidden Persuaders*, by Vance Packard, became an instant best seller in the late 1950s when it alleged—falsely, as it turned out—that consumers could be conditioned to buy products by subliminal suggestions flashed on screens for microseconds. The excitement occasioned by this claim entirely swamped its dubiousness. A decade later, B. F. Skinner urged us to reach *Beyond Freedom and Dignity*, where we would find programs to modify human behavior.[17]

Everyone could be conditioned for virtue. It was a prospect which, though wildly improbable, was enough to make Puritans perspire.

However, the most serious consequence of excess universalism is, ironically, what it most condemns—rising crime and fraud, which must eventually cripple the whole culture. As particular individuals slip first into delinquency, then into criminality, they find their persons increasingly excoriated in favor of abstract moral principals: "I hate you because I love Honesty." There is nothing in this process that deters criminality and everything that compounds it, as the criminal angrily rejects the social standards that dwarf him and reciprocates rejection.

Analyzers Extraordinary

The United States is also preponderantly analytical, spending more energy deconstructing than constructing. This "Anglo-Saxon empiricism" is a part of its British and Protestant heritage. None in the cultures in our sample were as keen as Americans to strip phenomena to their "bare bones." This is probably the reason the United States excelled so greatly in the Machine Age. Machines are readily reducible to their parts, as is the process of belting out simple standardized products. But with the extraordinary growth in complex systems joined by information, cultures that put the whole before the parts, such as Japan, France, and Germany, may now have an advantage.

This value has a profound influence on business practices. Cultures that analyze may intend to put the pieces together again, but as in the rhyme about Humpty-Dumpty, the egglike creature shattered beyond repair, the job is never completed. Similarly, integrating cultures may hope that once the grand theory is completed, the details will be mastered; but often they never do get down to the facts. The choice of analyzing versus integrating can be a critical one, and perils lie in either direction. Peters and Waterman warned of "paralysis through analysis" along with the dangers of spending your time counting bodies while you are losing a war.[18] However, as demonstrated by the disastrous effect of Marxism on wealth creation, the Miasma of Mountainous Theory also has its dangers.

The Dilemmas Methodology

We measured the analytic vs. integrative orientation in two ways. First we posed two extreme ways to describe a company:

a) A company is a system designed to perform functions and tasks in an efficient way. People are hired to fulfill these functions with the help of machines and other equipment. They are paid for the tasks they perform.

(b) A company is a group of people working together. The people have social relations with other people and with the organization. The functioning is dependent on these relations.

Respondents were asked to choose between these descriptions for themselves. The answers are set out below. Once again the United States is at the opposite end from Japan, which is by far the most synthetic of any nation sampled.

Table 2-3   Company a Set of Tasks

Tasks and functions	USA	CAN	BEL	NL	AUS	SWE	UK	IT	GER	SIN	FRA	JAP
	74	69	68	61	59	56	55	46	41	39	35	29

We see that the United States is the most analytic and reductive culture of the twelve we measured, while Japan and Singapore in Asia, and Germany and France in Europe are the most oriented to larger, integrated wholes.

We also sought to discover how legitimate it ws to reduce and analyze a company to a set of profit figures, confident in the belief that you had thereby distilled its value. This was a reflection of General Motors' famous boast that it was not in the business of making automobiles but of making money. We asked our managers to choose one of the following as an accurate statement of the proper goals of a company:

(a) The only real goal of a company is making profit.

(b) A company, besides making profit, has a goal of attaining the well-being of various stakeholders, such as employees, customers, etc.

Which of these opinions do you think most other people in your own country would think better represents the goals of a company, (a) or (b)?

Table 2-4   Analyzing vs. Synthesizing—"Only Goal Profit"

Profit only	USA	AUS	CAN	UK	IT	SWE	NL	BEL	GER	FRA	SIN	JAP
	40	35	34	33	28	27	26	25	24	16	11	8

Although only 40% of American managers still cling to "the bottom line"—down from the high forties when this research began seven years ago—the United States remains higher on this dimension than anyone else. Only 8% of Japanese managers agree with such reductiveness, only 11 percent of those in Singapore.

As the "bottom liners" see it, other responsibilities of the corporation may be important, but none are affordable and all are derivatives of the capacity to trade profitably and deliver to shareholders the returns which make continued investment worth their while.

As the multiple criteria managers see it, there are many strategic trade-offs. You can buy greater market share, train your human resources, increase volume, and learn more rapidly if you shave your profits wafer thin, or accept losses for a period. Indeed, you can force United States rivals to withdraw from competition by making it unprofitable for them. For Americans this is "dumping" and "cheating." All businesses must have a chance to compete "fairly," that is, make profits in the short term. It is destructive to engage in predatory practices that remove from whole industries the opportunities to profit, an argument which is entirely consistent with a culture that sees profit as "the specific of specifics," and the chief index of business virtue.

Americans tend not to see anything except the atoms they have analyzed out. "Give me the facts!" Harold T. Geneen of ITT was reported as saying, "the cold, unshakeable facts." He wanted these without gloss, without qualification, and especially without excuses. Flanked by his staff of data gatherers, each divisional manager would take his turn on the hot seat while "the facts" arising from his performance were examined and explained.[19]

Now, the idea that "facts do not lie" is contained within the word *data*, literally, "things given." If the scientist detaches himself from the "things given" he will see these as they really are, not how he would like them to be. The eye is a retinal mirror on which the images of objects fall. Try to interpret facts, place them in your own context, connect them in particular ways to suit your purposes, and bias has crept in! There is certainly some truth in this. Cultural perspectives are always partly true. You gain by adopting them and you lose.

Analyzing allows you to look at business in microscopic detail. Examine part by part, faults reveal themselves. For example, sales volume is up, but margins are slipping. Deliveries are up, but more are late. Bad debts are down, but late payments are up. Defects are down on established products, but up on newer ones. Problems are pinpointed and corrected.

Yet the idea that "facts don't lie" or that reality is "objective" is less a proven proposition than a cultural preference, especially strong in America and Great Britain. Facts are interpreted by the context in which we see them. To regard these facts as somehow more "basic" than their contexts is not obvious in large parts of the world, especially Asia. For example, a steep rise in profits may be an "unshakable fact," but it could be most unwise to rely on this as an unambiguous sign of virtue. Depending on the context, this could mean the company has switched to larger, gas-guzzling cars with higher margins, that less value is being given to consumers as compared with shareholders, that the volume auto business is being ceded to Japanese imports, and that the whole industry is headed for a precipice.

It would be equally plausible to argue that context does not lie, that improving relationships and valuable information flows between the company and the customers will take care of any unpleasant facts that customers may unearth. The famous axiom of Japanese management, "Crisis is opportunity," places alarming facts in the context of managers' ability to redeem such errors and greatly improve performance.

What may really be at stake here is the belief in objectivity as an ideal, which even if impossible should be approached as nearly as possible, versus the acceptance that all knowledge is relational, joining the knower to the known, and that attention without intention is neither possible nor desirable.

Mechanism and Organicism as Metaphors

Insofar as technology and machinery constitute a major part of what a business does to create wealth, the analysis of such machines into their specific parts is obviously sensible. A machine is constructed from its parts, and if you want to understand it you take it to bits. Most products are similarly assembled from their parts, each of which is typically supplied by a different department within the organization. The very word "organization" comes from *organon*, meaning instrument. An organization is an instrument to accomplish tasks, modeled on the way the parts of an efficient machine operate. Markets are also conceived of as machines, hence "the market mechanism," which balances millions of items of supply against items of demand and has more than a passing resemblance to Newton's perpetual motion machine.

Indeed, the semiconscious metaphor underlying the way Americans and their analytic bretheren think is the notion of the corporation as a mechanism, while the Japanese, Singaporeans, French, and Latins generally tend to think of the organization more as an organism.[20] The former is analyzable without being destroyed, the latter must stay connected to live. The former is sufficient unto itself, the latter needs nurturance and natural sustenance from its environment and is interdependent with its whole ecology. The former is nothing but the parts of which it is constituted, the latter generates higher levels of meaning, purpose, and direction which transcend its parts.[21] Thus, for Anglo-American corporations, employees are "human resources" on a par with capital resources and raw materials. These aggregations of units can be hired, fired, and acquired as if they were physical things without living connections. Organizations are downsized, rationalized, restructured as if they had no meaning to the people within them and these goods (literally, good things) suffered no trauma by being decimated and divided. No wonder that managers in British Petroleum speak of BOH-ICA (bend-over-here-it-comes-again).

An interesting mechanical metaphor is Michael Porter's concept of the value chain. Corporations are increasingly linking themselves together across national borders, so that cheaper manufacturing assembly can be done in countries where wages are lower. In a recent book, Porter invites us to calculate, link by link, the most cost-effective world location for different operations.[22]

But this concept fails to consider the quality of connectedness. For example, Apple Computer decided to assemble in Singapore because it was cheaper. To the company's amazement, the Singapore assembly plant was outperforming American and European assembly operations within months of start up. The real gain was achieved by connecting Singapore to Apple's international operations and having them teach assembly to the rest of the network.[23]

Perils of Negotiating

Preference for analyzing versus integrating is much encountered in the course of negotiating and is the source of great difficulty and stress. Americans and Northwestern Europeans like to "get to the point." "What's your proposition? Can we do business? I'll send you a FAX with the terms of a suggested contract." No one wants "to beat about the bush" because "time is money." Friendships and goodwill are not virtues to be slighted, but there is time enough to deepen any relationship after having assured ourselves that there is a likelihood of genuine commercial gain. After all, the world is full of people with whom it might be nice to drink tea, but not full of potential business partners. So "let's get down to the basics. What have you got?"

Many other cultures, especially in Asia, find this approach rather crude and mildly offensive. In their view, the more genuine scarcity is not of products or profits but of people one can trust, with whom it is possible to form multidimensional connections involving the exchange of complex information. It is best for several reasons to approach such persons with circumspection, to discover how sensitive, responsive, and subtle they are before moving on to specific inducements which might lead them to feign such solicitude. A person who cannot wait to horse trade may not be worth trading horses with, caring more for gain than for the partnership. Such people may depart as abruptly as they arrived, thus wasting all the effort invested by their partners. American and Asian approaches to negotiation look rather like this:

USA   JAPAN

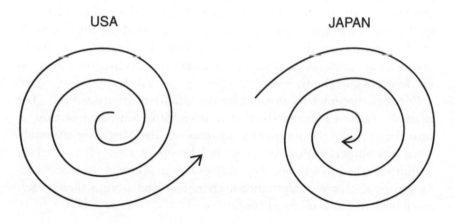

The spiral on the left starts at the center and circles outward. The one on the right starts at the outside and circles (slowly) inward. The former is typical of the United States and much of northwest Europe; the latter is typical of Japan and some Latin countries.

What seems to Americans to be an intolerable ritual of individuals waltzing around each other while making remarks of a vaguely benign and ritual nature, is for the Japanese full of clues to the quality of relationship to be expected with the other person. That the discussion appears to be about nothing pertinent to business only makes those clues more significant. According to this view, the real waste of time is having relationships sour after one has spent three or four years nurturing them. Who knows what human qualities may be needed to sustain this relationship in the future, so why not meander to discover the other's full range of attributes? Moreover, "to give sometime time" is a mark of respect (see Chapters 4 and 7).

In the view of most Americans, whether you like an individual should be separated from whether you want that person's product. The proposition is logically independent of the parties, and only "backward" and "primitive" people from the American South insist on talking about fishing for several minutes before deciding whether or not to buy. (This may be one reason that the Japanese prefer to locate many of their plants in the South.)

Because the human connection is, to Singaporeans, the Japanese, and the French, more important than specific contract terms, they may expect—or at least hope—that contracts can be scrapped and rewritten in the light of changing situations in order to maintain a mutuality of benefit for both partners.[24] This strikes most Americans not simply as illegal, but immoral and hardly what they have hired expensive legal talent to do. The contract and its terms are a pledge of "your word" (note the exaggerated specificity—not even many words, but one). The contract is, of course, a derivative of the covenant with God by which the Puritan pledged his soul (another distillation of virtue). For many cultures, however, virtue is irreducible to words or souls. It inheres in the broader context, not in "the law" but in its spirit or meaning within altered contexts.

The Japanese habit of indirect "circling around" is also seen in their *ringi* decision making, in which a decision is passed around in a circle and ritually initialled by all the major players. In contrast, Americans admire quick and incisive decision making by tough leaders. It is a much debated question whether the time "wasted" by circuitous deciding is not made up when the decisions are implemented more smoothly and with fewer snags. Our interest is less in settling this argument than in showing that there are two entirely plausible, yet opposite, approaches to such issues.

The Limitations of the Analytic Mind

While it would be foolish to try to run a business without analyzing its operations, it is quite difficult to achieve wholeness by first analyzing and only later recombining the parts. The problem with this procedure is that qualities of production and service not entirely contained within each part are lost sight of, especially design, total quality, and fit with the human customer. We lose "the between." As William Wordsworth put it:

> Our meddling intellect
> Misshapes the beauteous forms of things.
> We murder to dissect.[25]

Moreover, to subject all phenomena to analysis can confuse your method with what you are studying. There is the famous story of the learned professor who diced some cheese with a kitchen gadget and then wrote a learned dissertation on the cubic nature of cheese.[26] For example, you can break a pearl necklace down into one hundred and fifty pearls, a thread, and a fastener, but you have lost the idea of "necklace," not to mention the neck of the lady it adorns and the impressions she creates on others. Wholes have meaning, design, beauty, purpose, forms, and relationships with people, not present in their parts alone. Wholes join the person to the product, to the information and the service incident to the product. Quality is seamless.

While machines, as we have seen, can be easily analyzed, living systems, their expressions, and creations have qualities of connections which analysis actually destroys. The culture that puts parts before wholes is left with the pieces: statistics without meaning, inventories without purpose, tasks without integration, functions without coordination. In the words of Gareth Morgan, you get a rationality of parts, separate departments, but an irrationality of the whole organization.[27]

It is also important to see that a culture can be adept at connecting while not capable of analyzing properly. Such was the case with American Indian culture. America's Western expansion, during which the Indian tribes suffered defeat and the destruction of a life-style of hunting and gathering, pitted a Western analyzing culture capable of manufacturing rifles against a connected culture ecologically dependent on its land. Chief Seattle, in his famous letter to the United States president had difficulty with the conception of property as divided and separately sold. From his perspective, the land joined everyone in a sacred brotherhood. In one sense, the American Indians could be regarded as "primitive." They could not grasp the principles of analysis at all. Today we face rather stiffer competition. Our rivals understand analysis as well as we do while retaining holism for social and human purposes.

Business cultures highly involved in analytical specifics tend to be Philistine. They know "the price of everything" (since price is a specific), but "the value of nothing" (since value is an integral system). The belief that business was prosaic, ugly, and uninspiring haunted both the U.S., British, and Northwest European economies during the late 1960s and early 1970s, when millions turned their backs on business as a worthwhile moral commitment. Although fashions have now changed, a decade of disenchantment is not easily recoverable. Moreover, business success is not seen as it is in Japan, Holland, Sweden, or Italy as a choice for idealists or those dedicated to aesthetics, but for those who want to "get ahead" and "make a buck." Those business cultures greatly depending on analysis find it difficult to capture the imaginations of employees in superordinate goals or larger visions. They tend to get stuck with more of some specifically defined objectives, more money, more profit, more customers, products, or turnover. Their TV offerings are divided into spots, slots, and breaks, while their politicians are reduced to one-liners and sound-bites. One tends to feel like someone trapped in a *Guinness Book of Records* exhibition or shut inside Ripley's *Believe It or Not*, with their "fastest, longest, tallest, biggest, fattest" exhibits. Size and volume become very important in what the Japanese regard as an "obvious culture." The largest canyons, the tallest skyscrapers, the most visited museums, all must vie through a few simple dimensions. We very rapidly exhaust the possibilities and are left with only the grosser extremities, 600-pound men and 90-hour pole squatters, hailed amid superlatives: "terrific, giant, dynamic, wow!" Even the genius of Steve Jobs is reduced to calling the Macintosh computer an "insanely great machine."[28] In this linear world of extensions, shooting onward and upward, there is nothing else to say.

America's strong analytical bias has also shaped her management practices. Management by Objectives invites subordinates to set their own specific objectives against which they will be measured and rewarded in the period to come. There are job descriptions, job enrichments, job satisfaction, the rate-for-the-job, and jobs and "slots" into which employees are "fitted." The first question in an interview typically inquires whether the candidate's qualifications fit the job description.

The traditional organization of the American factory followed Adam Smith's dictum that the wealth of nations is created by divisions of labor. It is, of course, equally true that such divisions must be integrated, but the emphasis on divisions looms larger in analytical cultures. Early in this century, the work of U.S. factories was so finely divided as to grossly simplify each job, which was often reduced to endlessly replicated hand motions, carefully timed and specified. Although claimed in the United States to be universally valid, this approach was, in reality, an adaptation to particular American conditions. The workforce was often multiethnic, low skilled, and foreign speaking. The workers were deemed capable of some manual dexterities but not of thinking or conferring with each other. Simplification of tasks kept wages low, allowing new immigrants, desperate for work, to replace "troublemakers." In the politics of the factory, a policy of divide-and-rule emphasized the existing bias toward division. Low job satisfaction raised turnover, which reinforced the need for subdivided simplicities, since new "hands" were constantly having to be hired and inducted into the plant. For one of the lasting legacies of cultures highly involved in analysis is the separation of head and hand, thought and action.[29]

The result was that the United States became the world's leader in the mass manufacture of relatively simple products in steady demand. American workers were trained to fit the logic of machines and to become extensions of the machines they worked with. Some unions grew powerful, defining themselves in the same rigid job categories by which they had originally been demarcated and, by contriving scarcities in key subspecialties, forced up wages in the midcentury, passing on the costs to consumers. Simplified, divided labors earned high wages.

The situation began to unravel in the mid-1970s and 1980s, when the proportion of U.S. goods subject to foreign competition jumped from 18 to 80 percent.[30] Third World countries, whose factories had been purpose-built by U.S. contractors to the same specifics as U.S. factories, found they could engage in simple mass-manufacture at a fraction of the wage rates paid to U.S. workers. America fought back, but in the same cultural paradigm as before. They moved their manufacturing abroad to wherever wages were lowest. To the division of thought and action, of brain work and manual work, new geographical divides were now added. The "Hollow Corporation" had its brains in Chicago and its hands in Mexico or the Philippines. There can be no more vivid example of how the urge to analyze and divide can overwhelm the capacity to cohere.

Climbing the Knowledge Ladder

There are, of course, alternatives to competing at simple manufacturing. The answer discovered by many developed economies is to climb the "knowledge ladder" toward goods and services with higher value added and increased levels of complexity.[31] But this leads one away from long manufacturing runs and the world of specialized and specified standards, into short-run, flexible manufacturing, frequent tool changes, just-in-time deliveries, and self-managing work teams with the discretion to solve problems and with considerable skill and sophistication. [32]

Here one worker may run six machines or more, their cycle times calibrated to fit his or her convenience and rhythm of work. No longer is the worker an extension of a machine or of the mechanized assembly line; rather, multiple machines are extensions of the human system that coordinates their working. The "new" manufacturing is more integrative and connected, and less analytical and specific than the "old" manufacturing. America's analytic bias, which gave her substantial advantages in the Machine Age, may now be of declining utility. Sophisticated manufacturing requires that an increasing richness of information be communicated among employees. This may require cultures more comfortable with multiple, connected perspectives.

It is analytical bias that brings us bureaucracy, the traditional factory visited on the office, where a sequence of clerks check different sections of an insurance claim. The pathologies of bureaucracy are well known: its incapacity to deal with problems not anticipated by its own rational organization, its impersonality, detachment, neutrality, and alienation. [33]

There is another important reason that analytical cultural biases are ill suited to an environment becoming more complex by the hour. You can break down simple operations, but to break down complex ones is to drown in thousands of details. Box 2-1, "Scientific Management Survives at McDonald's", breaks down the serving of hamburgers into a checklist of thirty-one observations. [34] Yet this is equivalent to roughly one manufacturing step, since this checklist does not deal with frying the burgers. Consider the manufacture of forklift trucks, which has two thousand manufacturing steps. An observational checklist of the same rigor as that used by McDonald's would require sixty-two thousand items to be observed and individually checked on, clearly a ludicrous proposition. Analysis as a cultural trait is reaching the limits of its usefulness where it is not qualified by more holistic perspectives.

The Hunt for the Unicorn

Perhaps the most limiting aspect of analytical thinking is the reduction of the multiple values with which an organization must deal to arrive at a single figure or dimension, that of profitability. It is not hard to see from whence the criterion of profitability got its good name. It is an extremely important way of feeding back to a private enterprise the degree to which it is succeeding or failing to serve customers. Beyond

Box 2-1

Scientific Management Survives at McDonald's

A management observation checklist used to evaluate the performance of counter staff in a fast-food restaurant

Greeting the customer	Yes	No
1. There is a smile.		
2. It is a sincere greeting.		
3. There is eye contact.		
Other:		

Taking the order	Yes	No
1. The counter person is thoroughly familiar with the menu ticket. (No hunting for items.)		
2. The customer has to give the order only once.		
3. Small orders (four items or less) are memorized rather than written down.		
4. There is suggestive selling.		
Other:		

Assembling the order	Yes	No
1. The order is assembled in the proper sequence.		
2. Grill slips are handed in first.		
3. Drinks are poured in the proper sequence.		
4. Proper amount of ice.		
5. Cups slanted and finger used to activate.		
6. Drinks are filled to the proper level.		
7. Drinks are capped.		
8. Clean cups.		
9. Holding times are observed on coffee.		
10. Cups are filled to the proper level on coffee.		
Other:		

Presenting the order	Yes	No
1. It is properly packaged.		
2. The bag is double folded.		
3. Plastic trays are used if eating inside.		
4. A tray liner is used.		

5. The food is handled in a proper
   manner.   _____ _____

Other: _____ _____

Asking for & receiving payment   **Yes**   **No**
   1. The amount of the order is stated
      clearly and loud enough to hear.   _____ _____
   2. The denomination received is clearly
      stated.   _____ _____
   3. The change is counted out loud.   _____ _____
   4. Change is counted efficiently.   _____ _____
   5. Large bills are laid on the till until the
      change is given.   _____ _____

Other: _____ _____

**Thanking the customer & asking for repeat
business**   **Yes**   **No**
   1. There is always a thank you.   _____ _____
   2. The thank you is sincere.   _____ _____
   3. There is eye contact.   _____ _____
   4. Return business was asked for.   _____ _____

Other: _____ _____

providing information, it provides resources for the successful to continue their good work, while progressively diminishing the resources of those who are failing. The net effect of this process in the whole economy is to shift all available resources away from those who utilize them poorly and toward those who utilize them well. It is also a well-deserved reward for the enterprising, that they should be encouraged to expand in proportion to their success.[35]

The profit criterion also distinguishes the prosperous times of the West and Pacific Rim from the seventy-four years of abject failure that has characterized the Soviet system, along with the stagnation of the Eastern bloc, following World War II. Profitability has thus been a beacon shining in the darkness of the Cold War, a symbol of freedom itself, an index of personal achievement and a verdict deliverable by individual consumers against the organized force of businesses large and small, a message to the mighty and overbearing that they are only as good as "dollar ballots" cast in their favor by ordinary men and women. No organization willingly abolishes itself. Only markets can do this job.

Indeed, the problem is not with profitability as a value or a necessary condition for free enterprise. The problem lies with profitability as an exclusive criterion, a sufficient condition, that is, with profitability per se, meaning "as a thing." What could be harming America and the West is not the care taken to assure that companies are profitable, but the belief that if they are profitable, then everything else must be all right. The problem lies in the reduction of multiple interdependent signs of organizational health to one be-all and end-all. Elsewhere we have called this the "Hunt for the Unicorn," the attempt to avoid conflict, dilemma, and ambiguity by putting one's faith in the bottom line, the unicorn's pure and mystic extremity, the animal that never was. Box 2-2, "Eight Objections to Profit Maximization," argues that, strategically, the attempt to maximize profit by itself can lead to disaster and is easily defeated.

Box 2-2

Eight Objections to Profit Maximization

Strategies aimed at profit maximization have the following serious drawbacks:

1. Profit comes too late to be used to steer a company effectively. This is because your present profit may be the result of decisions made many years ago but just coming into fruition. It is like trying to steer a boat by the wake left several miles behind.

2. Profit, like happiness or self-fulfillment, is more easily attained by indirection, by not thinking first and foremost of yourself and what you want, but by focusing on the needs of customers. A short trip through a kindergarten should convince us that self-concern does not have to be learned but the understanding of others takes a lifetime.

3. Profitability conflicts with values of greater priority, which is not to say values of greater importance. We have to gain a customer's allegiance before she or he provides our profit, to invest before the payoff, to care about our product before we ask others to care. Taking profits out of an organization now will typically slow its growth later, while emphasizing growth now will increase profits later.

---

4. Profit-maximizing strategies are too predictable and too easy to defeat. Your rival need only remove the profitability from your contest and wait for you to drop out in frustration.

5. The more you profit initially in a new market, the more entrants will rush to exploit this same opportunity. But if you have learned much while profiting modestly, they may leave you alone.

6. If top management goes for the highest returns it can get, do not be surprised if your workers and star employees make similar suboptimal demands on you.

7. Profiting may not be applicable to all units in a strategic alliance. For example, if your Japanese competitor has a bank, an insurer, and a trading company not extracting the highest price from him, then he can gain a cost advantage over you.

8. Where profits alone are pursued, a company can damage the integrity and coherence of what it knows, hopping from automobiles, to aerospace, to information services, with few logical connections between the bodies of necessary knowledge and skills.

Source: *Charting the Corporate Mind*, Charles Hampden-Turner. New York: Free Press, 1990, pp. 205–220.

3

The Triumphant
Individual Within

We believe in the dignity, indeed the sacredness of the individual. Anything that would violate our right to think for ourselves, judge for ourselves make our own decisions, live our lives as we see fit, is not only morally wrong, it is sacrilegious. Our highest and noblest aspirations, not only for ourselves, but for those we care about, for society and for the world, are closely linked to our individualism. Yet . . . some of our deepest problems both as individuals and as a society are also closely linked to our individualism. We do not argue that Americans should abandon individualism—that would mean for us to abandon our deepest identity. But individualism has come to mean so many things and to contain such contradictions and paradoxes that even to defend it requires that we analyze it critically, that we consider especially those tendencies that would destroy it from within.[1]

Habits of the Heart

IN THE PREVIOUS CHAPTER we saw that American managers were far more oriented to universal codes and standards than to particular relationships and exceptional circumstances, and were far readier to analyze and reduce than to integrate and construct. This chapter adds more detail to the picture of the American style of wealth creation by examining the next two processes identified in Chapter 1 as vital to creating value. These processes, and the dilemmas that characterize them, are: #3. Managing Communities of Individuals (individualism versus communitarianism) and #4. Internalizing Outside Events (inner-direction versus outer direction).

47

American managers are by far the strongest individualists in our national samples. This means that they regard the individual as the basic unit and building block of the enterprise and the origin of all its success. They are also more inner-directed, i.e. they locate the source of the organization's purpose and direction in the inner convictions of its employees. No culture is as dedicated to making each individual's dream come true. Americans believe you should "make up your own mind" and "do your own thing" rather than allow yourself to be influenced too much by other people and the external flow of events. Taken together, these are the prime attributes of entrepreneurship: the self-determined individual tenaciously pursuing a personal dream.

The imprint of these values on the American style of wealth creation is unmistakable. No other culture in the world has profited so greatly from entrepreneurial endeavours. Inspired and brilliant men like John Hopkins, Matthew Vassar, Leland Stanford, Andrew Carnegie, and the Rockefeller and Vanderbilt families accrued enormous economic power. The world eats what Philip D. Armour, Clarence Birdseye, and W. K. Kellogg once devised. We fly and travel thanks to Donald W. Douglas, William E. Boeing, and George M. Pullman, and stay with Conrad Hilton. We drive thanks to Henry Ford, Benjamin F. Goodrich, and Paul Getty, and shop with F. W. Woolworth, Samuel H. Kress, James C. Penney, Richard W. Sears, and Alvah Roebuck. Many a small nation does not have an exchequer with as much money as the Ford, Rockefeller, Getty, Mellon, or Carnegie foundations. Yet most of these individuals started with little or nothing.

American culture encourages the individual to "be all you can be." Even today, America leads the world in Nobel Prizes won, in the total number of new patents, in the number of new jobs created annually, in new business starts (averaging around 700,000 per year from 1985–90). The availability of venture capital to outstanding individuals is the most abundant in the world. The capacity of Americans to reinvent themselves remains unprecedented. Moreover the whole society is organized to benefit individuals, with an extraordinary 66.3 percent of GNP going for personal consumption.

Yet once again this extraordinary strength leaves America vulnerable, because while America extolls individualism, it ignores the needs of the larger community upon which even the strongest individuals must depend. The Fortune 500 have been shrinking both in employees and their contribution to the economy. "Big" is ceasing to work in America, whether big corporations—IBM, Ford, GM, Sears Roebuck—big government, or big cities. Labor relations remain poor. Education is in trouble. Social programs have not simply failed but have proved disastrous. Communities seem helpless to stop epidemics of drugs and crime. Inner-directed individualism is half the solution only.

Another downside of individualism, especially powerful when combined with inner-direction, is that American managers are so transient and footloose occupationally, so determined to march to their own drummers and to extract value from groups and corporations that bankruptcies have reached epidemic proportions, 68,000 a year, many of large companies. The Fragile Corporation may not survive those who feed off it. Groups need nurturing too. In regarding corporations as "social technology," mere instruments for individual gain, American institutions may have weakened themselves in their contest with the more community-minded Germans, French, and Japanese.

Inner direction has its downside too. Fervent believers in "the soul within" may blaze with achievement fantasies and fight for self-fulfillment, but as the world fills up with man-made systems, perhaps it is not the fittest who survive but the fittingest, those who can adapt fast to an environment changing before their eyes. As external change speeds up, it is those who best ride the turbulence of furious international currents who prosper. Japan, Sweden, and Holland have all been subject to overwhelming external powers and keep their antennae tuned to the world outside, and while Germany and France are champions of inner conviction, their less individualistic approaches help them build communities of customers and suppliers in lifelong, durable relationships. Only in America does the "inner man" talk so exclusively to the triumphant individual.

The Puritan Legacy

American individualism originated in Puritan ethics, especially in the belief that each individual, whom God had chosen as a "saint," had a personal unmediated capacity to approach God, to form a covenant or contract with Him and serve as His earthly agent in building the Kingdom of Heaven on American soil.[2] A divine CEO delegated individual responsibility to agents. To this day there are pews in New England churches in which the worshiper is screened from those next to him, but pointed toward the altar to gain a private audience. While Catholics approached God as a community, the Puritans came separately, joined by the Bible and by the object of their allegiance.[3] The persecution of

Puritans in England precipitated their "errand into the wilderness" to establish the Pure Community in the New World. In what must have been a highly selective process, certain persons were willing to uproot themselves from the only society they had known, severing bonds in the process.

The idealized life was that of the artisan-craftsman, typified by Benjamin Franklin, and the gentleman farmer of independent means symbolized by Thomas Jefferson. In Hawthorne, Emerson, Thoreau, and Melville the self that earns money and owns property yields to the self that is cultivated, learned, and resourceful. Yet the persisting tension with society remained. "Society," wrote Emerson in *Self-Reliance*, "everywhere is in conspiracy against the manhood of every one of its members."[4] Public group opinion, he believed, sapped the integrity of the person. In his poem *Freedom*, Emerson slights even family and home. Like Horatio Alger, you have to be orphaned to be truly independent.

> Freedom's secret wilt thou know?
> Counsel not with flesh and blood
> Loiter not for cloak or food,
> Right thou feelest, rush to do![5]

American self-help did not end with emigration from Europe to the New World. There was an extended trek westward, with a frontier the length of a whole continent. The United States was thinly populated by native Americans, so that in many essentials the land was for the taking. The opportunities available to individuals, soon to be followed by wave upon wave of new immigrants, is probably unprecedented in the history of the world and is unlikely to ever be repeated. If American culture was shaped by this rare experience, we should expect that culture to be as untypical as was the experience. Individualism worked for Americans so well that the culture is indelibly marked by its success.

No wonder, then, that popular American culture celebrates the "man alone": Han Solo of *Star Wars*, Rick, the hard-boiled, cynical saloon keeper in *Casablanca*. Such individuals are typified by Lone Rangers, Lone Eagles, innovative seagulls, hard-bitten detectives, mountain men, mavericks, lovable bank robbers, pool sharks and con men, junk-bond salesmen, grand acquisitors, even Colonel Oliver North. TV series end routinely with heroes riding off alone into the next episode.

A community in this view is but the sum of its individuals and their strivings with a few collectivist impedimenta thrown in. Herman Melville caught the spirit:

'Take a single man alone, and he seems a wonder, a grandeur and a woe. But from the same point take mankind in the mass, and for the most part they seem a mob of unnecessary duplicates.'[6]

It was the great entrepreneurs who effected first Britain's, then America's, industrial revolution, who defied the values of landed gentility and inherited privilege, struck out on their own and transformed the world. Watt, Arkwright, Carnegie, Mellon, Ford, Rockefeller—the roll call of capitalism's great individuals is part of our folklore. The latter four became great through massive acquisitiveness and great again through massive charity.

The point is not that these individuals thought only of themselves. Great Britain owes Andrew Carnegie much of its public library system. Individualism, properly understood, leaves you free to be selfish or self-sacrificing. The doctrine holds that whatever the choice, the individual is its origin. Heroes of popular culture typically put their lives on the line. Hence, in *Star Wars*, Han Solo rushes to the rescue of Luke Skywalker—even their names reflect mythic separations. Rick of *Casablanca* joins the battle against fascism at the cost of his love life. As Robert Bellah has pointed out, the American myth's hero "again and again saves a society he can never completely fit into."[7]

The straight shooting of the ranger, his special sense of justice, his total incorruptibility destines him to "defend society without really joining it." The value of American heroes to their society is that they "stand alone, not needing others, not depending on their judgment, and not submitting to their wishes," yet this individualism is not selfishness. Indeed, it is "a kind of heroic selflessness. One accepts the necessity of remaining alone in order to serve the values of the group."[8]

We may, therefore, miss the many subtleties of American individualism if we confuse it with just one of its varieties, i.e., with selfishness and greed. A cultivated, compassionate person may reach out to the oppressed, as did millions during the Civil Rights Movement and the protests against the Vietnam War. It is no coincidence that the American left calls itself "liberal," a term generally reserved for free-marketeers in other countries. The likely reason is that all motives, including prosocial ones, are deemed to arise from the personal choice of free individuals. There is no ethos in the United States that puts the community before the individual. There are only individuals more or less committed to forming communities.

One reason the radical surge in America collapsed so suddenly and so totally that it seems scarcely to have taken place at all, is that it created almost no permanent groups or organizations. The movement rejected self-interest and, with it, any reason for building lasting organizations that might stifle self-expression. The protestors' rage against acquisitive individualism was quite genuine, but they brought into the streets an alternative selfhood, and there remains from those years only a parade of colorful personalities, "beautiful people," whose higher sensibilities cried out against injustice. The way in which the liberals of that era thought was captured by Martin Luther King. You joined the Civil Rights Movement because you shared a dream, because you sought to develop your "soul-power," and because "suffering is redemptive." "The individual who breaks the law that conscience tells him is unjust and willingly accepts the penalty . . . is in reality expressing the highest respect for law." Each person carries a new just code within his selfhood. King's dream was that one day men "will not be judged by the color of their skin, but the content of their characters."⁹ The ideas were individualist to their core. When three civil rights workers were slain in Mississippi, Ben Shahn designed a famous poster invoking the words of the British poet Steven Spender. This is an example of Compassionate Individualism, but it suffers from a recurring problem. The person making the protest, about three other persons making a protest, does in the end draw more attention to the beauty of the individuals concerned than to the desperate needs of the communities they sought to serve. A morality that starts with the individual and his or her outraged conscience often ends in celebrating "the great" and not the downtrodden.

In any event, at this time of writing, Compassionate Individualism is out of political fashion and Acquisitive Individualism is back in with a vengeance, as it was in the days of the robber barons, the great trusts, immediately prior to the Great Depression. The 1980s are even now being lamented in the media as "the age of greed and excess." Herein lies an important lesson. What distinguishes individualism from communitarism is less any aim or motive of individuals than the tendency to see one or the other as the basic entity to which values accrue. Individualism holds that "in the beginning" was the individual who formed a contract or religious convenant with other individuals, thereby forming a voluntary association or group, be it Salem Village, Alcoholics Anonymous, or Mothers Against Drunk Driving. It follows that if these freely associating groups choose to serve the wider community, then that is fortunate for society and a credit to those individuals, but their choice is no one's business but their own—within the boundaries of the law.

The consequence of the logic is that while individualism may not result in selfish conduct, there are very few sanctions within an individualistic society like the United States to prevent this happening. In combatting selfishness we are reduced to showing that Scarlett O'Hara in *Gone with the Wind* has made herself personally unhappy by her ruthless exploitation of her social environment. We are not invited to champion her convict laborers against her. Thus, in the war of Self verses Others in American letters and media the very battle takes place within the self, with personal fulfillment and happiness as the prize to be enjoyed for social sensitivities.

The Curious Birth of Classical Economics

It is not a trifling matter that individual self-interest has been enshrined within the very foundation stone of neoclassical economics—the currently reigning orthodoxy in the English-speaking world. Adam Smith's famous doctrine of self-seeking at the roots of Homo Economicus is perhaps the world's leading example of cultural bias and historical circumstance disguised as a principle of science.[10]

Adam Smith published *An Inquiry into the Wealth of Nations* in 1776, the year America won her independence. The book became virtually a manifesto for the end of mercantilism and the beginnings of laissez-faire, and a charter for American economic liberties. It is certainly the most influential book on economics ever written. In two much-quoted passages Smith wrote:

> It is not from the benevolence of the butcher, the brewer or the baker, that we expect our dinner, but from their regard to their own interest.[11]

> [The individual] . . . intends only his own gain, and he is in this, as in many other cases, led by an invisible hand to promote an end which was no part of his intention. Nor is it always the worse for society that it was no part of it. By pursuing his own interest he frequently promotes that of society more effectually than when he really intends to promote it. I have never known much good done by those who affected to trade in the public good. It is an affection indeed not very common among merchants, and very few words need be employed in dissuading them from it.[12]

Smith was extremely influential in the development of American economics and social thought. He was also the darling of America's great entrepreneurs. Samuel J. Tilden, a lawyer for the railroad interests and presidential candidate, made a famous speech at a testimonial dinner for Junius Morgan, John Pierpont Morgan's father:

> You are, doubtless, in some degree, clinging to the illusion that you are working for yourself, but it is my pleasure to claim that you are working for the public (applause) while you are scheming for your own selfish ends, there is an overruling and wise Providence directing that most of all you do should rebound to the benefit of the people. Men of colossal fortune are in effect, if not in fact, trustees for the public. [13]

In other words, a universalist dispensation redeems self-interest for the public good.

It is very easy to see why Adam Smith might have believed strongly in the ideas presented in these passages. He was, after all, an employee of the ruling class, a tutor to the son of the Duke of Buccleuch. Like many contemporary academics, he had greater sympathy for those attacking the elite than for his own paymasters and the class then rising to challenge landed privilege, the bourgeoisie. Smith was also rightly sceptical of the vaunted "benevolence" of this landholding elite and their "charity" toward tenants, peasants on the large estates, and toward tutors. Merchants, whom he did not much like, as several passages make clear, were at least openly self-seeking, whereas he saw his patrons as secretly so, yet pretending to an affection for the public interest.

It may be a major irony of economic history that what Smith intended as a sideswipe at some rather pretentious acquaintances has been refurbished into the motivational core of economics. It is, of course, true that the affection one feels for oneself is more tangibly real than are posturings by the powerful about the public good, but Smith elided two separate issues and confused them both. He argued that more affection is felt for a real person than for an abstraction, "the public good." He confused this with a second argument, that self-interest is more salient in human nature than benevolence, and he skewed the issued in his own favor by attaching self-interest to the individual reader and benevolence to an abstraction. Of course, benevolence is weaker and less genuine when expressed toward "society," rather than toward particular persons within that society.

There is only one way to give an individualist pause, and that is to ask, Could a capitalist economy be organized on precisely opposite premises? Could it be argued that benevolent relationships with customers and fellow employees is the basic cultural norm and obligation, from which the self-interests of those who are parties to these relationships will subsequently emerge—as if by an invisible hand? Why is it somehow more true that benevolence follows from self-interest than that self-interest follows from benevolence?

Let us, then, rewrite Smith's argument, but designate a real economic actor to whom benevolence might reasonably be shown, the customer. Is it plausible that concern for the customer is but posturing?

> It is not because he cares for you, the customer, that the brewer, the baker, or the butcher provides for your dinner, but becasue he cares for himself.

> [The supplier] . . . intends only his own gain and is led by an invisible hand to serve you, his customer, although this was not part of his intention. Nor is it always worse for you that the supplier does not want to serve you. By pursuing his own gain he often serves you better than if he consciously tried to benefit you. I have never known much good done by those who claimed to like their customers. It is an affection indeed, which few merchants have.

A few moments of reflection on the two sets of passages in which "self" and "other" are rendered as real people reveals the perversity of the argument. Benevolence is wholly compatible with customer service, and to provide another person with a product you have made with pride and care can be an act of genuine affection from which, additionally, you earn your living.

Three cultural biases, felt very strongly by Americans, underlie the belief that economic self-interest must have primacy over social concern. First is the analyzing bias encountered in Chapter 2, sometimes called "nothing but-ery." According to this view, motivations, and much else, must be broken down to the smallest possible atomic unit and be shorn of all contradiction. Hence we are forbidden to couple self-interest with benevolence, since these are "opposed categories" and the rules of logic derived from Aristotle oblige us to separate "A" from "not-A." We must get rid of one or the other. Second, the individualistic bias makes sure that it is benevolence and social concern that we get rid of. The individual is considered prior to any relationship formed or feelings expressed. It follows that self-interest is "basic," while benevolence is "nothing but" an expression of that individual. "My self is interested in helping others," perhaps because of the vicarious thrills received or pleasure in others' gratitude. Third is the sequential bias, discussed more fully in Chapters 4 and 7.

The Individualist Corporation

American corporate practices are also highly individualist. It is no coincidence that the United States pioneered piecework incentives, whereby each individual worker is paid according to the number of pieces produced above a fixed standard. Management by Objectives assumes a free commitment by the individual to an objective important to the organization. You are rewarded according to your performance of a contract freely entered. That this does not appeal to much of Latin Europe, the Middle East, and Asia is a consequence of differing suppositions. If your relationship with your boss or supervisor is the origin of productivity, why should you be paid as if he, or your work colleagues, had no share in this? If it is important to think of the customer's interests, why introduce the temptation to load him up with excess stock, so as to hit a private sales target? Individualism clearly illumines some motivational dynamics but obscures others.

Measuring Individualism—Organization

To try and learn more about whether our group of managers identified themselves more strongly as lone individuals or as members of groups, we posed the following dilemma:

Suppose you, as a manager, are in the process of hiring a new employee to work in your department. Which of the two following considerations are more important to you:

(a) The new employee must fit into the group or team in which he/she is to work.

(b) The new employee must have the skills, the knowledge, and a record to success in a previous job.

Obviously, the person who choose (a) is more sympathetic to group goals, while the person choosing (b) has greater concerns for the needs of the individual.

Table 3-1   Personal Ability or Fitting In?

Individual capacity	USA	CAN	AUS	NL	GER	UK	BEL	IT	FRA	SWE	JAP	SIN
	92%	91	91	88	87	71	69	62	57	53	49	39

We got similar results when we asked the managers to express their preferences for "two different kinds of jobs:"

(a) Jobs in which no one is singled out for personal honor, but in which everyone works together
(b) Jobs in which personal initiatives are encouraged and individual initiatives are achieved

Table 3-2   Individual Honors Achieved

Personal initiatives encouraged	USA	AUS	CAN	SWE	NL	UK	GER	BEL	IT	FRA	JAP	SIN
	97%	97	96	95	92	90	84	79	69	69	49	39

It should not therefore surprise us that top U.S. salaries are astronomical by European and Asian standards. In November 1988, *Fortune* (the name is no coincidence) asked, "Are Europe's Bosses Underpaid?" This journal reported that Lawrence Rawl of Exxon earned $5,523,000, while Sir Peter Walters and L. C. van Wachem, the British and Dutch heads of BP and Royal/Dutch Shell, earned $582,000 and $500,000, respectively. Shell is as large and as profitable as Exxon. Lee Iacocca earned $17.5 million, Edzard Reuter of Daimler-Benz $1.2 million, and Tadashi Kune of Honda $450,000. It was Chrysler that needed bailing out, while Honda's growth has been dazzling. Jack Welch of GE received $12.6 million in 1987, as compared with $290,000 for Ichiro Shinji of JVC in Japan. Salaries in Singapore rarely top $150,000. South Korea's salaries are about 75 percent of Japan's.

By May 1991, even the American media was asking why top salaries, already high, were rising so much faster than those at a lower level. *USA Today,* hardly a radical organ, reported that the salares of CEOs during the 1980s had increased 212 percent, while the average factory worker had received only 53 percent, less than the rate of inflation. CEOs in America earned eighty-five times as much as the average worker, compared with thirty-three times in Great Britain, twenty-five times in Germany, and seventeen times in Japan. Moreover, in several cited cases, the salaries of CEOs had soared while the fortunes of their companies had slumped. For example, Stephen Wolf of United Airlines received 1,272 times the starting pay of flight attendants in 1990, a year in which profits declined by 71 percent. His salary was increased, although flight attendants had not had a pay raise for five years.[14] This was the height of the boom. His salary was later reduced.

All this, of course, is the logical outcome of accelerating individualism in a culture where the norms of community appear to be steadily weakening. These individual executives are largely their own judges in a culture that holds the individual to be supremely important. If, therefore, he or she does well, is there any sum that such a person does not deserve? If profits are slumping, is this the time to lose valuable executive talent, or should we pay even more to keep and attract the best?

What is worrying many friends of America is that there appears to be a long-term erosion in the whole nation's sense of being a community.

The Myth of the Triumphant Individual

The problem lies not with considering the welfare and fulfillment of each corporate or American citizen. This is obviously vital to civilized conduct. America's championing of individual human rights is as important today as it ever was, and a community is only as good as the morale of the individuals who constitute it. Nothing said in this chapter is intended to minimize in any degree the verdicts delivered by individual human beings upon their life and times. There is no other reliable testimony.

It is a particular variety of individualism that may be sapping the strength of America and some of her Western allies. We follow Robert Reich of Harvard's Kennedy School in calling this "the Myth of the Triumphant Individual."[15]

The problem is quite easily stated. The individual's nobility, independence, courage, and conviction are persistently polarized with the conduct and opinions of the group, which frustrates the individual, marginalizes and seeks to corrupt him or her, before being saved from its own mediocrity by the hero's unflinching rectitude. The flaw in this scenario is that communities consist of many individual members. Indeed, there must, by definition, be more of these wretched groupies than the He-who-stands-alone type of individuals, (we dropped gender equality here because we suspect that women, who do more nurturing, are less extreme on this issue). It follows that this particular American myth requires a ratio of heroes-to-patsies of at least twenty to one. How many despicably cowardly townspeople in *High Noon* does it take for Gary Cooper to stand alone? Indeed, virtually the whole town has to run out on him to establish his heroism.

Yet as a matter of practical accomplishment, how often does it occur that a collectivity is redeemed by an itinerant stranger who hardly knows its members or their situations? Of course, it is possible that the judgment and self-interest of one lone CEO-plus-parachute, one consultant, acquisitor, or arbitrageur is correct, while the judgments of those working in the company for many years are wrong, but what makes for heroic drama may miss the day-to-day probabilities and less heroic realities. For the truth is that power and decision in all developed economies are exercised by organizations and collectivities. To despise the collectivity but applaud its members, no sooner do they register dissent, is a curious strategy for organizational development. The Myth of the Lone Hero tells of organizations immensely enriched and saved from their fate by outsiders, but why does the collectivity never seem to learn and must be saved repeatedly? Common sense suggests that if organizations are really the beneficiaries of so much saving, they should, by now, be the wiser for it.

Everything we know about the development of personality and independence suggests that families, friends, schools, peers, and organizations play a vital part in personal development. People do not grow in conviction and independence through being rejected, but through being loved, accepted, and supported. Once they have developed in this way they can stand by their convictions and withstand rejection, but this, paradoxically, is a tribute to the sheer number of occasions they have found support for their initiatives from companions and the quality of the groups in which they have enjoyed membership.[16] And their motive for telling the group the truth as they see it is often their respect and affection for that group. The problem, then, with American individualism is that it scorns its own origins in the supportive community. The dauntless entrepreneur is a self-made man. This may be a good political argument for keeping the money you have accumulated, but it is a very dubious claim in reality and one that sells short the many who sustained you.

If it is true that the nurturant community is "the cradle of individualism," then it follows that many changes could be made to organizations, shaping them as communities that could increase rather than decrease the individuality of each member. We may achieve some of this by extolling achieving individuals and increasing the size of their rewards, but to focus only on individuals is to miss all the ways social and collective arrangements can be altered so as to enhance individuals and their performances.

For example, it has been known for more than thirty years that if a bonus is paid to a whole group of workers, then the group is likely to support and reward with their friendship and respect the higher performers and more creative individuals within that group. But if the bonus is paid to individual high performers or to individuals identified as more creative, the group is more likely to gang up on those most favored by management, discourage their performance, and punish their originality.[17] In short, outstanding individuals may benefit more from rewards paid to their group than to themselves. Yet American corporations have tended to dismiss such discoveries as being inconsistent with cultural individualism. Cultures "see" what they are predisposed to see and ignore the rest. Collective ways of enhancing individuals tend to be underutilized in U.S. corporations, and in the end it is the individual who suffers.

This helps to explain the number of American consultants who have invented ways of enhancing quality and productivity which corporations in their own country ignored, and which the Japanese adopted with enthusiasm. The concepts of Edward Deming in regard to quality circles, and of Joseph Scanlon about self-managed groups, found acceptance in the United States only after Japanese corporations had turned these to competitive advantage against the country of their origin. The extraordinary success of such books as *The Organization Man*, which argued at length that American individualism was being betrayed by the group ethic of organizations, demonstrate the extent to which the very existence of corporations is felt to be a collectivist betrayal of those colorful entrepreneurs who initially industrialized America.[18]

Only America and the other English-speaking economies, the United Kingdom, Australia, and Canada, allow individualists like T. Boone Pickens, Lord Hanson, Rupert Murdoch, and the Bellsburgs to acquire and disintegrate huge corporations, the slothful collectivity shaken by the scruff of its neck by enterprising individuals. Other nations prefer friendly takeovers and seek to avoid the social trauma attendant on constant acquisitions and divestitures.

If the organization is but a vehicle for our personal aspirations, then we owe it no loyalty. We posed a dilemma to managers to see how great was their commitment to the organization:

If I apply for a job in a company,

(a) I will most certainly work there for the rest of my life.
(b) I am almost sure that the relationship will have a limited duration.

Table 3-3   Limited Commitment to Organizations

Short duration	USA	CAN	AUS	UK	NL	GER	SWE	FRA	IT	BEL	JAP	SIN
	99%	96	96	94	89	83	81	79	72	71	41	32

U.S. individualism also shows up in chronic levels of high turnover. Can a corporation take the long-term view if executive turnover is running at 20 to 30 percent, so that most managers are gone within three to four years? Can organizations develop if the dominant attitude of employees and shareholders is that the company exists for their private benefit? Arie de Geus writing in the *Harvard Business Review* recently argued that corporations that compete successfully are those that learn faster than their rivals about changes in their environments.[19] But can a mere container of churning human ingredients be said to learn at all? Individualism risks reducing knowledge to what can be carried off in the heads of itinerant experts.

A major problem faced historically by individualistic economies has been called "the tragedy of the commons." During feudal times in England all freeholders had the right to graze their animals on common land, but as increasing numbers exercised this right the lands were overgrazed, seized by powerful landlords and enclosed, usually for sheep farming. Millions of individuals lost their livelihood through the exhaustion of a common resource. This is not an isolated incident but a recurring problem, known to economists as "free riding."[20] The self-seeking individual must logically advance a private interest in free public goods until these are used up. Would not the individual stop short when such destruction seemed imminent? Unfortunately not, as revealed in a recent *Wall Street Journal* article on America's depleted fisheries (see Box 3-1).

There are some curious ironies in the individualism-communitarian dilemma. We personally know at least two hundred academics-cum-consultants in the general area of organizational development, effectiveness, and strategy. Almost to a person, these individuals tirelessly teach the arts of better relationships, arguing that organizations should be better integrated, more connected, coherent, harmonious, responsive, cooperative, responsive to ecological issues, etc. Yet, who are we? We are itinerant globe trotters and academic individualists, loosely organized at best and disconnected from the very organizations we seek to make more whole. The whole consultant culture is American; the very idea of sending a wise individual to mend a group is an individualist concept.

The paradox is caught in the dedication by the Canadian Henry Mintzberg of his book *Mintzberg on Management:* "To those of us who spend our public lives dealing with organizations and our private lives escaping them."[21]

Are we so different from the early Puritans, turned out of the medieval monasteries onto England's highways, talking passionately about the City on the Hill and the Pure Community, but in reality passing through

---

Box 3-1

**Seize the Fish While They Last:
The Tragedy of the Commons Repeated**

Under the headline "Dead in the Water: Overfishing Threatens
to Wipe Out Species and Crush Industry," a *Wall Street Journal*
(16 June, 1991, p. 1) article by Lawrence Ingrassia recently
reported:

> Off Cape Cod, Mass. On a brilliant sun-splashed morning,
> Frank Mirarchi lowers the net from his 60-foot trawler into
> the gleaming blue water of the Atlantic near Stellwagen
> Bank, long one of America's richest fishing grounds.
> But when he hauls it in 2 hours later it holds just 350
> pounds of fish—half what he would have caught in the early
> 1980s. As usual, the net has swallowed almost no large
> codfish and flounder. Many fish have barely reached the
> legal minimum size for keeping. As for haddock, one of the
> most prized species in these once-teaming waters, not one
> is to be found . . . Where have all the fish gone? Mostly they
> have been caught—and over a period so ominously short
> that the future of one of America's oldest industries is
> threatened.

The article goes on to credit the present problem to the new
fish-finding electronics and the successful assault on quotas. All
concerned caught more fish . . . for a while: "Many New England
fishermen find themselves in dire straits, victims of a get-it-while-
you-can mentality that could exhaust stocks beyond recovery. . . .
'It's greed, 90% of it is greed—the future looks very dim,' says
Marty Manley, a scallop boat owner in New Bedford, the fabled
whaling town described in Melville's *Moby Dick*." The article goes
on to describe similar crises off Alaska, the Gulf of Mexico, and
along the Pacific Coast.

Yet this does not stop "fishermen crowding public meetings to
berate bureaucrats over proposed conservation measures."
"Straining to pay off mortgages on expensive boats, many fishermen say they don't have the luxury of *not* catching as much as
they can as fast as they can." Many deny that overfishing is the
problem and blame pollution. After quotas were lifted in 1982 as
part of a nationwide backlash against regulation, the 1983 trawler
catch reached 410 million pounds, by 1989 it had dropped to 234

million. Many fish are now too small to have spawned. The 22-inch gray sole spawns four times in its life. But most are now caught at 14 inches and have only a 50 percent chance of having spawned once. Fishermen interviewed explain what the crunch has done to them. "The majority are caught up in a rat race . . . If I hadn't paid off my mortgage I'd be fishing day and night . . . we're fiddling while Rome burns."

and preaching for our supper . . . and in many cases ending up as pilgrims in the New World? Community is for others and for the future, the lone trek is for today. We can be for a more collective approach and still behave like people who carry this saving knowledge within their lonely souls.

Finally, individualism, especially in its more extreme expressions, is better adapted to consumption than to production. We consume as individuals, and year by year the sheer variety of products and services encourages us to strike individualized postures and personalize our styles. In contrast, the creation of products is a more disciplined group effort. That the manufacturing of the most individualist countries appears to be in decline—while too much consumption chases too few goods, fueling inflation—appears increasingly as an affliction of individualist economies, at least among developed nations.[22]

The Inner Individualist

Almost no issue distinguishes the American mind-set from most Asian and Latin cultures more than the idea that persons can and should exercise control over their environment from within themselves (inner-direction). In the American view, each person is responsible for her or his own destiny. To blame fate and adverse circumstances is an attempt to excuse ourselves—the hard luck story of the perpetual loser. Almost by definition, the successful competitor has controlled the game, while the unsuccessful has let the play control him. William Ernest Henley immortalized the inner-directed person when Britain was more successful than it is today:

> It matters not how strait the gate,
> How charged with punishments the scroll,
> I am the master of my fate;
> I am the captain of my soul.[23]

It is possible to be thoroughly individualistic, as are the Dutch, and to still believe that your environment exercises considerably more power over you than you do over it. The Dutch have learned through their long battle with the sea that enormous powers are located in their environment. This does not, however, remove from them the responsibility for surviving. It is just that small countries like Sweden and Holland do not generally see their members as "commanding" world events in the style of Americans or the British, but still stress personal responsibility. For Americans, however, individualism and inner-directed control combine, and the lone hero has both.

The belief in "being your own man," that "the buck stops here," that when "the going gets tough the tough get going," that superlative FBI professionals are "untouchable" and unsullied by corrupt environments, is so obviously true for Americans that negations of this ideal make them cringe.

Indeed, Americans are repeatedly warned against "other-directed-ness" or "outer-directedness" as a creeping malaise. In a series of books published in the 1950s and 1960s, Erich Fromm warned that the "productive personality"[24] pushed from within by personal conviction was yielding to the "marketed personality," who contrived to package attractively his or her personality for outside approval. David Riesman echoed this theme in *The Lonely Crowd*.[25] America's great entrepreneurs had been inner-directed, but now superficial changes in image and appearance and spurious advertising drove the economy to conform to ephemeral fashions. In Arthur Miller's *Death of a Salesman*,[26] the protagonist, with nothing of substance to offer the world, slowly collapses into despair and suicide as his customers, colleagues, and children desert him and his ambition to be "very well liked" is frustrated.

We administered a questionnaire to our multicultural samples of managers, asking for agreement or disagreement with the following pairs of propositions:

(a) Unfortunately, an individual's worth often passes unrecognized no matter how hard he or she tries.

(b) In the long run, people get the respect they deserve in this world.

(a) This world is run by a few people in power, and there is not much the little guy can do about it.

(b) The average citizen can have an influence on government decisions.

(a) It is not always wise to plan too far ahead because many things turn out to be a matter of good or bad fortune anyhow.

(b) When I make plans, I am almost certain that I can make them work.

(a) Many times I feel that I have little influence over the things that happen to me.

(b) It is impossible for me to believe that chance or luck plays an important role in my life.

(a) Most people don't realize the extent to which their lives are controlled by accidental happenings.

(b) There is really no such thing as "luck."

The answer of the inner-directed individual is, of course, (b). The average percentage of managers in our twelve countries supporting the inner-directed option were as follows:

Table 3-4

	USA	GER	CAN	AUS	FRA	NL	UK	IT	BEL	SWE	SIN	JAP
Inner directed	68%	65	64	61	60	55	51	49	48	45	42	41

What is registering when we ask these questions is a less than full endorsement by other nations, especially Japan, of the American ideal of the individual steered by inner-conviction. Managers of Asian nations tend to see themselves as driven by external forces, often out of their control. They are caught in a maelstrom, in the tides of great events. The ideal is not that of Superman or the Incredible Hulk, who show a strength superior to natural forces, but "The Way of Monkey," a figure in Japanese pop culture who uses agility and wit to redirect the force and momentum of his opponents.

Japanese religion, for example, is Shinto, literally "the way of the gods." Godlike forces (*kami*) exist in nature, in streams, winds, tides, and crops, and, by extension, in markets and flows of information. The art of life is to go with such forces. They may behave arbitrarily and randomly, but one must still adjust. Even in contests where the idea is to win, the preferred means is to go with the strength of your opponent, changing only its direction and consequences in a way that shows mastery. We see this in jujitsu, aikido, and other Asian martial arts with their curious combination of combat and mental aesthetics.

The Limits of Inner-Directedness

Yet even if outer-directedness has its judo tricks, there can surely be no substitute for creativity that correlates strongly with inner-direction.

The person who creates is steered from within, by the new connections formed in the mind's eye. Here Americans easily out-distance their rivals as, for example, in the number of Nobel prizes won and in the availability of venture capital, a vote of confidence in the creative capacities of the entrepreneurs involved. So long as America leads the world in sheer inventiveness, can much go wrong? American culture rings with praises of lonely inventors, short-changed by the arid corporate environments—for example, the developer of the Tucker automobile years before its time. As the myth tells it, some farsighted individual saw it all (for example, the defects in the O-ring seals on the Challenger spacecraft), but groupthink blocked the avenue of expression. So should we not extol inner-directed voices of conscience even more? Let us consider for a moment quite another approach.

Meredith Belbin, a British management researcher on the effectiveness of management teams, thought he knew what a good team was.[27] He administered tests of intelligence and creativity to executives attending courses at the Management College at Henley. He found a team of seven so unusually intelligent executives that he christened the team "Apollo," after the U.S. space expedition. He found seven people of such unusual creativity that he put them in their own team as well. He called them "the Plants."

That the team of superlatively intelligent and unusually creative people would win a business game demanding intelligence and creativity seemed a bit too obvious to test. But test it he did. Of eight teams, the Apollo team came in last and the Plants came in sixth. The experiments were frequently repeated, and again and again the whiz kids realized but a fraction of their potentials and came in nearer last than first.

So what had happened? The high-IQ executives turned out to be brilliant critics and evaluators who clawed each other to ribbons. The Plants spewed out ideas that no one else would pick up and run with. Brilliant individuals can be collectively sterile and, while their frustrations make good drama, that is all they make. Belbin found that at most a team needs one or two critics and only one or two "Plants." The reason for this was that for every idea suggested, another team member was needed to receive and recognize it, a third had to find the necessary resources, a fourth had to champion the product and push it through, a fifth had to evaluate and improve it, a sixth had to insure that it was complete in all its details, and a seventh had to maintain the group's morale. Although one person would occasionally play two roles or more, overall success was a question of balance within the team. While it often took one person to invent an idea, it took the whole team to innovate; hence, while idea generation may be individual, innovation is collective, while invention is resolutely steered from within, innovation requires team members to "tune in" to a frequency originating outside themselves. Roger Harrison has likened an innovative corporate culture to an improvising jazz band. One player tries a new rhythm, and the others follow if they approve, or go off at another angle if they do not.[28] All players are directed from outside and from inside themselves.

Innovation can be seen as the culmination of inventiveness, the point at which the company begins to recoup its costs. While we have not been able to find figures on the ratio of inventions to innovations, Polaroid estimates that only between 5 and 10 percent of its patented inventions pay off as innovations. That shows just how much of the battle remains to be won after invention. There is considerable evidence that the United States invents well but innovates not as effectively, letting outer-directed cultures get to market faster with those inventions turned into innovative products by whole teams. Robert Reich has commented:

> Several product histories make the point. Americans invented the solid-state transistor in 1947. Then in 1953, Western Electric licensed the technology to Sony for $25,000—the rest is history. A few years later RCA licensed several Japanese companies to make color televisions—that was the beginning of the end of color-television production in the United States.[29]

This pattern has been repeated time and again. Once the inner-directed invention has come from the United States outer-directed improvements, elaborations, details, and champions for that product mobilize in Asia to create a more attractive product for the consumer. So it would appear that cultures with an internal locus of control get a head start, while those with an external locus of control catch on faster to what is happening elsewhere and then catch up.

Unfortunately, even this pattern is becoming obsolescent. The idea that Americans "start faster" but outer-directed cultures "finish faster," assumes a race with a beginning and an end. A product is invented, developed, and sold, grows to maturity and dies. Then there is another invention and another life cycle. All the inner-directed nations have to learn is how to keep their lead. But products are increasingly forming "food chains," as the Japanese call them, or "product generations." The number of starts and finishes is decreasing; instead, there are continuous incremental developments in which A and B beget C, D, and E, who beget F, G, H, I, and J, and so on. Reich makes this point well:

> Color televisions evolve into digital televisions capable of showing several pictures simultaneously; video cassette recorders into camcorders. A single strand of technological evolution connects electronic sewing machines, electronic typewriters and flexible electronic workstations.[30]

The race with a start and a finish has turned into something resembling a relay race in which you must rely on the previous runner to pass the baton. The faster finishing speed of your teammate sets you off in front of your rivals. The greater resources generated by more marketable products can be reinvested in R&D. Everywhere teams are replacing individuals. The Japanese, as discussed in later chapters, make extensive use of the concept of a relay race in their development and manufacturing.

The problem with extolling the inventor or entrepreneur with a Big Idea, Reich argues, is that your workers who "merely implement" such an idea come to be seen as drones, to be replaced by drones in Mexico, the Philippines, or Panama if their wages won't come down. But bringing the best innovations to market requires collective entrepreneurialism, with workers who solve problems, cut costs, and help to get the product redesigned for more effective manufacturing. Products do not sell simply because they are new, but because they are convenient, user friendly, well designed, simplified, cheaply priced, and refined. It is the community of employees who achieve these goals, not the genius with the Big Idea.[31]

One problem with the Big Idea is that it goes in one ear, and then around the world by satellite to set off races to market as surely as if you had fired a starting pistol. Big Ideas are easily learned about and, with a few changes, a manufacturer can get around most patents. In contrast, the process of moving from invention to innovation is private to each company, immensely complex, particularistic, communitarian, and sociable. Such unique cultures cannot be stolen or imitated as can the universal, codified patents Americans so admire.

America's preponderant inner-direction may be responsible for its spectacular record in starting up new companies and creating new jobs, but this leaves the companies very vulnerable as they approach their "organizational phase," the point at which they must serve a maturing market. At maturity, markets typically subdivide into hundreds, or even thousands, of niches, and the quality and variety of such products, rather than their very existence, is what makes them competitive. The complexity of this phase moves far beyond the founder's original vision and seems best served by extended terms working collectively to respond to myriad patterns of changing customer demands. As MIT's Commission on American Productivity has shown, it is at just this transition point to maturity that Japanese industry strikes and makes massive inroads.[32]

As the world develops and more and more products are more and more connected by skeins of information and seminal ideas, how much sense does it make to claim that we are or should be steered by those ideas that are currently within us? There are increasingly more bodies of relevant information available than any one brain can encompass; even Nobel prizes are increasingly being awarded to teams and partnerships. The chance of a particular individual's "thinking of it first" becomes more remote all the time, even as the danger of reinventing the wheel increases. One response to the sheer volume of innovation is to scan the environment more thoroughly, while reducing complaints about products "not invented here."

"Controlling" your environment with the exercise of personal willpower creates interesting problems. If everyone tries to do it, who will willingly *be* controlled? The consequences of trying to subdue the ecology of the planet are already evident. As international markets grow ever more turbulent, and as the number of competing nations increases, does not the ideal of personal control become increasingly unattainable? *Fortune* magazine still celebrates annually America's "ten toughest bosses"—a recent example is so tough, "he tells you when you can go to the bathroom." But this must logically entail several subordinates waiting to get permission, hardly a ringing endorsement of American managers as a whole. Recent additions to *Fortune*'s Hall of Fame are: "Loose Cannon," "Old Blood and Guts," "Cost Buster," "Detail Monger," "Megabrain," and "Commando."[33] Yet all these paragons of inner-direction need other managers to play "dead meat," "cost overrun," and "cannon fodder." It is hard to see any gain for the organizations as a whole.

The inner-directed view also encounters difficulty in world marketing. What if the foreign customers' views and wishes cut across those of their U.S. supplier? Customers do not as a rule share the logic of those who designed their products. They want to use them for quite other reasons. Hence, to be customer-oriented is to be outer-directed.

Fighting Each Other in the Face of International Challenge

Perhaps the gravest limitation of America's inner-directed individualism at the present juncture in the struggle for world trade is its incapacity to close ranks in the face of international rivalry. America rallied its sense of community in the Great Depression, in World War II, and following Sputnik, when faced with the Soviet challenge in outer space. On each occasion, massive resources were made available for the common good, but America's current economic crisis is different because it believes the only prescription for economic success is individual competition and more individual competition. Facing the Japanese challenge as a community and society, fighting to maintain its position, is permitted in war, in space, but not in economics! Instead, there has to be greater, not lesser, rivalry among Americans with each other even as America's international rivals make massive inroads upon her markets.

At issue here is what is the competitive entity? Should we compete as individuals, as single organizations, as clusters of organizations (sometimes called value-added chains), as entire industries (electronics, metals, ceramics) or as whole nations? Michael Porter has argued that it is the cluster, i.e., the company, its suppliers, bankers, customers, partners, and even competitors, which, by exacting higher standards, develops competitive power.[34] If he is right, then maximizing the salary of just one CEO or the profit of one partner may be suboptimal.

Inner-directed individualism prevents the United States from forming the cooperative structures necessary to compete internationally at the level of clusters, industries, or nations. America's historical experience with large economic combinations is almost entirely negative. In 1890, Senator Sherman proposed the Sherman Antitrust Act, specifically aimed at the Standard Oil Trust and a large number of new trusts controlling the supply and price of whisky, sugar, beef, lead, and linseed oil. These had combined against the consumer and were extracting huge profits by monopoly power. Antitrust policies were pursued by Teddy Roosevelt after the turn of the century, and again by President Taft. This was the era of the Muckrakers, fearless individualist writers challenging the dark of collusion of the combines. Ida M. Tarbell's *History of the Standard Oil Company* set the tone and was followed by *Frenzied Finance*, by Thomas W. Lawson, *The Story of Life Insurance* by Burton J. Hendrick, and Upton Sinclair's *The Jungle*, among many others. But is not collusion the inevitable consequence of joining together individual self-interests? The only reason they will work together is to take advantage of a third party. America's whole experience of such relationships is that they become cozy, comfortable, corrupt, back-scratching, and relatively effortless. Without the spur of competition the self-seeking go slack. For there is just as much self-interest in doing less for your money as there is in earning extra rewards. Rather than joining with each other to fight international competitors, such as the Japanese or Germans, American combines will, it is feared, go after the easier and softer targets of American domestic consumers, as did the Detroit "Big Three" automakers on the eve of the Japanese invasion. Such predatory combinations are not simply industrial,, but have in-cluded trade unions, professionals, and government regulators, all dis-trusted in their collaboration and all thought to be looking for a victim, the public interest.

We decided to test the proposition that Americans see cooperation as collusion against consumers, while some other nations believe that national players can bond together in the face of foreign challenges. We posed the following dilemma:

Two friends were discussing the way businesses interact.

One said: "If you allow businesses to cooperate with each other, they will usually collude against consumers and the larger society by agreeing together to raise prices and/or restrain trade. They will do this for the obvious reason that it is in their self-interests to do so. Compe-tition and still more competition is the only answer to this tendency."

The other said: "If you allow businesses to cooperate with each other they will usually pass on to their customers any enhanced effectiveness and economies of operations in the form of expanded trade. They will do this for the obvious reason that it is in their own and their customers group interests for this to happen. Cooperating in order to compete with the wider world is the only answer."

Table 3-5   Competition as Antidote to Collusion

Ever	USA	UK	CAN	AUS	IT	NL	BEL	FRA	GER	SWE	JAP	SIN
more competition	68%	65	64	62	51	50	48	45	41	39	24	19

Here we see that Europe, for the most part, leans away from American and British beliefs that unholy alliances will be formed by conspirators against the public interest wherever local competition is relaxed. It is this approach that allows Europe to compete as a trading bloc with Britain's rather reluctant agreement. Note also how logically all cultures proceed from their premises. If each of us is basically out for ourselves, of course we will sock it to consumers where we can. And in conditions of intraindustry collaboration we can! Yet few thinking intelligently about how clusters and whole industries within Singapore, France, Sweden, or Germany could compete better in world markets would recommend that they gang up on their own domestic consumers by doing less while earning more. National survival depends on all members of a cluster getting the very best from each other, i.e., cooperating. But note that American fears of collusion are not groundless. Japanese industry forces its own consumers to pay more than the world price. Regulated European airlines do less for more money than U.S. airlines. Both sides of the dilemma have perils.

Finally, the joining of individual self-interests has the tendency to create predatory combinations, whether trusts, trade unions, professions, or governments, with the result that combining per se becomes discredited and is seen as a prelude to victimizing unorganized individuals. The consequence has been a marked reluctance by Americans to cohere competitively at the level of clusters, industries, and the whole economy. America has responded in the last decade to foreign incursion into her markets, not by uniting, but by dividing, by giving more to her rich while abandoning her poor, by trying to break unions when industrial partnership is vital, and arguing in effect that the only way of holding off the Japanese challenge is for American corporations to compete more vigorously with one another. One consequence has been what Lester Thurow has termed *The Zero Sum Society*,[35] where anyone's gain is deemed another's loss, and so all interest groups refuse to budge. In the face of her greatest challenge, the nation is effectively immobilized by gridlock, as when automobiles crowd the intersections by jumping traffic lights and a whole city locks itself into immobility.[36]

4

When You're Racing with the Clock

> When you're racing with the clock
> The second hand doesn't understand
> That your back's all ache
> And your fingers break
> And your constitution isn't made of rock.
> The Pajama Game

THE AMERICAN CULTURAL "FINGERPRINT" is now emerging more clearly. As we saw in Chapter 2, the belief in a universal objective order in which the corporation is a perfectly tuned machine, responding to a market mechanism, is the image created by combining universalism with analyzing. Yet these mechanisms are operated by infinitely independent and courageous persons guided by the steadfastness of inner-convictions, an image created by combining individualism with inner-directedness. Problems arise not from this vision itself, but from its incompleteness, not from what it includes, but from what it ignores: the exception, the particular, the whole, the community and the demands of a shifting external environment.

We now come to our fifth process of wealth creation: #5. Synchronizing Fast Processes. Jobs need to be done quickly, but must also be completed "just in time" so as to be synchronized with the next step or parallel process. Time can be conceived of as "a race" or as "a dance." In a race we dash for the finishing post. In a dance, all the dancers'

73

steps are elegantly coordinated. The first view of time is sequential, the second, synchronized. The first encourages products to be worked on one after the other as on an old fashioned assembly line, the second encourages multiple operations to be done in parallel processes, before being combined at precisely the right moment. Both approaches are valid and useful. But cultures tend to be far more comfortable with one way of working than the other.

Time cannot be seen or touched. It is not a thing at all, but an experience of the human mind. Hence, how you think about time and conceptualize it tells you much about yourself and your culture. There are two ways in which cultures conceive of time. Time can be thought of as sequential, that is, moving forward, increment by increment, in a line. It is objective. All will pass before us like the windows of a lighted train at night, compartment by compartment. The Greeks had two gods of time: Chronos, the god of sequential time, and Kairos, the god of time and opportunity, which we refer to here as synchronized time. Kairos, who telescoped time, seized the chance to make past experience work with present resources, to gain future objectives. In this circular view of time, the present feeds back experiences to correct our future aims. It is subjective. All we really experience is "now," and past and future are but our ideas about the events we remember or anticipate. These ideas are also here now, synchronized in the present.

The U.S. view of time is largely sequential. No wonder then that the United States was the first business culture to have workers and managers compete against the clock to complete tasks in ever-shorter time intervals, with machines and assembly lines running ever faster, with employees in hot pursuit. The Model-T Ford emerging every few seconds from its Detroit assembly line is an early symbol of America's preoccupation with speeding up. The salience of computers that calculate in split seconds and the admiration for the "quick buck" made in an instant on the money markets by "keyboard entrepreneurs" are two contemporary manifestations.

The downside is an unwillingness to take time, to invest long-term and to grasp that as products grow in sophistication, the synchronizing with each other, so that a single worker runs six machines, may be as or more important than doing any one sequence fast. Higher speed is of no avail without coordination. High tech needs high touch," and the slogan is not enough. The "slow buck" has no appeal, but the reality is that complex products take years to develop, refine, and market, especially in large organizations where the dance of time must be painstakingly choreographed and constantly improved. In modern factories the worker is the Machine Master, not the slave of mechanical efficiency.

The United States, Great Britain, Sweden, and the Netherlands seem more oriented to faster sequences. Japan, Germany, and France are more concerned with synchronization. In "rationalizing" the corporation sequentially, people tend to be seen as a cost and waste, mere components of superefficient machines. In coordinating the corporation synchronously, people tend to be seen as sources of intelligent communication. Synchronous conceptions can be used to justify the retention and development of human resources and the insistence on working in smart teams.

An Investment Decision

How we think of time may greatly affect decision making. Take the idea that HDTV (high definition television) is a major technology of the future which in time will make contemporary TV obsolete. In the linear conception of time we and our money are present in this moment, but any mass market for HDTV is not yet here, but potentially somewhere in the future. Even if we grant that it will come, the question is when? five years, ten years, fifteen? We could go bankrupt in these intervals. An investment made today that starts to pay us back a decade later is a very doubtful proposition. Its "present value" could be quite low once we had discounted future cash flows for their remoteness, for their uncertainty and for inflation.[1] Doing something today and hoping to make a difference ten years hence is quite optimistic!

Suppose we consider the identical situation, but use a different conception of time. When we consider investing in the HDTV market, we envision an imagined future combined with a strategic present drawing upon a remembered past. Moreover, what we contribute to HDTV today will keep coming back to us, like the many happy returns of our birthdays, except that these returns will be packed with information and opportunity (but not money), allowing us to help HDTV arrive sooner rather than later. And when it arrives, not only will we be more expert than our rivals, we will be part of it. In the first way of thinking, you have to "catch the train before it leaves the station." In the second way, you are "part of the process of learning and developing." Of course, both views are useful and legitimate. HDTV, or the train, may never come. You could lose your shirt. Alternatively, if and when it comes, you could already be on board if you joined in the planning of its journey.

The Circles Test

To measure the extent to which cultures think of time-as-sequence or time-as-telescoped into "now," we employed the Circles Test, designed by T. J. Cottle.[2]

Think of the past, present, and future as being in the shape of circles. Please draw three circles on the available space (a half sheet), representing past, present, and future. Arrange these circles in any way you want that best shows how you feel about the relationship of the past, present, and the future. You may use different size circles. When you have finished, label each circle to show which one is the past, which one the present, and which one the future.

This is known as a projective test. Respondents drawing their circles project their own conceptions of time upon their configuration. Let us for the time being assume that most of our respondents saw the future as larger than the present, and the present larger than the past. This leaves us free to concentrate entirely on time-as-stretched-out versus time-as-telescoped. The pure conception of each view would look like this:

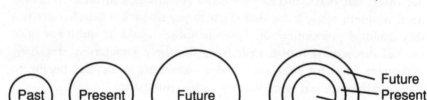

In practice, as we shall see, only some cultures see time as entirely separate episodes, and few of our managers saw it as without direction, that is completely telescoped, although some Eastern mystics might have done so had we inquired. Most cultures see time as progressing and recurring, as extended and interactive.

The results are set out in Box 4-1. Here we see that Americans are among the most sequential of the cultures researched, whereas the Japanese synchronized and condensed time more than any other groups of managers, while still maintaining a direction toward the future.

Box 4-1

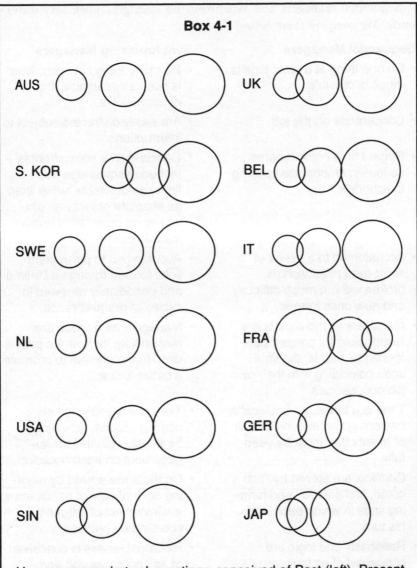

AUS

UK

S. KOR

BEL

SWE

IT

NL

FRA

USA

GER

SIN

JAP

How managers in twelve nations conceived of Past (left), Present (center) and Future (right). Circles placed apart reveal sequential thinking. Circles overlapping reveal synchronous thinking with a seminal future and remembered past, present, here and now.

Sequential managers and synchronizing managers work very differently. We compare them below:

Sequential Managers	Synchronizing Managers
• Do one thing at a time; time is tangible/divisible.	• Do many things at once; time is seen as intangible and elastic/flexible.
• Concentrate on the job.	• Are easily distracted/subject to interruptions.
• Regard time commitments seriously; emphasize keeping to schedule.	• Consider time commitments (schedules/agendas/deadlines) as desirable rather than as absolute objectives; emphasis on completing human transactions.
• Accustomed to a series of short-term relationships, broken without much difficulty and new ones formed.	• Accustomed to permanent links formed through a lifetime and periodically renewed in cycles of reaquaintance.
• Managers as individuals are responsible for present performance, that is, the time span coinciding with their own job occupancies.	• Managers as a group are responsible for how the past is used in the present to promote a better future.
• Time is a threat, an implacably hastening and expensive train of events that must be used fully.	• Time is a friend who keeps coming around, providing fresh opportunities for engagement on each occasion.
• Conflicts are solved by "first come, first served" and forming lines in which each waits his turn.	• Conflicts are solved by meeting several sets of needs from a minimal set of carefully coordinated processes.
• Rationality and logic are conceived of as fault-free, direct sequences of causes and effects, premises and conclusions.	• Reasonableness is conceived of as encompassing and synchronizing several aims and objectives into an inclusive process.
• Products are regarded as maturing over time, going from high novelty and profitablity to routine operations, lower margins, and eventual death.	• Products are regarded as self-renewing over time, the "genes" on one product giving life to the next generation and the next.

A Country In a Hurry

To visitors, the United States has always appeared to be a country in a hurry. The Puritans were not, like those of other religious persuasions, awaiting the afterlife in quiet contemplation. They had God's earthly kingdom to build and, given seventeenth and eighteenth-century life expectances, a perilously short time in which to build it. Andrew Marvell, tutor to Oliver Cromwell's ward and assistant to John Milton, was less puritanical about sex than about time in his famous "Ode to His Coy Mistress".

> Had we but world enough, and time,
> This coyness, Lady, were no crime . . .
>   But at my back I always hear
> Time's wingèd chariot hurrying near;
> And yonder all before us lie
> Deserts of vast eternity.[3]

This attitude toward time as a precious commodity, rushing through our lives with the speed of an express train, is captured in English and American proverbs and axioms: "Time and tide wait for no man"; "Procrastination is the thief of time." Benjamin Franklin had much to say on the subject: "Remember time is money"; "Nothing is certain except death and taxes"; "Dost thou love life? Then do not squander time, for that's the stuff life is made of." Clearly, the longer a sequence takes, the more time, money, life, etc. is wasted.

No wonder, then, that Americans were the first to conceive of the factory as governed by the stopwatch and by time-and-motion studies that would resolve all conflicts between managers and workers by calculating the most efficient and speediest sequence of workflows. In place of the "arbitrary foremen," believed by Frederick Winslow Taylor to be the powder keg of many strikes and walkouts, would be the least costly and most productive sequence of motions by people and their tools.[4] Time is the Puritan's Great Disciplinarian and Cost Accountant. In the American musical satire *The Pajama Game*, the workers sing, "Hurry up! Don't waste time! When you're racing with the clock the second hand doesn't understand." Even their futures are calculated in increments of time:

> Seven and a half cents isn't worth a hell of a lot
> Seven and a half cents doesn't mean a thing
> But give it to me every hour

> Forty hours every week,
> That's enough for me to be
> Living like a king . . .
> I've figured it out . . .

A strong bias toward sequential thinking about time has clear benefits in spurring the spirit of "get up and go," in conveying urgency, in using the clock as your competitor in the absence of other rivals. American aptitude tests are completed at high speed. To think more slowly than others is to fail, to waste your would-be employer's money. It came as a surprise to one of the authors at the Harvard Business School that if his Written Analysis of Cases was as little as two seconds late it would be marked as such by a policeman! Time is obviously essential in planning the convergencies of activities toward agreed outcomes. Those who crowd their busy schedules with appointments probably get more done. Kipling advised the nation's youth:

> If you can fill the unforgiving minute
> With sixty seconds' worth of distance run,
> Yours is the Earth and everything that's in it
> And—which is more—you'll be a Man, my son![5]

"Time management" remains a major topic in the United States. Airline magazines sell leather portfolios in which "time cards" can be arranged in straight rows. A recent preoccupation is time-to-market, that is, the time it takes for a product to go from conception to the customer. Others measure time-to-break-even or time taken for an investment to be repaid. Future cash flows are discounted in proportion to the time taken to realize them.

Clearly the whole Industrial Revolution and the factory system were created by the willpower of sequential thinkers seeking to accelerate the speed of timed manufacture and assembly. Economists conceive of value being progressively "added" to products as they move down imaginary lines. Computers cannot do anything that was not first programmed into them, but they perform much faster than human workers, taking just seconds rather than hours. It is not hard to see why those cultures that saw time as a relentless pursuer or a conveyance leaving on schedule, whatever our pleas, and that regarded the human life span as a desperately short interval in which to justify oneself to God, have brought industrial development to the world.[6]

Limitations of the Sequential Approach to Time

Once again it is not wrong to think of time as a moving conveyance. The concept is incomplete. Cultures suffer not from what they include, but from what they omit. To get products through the factory and out the door in the quickest possible sequence is clearly an important consideration. Manual workers, sequentialist cultures believe, should work by small, successive increments, as fast as possible. Talking, joking, horseplay, fraternity, and resistance are all impediments to the progressive acceleration of work. It follows that trade unions are sheer impediments. Or are they? Suppose the real gains in productivity come from thinking intelligently about what you are doing and then on the next go around doing it smarter? Suppose that more and more effective synchronization of work efforts is the secret, with past errors quickly fed back to improve present and future operations? Weak bonds among workers could mean that important lessons are not learned. The German union, IG Metal, has that country's largest library and research collection on how improved work conditions and worker solidarity improves productivity.

Recently, American business has begun to reproach itself for its short-termism.[7] Chapter 8 reveals that in a poll of international managers, American corporations are eighteenth of thirty nations in their "capacity to take a long-term view," while Japanese corporations are first. But is not this the direct result of a sequentialist viewpoint? If "time is money" and time is hurrying past you at a rapid rate, then the more money you make in the shortest time the better. You can improve the time-money ratio, either by making more money in the same time, or the same amount of money in a shorter time. It follows that a longer-term span represents a cost to be avoided. Creative accounting and tax avoidance beats manufacturing.

In purporting to explain American short-time horizons, The MIT Commission on Industrial Productivity cited the greater equity financing of American companies by shareholders who want their dividends this year and every year, which results in a higher cost of capital to American companies, which means that potential new investments have a higher hurdle rate to jump and must pay back more money sooner to be considered viable. Cost of capital is also kept high by the low rate of American savings, as compared with that of Japan and much of Europe. Moreover, the salaries of top American executives are tied to annual or even semiannual profit figures. In the longer run, these executives are retired and/or parachuted to earth amid billowing fabrics of gold.[8]

But these factors do not "cause" short-time horizons, they merely repeat again and again the original cultural pattern. Investors, managers, workers, bankers, and savers increasingly want theirs now, or in the shortest possible time interval, so as to exercise additional individual discretion. It is an inseparable aspect of American individualism that for each one of us time is running out, in a way it does not run out for our communities or our corporations, who are renewed by new members and rising generations. The Mitsui Corporation is over 600 years old. But for each separate corporate employee longevity is a different matter.

Paying top executives according to current profit figures is a well-meant effort to hold them individually responsible for results and reward them in proportion to their own success in rewarding shareholders. The flaw in these calculations is that today's profit figures are usually the result of accumulated efforts and good decisions made over ten or twenty years previously which are currently bearing fruit. Giving top executives bonuses based on these accumulations is like overpaying the person who waves his fingers over the player piano on which the tunes were programmed many years earlier. In practice, it is not possible to calculate what a current CEO owes to the corporation as a community, which has learned and gathered expertise over time, and what that community owes to him for his contemporary activities. All we know for certain is that lavish bonuses and handshakes transfer money from the incorporated carrier of long-term commitments to the short-term extractor of personal benefits, and we must expect the longer-term viewpoint to suffer as a consequence.

For if, in fact, the top manager is receiving rewards owed to the work of his predecessors, but does not acknowledge this and accepts most or all of the credit for current results, why would he bother to think of those who come after him? Let them make bold contemporary decisions as he has and earn their keep! The doctrine of individual responsibility ties each manager to shortened contemporary time spans. Proximate results are laid at your door, but distant results at another's.

One's conception of time is also important to morale in general. Those who believe that time is a running reaper, waving his sickle, will experience the passage of a time as a threat. Those who see time as someone who comes around again and again to seek their engagement in new opportunities will see time as a friend. Suffice it to say that so long as time is conceived of as racing against individual Americans and using up their lives unprofitably, so will short-term profit extraction be experienced as a victory over time by the individual. As a Japanese executive told Peter Senge in a seminar, "For Americans time is the enemy. For the Japanese time is an ally."⁹ The North Vietnamese said something similar during the Vietnam War. They would persist, they said, as they had for eight hundred years. Americans would give up.

In *The Fifth Discipline*, Peter Senge argues that cybernetic circles or feedback loops (of the kind that Japanese managers spontaneously drew in Box 4-1) take the fear out of time where opportunities are seen to recur.¹⁰ The past has not flown amid bitterness and regret, but represents itself to those grown wiser through reflection. And the future is a recognizable friend completing a familiar cycle, not an alien epoch. It is this cyclical view of time that gives the Japanese and other time-condensing cultures their respect for age and hierarchy. In America, someone "over the hill" is a shrinking object, fast receding.

Yet perhaps the greatest foreshortener of time is the largely Western concept of rationality and the need to justify our decisions by numbers. In the process of logical or technical reasoning, premises are demonstrably linked to conclusions or causes to effects. The shorter and the more direct are these connections, the sounder we consider our rationality. But if we do something now in the hope of producing an effect in ten to fifteen years, then the likelihood of uncontrolled variables intervening in so long a causal chain is exceedingly high. When the value of some event so far ahead is rigorously discounted for risk and uncertainty, its "present value" dwindles to almost nothing. The investment is hard to justify, especially where monetarist policies have so forced up the lending rate that one would get a better return from idle funds put in a bank. Hazarding money on technological innovation is hardly "rational." Given the quick returns available from financial restructuring and "paper entrepreneurealism," it barely makes sense to produce more than a shrinking range of manufactured goods.¹¹ In contrast, a cybernetic view, or encompassing reason, with a circle of "opposite" values like the heaven and earth, fire and water of the I Ching, sees any value created now as persisting and returning to reward its instigators.

Finally, the sequential orientation gives American managers their attitudes to the birth, growth, maturity, senescence, and death of products themselves. Attitudes toward the human life span are projected on the products a culture makes. One possibly unintentional consequence of the sequential view is that products Americans make, like Americans themselves, are more celebrated in their youth than in their maturity. "Don't trust anyone over thirty," declared the Hippies, followed by the Yippies, followed by the Yuppies. The accent is forever on youth, and so it is in the claim to have created "new jobs" in the 1980s, while the Fortune 500 contracted into their senility. The fact that many of these jobs substituted "old" manufacturing for "new" boutiques and restaurants, paying a fraction of the wages, did not dent the general enthusiasm. Sequential Americans have a different vision of economic renewal than the synchronous Japanese, Germans, and French. For Americans, renewal is via Schumpeter's "gale of creative destruction." Existing companies are pushed to the wall and disintegrated by thrusting new enterprises, their resources carried off like booty to be put to better use by younger and livelier competitors. "Move aside, grandad!" In contrast, synchronous companies seek to procreate, to find a logic or "genetic code" by which their products will endlessly renew. This is not unknown in American companies, witness John Sculley's book *Odyssey*, which depicts Apple Computer's developments as an endless journey of discovery, dropping off products at ports of call while putting "wings on the mind." But such metaphors are rare in North America and Great Britain.

The belief that products and markets are shortly going to die tends to be self-fulfilling and leads to strategies of frantically milking the aging "cash cow" while she still has something to give shareholders. In addition, money may be siphoned off to give to "growth industries." The consequence is that there is now a subspecialty of strategic management known as "the management of decline," one of the longer suicide notes in management literature. "Old" companies denied the resources necessary for renewal will, of course, die on schedule. The idea that these declining properties do not carry within them the seeds of information and experience from which newer industries can learn is strange indeed. Does a textile company have nothing to teach a maker of ultra-suede or high-fashion fabrics?

Are relatively young employees in old industries to stumble into the grave with their technologies and products? We seem to be mesmerized by metaphors of mortality into creating the equivalent of "granny farms" amid our product portfolios, and then we work these till they drop.

All this has about it an air of rational inevitability. If you start with the premise that corporations exist primarily to make money for shareholders and have no independent right to life, if you note that pension fund managers now manage the bulk of all share transactions, if you consider that those they represent will quite soon be dead, then the surprise is that anyone ever looks ahead for more than a few years. Nor should the massive mortality of U.S. corporations surprise us. They merely imitate their masters and beneficiaries.

We take up the subject of time further in Chapter 7, where we consider how Japanese managers operate in a synchronous mode. While U.S. managers tend to follow a logic of profit and payback, trying to get more for their buck, the Japanese follow a logic of synchronized and developing technologies. While Americans "push" their products through sequential stages from conception to distribution, the Japanese tend to "pull" developments in parallel, toward future synchronized rendezvous with their customers. While mass manufacturing is the product of sequential thought, flexible manufacturing is the consequence of fine synchronizations. While American hierarchies are "chains" or sequences of command, Japanese hierarchies are ever-larger coordinations of past, present, and future events.

5
Level Playing Fields

IN THIS CHAPTER we turn to our last two wealth-creating processes: #6. Choosing Among Achievers (achieved status versus ascribed status) and #7. Sponsoring Equal Opportunities to Excel (equality versus hierarchy). The American belief in the virtues of both achievement and equality has profoundly influenced everything Americans think about business, beginning with the common conception that business is a game. To Americans, economic achievement is a series of short-term contests in which individual corporations show their metal. Thus Pepsi-Cola takes on Coca-Cola in a monthly competition for a half- to one-percent gain in market share in what John Sculley described as the Cola Wars. Every month, Nielsen presents the scores. Has the Pepsi Challenge gained against Coke's Southern bastion? Gains of a fraction of a point are celebrated, and repeated losses lead to serious doubts about certain executives' futures with the company.[1]

It is for this reason that the U.S. and U.K. corporations so often set up "internal markets" within the corporation in which profit centers compete for resources. These contests never end. Players vie with each other to their dying day with even the corporation up for grabs. You never give up on your own potential, nor by extension on others' potential. There is a New World, a wide open frontier before you. This is not simply a "second chance" society for immigrants but a third, fourth, nth chance for the eternal aspirant.

It is quite otherwise in certain economies. Students compete ferociously in Japanese and French high schools, but once accepted into

87

corporations they will have status ascribed to them by the company, whose hierarchy will accept responsibility for bringing out the best in them. This status will grow automatically with age and experience. Such hierarchies are not unfair because everyone ages over time and will rise as high as the qualifications ascribed to them allow. (But note: long-term orientations are necessary for this fairness to emerge.) The metaphor is not of an internal game or contest, although the larger corporation is competing with outside rivals, but of a family, a garden, a cadre with seniors and juniors tied by bonds of *giri* (Japanese for moral indebtedness and deep obligations of gratitude).

There are problems with both the Level Playing Field and the Family or Garden. If everyone competes with everyone in endless contests, who will coach, mentor, or develop juniors? Who will feel sufficiently secure in their own status to care about the corporation or customers? Will honest feedback be given to subordinates eyeing one's own job? Even a game needs sponsors and honest judges. Where will they come from?

Yet Americans know the Family model only too well and mostly disapprove of "paternalism," "nepotism," "ethnic blocks," "bosses," and ties that should have melted years ago. To have senior managers behave like "handkerchief holders" and get "cosy" with subordinates is a very doubtful enterprise. No wonder, then, that loyalty and devotion to the corporation is rare.

The Dilemma of Ascribed vs. Achieved Status

Should managers have status ascribed to them on account of their age, education, family background, or membership in a group, or should they earn that status by achievement? Most American and British managers would answer unhesitantly that status should be earned. What other basis is there for preferring the claims of one competitor over another? Should we give people a head start for being white or black, for belonging to a certain religion, for being older, for having titles or distinguished parents or ancestors, or because they are related to the boss? Most kinds of ascriptive status seem not simply wrong morally, but stupid in a practical sense and likely to block the higher levels of an organization with nonperformers.

Achievement is close to being the cultural bedrock on which the United States is founded. Other sources of status could not survive translation to the New World. If your neighbor is Norwegian and your doctor Ukrainian, who cares that you come from "a prominent family in

Kent"? If your parents speak only Yiddish, what is their experience worth to you in America? Some people adapt and others cannot, and only achievements can tell who is "making it" and who is not. Those cast upon a foreign shore can use their skills, not their connections to those they left behind.

The American War of Independence was led by its merchant class in the northeast who wished to end their ascribed status as colonialists and primary producers of raw materials for manufacture in Britain. America's new achievers wanted to run their own production and won this right by force of arms. The Tories, with their friends in England and in the colonial governor's mansion, with their large landholdings and crops, were thwarted. Status now came neither from royal or noble connections, nor from land, but from what you had done to set up an industrial infrastructure to rival Britain's and eventually overtake her.

In no other nation in the world was there a canvas of such vast and empty proportions on which new human achievements could be inscribed. Factories, towns, roads, railways, and monuments were swiftly established by people from God knows where, but whose visible contributions could not be denied. And they were here now, not buried in the churchyard or doubtfully connected to earls and lords who, as Andrew Carnegie observed, had "done dirty deeds for kings."[2] While achievement orientation has an obvious connection to individualism, the "achieving unit" can be the person, the group, the division, or the whole corporation.

But the case for status by achievement is not simply explicable in terms of an unusual American experience, it would seem rather to have universal application to management and effective organizations everywhere. It is surely in the interests of any organization that the best employees should rise in their influence and the mediocre or poor should decline or move elsewhere. Employment contracts offer payment in exchange for work. What could be fairer than to pay more for better work and confer recognition, status, and rewards commensurate to what the organization has received? It partakes of natural justice, especially when the individual is seen as directed from within.

However, status by achievement works equally well at levels above the individual, allowing groups, profit centers, and whole organizations to be masters of their own destinies. It provides feedback on how the whole organization is doing, facilitating identification of individuals with that organization. By moving more resources toward achieving groups it invests in success and magnifies ability. Status by achievement is pragmatism and empiricism applied to progress, rewarding best who or what works best. Without achievement we could not discover where our potentials lie. Achievement is the reality test for human potential.[3]

The ideal is to mark out a universalistic playing field, carefully specify rules and points, let all individuals compete in their inner commitment, and recognize the highest achievers. In such a contest every other advantage save sheer ability and will to win should be minimized. To Americans and to those like them, educated there, all this seems so self-evidently right, that those who disagree must have some base motive or be carrying the baggage of ancient snobberies. Nevertheless, we decided to measure achievement orientations versus one particular kind of ascription, that based on age. We chose this because everyone grows older, and ascribing status to age is not unfair or arbitrary in the way that ascribing status to people on the basis of class, gender, or ethnicity is unfair. Statements used in our scale include the following:[4]

Becoming successful and respected is a matter of hard work.
It is important for a manager to be older than his subordinates.
Older people should be more respected than younger people.

Table 5-1   Proachievement, Antiascription—Based on Age

Status by achievement	USA	AUS	CAN	SWE	UK	BEL	GER	FRA	IT	NL	SIN	JAP	KOR
	63%	62.2	61.5	61	60	59	58	57	53	50	44	42	37

The scores are surprisingly close, only 21 percent separating the United States and Japan. One reason for this, we argue, is that status by age does not foreclose status by achievement. For, of course, nations that give the ascribing of status priority over achievement are not necessarily negating achievement, but may be trying to reconcile it with ascription, to ascribe in ways that makes achieving more likely than it might otherwise be. Could this be of value?

What seems to work well in Japanese and Pacific Rim economies is to increase the status of employees as their experience and periods of service with the company lengthen. As employees age, the expectation that they will be of greater influence and value increases. Like most social expectations, this one tends to fulfill itself. The employees to whom more respect is given achieve more. Such a system is deemed fair because everyone ages. So everyone's opportunity to succeed over a lifetime with a company is the same—within their educational cohort. The logic of this process is that older people have more experience and should teach and act as mentors to their juniors. This would be true even if a senior had not been particularly successful. The "lessons" are still there.

But such a system will only work if the upper reaches of the company are not littered with "dead wood" for which the organization must pay higher salaries. How could this perilous possibility be avoided? By the company assuming major responsibility for the development of all its employees. It is this qualification that transforms the policy of paying-for-experience and probably distinguishes ascriptions that facilitate wealth creation from those that fail to do so. A company, knowing it must pay more as its employees age, will make sure that they mature in all possible ways, as well and grow more valuable to their company in that process. To fail to invest continuously in their upgrading would be disastrous. Such cultures are not deemphasizing achievement, but seeking it by indirection. The ascription of status to older employees is intended to be self-validating and to result in higher achievement.

The Perils of Pure Achievement

The question for Americans then becomes not whether status by ascription should replace achievement, but whether it can, in certain circumstances, augment it. For "pure" American achievement criteria have their perils as well as their pluses. What are the problems associated with pay-for-performance and promotion-by-achievement? There are serious conceptual problems in separating "the achiever" from the organizational context in which achievement has occurred. If many employees pull together to achieve a creditable performance, how do we handle their relative contributions? And if we err in assigning credit, will they pull together the next time?

The problems attendant on pay-for-performance are notorious and have been detailed by Chris Argyris and Donald Schon. Supervisors are reluctant to give employees negative and costly evaluations, unless there is a sufficiently strong bond between them so that criticism does not make matters worse. What happens in practice is that emollient words and vague assurances paper over a potentially tense situation, and those rated "excellent" escalate hugely so that everyone is good and glad and defensively bland.[5] The paradox and irony is as follows. Only strong relationships can withstand critical feedback, yet if the relationship is strong the employee may work well for that reason. In this event, extra cash for extra performance simply adds to corporate costs and discourages those who don't receive it.

The public recognition of high achievers at a relatively early age makes them mobile and footloose. They will sell themselves to the highest bidder and then sell themselves again. Scarce talent is bid up. Salaries escalate, and customers must pay for them.

Another problem with emphasis on pure achievement is that it inevitably creates its antithesis, "pure losers." Indeed, many areas of competition create in more people more frustration than fulfillment. An organization's top echelon excludes more than it includes. For every glamorous film star who succeeds, twenty or more attended "the meat market" and were told, "Don't call us, we'll call you." Since being somewhere in the middle can hardly be called achievement, it may be said that a majority fail relative to their aspirations while being reminded that they have only themselves to blame. The race was to the swiftest.

America's growing number of losers are thus subject to a double bind. On one hand, there is massive ascription of low status to poor urban and rural ethnic groups, especially those with darker skins, but on the other hand, there is a generalized belief system that claims that they could and should have achieved on their own. This combination of unadmitted prejudice and stigmatization, combined with condemnation for not having succeeded, constitute what Richard Sennett and John Cobb have called *The Hidden Injuries of Class*.[6] That these groups "achieve," after a fashion, through crime, drugs, and prostitution, is not altogether surprising. Losers tend to become enraged with the rules under which they lost. It might be better to admit that ascription of status occurs and is massively influential in later achievement or failure. Ascribing status gives great potential powers to leaders, top managers, and supervisors. They are able to distribute to key parts of their organization self-fulfilling mandates to achieve.

In contrast, waiting for achievements to occur and then attributing them to the sterling character of the separate individual allows a company to avoid responsibility for more general improvement. It can fire, promote, and "hunt heads" with the help of consultants instead of joining to educate the whole work force. The good employee would have achieved in any case, so why waste money on the rest?

There is a crucial flaw in moralizing about the individual's sole responsibility for succeeding or failing to achieve. There are in all relationships that seek to evaluate performance a person whose role it is to achieve and a person whose role it is to recognize that achievement and improve the social environment in which it occurs. To tell competing employees that "it's all up to you" shifts from the supervisor to the employee the entire responsibility for achieving or otherwise. The supervisor is talking about achievement but not modeling it, and fails to address the question of what he or she or the company might do to improve performance in everyone.

Lack of achievement can be repaired in at least two ways: by each individual subordinate trying harder, and by "the game" being improved so as to elicit more of the employees' enthusiasms and potentials. Senior management is responsible for such elicitations and for the total quality with which work is performed. To ignore this passes the buck from organizers to contestants and fails by its own criterion, the personal responsibility of all concerned. The individual is linked indissolubly to the community as an arena in which achievement is first defined and then consummated.[7]

Only if status is also widely attributed can a culture decide which contests are worth entering and trying hardest to win. The problem with judging achievement solely by its monetary rewards is that $10 million made by increasing the use of credit cards is deemed equivalent to $10 million made by exporting high-temperature superconductors. Yet the impacts of these two strategies on the American economy may be very different. Given the chronic deficit in the international balance of trade, America's low savings rate and tendency to inflation, controlled after a fashion by high interest rates, the pushing of credit cards is part of the problem. The export of superconductors with a potential for world leadership, lasting decades, is part of the solution. A nation that cannot clearly confer greater social prestige upon solutions than upon problems will have difficulty improving its overall performance. Not all "achievements" are worth achieving.[8] It is increasingly important to confer status on various endeavors before they succeed. These include partnerships, joint ventures, new projects, strategically key technologies, and customers vital to one's future. Wait for these to succeed or fail, and it is too late. In a very real sense, the attribution of status to this or that initiative is part of strategic thinking. You must ascribe value to create value.

For several nations, France especially, but also Japan, the time for competitive achieving is while the employee is at school. Once recruited into the organization on the strength of school records, status is attributed to the brightest, and these go on to shine with the corporation as their impresario. The system of mutually reinforcing ascription and achievement seems to work best.

The Dilemma of Hierarchy vs. Equality

Our discussion now brings us to perhaps the most puzzling cultural distinction, that between cultures whose hierarchies are relatively steep and those whose hierarchies are flat. It seems self-evident to American-educated authors, such as we, that hierarchies need to be flat when so much complex knowledge is being exchanged. Most discussions within corporations do not take place between achievers and nonachievers, but between peers. On the issue of remodeling an automobile's gas tank, whose expertise is most relevant—the safety engineer, the fuel engineer, the performance engineer, the general manager, the cost accountant, the quality control supervisor, or the test engineer? In practice, it is not possible to know whose knowledge is more authoritative until the problem has been thoroughly explored. The custom, then, is to treat all potential sources of information and solutions as if they were equals, pending the outcome of discussions.

Even where it is discovered that, for instance, the fuel engineer has the solution, that authority might not carry over to the next problem, how to increase the effectiveness of the bumpers, for example. In effect, therefore, the structure of equality remains the best way of facilitating the process of discovery. It seems obvious to most Westerners that it is extremely unwise to assume that "the boss knows everything about what should be done." This is rapidly becoming impossible.

The accepted wisdom, based on considerable research, is that simple products and technologies can be run by steep hierarchies, because the total task can be encompassed by a single mind, but that complexity requires many sources of knowledge and multiple authorities, all needing to be reconciled.[9] The lone boss standing at the apex of his chain of command cannot know enough about rapidly changing conditions in the field. Instead of a centralized system issuing inflexible orders from above, what is needed are high degrees of local initiative, which respond to customer demands and learn rapidly from the environment. All such arguments make for flatter hierarchies. Surely the whole world understands this—or would be wise to do so.[10]

This is indeed how we think in the United States, Britain, and much of Northwestern Europe. Before we consider alternatives, let us check the research. We presented our samples with several hierarchical shapes, varying from steep to flat. We asked managers from different countries to choose the shape most resembling their own organizations. These are set out in Box 5-1, with the most hierarchical cultures at the top and the least hierarchical at the bottom.

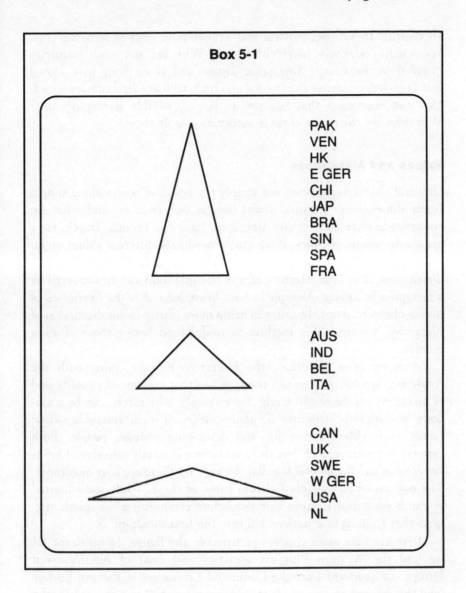

Box 5-1

PAK
VEN
HK
E GER
CHI
JAP
BRA
SIN
SPA
FRA

AUS
IND
BEL
ITA

CAN
UK
SWE
W GER
USA
NL

At first glance, Western presuppositions are confirmed. There, at the flattest end, are the Netherlands, the United States, West Germany, and Sweden, strong economies all, while Pakistan, Venezuela, and China are all underperforming economically and autocratic politically. But then we notice anomalies. Hong Kong, Japan, and Singapore are among the more hierarchical countries of the world, yet are also among the most successful. In Europe, Austria and France have enjoyed some success, yet remain relatively hierarchical too. Why are not such countries crippled by autocracy? Singapore, Japan, and Hong Kong have moved into knowledge-intense electronics and high-tech at extraordinary speed. How can economies that kow-tow to bosses possibly accomplish this? Why does not the power of their autocrats cripple them?

Values and Metaphors

Cultural characteristics are not simply the result of scores along simple linear dimensions. Cultural traits overlay one another, and what we recognize as characteristically American, Japanese, French, Dutch, etc., are combinations of traits. If we cross-coordinate different values on an axis (see Fig. 5-1), then we create quadrants, each of which have two dimensions. The characteristic of any one quadrant can be conveyed by a metaphor or analog. Metaphors have been defined as the likenesses of unlike characteristics. In order to bring more clarity to our discussion of hierarchy, we used this method to understand better those of each culture.

When we cross-coordinate the Hierarchy-Equality value with the Analyzing-Synthesizing value, then we see that systems of equality and of hierarchy can be of two kinds. For example, a hierarchy can be a top-down bureaucratic structure of subordination, or it can resemble a close family with elders caring for and developing younger people. Both systems are hierarchical, but their ambience is totally different. One is impersonal and the second familial. In Fig. 5-1 there are four quadrants. The nations of our sample fall into three of these, while some limited research we did in Eastern Europe, before communism collapsed, suggests that Eastern bloc nations fell into the first quadrant.

There are four main clusters pictured in the figure. In quadrant III we find the Western Pluralist societies and most of Northwestern Europe. In quadrant I are the Command Economies of Eastern Europe (and the defense sectors in Western economies) and in quadrant II, the family-style organic ordering economies of Asia, southern Europe, and Latin America. In quadrant IV are the Structured Networks which typify Germany and which a Federal Europe, if it emerges, may resemble. "Western Pluralism" conveys a contest among separated and analyzed ideas, each raising its voice to get a hearing. "Command Economy" refers to a hierarchy that plans and analyzes in advance, before issuing precise and detailed commands. This is the ideal of "Scientific" Social-

Fig. 5-1

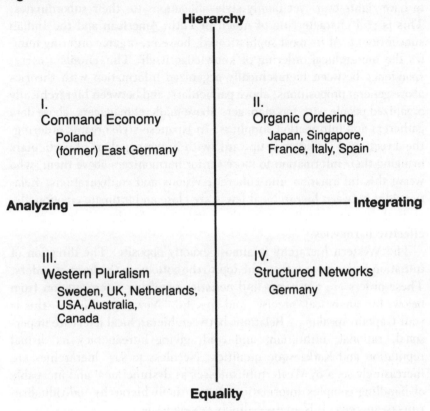

Hierarchy

I.
Command Economy
Poland
(former) East Germany

II.
Organic Ordering
Japan, Singapore,
France, Italy, Spain

Analyzing ──────────────────────────── **Integrating**

III.
Western Pluralism
Sweden, UK, Netherlands,
USA, Australia,
Canada

IV.
Structured Networks
Germany

Equality

ism, now discredited. "Organic Ordering" suggests a hierarchal ordering of organically related information, while "Structured Networks" suggest a more equal, yet structured, relationship between advanced-technology companies.

Command economies need not detain us. They are failures. Issuing specific orders from the top down turns subordinates into mechanamorphosed beings and makes the economy rigid and unresponsive. Western pluralism has thousands of separate ideas and ventures jostling each other for acceptance on a relatively equal footing. Since the latest knowledge is not necessarily in the possession of top managers, employees who might contribute to the solution of problems are treated as relative equals pending the outcome of discussions.

But of potentially great importance, and little understood by Westerners, is the process of organic ordering. At its most primitive it is a form of semifeudalism, in which those owning land and property are deemed to have rights over, yet family-style obligations to, their subordinates. This is still characteristic of much of Latin American and the Indian subcontinent. At its most sophisticated, however, organic ordering mimics the hierarchical ordering of knowledge itself. This entails a correspondence between hierarchically organized information with theories above general propositions, above particulars; and between hierarchically organized people with top managers above midlevel managers, above data gatherers and information suppliers. In Japanese-style organic ordering, the direction of initiation is upward, with junior suppliers of particulars bringing their information to more senior harmonizers above them, who weave this information into coherent visions and configurations. Relationships between hierarchical levels are close and intimate emotionally, as well as conceptually, since the parts must fit the whole to create effective harmonies.

The Western hierarchy is almost exactly opposite. The direction of initiation is downward, from the top to the bottom, in the form of orders. These orders are not vague and holistic, requiring interpretation from below, but analytical, precise, and specific: "Now hear this . . . this is your Captain speaking." Relations between hierarchical levels are impersonal, rational, utilitarian, and cold, giving bureaucracy its dismal reputation and Kafkaesque qualities. Needless to say, hierarchies are increasingly seen by Western businesses as dysfunctional and incapable of handling complex information. Yet without hierarchy individualism runs to anarchy. It is an exceedingly vexing issue.

We may say in summary that while a U.S.-type hierarchy is *propositional,* the top creates a strategy which says in effect, "Have I got a new microprocessor for you!"—which it then implements downward. The Japanese-type hierarchy is *appositional.* This word means "apposite, pertinent, well adapted." "What kind of microprocessors would you like us to make?" The bottom of the hierarchy feeds upward into the organization myriad, particulars about what customers want which are synthesized and adapted to by those higher up. Let us recall from Chapter 3 that being outer-directed to customers and subordinates is not low status, but high status. You skilfully adjust your organization to messages coming from the field. If, then, Japanese workers participate more in their corporations, it is because their roles are more crucial. They are not mere implements of the ideas of others, but furnishers of vital information that goes into the construction of new harmonies.

But we have yet to deal with Germany, in the bottom right quadrant, whose structured networks are both relatively equal yet densely integrated with each other. Germany's forte, as we shall see in Chapter 9, is its capital goods industries with formally structured mutualities between suppliers, industries, unions, and customers, in which, for instance, a supplier of printing machines needs to know the printing industry thoroughly and may spend a lifetime, even generations, with customers working on the most sophisticated technological improvements.

Hence, the terms *hierachy* and *equality* do not have the same connotations in Japan, Singapore, Germany, and other integrating cultures shown in Fig. 5-1, as they do in Anglo-Saxon discourse. Equality can be quite formal and structured in Germany, while hierarchy can be familial, affectionate, bottom-up, and information-intense in Singapore and Japan. (France has both family-type and bureaucratic-type hierarchies.) The crisis of authority and the breakdown of hierarchical order may therefore be a North American phenomenon,[11] extending to parts of Northwest Europe. The authorities who receive information are less out of touch than those who issue commands.

Just as we cross-correlated Analyzing-Integrating with Hierarchy-Equality so it is possible to do this also with Universalism-Particularism (see Box 5-2). Because American managers rate high both in Universalism and in Analyzing, we need a metaphor or analog that has both these characteristics. What works by universal laws, yet is readily analyzable into parts? One answer we found was a machine or mechanism. We might therefore expect American managers to think of their organizations as powerful machines and rational tools.

But suppose a managerial culture is more particularistic and synthesizing. What phenomenon contrasts with a mechanism in being particular in its shape and form, and also indivisible in its need for wholeness and relationship to an environment? The corresponding entity is surely an organism. Hence, in Part A of Box 5-2, "Twelve Metaphorical Bridges," we have followed Gareth Morgan in *Images of Organization* in suggesting that mechanism and organism are two major images which managers have of their organizations.[12] Yet because of cultural preferences shared by the United States, the United Kingdom, Australia, and the Netherlands, the image of mechanism is more likely to predominate. Because of the cultural characteristics shared by Japan, Singapore, France, and Italy, the image of an organism is more likely to predominate in those cultures. An interesting exception is Germany, with its machine systems, or integrated machines.

Box 5-2
Twelve Metaphorical Bridges

A.   *Images of the Organization*

Universalism

THE MACHINE	MACHINE SYSTEMS
USA, UK, Australia, Netherlands	Germany

Analyzing ———————————————————————— Synthesizing

THE ORGANISM
Japan, Singapore, Spain

Particularism

B.   *How Managers Conceive of Their Working Lives*

Individualism

THE DIKE	THE STAIRCASE
Netherlands	USA, UK, Australia

Outer-directed ——————————————————————— Inner-directed

THE ROLLER COASTER	THE BARRICADE
Japan, Singapore, Spain	France

Group/Organization

C.   *What Principle of Social Order?*

Individualism

LEGAL HARNESS FOR
SELF-INTEREST
USA, UK, Australia

Particularism ————————————————————————— Universalism

HARMONIOUS AESTHETICS OF RELATIONSHIPS	KONSENZ UND ORDNUNG
Japan, Singapore, Hong Kong	Germany

Group/Organization

D.   *The Logic of Economic Development*

Hierarchy

INDUSTRIAL POLICY OR
DESIGNER CAPITALISM
Japan, Singapore, France, Spain

Status Through ———————————————————— Status Through
Ascription   Achievement

LEVEL PLAYING FIELD
FOR FREE COMPETITION
USA, UK, Sweden, Germany

Equality

It may be asked why the bottom left quadrant is empty. This is because not all combinations are culturally viable, a culture that is analyzing *and* particularizing would have no principle of order or coherence.

In Part B of Box 5-2 we look at how managers conceive of their working lives and career paths by cross-coordinating Individualism–Group/Organization with Inner-directed–Outer-directed. This suggests four images. In the top right quadrant, Inner-directed individualists of the English-speaking democracies tend to conceive of their working lives in terms of a Staircase, or career ladder, climbed step by step by dint of personal effort. As a song in *An American in Paris* put it, "I'll build a stairway to Paradise/with a new step every day/I'm going to get there at any price/stand aside I'm on my way."

At the bottom left is the Outer-directed communitarian quadrant, occupied by Japan, Singapore, and Spain. These managers saw their working lives more as roller coasters, hurtling them up and down collectively, conveyed by forces beyond their control, but to which, if they hung together, they could adapt. An interesting variation are the Dutch, suspended between Individualism and Outer-directedness, at top left. We chose the metaphor of the dike, in honor of the little Dutch boy who withstood external threat by the individual initiative of putting his finger in a hole in the dike.

Finally, the French combine an Inner-directedness with group orientation at bottom right. We chosed the Barricade to symbolize this combination of communal revolutionary action with deep inner convictions about the reasoning mind.

We asked in Part C of Box 5-2 what Principle of Social Order guides different cultures? Nations that are both individualistic and universalistic emphasize a Legal Harness for Self-Interest. This typifies the United States, the United Kingdom, and Australia. Nations high in Group/Organization and Particularism stress the Harmonious Aesthetics of Relationship, often aided by rituals and ceremonies, like the Japanese *ringi*, in which proposals are circulated and initialed. The United States and other English-speaking nations generally try to control the individual self-seeking of their business protagonists by an elaborate network of universal rules and regulations, preferably made by the parties themselves through contractual agreement. The Legal Harness typically involves adversary proceedings in courts which enforce contracts and other obligations of defaulting parties. This helps to explain why America currently has between 650,000 and 700,000 lawyers, twice as many as in 1960, and estimated to reach a million by the year 2000. This is twenty-three times the number of lawyers per capita in Japan.[13] Harnessing individual initiatives via regulation is what gives Big Government in America its dismal reputation, but the more individuals breach the law to express freedom, the more the net of legal prohibitions tightens and the more government, bureaucracy, and interference are excoriated.

Again, the top left quadrant is blank because any culture that tried to be both individualistic and particularistic would court anarchy. However, Germany occupies the Group/Organization–Universalism quadrant. We call this *Konsens und Ordnung,* "Consensus and Order."

Next we asked, What is the Logic of Economic Development in different kinds of culture? We see in Box 5-2, Part D, that economies that value Status Through Achievement by way of Equality of opportunity fall into the bottom right quadrant and call for a Level Playing Field for Free (International) Competition. Here capitalism is a predefined "game" with clear rules in which nations compete, similar to the Olympic Games. The prizes for achievement are international markets, acquired corporations, and bigger profits. Nations compete on an equal footing with other "most favored nations" who subscribe to the GATT rules. This model is similar to that by which America refereed the advancement of her own ethnic groups. The logic states that those people or corporations that achieve most in a fair contest will best advance economic development as a whole.

For countries in the top-left quadrant, the logic of economic development is different. Certain technologies and key product areas have greater national importance ascribed to them and are given a higher position on a hierarchy of national priorities. For example, photovoltaic cells are targeted by Japan for reasons of energy saving and pollution control and as a vital strategic component within innovative products. According to this view, capitalism should be fashioned to a particular national design created purposefully by bureaucratic or political elites to gain world trade advantage. These cultures seek to manage competition to this end. These attempts may or may not succeed, but the intention is usually evident and is frequently referred to as industrial policy (but not where efforts are covert). Industrial policies are more easily accomplished in countries with strong, ascriptive elites, as in Japan, Singapore, and France.

The recent tensions between France and the United Kingdom about the future direction of Europe is a good example of clashing cultural paradigms. For Britain the EEC is a free market allowing a widened competition; for France the EEC is more an exclusive club, a distillation of the values of civilization, a grand vision of enlightened social policies. Is the EEC Commission to be a French-style ascriptive elite or the referee of fair and equal contest linking the United States with Europe? America's answer to the possibility of Fortress Europe is an enlarged free trade area including most of North America from Canada to Mexico. The struggle is to make the world resemble one's own cultural paradigms.

There are no nations in the bottom left and top right quadrants, since steep hierarchies impede achieved status and there is no point ascribing status to people if you wish to treat them equally.

Our twelve metaphorical bridges are a tentative beginning to understanding the highly metaphorical and integrative concepts employed by Japanese managers, a topic to which the next three chapters are addressed.

6

Harmonious Patterns of Particulars

WHEN WE ADMINISTERED our questionnaire to some Japanese executives, they seemed clearly upset. The dilemma that seemed to bother them most was about the man who was having a beer with his friend, the safety engineer, when an employee injured himself. Should he tell the safety commission what happened, or should he side with his friend? The senior executive present asked whether the group could confer before answering. He did not look very pleased with us. This was not the way our questionnaires are usually answered, but we nonetheless agreed. The group was out of the room for almost fifteen minutes. When they returned their leader spoke for all of them.

"Both alternatives are wrong," he said. "The answer is to promise your friend your support in the version of events which he wishes to present, but to plead with him, as a friend, to tell the truth. In this way, you can remain friends and the workplace will be made safer."

This answer is of unusual interest. It suggests that while Americans and Northwestern Europeans like to state universal truths and rules, and then require that particular situations and human relationships submit to those universals and be guided by them, the Japanese reverse these priorities. For them, the particular relationships of *honne*, a spirit of intimacy between persons, is the moral cement of society, and to the extent that such relationships are trusting, harmonious, and aesthetic, rules of wider generality can be derived from them. People who are alienated from their close friends are going to break the law anyway. We have always admitted in the West, that a loveless home and the breakdown of communities are among the origins of crime. Is it so illogical, then, to insist that affection for particular persons is the basis of a law-abiding society, that human relationships of mutual respect carry within them the seeds of social order?

Japan's strong orientation to particularism is seen in the extraordinary range of differences in its products, with its estimated 27,000 bookstores, 75 percent of its television presenting news and education, and dozens of products for every age group—for example, nine varieties of motor scooter for the female office worker between age eighteen and twenty-two. The image is expressed in art and gardening. A dynamic harmony is created from myriad differences, with no tree, leaf, flower, or stone like any other. Japan thus leads the revolution toward customized goods. But the tendency to treat particular customers with extreme consideration can lead to scandal, as when brokerage houses voluntarily repay the losses of their favorite customers, with money that has come from the less favored. Corruption typically takes the form of doing too much for special persons. It is also hard to see how, with its dislike of universal rules, Japan can exercise world leadership in America's place. To treat almost everything as particular requires an extraordinarily homogeneous culture.

In cultures where values are believed to clash and collide, the law of the land and a universal moral order is deemed to have supremacy over the private and particular wants of the person subject to that law. But in cultures where values are deemed harmonious and complementary, personal and particular relationships become microcosms of the larger social order. You behave toward others in such a manner that a universal law could be derived from your mutuality. Such an approach is much more flexible, and, to outsiders, "devious." The Japanese call it *tsukai-wake*, roughly "situational ethics."[1]

But if we are to judge Japan by the level of civil order and organizational harmony achieved in the last thirty years, by the fact that the level of crime was reduced in the years after the American occupation, while crime levels in several "universalist" cultures seem to be out of control, then accusations of amorality will hardly do.[2] The idea that crime or civic virtue has its origins in how you treat and are treated by particular close friends is not to be dismissed, and may be wise. And if you seek to reform your careless friend, the safety engineer, then perhaps your friendship might be the reason he chooses to tell the truth after all, whereas your insistence that you both submit yourselves to an abstract moral rule could have less appeal. Most Americans agree on what they ought to do as a witness before the safety commission, but what they actually do is a different question not asked in this research. Since the claims of close friends may be more powerful in practice than a loyalty to abstract codes, the harmonizing of social relationships with abstract codes could be the best guarantor of law and order.

The insistence by Americans and Northwest Europeans, that they know what the rules should be, and that it remains for the Japanese to obey them, was recently the subject of comment by Akio Morito of Sony.

> Americans and Europeans seem to think that their idea of how the world trading and monetary systems work, and should continue to work, should be universal, especially in the business world, and that since they believe they invented the game, the rules should never be amended. The system up to now has served them well, and there is no need to change.[3]

> If you go through life convinced that your way is always best, all the new ideas in the world will pass you by. Americans tend to think that the American system is the way things should work all around the world, but they should not be blind and deaf to how things are done in other countries.[4]

Two Different Principles of Social Order

Every society faces the same existential issues. For example, how do you differentiate yourself in the pursuit of different needs, goals, and labors, while also integrating yourself so that persons share a sense of order and of meaning? Differentiation and integration are basic biological necessities.[5] No living creature can develop without becoming more differentiated, better integrated, and retaining a vital balance between the two. The same rule applies to corporations. The more complex and creative their environment, the more differentiated and the better integrated a corporation needs to become.[6]

What makes Japan such a bewildering society for Westerners is that they have a completely different concept of social order, which is evidenced in their different scores on the dilemmas we put to them. As we saw in Fig. 5-2, the Japanese and the Westerners imagine the world quite differently. Where Westerners see machines and staircases, the Japanese see organisms and roller coasters.

It is essential to grasp that making particulars harmonious with each other is an alternative kind of social ordering to Western-style moral objectivity, with its Golden Rules applying to objectively describable situations. Harmonies are of overlapping kinds, emotional, responsive, dynamic, aesthetic, and relational. Elements within a situation, or persons within a group, are expected to reorder, rearrange, and recombine themselves until they have approximated this ideal. We see this in the way Japanese executives nod and bow to one another and in their liking for group calisthenics.

Our use of axes and quadrants to show the interaction of values is in itself biased toward some imagined Western universe of objective order. You are either in one quadrant or another. You have an objective location on two universal continua. So let us instead draw a figure consistent with the Japanese ideal of harmonious relationships. Our best effort in this direction is Fig. 6-1, which integrates, encompasses, and harmonizes all four of our polarities in a dynamic whole.

Fig. 6-1   Encompassing Western Polarities

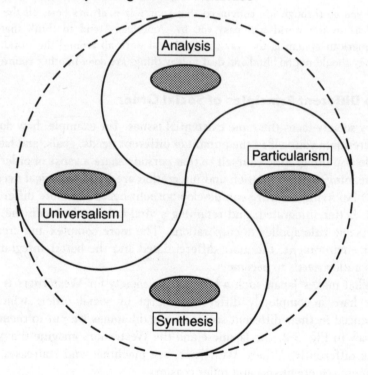

The contrast between the images in Fig. 6-1 is profound. Universals and particulars are all encompassed within a circle that ebbs and flows like the lighter, whiter mountain mist and the darker, heavier mountain mist that alternate in the original *Tai Chi*.[7] Moreover, each part is seen as part of the larger whole, just as particulars are microcosms of the universals that organize them. This is a very important insight, because parts and wholes, universals and particulars, can be seen as either excluding or including one another. What passes for holism and particularism in much Western discourse is the attempt to champion the whole against the parts and the particular against the universal. These views, championed by countercultural minorities within the United States and other Western nations, fail to grasp the genuine breadth of holistic thinking. To champion the whole against the part is to remain both adversarial and analytic. You are treating the ideal of wholeness as a thing separated from its parts.[8] Genuine wholeness views all details and all particulars are being encompassed within its pattern.

Hence, in Fig. 6-1 all four elements are enfolded within the larger context. You can conceive of them as moving clockwise or counterclockwise, as snaking to and fro, or as simultaneously interactive. The four oblong shapes convey a vital quality of the yin-yang, namely that all values have the seeds of their opposites within them. Just as universal codes are seeded with particular examples of those principles, so every part carries within it a capacity to relate to the whole.[9]

That the Japanese do not start with "universal principles" and derive right conduct from them is the subject of much hostile comment among Western observers, leading to the accusation that the Japanese are not moral at all! Hence, William J. Holstein, associate editor of *Business Week*, comments:

> Most Americans with any exposure to Japan know that the Japanese move smoothly from *tatemae* to *honne*. The former is the diplomatic, or official line, that you give to someone you don't really trust, the latter is the level you reserve for someone you have met many times and know well. . . . Slightly more complex is the notion of situational ethics. If a certain kind of behavior is appropriate in one setting, then it's entirely natural to the Japanese that another kind of behavior is appropriate for another setting. They find it quite easy to switch hats. . . . But where was the moral core? What truths did they hold to be self-evident?[10]

The answer is actually quite simple. "The good" is what fits finely and elegantly with other valued elements. Indeed, "the good" is not a thing or single value at all, but an elegant pattern and a fine arrangement, different at the level of intimacy, from the level of diplomacy, but beautifully arranged like flowers or like a miniature garden at any level. It is well done if all elements harmonize.

None of this prevents Western fulminations, even by long-term residents in Japan, like the Dutch journalist, Karel van Wolferen:

> The malleability, relativity and negotiability of truth in Japan; the claimed superfluity of logic; the absence of a strong intellectual tradition; the subservience to the administrators of law; and the acceptance, even the celebration of amorality; these are, of course, all causally intertwined. All extant civilizations who have developed religions and systems of thought acknowledge the existence of a truth transcending socio-political concerns. Neither Shintoism nor Buddhism has been of assistance here.[11]

Wolferen goes on to quote Edward Seidensicker, who, writing in *Encounter*, referred to the Japanese as

> pulverizers of all ideas. Seidensicker relates that, when Japanese university students were given a list of ". . . isms": Communism, Democratic Socialism, Liberalism, Humanism, Pragmatism, Existentialism, Nationalism, Hedonism, Empiricism, etc.—nearly half chose multiple and contradictory philosophies! One student marked them all. Nowhere do disparate ideologies rest more comfortably side by side than in the heads of the Japanese, and the total result is, of course, a raging anti-intellectualism.[12]

Yet this desire and capacity to reconcile "isms" may not be all vanity and foolishness. Polarized opinions have not been entirely benign in their influence on world history. Nor is the Japanese search for values' organization without its advocates in the West. No less a luminary than William James held that the inner consistency and integrity of one's entire value system was the crucial test of moral enlightenment:

> He knows that he must vote always for the richer universe, for the good which is most organizable, most fit to enter into complex combinations, most apt to be a member of a more inclusive whole.[13]

To condemn the Japanese in direct proportion to their deviation from popular cannons of American and Dutch morality may hinder us from understanding the subtleties of even our own thinking, from Erasmus to William James.

It is instructive to note that while 74 percent of American managers saw a company as "performing tasks and functions" as its primary purpose, 71 percent of Japanese managers saw "people with social relations working together" (see Table 2-3). The first vision is of things organized by rules. The second is of a web or harmony of particular persons.

We also posed the following dilemma:

Some people think that a boss is usually characterized by the fact that he can do his job more skillfully than others. Some people think that having power is what characterizes a boss. Which do you think is better?

We saw "doing his job" as an objective unit of success and the right of such persons to lead as a universal rule derived empirically from the analysis of such performances. This should, therefore, be an approach preferred by American managers. We saw power as the totality of human and technical forces working together in a harmonious pattern. This should, therefore, be the approach preferred by Japanese manager. Indeed it was.

Table 6-1   Universalized Skills vs. Powerful Combinations

Does job skill or power legitimatize the boss?

Job Skill	GER	USA	SIN	FRA	BEL	SWE	CAN	IT	UK	AUS	NL	JAP
	79.7	78.5	78.2	75.2	71.7	69.7	68.7	68.1	64.2	62.5	62.3	26.7

The difference is very large indeed, with Japan virtually on its own. Since the question is about what happens, rather than what should happen, the relative power orientation of the United Kingdom, Australia, and the Netherlands may be a matter of regret. They may feel that superior job skill should characterize a boss but does not always do so.

But the case of Japan is quite different. Here, power is the measure of the manager's success. William J. Holstein notes:

> When the Japanese talk about one another, they do not usually say, "I don't like him," or "He is not nice." A more frequent insult is to say, "He has no power," or "He has no influence."[14]

No wonder, then, that Holstein called his book *The Japanese Power Game: What It Means for America*, or that Pat Choate wrote *Agents of Influence*.[15] For most Westerners, power is a corrupting and subversive influence in which the moral order, by which the best performers rise to the top, is corrupted by the private agendas of empire builders and power seekers.

For the Japanese, the whole meaning of power must be seen within the context of harmonizing the patterns of particulars. You are powerful as a manager because the group you lead has combined its forces powerfully. Harmony means that everyone is cooperating to increase the effectiveness of the whole. Power does not usually mean that employees have been defeated or crushed, since in this event the energies of many could not contribute to the organization and its leader's sense of power. The aesthetic of relationship sees many particular persons with different skills, joined in one powerful unity. That, at least, is the ideal. In practice, of course, such ideals may be unachievable without subjugating at least some points of view.

The difference between the Japanese and the American attitude is striking. We posed a dilemma concerning an employee whose current performance has slipped.

A meeting is called to make a decision about the dismissal of an employee. He has worked fifteen years for the company and has performed his job in a satisfactory way. For various reasons, last year the results of his work dropped to an unsatisfactory level. There are no reasons to believe that this situation will improve. Members at the meeting are divided. Part of the group says that job performance should remain the criterion for dismissal, regardless of the age of the person and his previous records.

The other part of the group argues that it is wrong to disregard the fifteen years the employee has been working for the company. One has to take into account the company's responsibility for his life. Which one of these two ways of reasoning is more appropriate?

The choice to dismiss concerns a belief in a universal objective order, because the employee has clearly fallen short of "the standards" required of all employees. His current performance, analyzed out of the overall context of fifteen years and made into a separate objective measure, shows him as deficient. He is also in default of his contract, a contemporary objectification of his long relationship with the company.

The choice to consider the employee's long service and hold the company responsible to him, builds on the particular human circumstances of the man: Is he getting old and tired? Has the company failed to nurture him? In so considering, the manager concerns himself with the relationship of the company to the person and with the morale and harmony of employees generally. Could this be harmed if they see one of their members discarded?

Table 6-2   Failing by Objective Standards vs. Joining Together Particular Needs and Obligations

Criteria for dismissing long-service employees

Failing by	USA	CAN	UK	AUS	NL	BEL	JAP	GER	IT	FRA	SIN	KOR
objectively derived standards	77.2	75.0	42.4	40.0	37.4	36.5	33.8	31.0	27.5	26.2	21.0	19.0

Although Japan is not as considerate toward the failing employee as several other countries, U.S. managers are more than twice as likely to choose the argument pointing to dismissal, with over three-quarters regarding current performance as the only relevant issue. The Japanese managers, in contrast, tend to judge within a wider context, taking the whole of the surrounding circumstances into consideration. On this question, Singaporean managers are the most concerned for employees' particular circumstances. The situational ethic in this instance is not without moral sensibility.

The Objective Society vs. the Polyocular Society

Magorah Maruyama, a Japanese-American professor currently teaching at Aoyama Gakuin University in Tokyo, has described Japan as a polyocular culture.[16] This is in contrast to the American search for objectivity and has to do with contrasting attitudes to verification. How do we make sure that knowledge is accurate and reliable? U.S. culture, and much of Northwestern Europe, define the world as existing of objects located in "public space," where all detached observers would agree on their description. Consider, for example, "Profits went up 10 percent in the last quarter." This is neutral, disinterested, undeniable fact. All qualified accountants using the specified practices would agree. The Japanese take the view that all phenomena can be seen from multiple points of view, and that the additional angles make reality more whole and comprehensive. These two approaches are logical extensions of the cultural preferences for ordering objects universally, or for harmonizing particulars.

It may come as something of a shock to discover that prior to Western penetration, the Japanese had no word for "objectivity." It had to be invented once Westerners began talking. The word now used is *kyakkan-teki*, literally "the guest's point of view" (while *shukanteki* is "the host's point of view," or "subjectivity."[17] There is surely a hint of reproach in the first of these terms. The guest is not simply an outsider and a stranger, but is probably naive about the nonvisible relationships of the family being visited. The guest "sees" a number of separated people and, unlike the host, cannot know the patterns or the dynamics within the whole. The guest's objective gaze is partial and misses much. Whatever is gained in sharpness is lost by superficiality. The guest's view is *monocular*, Maruyama claims. Western objectivity isolates and objectifies as if a telescope had been focused. This indeed is how Western science originated, and we may have gone overboard in celebrating the methods by which this knowledge first reached us. Yet the same focused lens that clarifies the distant object makes the foreground and background fuzzy and cuts off the object from its field.[18]

So, if objectivity impoverishes us, is there another reliable way of perceiving? Maruyama starts with the reminder that we have two eyes and that the perception of depth and of wholeness derives from our brain's computing the difference between the images received by each eye. To see whole patterns and three-dimensional configurations, the brain must process particular differences. The importance of these differences is not confined to two eyes in a single head, but to differences between what four, six, eight, or a score of eyes might perceive from positions all around the phenomenon being scrutinized. Hence, the Japanese view is *polyocular*.[19] Every member of a quality circle or working team has an important vantage point upon an issue and sees different aspects. Products and services are themselves multidimensional, with as many facets as there are customers. The whole truth is always in the process of being discovered. There is no such thing as a completed product system to which no improvements are possible, since there is always another viewpoint to be taken into consideration. All employees can and must participate, because each has a new view to add. All customers must be listened to with rapt attention, because they may have another valid reason for appreciating or not appreciating what is offered. The polyocular Japanese culture is symbolized by the way its members depict nature and their taste in art and gardening. Rarely is any rock or tree like any other, yet all particulars achieve a dynamic wholeness.

But what has this to do with business? The notion of a world that consists not of objects, but of differences,[20] could be giving the Japanese a massive advantage in the information or knowledge revolution. The reason is that while traditional production manufactures objects, information is news of differences, symbolized by the "bit" of the computer with its binary code of 0 and 1. A culture attuned to a multiplicity of particulars or differences, in which it seeks to find patterns, may process information more easily than a culture searching for universal or uniform attributes among objects. Maruyama argues that arranging particulars or differences into wholes is a variety-enhancing process, whereas looking for universals among objects is a variety-reducing process.[21] The problem with "objectivity" is that those who claim to have it believe they need to look no further, need listen to no one else, and never alter their convictions. They have "the data," or "givens." But those pursuing polyocular knowledge will never be satisfied, never know enough. And it is nonsense to claim that the monocular or objective view is more scientific. In the last fifty years, science has plunged into a relativistic, holistic, transformative, and dynamic revolution. Theories of complementarity, uncertainty, catastrophe, chaos, and dissipative structures all require the combination of alternative viewpoints.[22] Research on the brain has found that it is laterally specialized left and right, in addition to being specialized fore and aft, so that "opposite" endowments combine.[23] Karl Pribram has likened the brain to a hologram in which light waves cross and form interference patterns. This is evidently closer to polyocularity than to the supposed "reflection of objects in the brain."[24]

Do we see evidence of polyocularity in the style of Japanese management? Yes, in many ways. A well-known method of the Toyota Production System is called "the Five Times Why." Employees of Toyota must never be satisfied by a single explanation, but must ask "why" at least five times.[25] Why, for example, has the tool bit broken six times in the last two months? Because—

• The metal being bored is too hard.
• The tool-bit is not hard enough.
• The speed of boring is too high.
• A better lubricant is needed.
• The machinist lacks skill/training.

The point is that all these reasons may be true, all represent different places to intervene in the system as a whole, and one or more interventions will prove the most satisfactory and the least costly.

Or consider the *kanban* procedure by which every part in a factory bears a label or *kanban* that describes which particular part it is, and the place it has in the whole assembly. In this way, every part carries attached to it a representation of the whole and is a microsom of that whole.[26]

Another well-tried Japanese process is know as the KJ method, and is borrowed from the Japanese anthropologist Jiro Kawakita. This was originally a form of anthropological investigation. Many particular evidences were gathered from the society being studied, and then the natives themselves were asked to make meaningful wholes from these particulars. As adapted by thousands of businesses, the KJ method uses *kama-kire-ho* (literally, the scrap paper method). Employees write down on small pieces of paper concrete descriptions of what they believe is wrong, or what they want the newly formed group to accomplish. These particulars are then organized by insight (not by categorization) into whole themes; later the different themes are connected into larger patterns, which are then implemented.[27]

Depersonalized Data vs. Personal and Tacit Knowledge

There is an important corollary to processes like *kama-kire-ho* and "creativity circles," in which everyone's ideas are first written down and later harmonized. The thinking is inductive, moving from the particulars to generalizations and syntheses. This contrasts with the deductive thinking preferred by Americans, in which universal propositions are tested by seeing if they do indeed produce the objective data that was initially hypothesized. Inductive thinking is able to deal with every minute particular in the workplace: "Shoji is too easily rattled," "If the part doesn't quite fit, refrigerate it first," "Yuki's dies are accurate within three thousandth of an inch—no one knows how she does it, nor does she!" When you think inductively, every detail from the factory floor, however subjective, personal, deviant, fallible, or idiosyncratic is included. Moreover, influence flows up from the work floor to those responsible for the larger system.

Deductive thinking works the other way, down from those who form hypotheses to the manual workers who do what the theory tells them. The whole notion of Taylorism, or Scientific Management, is that the scientific procedure is worked out in advance by the time-and-motion engineers and is then put into operation by blue-collar "hands" obeying white-collar "heads." The Japanese themselves see this as America's fatal flaw. In 1985, Konosuke Matsushita wrote:

> We are going to win and the industrial West is going to lose. There is nothing much you can do about it, because the reasons for your failure are within yourselves. Your firms are built on the Taylor model; even worse so are your heads. . . . For you, the essence of management is getting the ideas out of the heads of the bosses into the hands of labor. For us the art of management is the art of mobilizing and pulling together the intellectual resources of all the employees in the service of the firm. . . . Only by drawing on the combined brainpower of all its employees can a firm face up to the turbulence and constraints of today's environment.[28]

Nor does the hypothetico-deductive method tolerate tacit knowledge, personal knowledge, or vaguely defined bonds of affinity among workers.

In order to deal "scientifically" with "data" the human world must first be reduced to objective facts and hard units. Insofar as possible, these—along with workers—are expected to be predictable, controllable, replaceable, precise, and invariable—resembling objects that yield to the mastery of physical science. The preference is for highly codified knowledge, preferably numbers. That which cannot be expressed as an objective quantity is either ignored or transformed in its meaning to become objectlike.[29]

Hence, personal conversations become "bullets" of itemized assertion. Norms and values are treated like fly-paper, and their number of adherents quantified. They are carefully defined so as to polarize them with their alleged "opposites." Once codified at ludicrous levels of generality, the information becomes useless. The personal knowledge that "Shoji gets rattled" is something that his work group can deal with. But what is the group going to do with "The Contribution of Human Anxiety to Machine Malfunction"? Even if they could read and understand the paper, its applicability to their specific problem is doubtful.[30]

Several years ago the philosopher Abraham Kaplan contrasted the logic of discovery, which always includes inductive thinking, with reconstructed logic, the way Westerners write up the discovery afterward in a purified deductive form.[31] Box 6-1 shows how the Boston Consulting Group reconstructed the success of Honda motor scooters so that it fit the Western deductive mind-set of their clients.

In numerous cases, we do not know *why* we know. Particular workers have extraordinary and particular skills that cannot be codified and may even be unarticulated and tacit: "I know how you feel," "I know this part is faulty," "I know this machine." To downplay such knowledge because you cannot codify it and generalize from the code, is to deny recognition to a vast array of human potentials. As Professor Daisetz Suzuki explains, the Japanese see *prajna*, "an intuition of the whole," as the source of *vijnana*, "reason." You first intuit a whole pattern; only then does reason go to work on this.[32] It does not matter that skills are tacit, vague, or indefinable, what matters is that they make a noticeable difference to the whole operation of the group and the plant.

The Japanese also prefer uncodified approaches in marketing. They are not keen on questionnaires, but prefer to talk face-to-face with customers. Increasingly, they bring out a particular product on a very short time-cycle, to see whether the customer approves or complains. In launching their Honda motor scooters in the United States, they discovered through personal conversations that the narrow oriental saddle

Box 6-1

An American Consultant Reconstructs Honda's Achievement

Honda motor cycles' amazing achievement in first the Japanese market, and later the American, is an oft-told tale, but its telling is instructive. The Boston Consulting Group hired by the British government to explain the demise of the British motorcycle industry, pointed in its report to Honda's "huge production of volumes in small motor cycles for the domestic market, and that volume-related cost reductions had followed. . . . This resulted in a highly competitive cost position which the Japanese used as a springboard for the penetration of world markets."

Subsequently revised as a Harvard Business School case study, the authors explained that the Honda machine retailed for $250, compared to much more expensive and high powered U.S. and British machines. Moreover, Honda had seven times the number of designers and engineers compared to its rivals, thereby achieving higher production per man hour, and higher investment in net fixed assets. Honda had boldly "redefined the market" away from leather-jacketed macho men toward ordinary Americans, thanks to its inspired advertising theme, "You Meet the Nicest People on a Honda" (not Hell's Angels or Satan's Slaves). Sales rose from $500,000 in 1960 to $7.7 million by 1965; a whole new middle-class market had been created.

Richard Pascale, co-author of *The Art of Japanese Management*, arranged to interview the six retired Honda executives most responsible for this feat in a Tokyo hotel. Their story was quite different.

They were initially overwhelmed by America's sheer size, the ubiquity of the automobile, and the rudeness and shoddiness of the motor-cycle business. "In truth we had no strategy other than the idea of seeing if we could sell something in the U.S.," Kihachiro Kawashima, the ex-president, explained. They aimed to start in July 1959 and compete with other large European imports. Four of them rented a Los Angeles warehouse and a one-person apartment, so that all save one slept on the floor in turns.

Disaster came early when Honda's 250 cc and 350 cc bikes failed to withstand the faster and longer driving typical of the U.S. Their clutches gave out and leaked oil. The defective samples were air-freighted back to Japan for modification on a twenty-four hour schedule. But the launch was wrecked without saleable stock. There were, however, a few 50 cc Supercubs, thought to be unsaleable in 'jumbo-sized' America, but used by the executives themselves to putter around L.A. These attracted a lot of attention. Then a buyer from Sears called. So Honda tried to save its aborted launch by pushing the 50 cc, and because "macho" cycle dealers scorned it, they tried sporting good stores.

As for "strategically redefining" the market through advertising, this too was a lucky happenstance. The famous campaign about "Nicest People" was dreamed up by an undergraduate student at UCLA for a class project. His instructor introduced him to Grey Advertising, who purchased the idea. It was adopted despite major opposition.

So is BCG's version wrong? No, but it is reconstructed in an idealized form after the event, so as to be sold to clients. It is perfectly logical, but this is not the logic by which the strategy actually emerged. Reality is full of mess and error.

Source: "Perspectives on Strategy: The Real Story Behind Honda's Success," Richard T. Pascale. *California Management Review* 26 (3), pp. 47–72.

uncomfortably bisected the broader occidental ass—hardly a subject for questionnaires.

Product Standards vs. Seamless Quality

Almost no issue is more important in world-class competition than the question of quality. As products grow more and more extensive, comprising not even separate office machines, but productivity systems; not just domestic appliances, but coordinated systems for the home, so the reliability of each particular part becomes crucial to the functioning of the whole. Quality is especially critical to complex, knowledge-intensive, high value-added products, the markets which the Japanese have targeted and taken. We do not tolerate errors in the computer we use for personal banking. To the extent that electronics are becoming extensions of our own minds and bodies, fault-free operation is vital.

Quality also interferes with the calculations of economists. Theories of perfect competition and markets which "clear" to find their own level, balance of payments' problems that adjust "automatically" when the dollar or pound loses value against the yen and makes American or British goods cheaper, simply cease to work if the products themselves are not homogenous. And the quality revolution means that increasingly they are *not* homogenous.[33] Companies are obliged to buy the highest quality, as opposed to cheapest components, simply to keep abreast of competition and reduce the chance of malfunctioning in finished assemblies. It is the Japanese who have introduced to world markets the concept of one defect per million, as opposed to one hundred or one thousand. Once this becomes possible, customers will accept nothing less—the massive accretion in the value of the yen notwithstanding.

Unfortunately, the American way of thinking, with atoms of uniform quality generalizing into universal laws, constitutes a search for sameness,[34] of which supply and demand curves and standardized units of output are just two examples. There is an irony here. Compared with Japan, says Maruyama, the United States is an exceedingly heterogeneous society in which scores of different nationalities have found a home. America's drive toward universalism, legalism, standardization, and "scientific" management is a robust attempt to bring order to this vast array of overflowing differences.

Japan, in contrast, is a very homogenous society in which minorities are not well assimilated. Yet it is this very homogeneity that allows that society to search for qualitative differences, to produce products in almost unprecedented varieties, and to allow every member of the quality circle to champion a different vision of excellence, so that the finished product excels in a multitude of details.

Americans traditionally inspect for quality.[35] For them, quality needs one more department, one more task, so "add an inspector" and have him reject products "not up to standard." First comes the universal law, "total quality," as it is now being called, then each atom of product "makes the grade" or fails to do so with workers or suppliers rewarded or punished accordingly.

The Japanese approach to quality is to create a seamless whole from an ever-increasing number of particulars. In this view, quality is integral to the whole process. It is everyone's responsibility, and all members of a work team should cooperate to ensure that nothing that is second rate is tolerated.

The Japanese approach seems to produce superior results for several reasons. American quality, by focusing on separate pieces, often misses the gaps between, i.e., the quality by which the whole is organized, which may not be the responsibility of any one group or person. Moreover, the inspection of parts tends to cause adversarial relationships between producers and inspectors, who must effectively cancel out a portion of the work that producers regard as finished. If there is no air in the inspector's tires when he wants to drive home, he gets the message. Finally, producing "up to standard" assumes the correctness of the standard, but in practice it may be too high, in which case producers resent it, or too low, in which case they take a breather and earn some easy money. In any event, standards require constant revision where performance improves. In this process, theory and practice tend to clash.[36] Japanese quality is pushed higher and higher by the initiatives and learning of the workers themselves.

Although the words *total quality* have now been borrowed from Japan and widely used in America, they may not have the same meaning. Total quality in the American context too often means impossibly high, theoretical standards foisted by engineers on workers, in short, business as usual.

Either One Value or Another vs. More Valuable Combinations

The Japanese not only have a different approach to quality, they see "value" and values creation in a different light, yet one that follows their cultural orientation. Americans tend to segment values into either-or. Indeed, "market segmentation," "niche marketing," "price bands" are all the rage. There is nothing wrong with such approaches. The problem is rather in what is *not* seen.

When we divide, for instance, "convenience foods" from "luxury foods," "health foods" from "gourmet foods" and decide that we will aim for the "health-convenience" market because this "segment" has fewer offerings, then what we miss is the realization that convenience foods can also be luxurious, healthy, delicious, and less expensive than others.

No less an authority than Michael Porter has assured us that there are two "generic strategies," each unique and, hence, exclusive. You can be the "low-cost producer" or go for "a premium product" and charge extra. You can focus on one or a few products or supply the entire range, including less popular items.[37] Again, this approach is not mistaken. It is true that you may fall somewhere in between, impressing the customer with neither your cheapness nor your quality, but it is a very partial view, and very American. What is misses is that even the buyers of premium goods will prefer those that are relatively cheaper. You can focus and then rapidly extend the range. We have seen the Japanese gradually capturing a larger and larger share of the world automobile market by producing first low-cost cars that happen to have premium qualities, and now premium cars that undercut Rolls Royce, Jaguar, Cadillac, and Mercedes. Japanese cars are safe *and* high performing, compact *and* roomy, economical in gas mileage *and* quick to accelerate.[38]

In Anglo-Saxon classical economics, choices are irrational and subjective. One consumer likes strawberry ice cream, another raspberry.[39] The only objective facts are the level of demand at particular prices.[40] One choice typically obviates the other, and, as Jeremy Bentham put it, "pushpin is as good as poetry," maybe better if the price is higher. Hence the economist is uninterested in human needs. What he knows is demand. Nor are there any rational grounds for believing one product to be better than the other in the absence of such demand.

The Japanese view appears to be quite different. A product is as valuable as the number of *particular* human satisfactions that have been wrought into the *whole* combination. Of course, the consumer must demand this values combination, but the more values by more people that have gone into its making, then the more satisfactions by more customers will go into its consumption. The larger the values combination, the more potentially valuable the product, the higher its quality, the more multifaceted and, hence, wider will be its appeal. In short, wholes are more valuable than parts, and products develop not simply in complexity but in the range of what is encompassed. The polyocular approach seeks to reconcile many points of view into a choice combination, rather than a choice between one flavor and another.[41] Of course, both approaches are valid, but the either/or approach is more appropriate for the ice cream vendor, and the choice combination is more appropriate for the purchaser of computers, video recorders, and fax machines, where the product greatly complexifies over time. World market trends seem to suggest that Japan increasingly dominates those products that fit its thought patterns.

Terms, Objective, Aims vs. Improved Relationships

Polyocularity also shows up on the gradual and seemingly circuitous manner in which the Japanese build their business relationships. This indirect approach to forming relationships makes good sense if your view is polyocular and you are willing to take time and trouble to build robust, long-lasting relationships. The very real danger is that you will be deceived and exploited by your partner several years hence, when an enormous amount of time and effort has gone into the partnership. How can this be avoided? The answer is to look for many small and particular instances of how the potential partner behaves when he is not focused upon his own personal gain. Anyone can sustain a program of deception when narrowly focused on a particular goal, but to relax, to show interest, to respect the dozens of unfamiliar particularities in which your host engages when there is no specific goal to be achieved, this reveals the kind of trust and human responsiveness that the Japanese are looking for in partners.

For example, in *Japan Inc*, "a comic book for graduates," published in the United States by Stanford University Press, the "Mitsutomo Company" is visited by officials from an unstable Arab company whose representatives insist on talking business straightaway—a sure sign of danger and unreliability. The Japanese hosts are astonished. Can those who grudge the time to cultivate relationships be trusted? Can they be anything more than impatient self-seekers, who will abandon the relationship as soon as they encounter their first inconvenient obligation? We note in passing that the very existence of "comic books for the educated" shows Japan's greater reliance on whole pictures and images rather than printed words alone. In English-language publishing, pictures are usually for artists, children, and the half-literate readers of tabloids.

The polyocular approach to relationships also helps to explain "the seeming indifference of Japanese business to a small print" and precise legal terms of contracts.⁴² There have been horrendous misunderstandings between Japanese and Western negotiators about how much the specific terms of a contract matter when the circumstances have radically changed. The most notorious case occurred in 1976–77, in the sugar dispute between Australia and Japan. Japanese refiners agreed to a long-term contract to buy Australian sugar in the autumn of 1974—a time of acute crisis for Japan, since the world price of oil had quadrupled and, with it, the nation's import bills. However, the price of sugar fell precipitously, and Japan found herself contracted to pay $160 per ton above the world price for five years. The Japanese immediately asked for a renegotiation of the terms, on the grounds that mutual benefit to the parties required it. Japanese-Australian relationships were more important than the atomistic price agreed to before world sugar prices slumped. But the Australians took the view that a price was a price. The Japanese had given their word and must keep it.⁴³ Great bitterness and deep misunderstandings ensued. The Japanese view was summarized by *The Japan Economic Newspaper*:

It is true that a contract is a contract, but when customers are in a predicament, we believe that assistance is routinely extended to customers from a long-term viewpoint, even in Australia.[44]

Certainly, Japanese suppliers extend such assistance to their customers. For example, if heavy snow falls in Tokyo so that cinema audiences shrink, the film distributors offer generous rebates to movie houses. If a female customer for a tube of lipstick cannot get the shade she requires, a dispatch rider is often called to deliver it. Looked at analytically on an item-by-item basis, the delivery of a single tube is not cost-effective. But looked at as strengthening the relationship between customer and retailer, and retailer and supplier, it makes very good sense. The "extravagant" act of generosity toward the customer tends to evoke her loyalty and patronage. She will likely make it up to her supplier. We can characterize the difference between Japanese and U.S./Australian approaches as following the "letter of the law" in U.S./Australian cultures and the "spirit of the law" in Japanese culture.

Westerners assume that the less ambiguous are the terms and the more literally they are enforced, the fewer will be the attempts by self-interested parties to bend the interpretation in their own favor. The Japanese assume that the more ambiguous the terms and the more liberally they are interpreted, the easier it becomes for ongoing relationships to develop and mature even in radically altered circumstances. In the U.S./Australian view, universal obligations attach to precisely defined contractual items. In the Japanese view, whole relationships develop and mature from the particular and changing needs of partners. The really vital question to be faced is whether Japan has lower "transaction costs," as a result of building relationships of trust and mutuality, than Americans do by negotiating enforceable contracts and extensively litigating conflicts.[45]

There follows from Japanese preferences a marked reluctance to say no, and Westerners may get angry when they believe they have won agreement, but nothing transpires. So notorious is this Japanese unwillingness to contradict or confront foreigners that Shintaro Ishihara, the Japanese right-wing politician has recently written a best-seller, *The Japan That Can Say No*, calling upon his countrymen to imitate Westerners in championing basic ideas and fundamentals.[46]

The reason Japanese managers hesitate to say no is not hard to discover; they are addressing themselves to the relationship with the foreign partner and not to the concrete things being asked for. The words "Yes, but it is difficult . . ." accompanied by meaningful pauses, means "Yes, you have a right as a partner to ask me, but no, I can't do this particular thing." Yet Americans hearing these words then go away believing they have won assent to their proposition.[47]

For Americans, an orderly framework is constructed out of specifically agreed points. These terms must be agreed to first without backsliding and equivocation, since without carefully defined parts you cannot build a whole. It is, therefore, crucial to know whether the Japanese agree or not, point by point. For the Japanese, many of the particular wants of both parties need to be accommodated through a whole relationship, preferably flexible, loose, and friendly. The actual points matter far less than building the relationships, inasmuch as the greater the mutuality and the trust, the more it will be possible to include the widest range of particulars sought by either party. Moreover, particulars are frequently interchangeable, there being many alternative ways of satisfying a particular want. "Yes, but let us go on trying to help each other since other ways can be found." It is for this reason that Japanese negotiators not infrequently renege on specific points, because when they come to think of it, a certain item does not fit the emerging whole. In such cases, Westerners are often furious.

Of course, the Japanese have no trouble saying no to each other, which, according to one American researcher, they do "more often but more politely than Americans."[48] The politeness is part of the same pattern: maintain the relationship at all costs, but be constructively critical within it. As the Japanese learn American ways they tend to become more outspoken. Akio Morita recalls that he flatly contradicted Donald Regan, then treasury secretary, who accused the Japanese of manipulating the value of the yen.

> At the Hakone meeting, my countrymen were very much surprised to hear this jarring note of disagreement in the midst of a bland and pleasant conference. At these meetings the Japanese usually sit politely saying little or nothing, and thus fail to make new friends. That is a major Japanese problem. At the recess, some younger Japanese came up to me and said they appreciated my defence of the Japanese position, but some of the older Japanese came to me shaking their heads. "You were rude to our guests who have come from so far away to be with us."[49]

Bricklayers vs. Stonemasons

Akio Morita has compared the American factory system to the Japanese by using the metaphor of the bricklayer versus the stonemason. The Americans have the framework all laid out in advance and proceed to order their different bricks to fit the slots available. Workers have standardized skills, which vary by speciality, so you hire a specified skill to fit a predesigned job. The Japanese order irregular lumps of stone, which the mason or manager then shapes so that they fit together harmoniously. The stones are not specialized, but have the capacity to be shaped for many purposes.[50]

This makes the concept of the team and of teamwork quite different in American and Japanese cultures. American team membership begins with a demand for consensus. You must agree to put your paid specialty at the service of the overall framework. You must agree to do so much work for so much pay at a stipulated level of competence. Your contribution is known in advance, is contained in your job description, and has a market price dependent on its scarcity. Labor, then, is an atomistic "thing," a commodity for sale, like pork bellies or bushels of wheat. The factory will produce a standardized and uniform product if each worker agrees to supply a standardized and uniform input. The "house" is thus constructed from "bricks" of different shapes, sizes, and functions, and is built up piece by piece according to a codified plan.

The Japanese view of the team and teamwork is crucially different. It begins with the heterogeneity of unshaped "stones" with a variety of potentials. Workers are encouraged to have multiple skills and are valued and paid for their versatility, the number of different roles they can play within the team. This allows teams to assume major responsibilities and to solve problems spontaneously as they arise, rather than asking the engineers for a new blueprint and the staff for new work procedures. The work is more varied, flexible, and challenging and may make whole levels of supervision unnecessary.

In practice, the standardization and uniformity required by American "bricklaying" makes the factory and the office into an enemy of freedom and individuality, so that production work, especially manufacturing, is not generally performed with enthusiasm or skill. Yet manufacturing is the cutting edge of Japanese competition, allowing their teams to self-organize spontaneously and deploy their varied talents in ever-new configurations.

Here the Western stereotypes of Japan interfere with our understanding. The Japanese do indeed "conform," if by this we mean that they strive to form jointly a harmonious pattern of work relations and regard this destiny as more important than personal gain. But they do not conform, save in superficial ways, dress, and luggage, to the skills and attainments of one another. The basis of harmony is to be heterogeneous, to have skills that are complementary rather than substitutable. To sing in harmony is to sing different tunes.

Hence, Maruyama conducted research among Japanese teenage groups. He found them to be spontaneously organized on the principle of heterogeneity, with as many different particulars as possible. One teenager would be the expert on compact discs, another on audiocassettes, a third on telephone cards, a fourth on baseball and pachinko, and so on. The principle was to bring the greatest possible variety of information on diverse pastimes to the group as a whole.[51]

The same patterns are found in architecture, art, and gardening. A room in a Japanese house does not have a single function, i.e., a dining room or a living room. Partitions can be moved and interior configurations changed, so that the same space serves multiple purposes. Not until the whole has been configured can you see the purpose of the room or the part it plays in the whole house. Furnishings are also modular and multipurpose. No rock or tree in a garden is like any other, and yet from all this heterogeneity the garden derives harmony and integrity.[52]

Bill Ouchi, a Japanese-American academic and consultant, has argued that while U.S. corporations tend to seek goal identity, the Japanese search for goal congruence.[53] Thus American workers are asked to agree that the company belongs to the shareholders and that their function is to earn a profit for the shareholders. It is not a very popular idea among those who contribute their lives while shareholders contribute their money.

In contrast, the Japanese expect workers to want higher pay and more enjoyment and zest at work. They do not expect workers to wax lyrical about owners they never see. They do expect workers to grasp that what they seek is congruent with what shareholders seek, i.e., that higher pay and higher performance harmonize with better dividends or growth in the share price.

Congruence also helps to explain the Japanese penchant for job rotation. Employees in the top 30 percent of the Japanese economy are expected to dedicate much or all of their working lives to the corporation they have chosen, but are constantly rotated so as to see issues from as many different angles as possible. Thus, graduates from top universities work on the factory floor for as long as two years and represent fellow workers in union activities. Ideally, the senior manager in his fifties will have personal experience of nearly every vantage point within the corporation. He can help harmonize differences because many of those differences are known to him.[54]

Pure Competitiveness vs. Cooperative Competing

The habit of Anglo-Saxon empiricism is to analyze concepts to their smallest ingredients or atoms. Competition shorn by Occam's razor of all qualifications and encumbrances is pure competition in which the sheer number of competitors has driven down the price to the lowest possible level, much to the benefit of the consumer. It is not that the supplier cares two hoots for the customer—he is forced to lower his price by his competitors, by the impersonal operations of the market mechanism. Red in tooth and claw, gnashing his teeth at rivals, he is yet compelled, despite the ferocity of his mood, to offer products and services that customers prefer. It is a curious doctrine when one thinks about it.

The Japanese are said to practice "managed competition," and this is a difficult concept for the English-speaking nations to grasp. Anything that reduces competition looks like a serious threat to the free market, which is *un*managed by definition. The whole point of the market mechanism is that no single supplier has control over the price, which then falls to the point at which the most efficient producers can still prosper. If markets are to be managed, then for whose benefit? Would not the economy be at once politicized?

"Managed competition" is thus a rather confusing concept, and insofar as it suggests moderating competition, it is not an accurate description of how the Japanese conduct business. Indeed, the advocates of pure competition in the West derive considerable comfort from the sheer intensity of Japanese competitiveness. Michael Porter points out that there are 112 machine-tool companies competing in the industry, 25 in audio equipment, 34 in semiconductors, 15 in cameras, and so on. This accounts for the high standards achieved by these "competitive clusters."[55] Akio Morita explains:

> The glory and nemesis of Japanese business, the life's blood of our industrial engine, is good old-fashioned competition. It is a severe competition, and sometimes it is so severe that I am worried about its export to other countries. . . . In Japan today, there are more makers of civilian industrial products than in any other country on earth, including the United States. And those companies—nine automobile makers and two heavy truck makers, more than one hundred machine tool makers and over six hundred electronics companies, for example—are survivors of the competitive struggle.[56]

So how does Japanese competitiveness differ from the purified conception in classical economics? To grasp this we must first understand that the Japanese do not polarize competing with cooperating as we do. Theirs is a cooperative competing in which particular competitors harmonize their talents, not by accident, but purposefully and through sociable motives.

The view of classical economics grows from the values of Britain and the United States. In this view, we start with separate atoms of product or units of sale, and these become subject to the universal laws of supply and demand, otherwise known as the market mechanism. This is a variation of Newton's perpetual motion machine, the central metaphor of classical physics that did so much to shape Western consciousness.[57]

The Japanese view grows out of Japan's own history and cultural preferences. It begins with a whole multitude of particular products being offered for sale and competing with one another, but from the seeming chaos there grow clusters of cooperation and harmony. Competing and cooperating, rather than being "opposed" processes, can intensify each other's power. The Japanese phrase *kyoryoku shi nagara kyosa* means "cooperating while competing."[58]

So hard is this for Westerners to understand that they see it as akin to treachery. William J. Holstein of *Business Week* comments:

> In the Judeo-Christian ethic you are either my friend or my enemy. You cannot be both at the same time. But to the Japanese mind this contradiction is not disturbing. As masters of long-term, low-level conflict, the Japanese find it only natural to embrace at one level and struggle at another. At the official level, *tatamae*, I can be polite to you. At heart, the *honne*, we can struggle . . . most Americans would call this duplicity, most Japanese call it natural.[59]

But this completely distorts the *wa* (harmony) of competing and cooperating which, so far from being deceitful, is a phenomenon of beauty and aestheticism in which no member of the culture is wilfully deceived. To claim that Japanese economic success is based on daggers beneath cloaks of good will is absurd. The transaction costs of cheating and misinformation are simply too high. The Japanese may seem ambiguous to us, but that stems from our failure to understand.

How, then, does Japan manage to be both more competitive and more cooperative than its major Western competitors? How do competing and cooperating harmonize? In the first place, by occurring simultaneously at different levels of the social system. The better employees cooperate within the organization, the keener will be the competition between that organization and others. There is neither duplicity nor contradiction in this fact. It is common sense. The individuals cooperate. Their organizations compete. The quality of the first increases the intensity of the second.

Competing and cooperating can also be phased over time. There is no contradiction in competing hard at school, for which the Japanese are famous, so that you discover where your talents lie, which will enable you to cooperate best with colleagues in the corporation. Here, the earlier competing is *for* the later cooperation. Who, after all, wants his teeth drilled by someone who has failed his dental exams? Competition in dental school is indeed in the interests of the patient.

Similarly, Japanese corporations seem to be able to cooperate in making joint representations to their government about "the future of the shipping industry" or "HDTV in the twenty-first century" and then return to their offices to compete as usual. Here there is both a separation by level, the industry as a whole having requirements independent of competition among its members, and separation by time. You agree this week on what is good for your industry and try the following week to take greater advantage of this than your rivals. It is the same as cooperating in basic research and then, as applications of this shared work become possible, starting to compete in bringing the best applications to market. The Japanese seem able to move back and forth between competing and cooperating modes.

It is important that we not confuse cooperating with *wa* (or harmony) since the latter is a far more subtle and inclusive concept, akin to the notion of *harmonia* in classical Greece.[60] Harmony is a value the West once grasped but has since largely lost. To avoid confusion we will use "cooperating" when we intend to contrast this phase with "competing," and we will use *wa* (or harmony), for the reconciliation of competing with cooperating so that they enhance each other. The failure of the Soviet and Eastern bloc economies results in part from the severance of cooperation from competition, and the idolization of the former. The economic success of Japan and the Pacific Rim countries results in part from harmonizing competing with cooperating.

But how do competing and cooperating combine into a single process? And what should this process be called? In our view they meet in the process of learning, both about the core technologies of the company and what its customers need and demand. The faster a corporation or a whole economy learns, the more it will prosper. By competing we learn to differentiate, contrast, and evaluate products and processes. By cooperating we learn to integrate, encompass, and facilitate the adoption of what we find to be best. Losers need to swiftly emulate winners and not be crushed or humiliated by losing. It is here we find the crucial characteristics of Japanese competition. It stops short of the destruction of its rivals, when it is clear who is winning; the loser is not just spared but learns from the victor the better ways of operating. Instead of competitive cooperation being a form of treachery, it allows a speedy transition from winning to teaching, from which even the loser can benefit. Akio Morita comments:

> But . . . there exists a fine line between competition and destructiveness. In China they say you should not break a person's rice bowl. In Japan it is understood that you must not destroy a worthy competitor—you must leave him his honor, his face.[61]

In fact, one-time "losers" in Japan have often come back with a vengeance. Japan's troubled steel companies have turned to metal ceramics and by-product gases. When the Japanese copper industry faced ruin because optical fiber was replacing copper wires, they moved into the optical fiber business and seized nearly 70 percent of the world market share. When sewing machines slumped, the suppliers hopped smartly sideways into electronic typewriters, printers, word processors, and office automation. In this they were helped by both government and bankers with loans allowing the workforce to be retained.[62]

To believe that cooperating and competing are harmonious appears to be culturally self-fulfilling; you are helped by governments and banks and so compete more aggressively. The American belief that these are contradictory creeds is also self-fulfilling. Those helped "go soft," become chronic wards of the state and parasites on the taxpayer. Companies that "cannot stand on their own feet" should be left to perish. Here classical economics activity supports what Schumpeter called "the gale of creative destruction," which brings us to our next major bifurcation.

The Mechanical Bureaucrats vs. the Organic Family

If you think of the company as a wealth-producing mechanism, then the competitive destruction of one company by another in a kind of demolition derby is clearly a good thing. Classical economics argue that if land, labor, and capital are being underutilized by their current managers, then it is far better that these resources be reallocated to more competent persons who can put them to better use and make more money for shareholders. The destruction of badly run businesses is to the inestimable benefit of us all. Interference by government, do-gooders, and sentimentalists who feel sorry for those who fall short of market disciplines is tragically misplaced, since we all suffer from the incompetence of those we seek to rescue.

But is a company like a machine? Or is this a habit of thought that has lingered on, a piece of vestigial Newtonianism designed to convince laypersons that economics is a science like physics? The Japanese view appears to be that the company resembles an organism that grows and develops, even more, it is a family with deep and affectionate bonds. Again, these metaphors derive from overall cultural preferences, with sizeable minorities of Japanese "mechanists" and American "organicists" arguing against the conventional wisdom. For English-speaking cultures, the economy is conceived of as an equilibrium machine which, like all machines, is nothing but the sum of its atomic parts operating by universal principles. In this system, rare, and hence valuable, skills will rise in the prices they command while lower, more common, and less valuable skills will fall.[63] The problem with this view is that machines are dead and their parts are things. Thus the classic metaphor greatly underestimates so-called *human resources*. Indeed, this very term tries to equate the living with the dead. The problem with asset stripping, hostile takeovers, and bankruptcy is that sensate beings are not "reallocated" without trauma, nor are disorganized people always as valuable as organized ones.

The Japanese, however, do not attack our views on classical economics, in part because they do not like to attack, but also because they see it as one outlook on truth, "the guest's point of view," but it is clear from the metaphors they use that they view the company chiefly as an organism to be nurtured, facilitated, and developed. In a garden, every growth is unique and particular, yet it forms an ecological and aesthetic whole. The most valued relationship is *sempai-kohai*, literally, elder brother-younger brother, and elderly family members, their status unassailable because of their greater age, go out of their way to nurture younger people.[64]

A favorite Japanese term is *nemawashi*, literally "binding the roots" when a tree is transplanted so that it will grow readily in the less familiar soil and will suffer minimal trauma by uprooting. Most Japanese change processes accompanied by variations of *nemawashi*. The use of tree analogies in the Japanese conception of organizations is quite common (see Sharp's Digital Audio Technology Tree featured in Chapter 7). Clover Management Research in Tokyo has developed a Lotus Blossom Method Diagram. Nippon Airways advertised its routes as tendrils of delicate flowers encircling their ports of destination, hardly the kind of metaphor Western airlines would use. The Japanese economy is frequently regarded as a "food-chain" with microchips, "the rice of industry," feeding numerous other products, "seeded" with little brains.[65]

Western corporations have embraced the idea of Kafka's castle as the paradigm of organized activity. The bureaucracy is legal-rational, cerebral, detached, instrumental, and bloodless. According to Max Weber, we must leave *Gemeinschaft*, forever, the intimacy of home and family, to operate *Gesellschaft*, the formal world of work.[66] The harder you compete when away from your family, the more loot you can bring home for domestic enjoyment. The world is split between the machine and the suburban garden, producing and consuming. No intimacy, affection, brotherhood, or rootedness is supposed to sully the world of work.

But, of course, such beliefs prevent the employment of the whole person, his or her passions, desires, dreams, and lifelong commitments. The idea is erroneous that Western corporations can match Japanese performance by appealing simply to a calculative mode of existence apart from the engagement of all human resources. The corporation has to stand for the fullest range of human aspirations. We are not going to win the Learning Race by deploying narrowly defined instruments for gain.

7

On Synchrony, Hierarchy, and Time

ONE OF THE CONSISTENT competitive advantages attributed to the Japanese is that of strategizing long-term. Their corporations persist, aiming more for growth than for profit, and fight for market share till others give up and withdraw. The Institute for Management Development in Lausanne publishes regular reports on comparative international competitiveness. When surveys of international managers inquire as to which country most successfully takes a long-term view, the Japanese top the list every year since the question was first posed (see Table 7-1).[1]

Table 7-1   Extent to Which Firms Take a Long-term View

Country	Rank	Country	Rank
Japan	1	Belgium/Luxembourg	17
Sweden	2	Australia	18
West Germany	3	United States	19
New Zealand	4	Italy	20
Finland	5	Ireland	21
Switzerland	6	United Kingdom	22
Singapore	7	India	23
Norway	8	Austria	24
Denmark	9	Mexico	25
Netherlands	10	Turkey	26
South Korea	11	Brazil	27
France	12	Hong Kong	28
Taiwan	13	Spain	29
Thailand and Canada	14	Portugal	30
Malaysia	16	Greece	31

Source: European Management Forum, 1989.

The Japanese view of time is based on the biological clock of cycles: daily cycles, seasonal cycles and life cycles, both within the person and within the wider environment. The ideal is to get these all working together, waxing and waning, tensing and relaxing, all harmonized into synchronized waves of pulsing energy. Machine cycles are synchronized with human cycles so that one person can attend to many machines, completing their operations at carefully timed intervals, which are reset and put back in motion by the machinist. Workers who are experienced and who work fast and accurately are often given longer cycles than those who are still being trained. What is important is that capabilities are synchronized precisely.

Very important in Japanese culture are generational cycles. The old and retiring pass wisdom and knowledge to the newly promoted. The same logic applies to products. They reach market maturity and then begin to subside, but not without passing crucial information down the generations. These dense clusters of cycles feeding back the information of growth and development necessitate a long-term view.

In joint ventures with Americans and British, the Japanese frequently exchange the opportunity to profit short-term, which they offer their foreign partners, for the opportunity to learn long-term and develop strategic technologies with spinoffs well into the future. They are notorious for accepting losses or very slim profits for many years rather than abandon a technology with a long future. What matters to the Japanese is not what shareholders get now, as it does in Wall Street and the City of London, but what the corporation as a community learns over time. The country and its corporations will last longer than each person, who is not simply expected to prefer the community to self, but to grasp the fact that knowledge and institutions survive for generations while the individual's tactical advantage is short. Or, as we say in the West, "You can't take it with you."

As discussed in Chapter 4, the American view of time is primarily sequential and the Japanese view is synchronized. We can see the interaction of these two viewpoints at any airport. People arrive and stand in line to check their baggage, first-come-first-served. Planes take off in sequence, according to prearranged schedules. Is there any other way of thinking? There is and there has to be, because Sequence A, people standing in line, is not coordinated or synchronized with Sequence B, planes taking off. What often happens is that people are still waiting to check their bags when they should be boarding. People with an hour or more to spare are ahead of people due to leave in ten minutes. The two sequences are impeding each other.

We all know what happens. An airline official walks down the line asking, "Anyone here for the 9:17 A.M. Paris flight?" Those destined for this flight are hurried away to check their bags at the gate. One sequence has been disrupted to maintain another sequence. The two sequences have been synchronized. The airline official has had to do something now for the aircraft to take off in the future.

In effect, all cultures think of time in both ways, as sequences and as synchronizations. Time would not be much use to us if people failed to synchronize their clocks and watches. All planes would take off late unless some passengers broke sequence. Cultures vary as their relative appreciation of sequence or of synchronies, in how strict their schedules are, and how readily altered in the interests of synchronizing with and accommodating other persons' priorities.

The Buddhist Influence

The origins of Japanese synchronicity are much speculated upon. We find particular appeal in the views of Takeski Umehara, philosopher and director general of the International Research Center for Japanese Studies in Kyoto (see Box 7-1, "The Civilization of the Forest: The Eternal Cycle"). Because Japan remains one of the most forested lands on earth, the ecology of the wild forests remains its major cultural metaphor. In Shintoism and in Japanese variations of Buddhism, the dead keep returning to this world to help redeem the living, much as leaves fall to the forest floor to nurture the ground. Hence, to live with nature is to live with the spirits of those who went before you, just as those now living will watch over future generations.

The importance of such religious beliefs to the argument here is not their truth or their falsity, but how they have shaped the modern views of time. When we die we both recede into the past and decompose underground, *and* come back again in our genes, in the memories of our children and our students, and in the accumulated experience stored within institutions. No view of time is more correct or scientific than any other. But synchronous and sequential time orientations have consequences for wealth creation, as we shall see, and they impart quite different meanings to the hierarchical structures found in Japanese and U.S. corporations.

Box 7-1

The Civilization of the Forest: The Eternal Cycle

Takeshi Umehara is perhaps Japan's most prominent and most controversial philosopher. Author of *Japan's Deep Strata* and *Exiling of the Gods*, he is a stern critic of Europe's postwar nihilism. He argues that the West's fading religious belief in an afterlife has left it cut off from the future and the long-term. The Occupation also exiled Japan's own gods which were mistakenly identified with "State Shintoism," a militaristic corruption of Japan's traditional culture.

This ancient culture is "the Civilization of the Forest." Because rice growing requires flat land and most of Japan is mountainous, the country remains 40 percent forested to this day. Lush, humid, luxuriant vegetation abounds. *Jomon*, the original forest culture, was not, therefore, eliminated by *Yayoi*, rice-paddy culture. The forest culture is reputedly the origin of Shinto, a polytheistic form of nature worship indigenous to Japan, which greatly altered the more recent importation of Buddhism.

The "other world" in this surviving forest culture is but a way station in a cycle of eternal return. There is no heaven or hell and no final judgment. All souls in the after-world become *kami*, spirits that return to the world to inhabit humans, animals, and natural forces. There are four Buddhist memorial days when the spirits of the departed return to earth to be with their families. They will also decide which among them will slip into the womb of a mother to be born anew. Japanese Buddhism lacks the asceticism of traditional Buddhism, and does not regard reincarnation as entrapment in earthy pleasures, but as an act of love and concern for the living. In *genso-eku*, preached by Shinran, the dead keep returning to save and sustain the living. Takeshi Umehara notes:

> Modern science has demonstrated that all life is basically one, and it has shown that living things and their physical surroundings are all part of a single ecosystem. . . . Even though the individual dies, his or her genes are carried on by future generations in a lasting cycle of rebirth. . . . The human race has finally realized that it can survive only in peaceful coexistence with other life forms.

Source: New Perspectives Quarterly 7, 3 (1990), pp. 22–31.

We now examine ways in which a synchronous view of time has contributed to Japan's extraordinary economic development.

The Psychology of Short-term and Long-term Mind-sets

If you are a manager sitting in a meeting with your colleagues and you conceive of the long-term future as far away, then you are not going to take it very seriously. Instead, you will do in the present what is most profitable and practicable so as to face the future in a strong position. But if you conceive of the future as being already here in your midst in the shape of assumptions, plans, visions, technologies, and expectations, and if you see it interacting with your past and present in an eternal now, then you are going to take it much more seriously. Let us examine the sequential and synchronic mind-sets in turn.

Sensing a future far off and separated from us by time intervals is like imagining a manifest destiny or monstrous dystopia beyond the horizon, yet tottering down the road to meet us. We may call it "global warming" or the "knowledge revolution" and view its coming with alarm or with hope, or we may regard all such prophesies with scepticism. The farther away such a future, the dimmer and more vague are its distant shapes and the more contingent is its eventual appearance upon intervening events. To spend good money now upon a mere contingency is to relinquish substance for shadow.

In the linear world of cause-and-effect, the past has "caused" the present, which will "cause" the future. The future is virtually unknowable because thousands of would-be "causes" are jostling each other to produce desired effects. It is no coincidence that "past," "present," and "future" resemble billiard balls behind which individuals with past records stand, cues in hand. How the balls end up only the aggregate of market forces can decide. Futurology, like astrology, is a dubious art. Objective knowing requires the present.

What the sequential mind-set does know is that a larger "ball" now can make possible a still larger "ball" in the next quarterly returns, which makes possible an even larger one subsequently. Shareholders will lend you more money in the future if your current results are good enough.

To sacrifice profits in this quarter on the grounds that you might make them up subsequently, flies in the face of how capital markets operate. People are going to lend their money, or withdraw it, depending on who appears to be the best bet. Any withdrawal of funds in the short-term could fatally damage future prospects. It is quite unjustifiable.

The synchronous view of the future as engaged with the present and the past is chiefly concerned with recurrences, i.e., seeds and seminal technologies, sown in the present to produce generation after generation of products in the future. What technologies might be logically targeted if we were looking for recurrences? We might consider steel, which repeats itself in product after product; so do microchips, semiconductors, biochips, machine tools, metal ceramics, photovoltaic cells, computers, telecommunications, optical imaging, robots, optic fibers, carbon fibers, etc.—precisely the products that the Japanese have targeted. These are the progenitors of hundreds of thousands of future products. They are the *kami*, or the nature spirits, returning from the past to watch over and inspire present and future generations. These are products whose "genes" eternally return and whose learnings fructify.

Recurring Japanese products do not stand on their own as units to be continued if they pay or eliminated if they do not. Microchips, for example, come in "generations," each conceived out of the life of its predecessor. They are like families that give each other mutual support in the process of reproduction. The nurture of "fathers" and "sons" may be vindicated in the profitability of "great-grandsons." The calculation is that the "gene pool," or the knowledge carried within the product, is generative of potent offspring.

Synchronous thinking also acknowledges "remote" connections, for example, the connection between school and cultural institutions and the effectiveness of the economy years later. Those who teach in Japan are valued and respected because the knowledge implanted in children is believed to recur indefinitely, and ten or twenty years is not long to wait before the results begin to be harvested. Teachers earn an (upper) middle-class salary because of their public role as "circulators."[1]

In America, anyone moved by idealism or nurturance to teach school or enter a caring profession pays the price in lowered salary and even public disesteem. There are several reasons: first, many teachers are paid from public funds and are seen as a present tax on something to be contributed by their students much later. Teachers also suffer from being on the wrong side of the public-sector versus private-sector conflict and from being seen as a "burden" and "overhead" on private enterprise. More specifically in the United States, they are paid from property taxes levied on many people whose children are grown or have been privately educated.

But the chief reason for low salaries is that any generous motives among those seeking to teach, care, or sustain others is subtracted from their salaries by market forces. If 25 percent more people offer to teach for motives of social concern, their price will drop proportionally, since the value of each as a commodity is now less. Only if teaching and learning are seen as synchronized with the economy long-term will adequate provision be forthcoming. Knowledge is not a separate "thing" but the germinator of an eternal rebirth.

The Pull of the Future, the Push of the Present

In a study undertaken by one of the authors of a Japanese-American joint venture in the design and supply of integrated circuits, it was found that the Japanese employed a "pull strategy," while Americans preferred a "push strategy." Within the pull strategy you agree with the customer to supply integrated circuits of a particular character and quality by a certain time, say two years. Given the customer's need for a particular performance in a specified time, you then calculate backward from that future rendezvous to see how all the necessary processes and elements can be synchronized on time and what it will cost to do this.[2]

The push strategy is quite different. It starts with the present and creates a schedule of sequential stages. The completion of each stage pushes the next stage into motion, and if nothing goes wrong, the product emerges at the end on schedule, often with the help of "progress chasers" chivying it along.

But, of course, things do go wrong, so we need to ask whether pull and push strategies are equally flexible and robust. Suppose, for example, an automobile manufacturer wants multiple sensors, which, in the event of a crash will inflate air bags, turn off the fuel, and unlock the doors so that rescuers can enter. It will take a further year of development to automatically smother the engine in fire-fighting foam. In the meantime, the manufacture of gas release pellets in the air bag has proved difficult—the product tends to explode during manufacture.

The pull strategy has multiple trade-offs in the likely event that the situation changes between contract and delivery. For example, the launch of "the safest car on earth" may be put forward or put back, or the safety specifications changed in view of imminent legislation. The supplier may not have solved the pellet problem and has to invest in an alternative technology. Whereas the cost of the integrated circuits was not a major problem, it has now become one. As the situation changes, the rendezvous with the customer's requirements can be renegotiated as often as necessary, even if this means changing the specs. What matters is that the optimal arrangement of integrated circuits be pulled on stage on cue. The customer is invited to trade off cost against quality, against timeliness, against modifiability by a subsequent technology now under development. Like guided missiles homing in on their targets, all elements of the customer's solution synchronize their arrival times, with extra resources thrown behind any component in danger of being late.

The sequential "push" strategy is typically more rigid, especially when attached to strict adherence to the original contract. The entire schedule is in jeopardy as the result of the lateness of any one stage, unless slack has been built in. With nearly all costs budgeted in advance, time tends to be the only flexible element, and hence increases and increases, causing the major "time-to-market" problems plaguing American companies. The relative shortness of the product cycle from design to delivery is vital. A Japanese integrated circuit company, with a six- to twelve-month cycle can have "three shots at a solution," while a company with a two-year cycle has only one. And, of course, the shorter your cycles the more likely you are to have the latest combination of circuits available at the time your customer wants them: push tends to be manifestly inferior to a carefully synchronized pull.

The issue is, of course, widely pervasive beyond the integrated circuit market. In "The Quiet Path to Technological Preeminence" in *Scientific American*, Robert Reich points out that the linear and sequential forms of American thinking are not simply mental but geographical and cultural. For Americans it starts with R & D, and research laboratories are frequently located in leafy and bucolic surroundings where the "creative types" have "space" to be geniuses originating breakthroughs.

> R & D often has relatively little connection to the rest of a company's undertakings. The proposals that emerge from the laboratories are scrutinized by market and financial analysts on a project-by-project basis, and only then, if approved, turned over to manufacturing engineers, technicians and production workers who design and execute the processes for making and distributing the products.
>
> The implicit assumption behind this series of events is that the product designs emerge essentially fully formed from research, after which they go into production. It is not unusual for American companies to put off any considerations of manufacturing until researchers have come up with a generic solution to a broad problem and the design engineers have transformed the broad solution into a specific design. This division prolongs product development times, and causes market opportunities to be lost.[3]

The contrast between this strategy, in which R & D pushes the sequence, and the Japanese synchronized approach is illuminating. U.S. companies typically proceed sequentially from research to development, to process design, to manufacturing, to product. There are, of course, feedback loops. Research, even in its countryside retreat, will hear about products that do not work, or those that need more development, but the main thrust is from research to product.

In contrast, Japanese companies may start the process anywhere, with a borrowed process design, with a product purchased from abroad which is then reengineered, or with the refinement and development of an American invention. The advantage of "pulling" all processes together in one place, toward a deadline in the future, is that you design for better manufacturability, research and develop for easier layout or quicker assembly. Instead of the R & D persons issuing instructions from their remote locations, those who design, manufacture, distribute, and sell the product can all address recurring problems and initiate recurring solutions to which designers and researchers can respond. The customer's future requirements drive synchronized circles of improvement and rapid redeployments of resources.

Companies pushed by the present state of their R & D activities are very likely to suffer from the "not-invented-here" syndrome. This is because of the one-way traffic of ideas through the sequence. It is the distributors and marketing people closer to the customer who are the most likely to discover something invented elsewhere, yet their capacity to enter the country retreats of their researchers is very limited, nor is their news welcome.

The Revolution in Flexible Manufacturing

There is a recurring pattern to Japanese-American competition. In complex manufacturing U.S. companies typically do well in the start-up phase. At this point, the product is so new and is demanded in such great quantities that it can immediately be supplied. Sheer inventiveness is highly rewarded. You can "toss the product over your shoulder and let them scramble for it."

But soon the market approaches maturity. The huge markets for single lines no longer exist but subdivide, like the Nile delta, into thousands of niches and tributaries. Customers now need elaborate, customized variations on a general theme, say, an automobile, and the question becomes, how can this ever-increasing demand for variation be met at the lowest possible cost? The problem is that varied products need frequent tool changes, larger inventories of parts, a more skilled, alert, and flexible work force, and better information flows. The Japanese tend to develop massive cost advantages over Americans as industries mature and products multiply. Why?

The sequential approach to time is what led Americans to their traditional mass manufacturing operations. The idea is to standardize products, increase the volume and speed of the manufacturing process, and have the products emerge at the end of the assembly line with minimum delay between sequential stages. The economics of scale are a function of both speed and volume, plus minimal delay in setting and resetting tools and fitting components to the automobile during assembly. In the interests of smooth and uninterrupted production, inventories of spare parts and subassemblies are held as part of work-in-process. This is thought necessary because customer demand is rarely smooth or continuous. Hence, fluctuations were traditionally buffered by holding inventories of parts, subassemblies, and finished or semifinished vehicles. Such production push is not incapable of variation, but the variations are usually superficial "add-ons": whitewall tires, cigar lighters, paneled dashboards, etc.

The Japanese have revolutionized the economics of manufacturing in several ways, all derived from synchronous approaches to a desired future state. By just-in-time delivery, spare parts are delivered by outside suppliers to the production process, minutes or moments before they are needed. This greatly reduces the costs of carrying, labeling, and moving the parts. Inventories are expensive. Over the years, immense effort has been expended on reducing set-up times, and number-controlled machine tools, capable of swift reprogramming, are the result of a key technology that was targeted and won. This means that the cost of working on two different vehicles is nearly as small as working on two that are identical. Variety of a fundamental kind, including different body shapes, can be produced to match, exactly, the constantly shifting patterns of consumer demand.

Time and costs are also saved by doing as much as possible in parallel rather than in sequence, a solution that occurs more readily to members of a synchronous culture. Of course, many operations must be done in sequence. You cannot assemble a window until the frame is in place. Nevertheless, sequences frequently overlap, as when a windshield is assembled while the frame is being prepared. Taichi Ohno conceives of the Toyota production system as an integrated series of race circuits, mediated by a baton-passing zone, where one "runner" hands over the baton while overlapping and running alongside the next. He argues for the adjustment of each circuit, so that the speed and stamina of the different runners are adjusted to one another. This is his definition of *work flow*, as opposed to *work forced to flow*, which happens when you use a mechanical assembly line. While this cannot always be avoided, the ideal work flow comes from the natural synchrony of people's work cycles, with the slowest persons having their cycles shortened so that these coordinate swiftly and smoothly with faster "runners" on longer cycles. Production leveling is essential to control waste-inducing fluctuations, as when one slower process holds up a faster one. Box 7-2 illustrates the synchronous structure of the Toyota automobile assembly line.

Given the flow of information from the showroom to the factory, automobiles can be ordered as they are being made, with the mix varying in proportion to shifts in demand. The vehicle comes off the assembly line with all the options the customer specified. Such highly synchronous "pulling" toward the customer's preference is now being adopted by many countries. Flexible manufacturing is increasingly the rule, not the exception, and America is learning from Japan. Nevertheless, the culture that invented flexible manufacturing from its own synchronous mind-set is likely to gain and retain the advantage, especially as manufacturing grows in complexity.

A particularly grim set of statistics are offered by the Tokyo office of the Boston Consulting Group. James C. Abegglen and George Stalk counted the number of manufacturing steps in different industries and correlated these with the proportion by which U.S. competitors employed more labor hours per unit than did the Japanese. (Note that the concept of "steps" suggests a sequence that may not in fact be required if the "steps" converge with one another.)

In steel mills, paper mills, and the manufacture of men's dress shirts, the Japanese and the Americans had a nearly identical number of labor hours, but in these industries there were only about eighteen to twenty-four manufacturing steps. In the manufacture of auto engines, with more than two hundred steps, American companies used 60 percent more labor hours, and in auto assembly and forklift truck assembly, with more than a thousand steps, Americans used 80 to 100 percent more labor. The advantages of synchronous strategies of "pull" toward final assembly increase with the complexity of work. Since products are

Box 7-2
The Toyota Final Body Assembly Line:
Synchronized Processes

This illustration is taken from Taichi Ohno's own writings on the Toyota system he designed. A varied series of Toyota vehicles proceed right to left along a central assembly line. When vehicle 20 is five places from having its engine installed, information travels to the engine preparation line where the engine required by this particular vehicle is completed in five stages. When it reaches the place now occupied by vehicle 16, information travels to the console box preparation line, where three steps are necessary to ready the console box, while the vehicle also moves three steps toward this rendezvous. The lines converging with the main assembly line are all synchronized. A *kanban* is attached to each set of components, detailing its description and its destination. However, workers learn to recognize the vehicle and its components by sight, so the *kanban* is used as a check. Processes A, B, C, D, and E are themselves subassemblies of parts delivered just in time.

Source: Toyota Production System: Beyond Large-Scale Production, Taichi Ohno. Cambridge, Mass.: Productivity Press, 1988, p. 49. Originally *Toyota seisan hoshiki*. Tokyo: Diamond Inc., 1978.

becoming more complex all the time, this could be a most crucial cultural advantage in the area of knowledge-intensive products.[4]

In the traditional American factory, milling machines, lathes, and drills are in separate sections, with human operators attached. Taichi Ohno made sure that in Toyota one operative ran at least three machines, their cycles synchronized so he could attend to them in turn. "This way," Taichi explains, "one worker operates many processes." This improves productivity.

Planning for Fusion and Creativity

Thus far, the distance to our future time horizons has been rather short. ICs were designed and developed for two- to three-year deadlines. This is hardly long-termism. But the Japanese do embark on projects of ten to twenty years' duration when they believe they are steering toward high probabilities of positive outcomes. What kinds of logic do they employ, and what accounts for the successes they seem to have enjoyed? Above all, is it remotely possible to "plan for creativity," or is this a contradiction in terms?

The Western tradition sees creativity as a flash of insight, an "ah-ha" experience in which two bodies or matrices of thought, considered remote from each other, are suddenly *bi-sociated*, to use Arthur Koestler's phrase.[5] If many other persons thought of making this connection, then it cannot be very creative! Innovative individuals are given genius status and credited with "thinking of it first." Yet when we look back on creative breakthroughs, the real wonder is how slow they were in coming. The soporific effects of chloroform were printed on the label of the bottle several years before anyone thought of using this compound deliberately to anesthetize. The movie camera was invented at roughly the same time by at least three people, and a vast number of cases of simultaneous invention have ended up in the courts. With the glider already invented, along with the gasoline engine, how long before an aircraft flew? As it was, the Wright brothers were barely ahead of others making similar prototypes.

According to this "group theory of creativity," because ideas like horse-drawn carriage and the steam engine are already in a culture, "the horseless carriage" is only a matter of time. We can foresee the synchrony of events likely to converge. The way to bet on a more prosperous future is to promote synchrony among two or more streams of technology, for example, machine tools and computerized electronic controls, perceiving that the mechanics of the factory will increasingly use electronic monitoring, signaling, and feedback.

The Japanese call this field "mechatronics," and it was deliberately set up through cooperation between corporations mediated by the Science Technology Agency (STA). As early as 1971, the Japanese government approved the Law for Provisional Measures to Promote Electronic and Machinery Industries. This arranged joint research projects with mechanical engineers, cross-fertilized with electronic engineers. It is not necessary that those making such arrangements be able to predict specifically what will emerge. It is only necessary to conclude that a majority of the advances in plant productivity will have their origins in novel combinations of electronics and mechanics. This is not a very controversial proposition, yet, pursued as a policy for future development it has proved extremely fruitful.[6]

Several examples are offered by Magorah Maruyama of Japanese projects set up deliberately for purposes of future synchrony. In one case, Seiko set out to challenge the Swiss watch industry long-term, using a quartz electronic resonant circuit. For this subsequent breakthrough, electronic engineers, quartz specialists, and jewelers were initially assembled and invited to synchronize their expertise. The quartz experts had never worked on anything so small, but the jewelers and electronic engineers were able to help them. The jewelers had never worked with electronics or quartz, but were helped by the other experts. A similar synchrony of expertise went into the design and testing of the Japanese bullet train. When it was foreseen that persistent vibrations could occur at certain speeds, aeronautical engineers sat down with locomotive engineers to solve problems of airflow.[7]

That the Japanese think in terms of both "hybrid technologies" and of interindustry technology fusion is illustrated in Box 7-3. A hybrid technology is one in which two or more technologies combine without altering their essential characters. For example, the electronic copyboard combines the technology of a blackboard with that of a fax machine. Anything drawn on the copyboard is encoded in a chip and may be reproduced and transmitted. Fax machines now come with telephones, copiers, and printers attached. HDTV is combinable with stereo sound speakers and video tape recorders.

More interesting still is technology fusion, so called because the component technologies are transformed through their synthesis. The Japanese call this *yugo-ka*. MITI introduced the concept of technology fusion in its 1986 white paper "The Fundamental Outline of Twenty-

Box 7-3
Hybrid and Fusion Technologies

The Japanese Approach to Hybrid Technologies

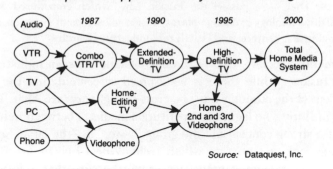

Source: Dataquest, Inc.

... and to fusion technologies
Interindustry Technology Fusion Index

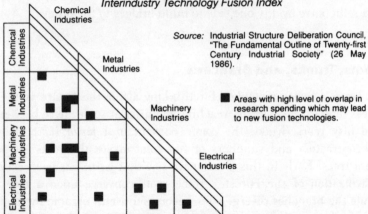

Source: Industrial Structure Deliberation Council, "The Fundamental Outline of Twenty-first Century Industrial Society" (26 May 1986).

■ Areas with high level of overlap in research spending which may lead to new fusion technologies.

Japanese hybrid technologies are technologies incorporated within the same system, but retaining their original form. In the illustration at the top, a Total Home Media System borrows audio, VTR, TV, PC, and telephone technologies to constitute an integrated system.

Where technologies fuse, the result is a new technology, thus Asahi Brewery, Kirin, and Suntory are combining their knowledge of fermentation with biotechnology, to develop new food preservatives, liquors, and medicines, while Sanyo's biolectronics represents the fusion of biotechnology, chemitronics, artificial intelligence, software, computer-aided design tools, neural nets, and VLSI design.

Source: Sheridan M. Tatsuno, *Created in Japan.* New York: Harper & Row, 1990, pp. 63–71.

first Century Industrial Society" (nothing less!). Sheridan Tatsumo reports:

> MITI believes that excimer lasers and ion implantation technology can be used in the manufacturing of propellers and x-ray mirrors. . . . In 1988 the Japanese Diet . . . passed the Fusion Law, which empowered MITI to establish technology exchange plazas, fusion management research centers, regional fusion centers, and "catalyzer" industry research.[8]

In American society, there is no one to stand between industries and suggest fusion. While there is widespread agreement that the future innovations of the economy must be cross-disciplinary (see Alvin Toffler's *The Third Wave*[9]), no legitimate institution mediates between industries. Without a strong concept of "the group," "we," or "the larger society," Americans lack an entity to which technological fusions are likely to accrue. Since individual industries cannot be sure that a fusion will accrue to their benefit (it could well accrue to the other party's), there is a reluctance by any one side to build bridges to the other.

Roots, Trunks, and Branches

In Japan a major metaphor for thinking about the future is the tree. Trees tend to grow slowly, reaching maturity at somewhere between five and fifty years. Kudo, the comic book hero of *Japan Inc.*, likens the subcontractors and suppliers of his company to the roots supporting giant trees. Early in this chapter we saw that Japan has been called the "Civilization of the Forest." Since roots converge upon a tree trunk while the branches diverge, this becomes a useful organic metaphor for the development of a corporation's various technologies in the future. The roots are the origins, the various logics of seminal knowing, while the branches bear the harvest of leaves, fruits, or flowers. And, of course, these harvests are seasonal and recurrent, with the inner logic of growth expressed with every springtime, while the tree also grows upward, foot by foot, as a function of time.

Box 7-4 gives one illustration of how the tree metaphor has been used for long-term strategy by the Sharp Corporation. Basic technologies, such as signal conversion, digital recording, thin film, symbol processing, and photography, feed into the trunk of the tree, and from this grow PCM adaptors, satellite receivers, microphone amps, multichannel recorders, synthesizers, electronic organs, digital filters, and tapeless microcassettes. Instead of analyzing each product separately, and asking

Box 7-4
Sharp's Digital Audio Technology Tree

Source: Sharp Corp. © Japan Management Association.

A typical organic metaphor of a living system, nurtured by seasonally recurring forces and carrying within its roots "genetic codes," which combine in the trunk to produce a harvest of differentiated products, reaching up to customers. The metaphor encompasses two cultural views of time: the synchronic and the sequential.

Source: Sheridan M. Tatsuno, *Created in Japan.* New York: Harper & Row, 1990, pp. 63–71.

whether it will meet the "hurdle" rate for return on investment, the corporation sees all products as outgrowths of knowledge and nutrients flowing up the trunk, drawn from the education-rich soil beneath. Upon the synchrony of these converging roots will depend the quality, quantity, and variety of the products. The branches reach out to customers, while the roots delve into earth for knowledge, ever spreading out and searching. This does not mean that the tree is never pruned back, or that all its foliage is valuable to customers. It does mean that growth takes care of the future, that products are self-elaborating, with connections among connections and branches of branches.

Amplifying Deviations

Thus far we have focused on synchrony, the coming together of loops representing past, present, and future, or different technologies or connectable ideas. But as we can see in Sharp Corporation's tree diagram (Box 7-4), all comings together also imply a spreading out again. To win in the marketplace your creative connections must result in unmatchable varieties of products, especially where markets are maturing and customization is demanded.

Magorah Maruyama has argued that both Americans and the Japanese have a fairly solid grasp of cybernetics, even if, as we have claimed, cycles come more naturally to Japanese culture. But he sees a crucial difference between two cultural varieties of cybernetics. For the most part, Americans are interested in the deviation-reducing feedback loop, the kind that detects errors and eliminates them. "Management by Exception" is a good example. The operations of the corporation are scrutinized only if they deviate from budget, plan, or estimated costs. The ideal is to restore the standard and reimpose controls. Investments in the future are not made unless they approximate target rules, and the farther you look ahead, the less and less do present rules apply.

But Japanese cybernetics and circular thinking tends to be deviation amplifying,[10] says Maruyama. What happens is that some happy accident, an idea or suggestion by a member of the work force, a chance occurrence (like the unexpected admiration for Honda's 50 cc Supercub) kicks off a small change which amplifies progressively to transform the entire system. Instead of selling macho motor cycles to black-jacketed gangs, Honda sells lower-powered scooters to "the Nicest People." What started as a seemingly isolated preference for the Supercub suddenly grew and grew into an industry worth hundreds of millions.[11]

This talent helps to account for one of the most devastating marketing strategies that Japanese *kaisha* (corporations) employ. They seem able to proliferate multiple varieties of a basic product in an extraordinarily short time. While flexible manufacturing is necessary to this process, it is not sufficient. What is needed in addition, is a view of serendipity, elaboration, and happenstance as benign, along with a lightning capacity to exploit accruing variations. What surfaces are differences between the suppliers expectations and the customers' needs, and the *kaisha* pounces on these differences to exploit them.

The now-legendary battle between Honda and Yamaha is a pertinent example. Yamaha challenged Honda with lowered prices, whereupon Honda fought back with a kaleidoscopic variety of new product introductions and scooters tailored to specific customer segments. In a market with only sixty varieties of motorcycle up to 1981, Honda introduced eighty-one new models in the next eighteen months, plus 113 product changes.[12]

This is not creativity as the West usually defines it, but is remarkably close to creation, as evolutionary biologists conceive of it, the process by which all animals and life forms have evolved via morphogenesis. Darwin's theory has been somewhat elaborated but not changed in its fundamentals.

It still appears that the wondrous variety of natural forms have evolved through those random deviations that best suit particular environmental niches, that this process involves millions of small failures and successes, the latter growing rapidly and the former disappearing. It has even been found that darker-colored moths in the vicinity of factories are better camouflaged from predators than their lighter brothers, while in less-polluted areas the reverse is true.

The Japanese may be unconsciously imitating evolution itself (albeit a much speeded up variety) by employing high degrees of minor variation, discovering and colonizing the niches into which these penetrate, and then turning minor variations into major ones, wherever customers selectively reinforce this deviance amplification. This approach has the virtue of minimizing risk and expense, since the initial deviations are small.

Another source of elaboration and variation is spinning products off from core technologies. The Japanese sometimes conceive of this process as resembling a mandala, with successive circles of elaboration spreading out. HDTV (high definition television) has been targeted by the Japanese for more than a decade.

Did enthusiasts for this technology do a discounted cash-flow calculation of paybacks starting in 1995? We doubt it. The answer to their eagerness to invest is that they see so many applications and uses for this technology that the real danger is that someone else will get there first. When a technology pays back a whole society many times over, which is not the same as paying back one firm by a specified date, then not to proceed is damaging.

Coordinations and Chains-of-Command

We must now address ourselves to the puzzling finding that although the Japanese appear more hierarchical than Americans, at least as measured by our instruments, this does not seem to slow or diminish their success. We shall also see that time, synchrony, and hierarchy are connected.

It may be recalled from Chapter 5 that we showed our samples of international managers five triangles of ascending steepness and asked them which triangle most resembled their own corporation. Figure 7-1 contrasts the triangle most often chosen by Americans with that most often chosen by the Japanese. We see that the latter view their own organizations as steeper, but only moderately so.

Figure 7-1

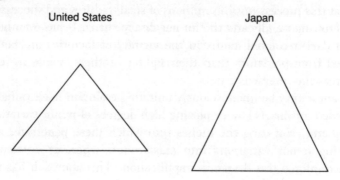

United States   Japan

Two of five triangles chosen by most American managers (left) and by most Japanese managers (right) as representing their own organizations.

There are numerous ways of defining hierarchy, and our research may have elided these. Within some definitions, Japan is clearly less hierarchical than the United States, if by this you mean equality-inequality of salary structures, the number of levels of status and skill, the number of exclusive privileges, i.e., executive washrooms, corporate jets, the number of distinctions in dress and decor, and barriers to junior employees' participation in the workplace.

However, the Japanese are, by American standards, far more deferential to superiors and to authority generally, employ a language indicative of the relative social standings of speakers and those spoken to, and are most reluctant to criticize openly or challenge those in charge. Hence the relative steepness of the Japanese triangle did not surprise us. More puzzling was their continuing success in the most knowledge-intensive fields despite such hierarchies. Much of our received wisdom states that the more complex the job and the more numerous the varieties of expertise necessary to a solution, the less can anyone at the top hope to know the answers, and the broader and more democratic must consultation be. Why, then, do not Americans gain the benefit of their flatter organizations and why do the Japanese not suffer more failures of complex decision making?

The first clues to an answer lie in the particular nature of Japanese hierarchies. Individualist nations tend to make much of the dauntless character, lonely decision making, and agonizing responsibility of the chief executive. He tends to be seen as the origin of vision, power, initiative, commitment, and strategy. There is a chain of command, down which his orders flow to invigorate the company. Clearly, as tasks grow complicated such a know-it-all becomes rare if not impossible.

The Japanese hierarchy is less a chain of command (since the boss is usually many, many miles from the customer) than a series of higher and higher, and more and more inclusive coordinations or synchronies resembling inverted Chinese puzzle boxes. The contrast is made in Fig. 7-2. The superior is the coordinator of initiatives occurring beneath him. He acts on behalf of the community, to synthesize and configure all the contributions of those reporting to him. There is, therefore, no necessary correlation between rank and the initiation of change and novelty. The leader spends his time listening, responding, nurturing, and deriving policy *ex post facto* from strategies that have emerged and from amplifications of unanticipated responses by customers.

For the sake of simplicity, we have assumed just four levels (Fig. 7-2). The downward arrows on the left illustrate the chain-of-command principle (there must, of course, be information going up). Note the gaps or psychological distance between the levels. The boxes on the right show that every higher step in the hierarchy encompasses the level below with closeness rather than distance. The superior is thus more of a

Figure 7-2

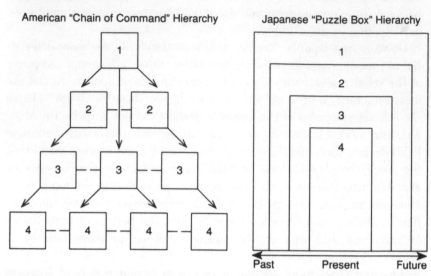

American "Chain of Command" Hierarchy   Japanese "Puzzle Box" Hierarchy

synchronizer-coordinator than a leader, responsible for what the subordinate does, but at a higher level of abstraction. This accounts for the curiously abstract statement in the report by MITI quoted earlier in this chapter, wherein the government agency purported to describe "The Fundamental Outline of the Twenty-first Century." The agency was advising industries on the advantages of technological fusion, but does this amount to "giving orders" to industry or to "government interference" so detested by Americans? Hardly, since the number of possible fusions are many and no industry is being told what it should do specifically.

The responsibility for choosing a precise set of actions belongs not to the apex of the hierarchy, but to those who interpret these broad directions specifically. This distinction is most important, because if B (boss) tells S (subordinate) exactly what to do, in specific and atomistic detail, then B essentially takes over responsibility for the effectiveness of that decision, and S may legitimately say, "I was just doing my job." His or her responsibility is decreased to the extent that B's is increased and hierarchy undermines the responsibility of the front lines. But if B describes the meaning and value of "improved service to the customer" and S interprets and achieves this in local circumstances far from the head office, then in no way is S's responsibility reduced, nor is the responsibility of B. Each is responsible for a different level of meaning:

B for outlining customer service as the company policy, S for performing that service in circumstances that cannot be foreseen from afar.

But, surely, is this not all done in U.S. corporations as well? It is to some extent—certainly many consultants advise it, but Americans find it difficult to carry through, for reasons outlined in earlier chapters as well as in this one.

The "puzzle boxes" in Fig. 7-2 are also importantly related to time. Each higher level of management looks farther past and farther forward than the level beneath it, encompassing not merely more people and more activity, but longer and longer time spans of discretion. It was the Canadian professor, Elliot Jaques, who first argued that status and fair pay are commensurate to how long you work without oversight and supervision. The lowest level may be supervised hourly, middle management monthly, division heads yearly, and top management every five years.[13] Long-term time orientation is thus a mark of high status. Jaques believes that the willingness and capacity to look far ahead is the crucial aspect of leadership potential.

Middle Top-down Management

While American management theory has a tendency to pit top-down management against the benefits of bottom-up participation, the Japanese have gone some way toward synchronizing the two. Professor Ikujiro Nonaka calls this "middle-up-down management," with the key role being played by middle management staff who actually create information from what the top and the bottom communicate to them. He quotes Tadashi Kume of Honda:

> I continually create dreams, but people run in different directions unless they are able to directly interact with reality. . . . Top management does not know what bottom management is doing. It is middle management which is charged with integrating the two viewpoints emanating from top and bottom. . . . There can be no progress without such integration.[14]

According to Nonaka, middle managers mediate between induction, with its bottom-up information, grounded in experience, and deduction, with its top-down, abstract values and policies emanating from on high. It is middle managers in the "compression chamber" who must reconcile contradictory demands and bring order out of chaos. They do this by creating information and proposals that embody both the top's policies and values and the bottom's day-to-day experiences.

In Japan, creativity occurs in conditions precisely opposite to those thought to induce creativity in the West. Instead of people being given space, time, and leisure in some leafy location, middle managers are compressed between contradictory demands from every side and are set urgent deadlines to come up with solutions. A Honda R & D manager told Nonaka: "Creativity is born by pushing people against the wall and pressuring them almost to an extreme."

Through dialogue, through interaction among seemingly contradictory positions, and through the operation of self-organizing groups, middle managers work out their resolutions, which are then proposed to senior management. This process has an important role to play in the generation of long-term plans and policies. Middle managers are able to work on plans, the fruition of which will coincide with their own rise to the top of the corporation as their seniority increases. In this way, people and policies develop as one, and a future leader may well find himself presiding over a policy he helped initiate fifteen or twenty years earlier. Akio Morita of Sony comments:

> Our encouragement of long-range plans from up-and-coming employees is a big advantage for our system, despite all the meetings. . . . It enables us to create and maintain something that is rare in the West, a company philosophy. . . . Even if a new executive takes over, he cannot change that. In Japan, the long-range planning system and the junior management proposal system guarantees that the relationship between top management and junior management remains very close. [15]

We see, therefore, that Japanese hierarchies are not simple conduits for direct orders from above. Senior managers lay down broad—very broad—outlines in which there is much freedom of interpretation, and act as sounding boards for proposals initiated by juniors. No wonder that Japan, even with its steeper hierarchies, delegates considerable authority downward, according to Institute for Management Development (IMD) surveys. Hierarchies may actually encourage an optimal flow of information where they mimic the structure of that information itself, with broad generalities, philosophies, and superordinate goals at the top, concrete data and unprocessed experience at the bottom, and an influential sense-making strata in the middle, creating new concepts to influence the long-term future.

Benevolence and Leadership

The final aspect of Japanese hierarchy, which makes it different from the old-fashioned autocracy that the West rightly condemns, is the tradition of benevolent leadership and of minimilist or fingertip control. Three concepts, *amae, sempai-kohai,* and *naniwabushi* will help us to understand the strong emotional obligations placed on Japanese leaders by their subordinates.

Amae can be translated only roughly, as a "reliance and dependence upon the indulgent love of an older person." In family relations it would describe an elder brother-younger brother bond (*sempai-kohai*) but is not confined to brothers.[16] The term is familial but not erotic. It denotes going well beyond contractual obligations to receive or give a very personal consideration. The Japanese do not make the distinction between *gemeinschaft*, a close-knit group with voluntary affections, and *gesellschaft*, an instrumental-contractual association suitable for work, first noted by Ferdinand Tönnies and now a foundation stone of Western sociology. For the Japanese, work relations should be familial and affectionate. You are not promoted to get away from less distinguished persons, but to take care of them. Promotion by seniority maintains this family connotation. Magorah Maruyama has suggested the word *aida-schaft* to describe the Japanese as having an orientation neither to work nor to family/friends but to relationships per se. For the Japanese, the relationship develops those related, rather than the other way around.[17]

Amae can be reciprocal if A depends on B in situation C, but B depends on A in situation D. In effect, superiors often depend on subordinates to do things for them. The unequal power in an *amae* relationship is an important part of the trust it instills. If A could have taken advantage of B's dependence but instead sustained him, *amae* is strengthened, benevolence is expressed. In a culture of accelerating complexity and runaway varieties of expertise, we are all increasingly dependent on each other's distinctive competencies. Inequalities of knowledge are everywhere.

Amae is most important in the forgiveness of honest mistakes and the willingness to learn from them. Akio Morita's statement quoted earlier, that you do not correct a child's mistake by disowning him is typical *amae*, or paternalism, as Americans would say. But, of course, if the relationship no longer exists because the mistake was fatal, elaborate apologies to survivors are in order. Hence, the President of JAL apologized personally to all the relatives of the victims of a recent airliner crash and then resigned. The fault was not with him but with the

American plane maker. However, *amae* had been breached, a trust broken.

Modesty is an important characteristic of Japanese leaders, Soichiro Honda marked the twenty-fifth anniversary of Honda in 1973 by resigning, taking up the postresignation title of Supreme Adviser, and touring Honda offices around the world. It is a crucial part of Japanese seniority that by living longer you have made more mistakes and can help others by owning up to this. His achievements were, he said:

> Merely the result of a series of mistakes, failures, and regrets . . . although my mistakes were never due to the same reason.

It is this "witness to error" role that justifies Japanese respect for old age. You have not necessarily been right, least of all before the event, but you have learned wisdom after the event and have learned not to repeat mistakes. In English-speaking discourse "wise after the event" is a sneer. In Japanese discourse, it is the gift of benevolent authority, the blessings of *kami* returning to earth to redeem their families and crucial to the whole process of cybernetic learning.

Amae relationships make possible a conflict-resolving mode called *naniwabushi*, in which the subordinate or dependent person throws himself upon the indulgence, even mercy, of the superior, offering respect and moral dependency in exchange for what is owed. *Naniwabushi* are ballads of the Edo period (1600–1868), a time reputedly of great peace. The ballad has *kikkake*, general background; *seme,* a narrative of events; and *urei,* the final resolution, often of great pathos. Hence, a debtor will explain the background, the recession, the narrative (his wife and children now eat dried seaweed), and the resolution: the superior will be the more magnificent for forgiving the debt. Robert M. Marsh, author of *The Japanese Negotiator,* comments:

> *Naniwabushi* is artful, premeditated, calculated—and in Japan it works. The more tragic and moving the story, the easier it is for the Japanese listeners to forget contracts or commitments. Indeed, listeners who do not compromise or show compassion in such circumstances would be condemned as cold-hearted and mercenary.[18]

What is happening, in effect, is that money or debt is being forgiven and valuable relationships maintained in exchange for the acknowledgment of the other's superior status. But it means that those rising in Japanese society will do so on the strength of indulgences shown to others. It is not the animal with the sharpest teeth that wins out, but he who accumulates moral debt through many *amae* relationships. The higher you rise, the more you must do for others.

Summary and Conclusions

Let us now take stock of the first seven chapters of this book, to see how they culminate in the short-termism preferred by Americans, and the long-termism preferred by the Japanese. The United States seems to be hampered in addressing economic problems in the longer term by the following cultural biases:

(a) A tendency to idealize the lawfulness and universality of the physical sciences, so attempting to trace events to their immediate "causes" (the universalism bias)

(b) An insistence on predicting events that have specific descriptions and on estimating the value of investing in these via detailed payback calculations (the analytic bias)

(c) A belief that new inventions and scientific breakthroughs originate in the transformative genius of creators (the individualism bias)

(d) An attempt to make the future predictable and controllable from within the conscious purpose of decision makers in the present (the inner-directed bias)

(e) The need to attach any successes in the future to persons currently operating (the achieved status bias)

(f) The preference for connecting future successes to achieving individuals who push sequences of events (the time-as-sequential bias)

(g) Strongly ambivalent feelings about hierarchy as making contests to control the future unequal (equality bias)

What appears to encourage Japanese culture to address the long-term economic opportunities and future is also present in their cultural biases:

(a) A preference for serendipitous connections and particular coincidences between economic opportunities (the particularistic bias)

(b) An interest in broad technological patterns of cross-connection, hybridization, and fusion (the bias toward synthesis)

(c) The belief that communities include many extant ideas, trends, and techniques, capable of, and destined for, fruitful combination, so that the sooner this happens the better (the communitarian bias)

The Benign Leader

Cartoons taken from *Japan Inc: Introduction to Japanese Economics.*

Our hero, Kudo, is still searching for a way to save the subcontractors to his company, now that 'Toysan' cars must shift operations to Europe and the EEC. He seeks out 'Boss Shijima', a mysterious elder, a resident of the threatened community, and a confidant of the Prime Minister. We see Shijima here 'in touch with nature', symbolically nurturing living systems in a 'generative' Japanese garden – a microcosm, says Maruyama, of the ideal of heterogenistic harmony. He has already arranged for Kudo to visit Princeton, where he will find the knowledge to build a center for biotechnology at Imahama.

(d) A belief that happy accidents and unplanned connections are bound to occur in the future, provided we constantly cross-fertilize and steer toward promising rendezvous (the outer-directed bias)

(e) A willingness to attribute importance and priority to key technologies that render thousands of other products more intelligent and valuable (the attributed status bias)

(f) A tendency to view the products so targeted as recurring in cycles of eternal return to inspire the living economy (the time-as-synchronous bias)

(g) A concept of hierarchy as associated with longer time spans of discretion and more and more relations of *amae* with "families" of subordinates (steep hierarchy bias)

This final idea may be the most important of all, since it replaces "the dismal science" of tough-minded business affairs, detached from the emotional lives of individuals, with "a joyful development" in which the feelings of all employees are at least potentially engaged. As the Japanese like to say, their business management is "wet," while that of Americans is "dry." But let the last word be that of Kudo, the communitarian cartoon hero of *Japan Inc.*

> Because of us, the Japanese economy is on the rise and Japan is becoming an economic giant, but what about the cultural side. . . ? At home, things haven't changed. . . . I think that when we begin to balance goods and feelings, the people and the country will become rich.[19]

8

The Logics
of Community

IN WESTERN POLITICS AND ECONOMICS there may be no term more reviled, no ideal so completely mired in disgrace as *collectivism*. Individualism and collectivism have contended since 1917, and almost everywhere the former appears to have triumphed, held in check in places like China only by the repressive nature of collectivist regimes.

Yet a study of the relative rates of economic development made seven years ago by Geert Hofstede shows that collectivist values, the belief in the need to serve the group, is a necessary, although not sufficient, condition for economic development. Japan, Singapore, Hong Kong, and Taiwan were all on the collectivist end of the scale, and all were also among the world's fastest developers.[1] A similar result was obtained in a study by Harvard professors George Lodge and Ezra Vogel and reported in *Ideology and National Competitiveness*. These two scholars created a measure of communitarianism—incoherence and rank-ordered nine nations on their index. The order was Japan, Korea, Taiwan, Germany, France, Brazil, the United States, the United Kingdom, and Mexico. They found that communitarianism correlated highly with annual compound growth rates over the previous decade, with increase in export shares of world markets, and with investment as a share of GNP.[2] However, collectivist cultures that did not place a high priority on business development—including Greece, Chile, Franco's Spain, and India—were not successful economically. The seeming anomaly of failing and succeeding communitarianisms is explained if we distinguish *statism*, the belief that the government can and must "command" the

165

economy, from *communitarian values,* the belief that whole organizations, societies, and economies can learn to act coherently to nurture higher rates of economic development. The idea that governments can unilaterally plan and control an economy is indeed dead, and the ever-growing complexity and turbulence of the world economy guarantees against its resurrection.

None of our seven cultures are statist, but several—the United States, the United Kingdom, the Netherlands—are highly individualist, and recently *all* individualist economies have been slow growers. The importance of communal values, the idea that in the midst of economic cyclones, the group, the organization, the whole economy and society is needed to sustain individuals—this conviction appears crucial to sustained economic development in the period of "late capitalism." The belief that individuals find self-fulfillment, even immortality of a kind, in serving their social group seems so full of competitive advantages that most of this chapter will be given over to the logics of community. We shall not, however, use the word *collectivist* since this is now associated wtih communism. We shall use *communitarianism* or *organization.*

We look for wisdom to Japan, easily the most communitarian of our seven cultures. Unlike Germany, which is also communitarian, Japan's culture reinforces communitarianism with outer-direction, the desire to be in harmony with the wider environment and nation, and by ascribed status, so that if the nation's leaders say a new technology or direction is important, it becomes so, along with all the persons involved. Hence cohesive groups can react with great swiftness to new environmental opportunities, often getting to markets first with American-invented products. The problem, as always, is the massive collectivist error, a whole nation rushing to disaster, as the 1941 attack on Pearl Harbor. More recently the organized push for the fifth-generation computer had to be called off. The sun also sets.

Japan seems to live by this outer-directed communitarianism. We say "seems" because once again Japan, in contrast to America, is not offering prescriptions for the world to follow and does not lay down codes of supposed universal validity. So we must observe what she does and says and infer her reasons. We will first show that Japan is more communitarian than individualist, more outer-directed than inner-directed, and more prone to attribute status to persons than to wait to see whether they achieve it. We shall then consider how outer-directed collectivism, with socially attributed status, serves community.

The Group First

We have already noted that the Japanese see capitalism as a system in which communities serve customers, rather than one in which individuals extract profits. We posed several questions designed to tell us more about communitarian values.

Our first question is of interest because by investigating the willingness of the individual to rely on the family as opposed to the state, it is independent of the capitalist versus communist argument. As expected, we find Japan, Korea, and Singapore at the communitarian extreme. The following dilemma was posed, and respondents were asked to choose one of two options:

> A man had a fire in his shop and lost most of his merchandise. His store was partly destroyed by the fire. He and his family had to have some help from someone to rebuild the shop as fast as possible. There are different ways of getting help.
>
> (a) It would be best if he depended mostly on his brothers and sisters, or other relatives, to help him.
>
> (b) It would be best to borrow some money *on his own* in order to get some construction people to rebuild his store.

As we see in the following table, the communitarian Japanese prefer option (a).

The results:

	SWE	CAN	USA	AUS	UK	IT	FRA	GER	BEL	JAP	SIN
On one's own	84%	80	79	75	74	69	68	67	61	50	38

The next question explores the willingness of the corporation to concern itself with the family, indeed, to act somewhat as a parent might. Respondents were asked to choose one of two options regarding the following dilemma:

> A company can fix the level of the income of its employees on various bases.
>
> (a) Some people think a company should take into account the size of the employee's family. In their eyes, the company is responsible for an extra compensation per child.
>
> (b) Other people believe that an employee should be paid on the basis of the work he is doing for the company. Therefore, the company does not have to take into account the employee's family.

The results:

Payment for work by individual only	UK	USA	CAN	AUS	NL	GER	BEL	SWE	FRA	SIN	IT	JAP
	95.5	94.6	93.7	92.0	91.1	90.5	90.4	89.3	88.0	65.2	67.0	32.4

Here, Japan is once again on the communitarian end. Should companies concern themselves with the breeding preferences of their employees? It seems very odd to Westerners, but at least the logic is consistent. The company must not simply act responsibly to employees, but encourage employees to behave responsibly toward others—in this case the employee's family. It may be strange to us, but it is not stupid. It is a very common finding in the study of corporate cultures, that the quality of the staff-customer relationship is a reflection of the staff-supervisory relationship, which, in turn, reflects how the supervisor was treated. Such patterns repeat themselves through communities, and it is clear that this is what the Japanese intend.

Moreover, Japanese companies typically go much further than those in other cultures in modeling themselves on family relationships. They admire *sempai-kohai* relationships, literally, elder brother-younger brother bonds between a mentor and a subordinate. They also admire *amae*, a form of "indulgent love," in which the elder gives more to the younger than he or she deserves and spurs the subordinate to attempted reciprocity and repayment. In this way, social bonds go far beyond contract or agreement and often involve an escalation of favors on both sides. Similar attitudes infuse relationships between suppliers and customers. You over-indulge your best customers. Japanese scandals often demonstrate this tendency taken to excess, since the money has to come from other, less-favored customers or from shareholders. It is for such reasons that on leaving Japanese friends at the airport, one may receive so many presents that considerable inconvenience, not to mention excess baggage charges, is incurred. Giving has an almost competitive intensity.

No wonder, then, that the image of the "good manager" in Japan is that of a highly socialized person, acting to help and sustain others, a "company man," not the American lone operator. In American films and comic books, the villain skulks beneath the group's protection, while the hero stands alone.

Falling on Your Feet

While a majority (76 percent) of American managers had an internal locus of control, believing that each man and woman has charge of his

The Communitarian Hero

A heated argument between Kudo, the communitarian hero, and the villainous individualist, Tsugawa, exponent of American ideals. Tsugawa wants to ditch the subcontractors to those Japanese auto producers who must now relocate abroad. Kudo fights back with the organic images typical of Japanese communitarian attitudes. The politicians advise the community to build an amusement park, but Kudo, assisted by a wise elder with contacts at the highest level, opts for a new high-tech centre. The subcontractors will all be re-employed at enhanced levels of knowledge-intensity and a more complex collectivity will be formed.

Cartoons taken from *Japan Inc: Introduction to Japanese Economics*.

or her own destiny and moral direction, only 44 percent of Japanese managers agreed, despite a questionnaire that made outer-direction seem rather weak and replete with excuses about luck and fate. In fact, the Japanese do not value "unconquerable souls" and steely inner convictions. A well-known Japanese axiom states, "Man alone is weak, but harmonized to nature he is strong."

It is an interesting question as to whether in an incredibly complexifying world most events, ideas, directions, trends, and forces are not in fact external to the individual. We are more and more buffeted by booms, busts, shocks, scandals, breakthroughs, and turbulence of all kinds. Japan was geographically created by volcanoes. Its seasons change abruptly. Earthquakes and tidal waves are common, and Tokyo itself is on major fault lines. Devastated by World War II, incinerated by nuclear and conventional bombs, and occupied by a culture of large-nosed aliens who rewrote their constitution and secularized their emperor, the Japanese had to be masters of resilience and adaptation in order to survive at all. That they survived and triumphed in the only expression of strength permitted them is a tribute to their extraordinary ability to ride upon a momentum originated elsewhere.

This is an ancient Japanese tradition. *Kami*, or gods, are thought to inhabit natural phenomena, winds, waves, mountains, forests, and fire. Nature is both powerful, terrifying, and beautiful.[3] To imitate nature, to identify with its might and majesty, helps human beings to survive and prosper (see Box 8-1). The Black Ships of Commodore Perry which forcibly opened Japan to the world, the atom bombs, the American occupation, the Korean War, the oil shock, the Nixon *shocku*, the massive appreciation of the yen, the onrush of new technology, the strength of market forces unleashed by the West—all could have sent Japan reeling. Instead, these forces were used as a judo artist uses the fierce momentum of an opponent, to propel Japan in the direction of economic development.

Hence, to appreciate Japanese-style communitarianism, we have to stress that it is not the grinding out of ideological axes, or the "correct" interpretation of Marxist texts, but an extraordinary capacity to be swept along and yet fall on your feet. Japan, with its chronic dependence on political allies and eternal sources of raw materials, is "open" to the point of vulnerability, yet every wound seems only to quicken her footwork. She has brought fast reactivity to a fine art. She steers in circumstances where all but the most resilient would stagger.

Box 8-1

Japanese Identification with the Strength of Natural Forces

In *Kagemusha*, "The Shadow Warrior,"—a classic Japanese film directed by Akira Kurosawa—the grandson of Lord Shingen, head of the Takeda clan, is being instructed by an attendant on the traditions of the clan.

ATTENDANT: "You know the Master's banner. What do the letters mean?"

GRANDSON: "Swift as the wind, quiet as the forest, fierce as the fire, immovable as the mountain."

ATTENDANT: "The Lord is that mountain, both in battle and at home. When his army moves, first come the horsemen, attacking swiftly as the wind. Second, the lancers advance, quiet as the forest. Third, the cavalry raids, merciless as fire. The land is behind them always, immovable as a mountain. Our Lord is this mountain, and that's why we call him 'The Mountain.' "

Status by Attribution

It is Japan's extraordinary capacity to steer and to persevere that merits closer attention. 58 percent of American managers believed that their status came from achievements. Only 27 percent of Japanese managers feel that way. How could such a strong record of achievement grow from a culture that appears to ascribe or attribute status to its members on other grounds, for example, their age and the kind of business they are in? What other grounds for conferring prestige are there?

The answer is that certain kinds of ascription encourage achievement, without diluting it or deflecting attention away from it. While some people are busy achieving, other people in a culture need to ask themselves and to decide what is worth achieving in the first place? Unless you are prepared to attribute status to the development of, say, photovoltaic cells, superconductivity, or microchips, achievements will simply follow the paths of least resistance and higher commercial payoff. Your culture will "develop" from making such movies as *Public Enemy*, in which 8 people died violently, to *Robocop* (32), *Rambo II* (62), and *Rambo III* (106).[4] This is a progress of a kind, and commercially profitable, but not development. Without the ascription of value to purposes more or less desirable, a culture will simply pander to its own excess, selling more and more addictive drugs like alcohol, tobacco, violent movies, and cocaine, because wealth and, hence, "achievement" is attainable thereby.

The point is not simply that certain business activities impoverish a culture, but that it is necessary to ascribe status to certain activities before they can succeed. Solar energy is not a "success," nor is nuclear fusion; nor is there a mobile phone yet created that gives you instant contactability, without wires, wherever you are. HDTV is not yet a noticeable achievement. Compact interactive discs have yet to revolutionize how we learn. The reason for ascribing status is to decide which of these potentials to pursue as a society. It is the same with partnerships, joint ventures, and shared enterprises. We have to believe in them before they come to fruition, or it will be too late to join the bandwagon. We have to say, "This is important to economic and social development, and, therefore, worth achieving." Without these initial value judgments a culture is without purpose or direction.[5]

Japan has been notable for asking itself, "Which technologies contribute most to the development of the economy as a whole?" To such technologies, high status and national priority are attributed. America did much the same thing, of course, with the revitalization of Europe through the Marshall Plan, with space exploration, and with the resistance, first of fascism, then communism. But all such exploits have been "world saving," in the sense of being beyond economics, although, ironically, the economic spin-offs proved invaluable. With the end of the Cold War and the pause of rivalries in space, the United States appears uncertain and notably reluctant to raise to the level of a national challenge its own economic difficulties. It refuses to regard certain products and activities as essentially more worthy of status than others. Markets must be the sole arbiters, achievement in reaching those markets the sole criterion of worth. Japan's great strength is that it seems able to break out of this circle of self-consumption, to idealize prospects not yet achieved but worthy of collective aspiration.

We shall now consider the various "logics of community" used by Japanese society, and how influences from outside are first absorbed and evaluated and then given the status of visions and aspirations shareable by all. Six logics result in noticeable cultural preferences for:

- Circular, not technical, reasoning,
- Knowledge-intensive enterprises,

- High market share,
- The *kaisha* as a community,
- M-forms and the *keiretsu*, and
- Cooperative technologies: the tools that make the tools.

Circular, Not Technical, Reasoning

We fail to understand Japanese thinking entirely unless we grasp its circularity and its simultaneous interactions. The Japanese create wealth by taking a large number of particular values, discovered perhaps in conversations with customers, and forming these particulars into more harmonious and, hence, more valuable wholes. It was at this point that universal conclusions might be drawn from the process and many atoms, or units of product, generated.

Figure 8-1 illustrates the same circular logic. Because the corporation concerns itself even with the welfare of employees' families and children, these families and children concern themselves even with the welfare of the corporation. They seem ready to pay 20 to 40 percent more for domestic versions of Japanese international products, to work for Japanese corporations, where possible, and to prefer their products over foreign offerings. The circle of reciprocity looks like this:

Figure 8-1   Circular Reciprocity

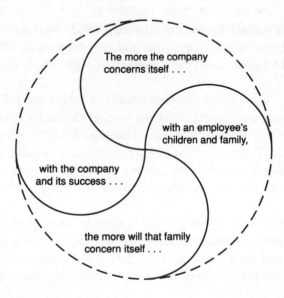

The more the company concerns itself . . .

with an employee's children and family,

with the company and its success . . .

the more will that family concern itself . . .

Circular thinking is vital to simultaneous enhancement of several members of a group, or several groups in an organization, or several organizations in a society. If the corporation pays more to employees with larger families or spends more on those who need to be rehoused, then all such efforts are wasted unless they "come full circle."

Reciprocal loops of this kind are by Western standards not rational, since rationality is judged from the standpoint of the single actor. To do "too much" for the customer (i.e., send one tube of lipstick by courier across town) is not cost-effective. Only if you put two persons in the loop and assume that the customer/employee will repay "excessive" solicitude with "excessive" loyalty or hard work does such "wasteful" caring make sense. This is helped by a powerful Japanese cultural tradition of feeling strongly obligated to parents, ancestors, and those in authority for favors received while young.[6] Subordinates thus feel the urge to repay kindness with prodigious feats of hard work. Japan's system of lifetime employment among the top 30 percent of its companies is not a "right," either legally or morally. (Legally, employment contracts are for one year only.) Lifetime employment is thus seen as an act of generosity and indulgence for which the recipient is beholden and which he or she should work as hard as possible to repay. Japanese unions in strikes against the company may choose their lunch break in which to strike, or may work harder immediately before and after the strike so as to compensate for the interruption. Is this "craven," "obsequious," "slavish"? If so, why strike at all? Or is it a "lovers quarrel" with the company, an acute awareness that wages can come only from production, and that weakening your paymaster is stupid? It may also contain a subtle message: "Here is the difference between our cooperation and noncooperation. Choose!" It is not without wisdom, albeit a circular variety with which Westerners are unfamiliar.

Of course, there are flourishing schools of cybernetic thinking in the United States, most especially at the System Dynamics Group at MIT, as recently expounded in *The Fifth Discipline* by Peter Senge.[7] But the very fact that Westerners need to teach themselves to think in loops, and that this discipline is the fifth and not the first, suggests that there is lacking for us the easy familiarity which the yin-yang has for many Asians.

The predominant American view is that the more the company does for its employees and their children, the less those employees will do for themselves and their families. The "paternalist" organization will have all its "dependents" suckling off corporate largesse. This is an individualist logic. If the corporation takes care of my family, that frees me to do my own thing! In the circular logic of community, we do even more for our families because the corporation has modeled that concern. We can also work harder than ever for the corporation, knowing that our families are being taken care of through those efforts.

Where the group is put first, it will accept responsibility for an error made by one of its members. Although the individual made the error, the group takes responsibility for not helping, teaching, or supervising him or her sufficiently. Group members may, of course, reproach the individual and make it clear that they want better quality work, but as far as the customer and senior managers are concerned, the group has accepted responsibility for the work of all its members. The seamless quality of the product is guaranteed by the seamless quality of the team.

Akio Morita of Sony complains loudly of the need of American managers to find fault and to penalize each other. The supervisor needs to prove it is not his fault, by sanctioning his subordinate instead. "You are individually responsible . . ." has the important implication " . . . and hence I am not." Morita recalls:

> The American director of a joint venture company in Tokyo complained to me that he was not able to pin down responsibility for an accident at his company and he asked why it seemed impossible to discover the name of the culprit no matter how hard he tried. I explained to him that the merit of his company lies precisely in the fact that everyone recognizes responsibility for the accident and to find one guilty party might destroy the morale of all. We can all expect to make mistakes. . . . I tell our people, "Go ahead and do what you think is right. If you make a mistake you will learn from it, just don't make the same mistake twice. . . . A child's mistake does not have to be dealt with by disowning him. It is more important to get to the cause . . . so that you can avoid the problem in the future."[8]

Morita recalls another occasion when he complained to American colleagues about a particularly exasperating employee:

> "What can I do with this guy?" I asked one day. They all looked at me as if I was slow-witted. "Why, fire him, of course," they said. I was stunned by the idea. I had never fired anybody and even in this case it had never crossed my mind. But to solve the problem by firing the man was the American system. It seemed so clear and straightforward and logical. I began to think America is a manager's paradise; you can do anything you want to do. Then a few months later I saw the other side of the coin.[9]

This "other side" turned out to be a top-performing sales manager who quit to join another company that offered him more money. Morita was aghast. "I couldn't believe my ears. . . ." A boss's freedom to fire had its corollary, the subordinate's freedom to take everything the company had given him and quit without regret or compunction. The very word *fire* is a celebration of cause-and-effect thinking in its purest form, a straight, logical progression. "Bang, he's gone!" As such it makes the Japanese deeply uneasy, because for them the consequences return. He who fires must have made a mistake when hiring. With the discharged employee whistling away like a bullet in the blue yonder, we shall never know how the cause might have been corrected. As for the firer, what will he learn—that people he does not agree with can be made to disappear?

Is there any reason to believe that the Japanese preference for thinking in circles and managing cybernetically is a cultural trait fundamental to their thought processes? Earlier we encountered the habit of "circling around" potential partners. We saw that the *Tai Chi* regards cyclicality as the most sacred and ultimate reality. We have seen that Shinto, being a form of nature worship, follows the cycles of the seasons. We detailed research studies in Chapter 7 that show that the Japanese, more than any other culture investigated, see past, present, and future in terms of interactive cycles. The Tokyo-based American consultants for the Boston Consulting Group, James Abbeglen and George Stalk, describe the strategy of the Japanese *kaisha* (corporation) as a virtuous circle of accelerated learning.[10] Another international consultant, specializing in transferring Japanese approaches to America, is Sheridan M. Tatsumo, the Japanese-American author of *Created in Japan*. Tatsumo also picks up the notion of the virtuous circle and ties it into the symbol of the mandala.

> Historically the mandala has played a central, though understated role in Japanese society. The mandala is used in Hinduism and esoteric Buddhism . . . a symbol meaning a circle, group or company. In Indo-Buddhist scriptures, it symbolized supreme inner enlightenment. . . . Japanese companies find that exploring creativity, using the mandala structure is a dynamic, whirling process. They set up the traditional *gonin-gumi* (five-person teams) which work together to develop and refine new ideas. These groups resemble planets revolving around the sun.[11]

It is not possible to visit a modern Japanese factory without seeing scores of feedback loops with virtually every important operation monitored electronically so that if malfunctioning, the machine shuts down automatically or signals the operator. Waste and scrap are routinely recycled.

The Point vs The Circle of Learning

Cartoons taken from *Japan Inc: Introduction to Japanese Economics*.

For Westerners, money making or profits can be 'the point'. For the Japanese, there are no still points – only eternal circles. Above, Kudo offers us his punchline on America and shows the Japanese alternative. But this is only one of many circles.

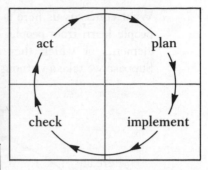

W. Edwards Deming's circle of quality was invented in the U.S. but adopted far more widely in Japan. Consider, for example, the intersecting circles that compose the logo of Toyota. Deming showed that quality goals increase production as well, while production goals tend to *decrease* quality.

Glossary of Circuits
Baton Passing Zone, baka-yoke, andon, autonomation, are all circuits of the Toyota Production System. Where the 'baton is passed' between employees working in relays you can exactly balance the strengths and weaknesses of 'runners'. *Baka-yoke* moves human intelligence into a machine so it regulates itself by feedback. *Andon* allows any worker to signal, using lights, that something is wrong with the work flow. *Autonomation* refers to learning circuits which are part human, part mechanical and increase both autonomy and automation.

From Circles to Helices and from People to Societies

What concerns us here is not simply circles that are self-correcting as people learn from people, but circles that progressively strengthen the elements of which they are constituted as whole societies develop. Suppose we take a virtuous circle in which

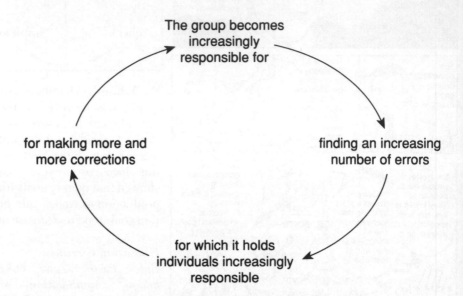

We have here a circle in which each element also increases. There is more group responsibility and more "errors" in the sense that small imperfections become "errors" as quality standards escalate, for which more individuals feel more responsible, hence more willing and able to make corrections. Because each element in the circle improves continuously, it makes more sense to see this as a developmental helix. Is there evidence that the Japanese think in helices as well as circles? There is. Professor Ikujiro Nonaka of Tokyo University has argued that Japanese management creates information by combining articulated, codified knowledge in which Americans are strong, with tacit, informal knowledge, which Americans tend to ignore. The weaving together of these two types of knowledge is represented by a helix (see Box 8-2).

A creativity cycle turned helix is suggested by Sheridan M. Tatsumo. He describes five elements of Japanese creativity: *sairiyo* (recycling), *Tansuku* (search), *ikusei* (nurturing), *hassoo* (breakthrough), and *kaizen* (refinement).[11] It is surely characteristic of the Japanese that they

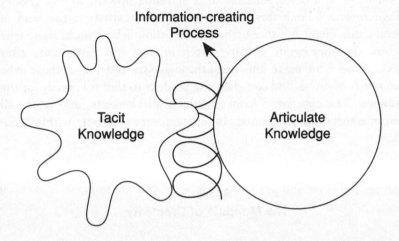

Box 8-2
Tacit Knowledge Joined to Articulate

Information-creating
Process

Tacit
Knowledge

Articulate
Knowledge

Professor Ikujiro Nonaka drew this helical process of generated knowledge which combines articulable with tacit knowledge. He believes that this is a crucial corporate advantage enjoyed by leading Japanese companies.

Source: "Organizing Innovation as a Knowledge-Creation Process." Center for Research Mgt, University of California, Berkeley, 1989.

approach creativity by indirection, by what most Westerners would regard as its opposite, *sairiyo* (recycling). You want to create, so you promptly recycle old ideas! But this approach is less "illogical" than simply cybernetic. Why create at all if there already exists something that will do the job, for instance, chloroform for the would-be anesthetist, or the gasoline engine if you seek to propel an airplane? Creativity needs elements to combine, thus recycling existing elements is a useful start. So is *tansuku* (search). Why "invent it here," when it has already been invented in America? The search process tells you about the state of the art. It is a commonsense preliminary. Next comes *ikusei* (nurturing), a culture of creativity within the corporation. Then comes *hassoo* (breakthrough), which is what most Americans believe to be creativity itself. But it is in *kaizen*, the refinement of creativity, that the Japanese excel. It is *kaizen* which they have traditionally added to products created in the West.

But what is of principal interest here is that the entire process is conceived of as a developmental helix spiraling upward to ever greater enlightenment.[12] From this we can infer that creativity is the work of several group members, those who recycle, those who search, those who nurture the appropriate culture (often in bars and restaurants after work), those who make the breakthrough synthesis, and those who streamline, improve, and complete the product so that it is ready for the customer. The cybernetic loops in which all elements, and hence all group members, are integrated also encompasses creativity within innovation.

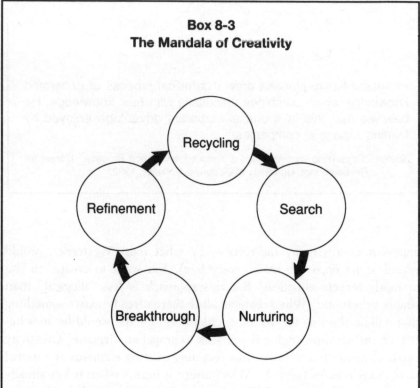

Box 8-3
The Mandala of Creativity

Sheridan Tatsumo's five-part cycle of Japanese creativity, based in Japanese folk arts such as wood carving, bonsai, rock gardens, flower arrangement (*ikebena*), paper folding (*origami*), folding fans (*sensu*) and hand-sewn juggling balls (*otedama*). The circle is self-transforming and developmental.

In cybernetic thinking, every element is both a cause and an effect, both antecedent and precedent. Every person in the circle is both subject and object, and there are as many polyocular ways of perceiving as there are elements in the group. Everyone's views of quality, creativity, and values inherent in a product are potentially important. No variable is independent. All are interdependent. Development is a process of mutual, helical empowerment, a process that imitates the building blocks of living nature. This helps to explain the frequent assertion that Japanese are incrementalists, taking many "small steps," that their major concern and target of investment appears to be in process as opposed to product, which is endlessly elaborated and improved. All these insights are consistent with continuous circular iterations.[13]

The Race for Knowledge-Intensive Enterprise

A fundamental principle of classical economics is that human wants are "value empty" and largely irrational, in the sense of being relative, subjective, inaccessible, and mere matters of taste. Why customers prefer tea or coffee is no concern of the economist. That they prefer one or the other will show up as a pattern of demand. Not until they have made their choices is there any reason to value coffee or tea more highly, and after they have chosen, the value of both commodities is their price. Lord Robbins, the British economist, put it plainly:

> So far as we (economists) are concerned, our economic subjects can be pure egotists, pure altruists, pure ascetics, pure sensualists. . . . Our deductions do not provide any justification for saying that caviar is an economic good and carrion a disutility. . . . Individual valuations are outside the sphere of economic uniformity. . . . From the point of view of economic analysis, these things constitute the irrational element in our universe of discourse.[14]

However, even Robbins's view is not quite value free. The economic actor must be able to "reckon the consequences" of spending that much on this pleasure, this much on that pleasure, or keeping the money in his pocket for later use. It is not an inspiring vision of human endowments and is not even adequate to our economic survival. The person is an alimentary canal with a calculating box above its mouth.

What this view fails to take into account is that producing and consuming certain products profoundly educates and changes all those involved. They are not the same people after their encounters with these products as they were before. Consider the design, development, and manufacture of a computer. The sheer volume of technical, intellectual, and social learning involved in such processes are incalculable. But the challenges do not end here. The computer needs to be distributed and sold to those who can realize the machine's full potential—or, rather, the full potential of their own minds and the accumulated experience of their companies acting through computers. Whole libraries of software must be transferred to those (and only those) who need'them and who know how to use them, along with the peripherals they need, all joined into a dense network of communications.

Simply to load customers with more than they can effectively utilize is an expensive mistake, while servicing ignorant and overburdened customers is a nightmare. In contrast, intelligent customers can dream up applications, create software, and discover potentials of which the supplier was even not aware.

All these levels of complexity are called *knowledge intensity*. Only economies with high levels of educational attainment, plus continuous learning on the job, are able to supply products with high educational contents while educating customers in their use.[15] And, of course, learning is progressive; the more you already know the easier it is to learn. The concept of "declining marginal utility" in economics, wherein more units of a particular product are worth marginally less to the purchaser, fails to take into account the nature of information and learning. We may be less inclined to consume a fourth cream cake, but the appetite for knowledge feeds upon itself, so that our tenth program could be more valuable than the nine previous ones.[16]

Knowledge is not given up in exchange for money in the same way as a cream cake. "You can't eat your cake and have it," but you *can* sell your knowledge and keep it. The knowledge revolution has destroyed many of the assumptions of scarcity that sustained the dismal science in its pecksniffery. As Romeo said to Juliet, "The more I give you the more I have." Knowledge, love, and growth defy the laws of entropy.

As if all this weren't enough, knowledge-intensive goods, that win buyers, typically command premium prices because the learning necessary to their supply is scarce.[17] Many nations can cut and shape leather to make shoes, but very few can supply computers to companies in ways that make these more productive and effective enterprises.

The same general principle applies to goods made internationally, such as automobiles. The design, the electronics, the automatic gearbox, and the high value-added, complex components will typically be made in Japan, and the assembly, hubcaps, seat cushions, and side mirrors are provided locally. The Japanese make sure that they learn faster than other communities.[18]

Even in joint ventures with U.S. companies, each culture gets what it wants. The problem lies in *what* Americans want. Robert Reich, writing in *The Harvard Business Review,* reveals the recurrent pattern. Americans supply the pure research and some of the invention and the marketing, the logo, and distribution. The Japanese supply the applied research, development, and manufacture—sometimes letting Americans assemble.[19] The Japanese contribution is a seamless whole, a body of accumulated learning that extends from applied research through development to complex manufacture, in which thousands of people learn an interlocking set of sophisticated procedures.

The American side of those joint ventures is as split and hollow as the Japanese side is integral. The Americans choose the "bread" on the top and bottom of a very nutritious sandwich. The pure science and the invention are typically American, but the process if patented can be imitated, and if developed with the help of university funds is often in the public realm anyway. On the bottom of the sandwich, Americans typically do the marketing and use their logo, thereby putting a domestic face on foreign goods and negotiating with their own culture, which the Japanese still find mysterious. And, of course, the American partner often enjoys good profits.

But what will happen after the joint venture has run its course? Will the Japanese still need a domestic face or will they drop their distributor, as Nissan recently dropped Nissan UK? Whatever they choose to do they will have learned more during their "marriage" with their Western partners than the partners learned, and they will have come out of it with the rarest and most valuable skills.[20]

The conclusion to be drawn here is that classical economics is simply mistaken in claiming that consumers alone confer value on products. Products have a greater or less potential to educate and to delight, which can be estimated before consumers choose, and which is either confirmed or negated by those consumers. What you do through a policy of deliberately increasing knowledge intensity is to raise the social stakes. You now have greater power to satisfy or dissatisfy, but where the level of consumer satisfaction remains constant, you will probably have added more value than before and left the members of your community better informed.

Simple manufacturers tend to get caught in the "low-wage trap." If you stick with making cheap footwear, then you cannot afford to pay

American workers more than comparable workers in Mexico and Brazil. The better education and training of American workers has to find its way into what they make in order to make their educations affordable by the economy. Only products that use and sell knowledge can pay back to their society the costs of educating citizens. Indeed, there is a case for arguing that simple manufactures should be phased out and purchased from abroad, thereby releasing employees for more intelligent and developmental opportunities.[21]

The failure to phase out soul-destroying work and substitute more challenging opportunities risks turning a whole generation of young people against business per se. This appears to have happened in the late 1960s and 1970s to American's baby-boom "radicals." At precisely the time that the Japanese economy was growing at 8 to 10 percent per annum, students in North America and much of Western Europe withdrew their allegiance from commerce en masse, most especially the members of elite educational institutions, in favor of the social challenges described by Presidents Kennedy and Johnson. What this "decade of disgust" cost the economy is still to be calculated, since those who dropped out might now be leading major corporations. Today business is back in fashion, but the damage is done.

Does industrial policy distort market forces? Not if this intervention takes place before competition has even started. Every company in every economy must decide which domestic and/or international contests to enter, and no one enters every field of commercial endeavor. What the Japanese government has decided as one of its several "logics of community" is that entering "high-knowledge" contests will develop more of its people. This decision is made before the market mechanism is even encountered. This has nothing to do, then, with antimarket policies. It is simply a choice to engage markets at higher levels of sophistication and to win or lose the more educative challenges. The Japanese government does not favor one computer manufacturer over another, for instance, Toshiba over Hitachi, but it does favor computers over flashlights or HDTV over radios. Within the computer and HDTV industries competition remains intense and market forces prevail.

Indeed, far from opposing market forces, knowledge-intensifying national or corporate strategy may be said to anticipate them. Low-knowledge manufacturing is going to gravitate to low-wage economies anyway, so why not abandon such activities before painful retrenchment and eventual bankruptcies are forced upon you? In the end, which government intervenes the least—the Japanese government that "advises" on the phasing out of low-skilled jobs, or the U.S. government that does nothing until the industries concerned are desperate, puts them on its "injured industries" list, and by invoking the myth of "voluntary restraints" by Japanese exporters then fights a desperate rearguard action against the force and logic of the market? Even where such historic preservation is successful, all that has been saved is a pocket of low-wage business in which the community must either accept an emiserating wage or see its jobs go overseas.[22]

That Japan and the Pacific Rim economies have been thinking in terms of upgrading the knowledge intensity within their product portfolios is revealed in research conducted by Bruce Scott at the Harvard Business School. He first rank ordered twenty-six different industries according to the "knowledge content" of their industry. This he defined as the ratio of R&D to total product costs. He then estimated gains and losses for all categories, to show that while Japan and the Pacific Rim countries were gaining in categories with high knowledge content, the United States was losing in these categories, but gaining in low-knowledge sectors.[23]

This situation is now aggravated for the United States by the decline in defense expenditures, the only legitimate avenue for funneling government resources into high tech. Unless something is done, America's edge in high-knowledge goods will continue to erode.

In fact, Scott's calculations underestimate the Asian gains in knowledge intensity. This is because considerable upgrading occurs within categories. Japan does not entirely abandon textiles, but turns to specialized carpeting and ultra-suede. It does not abandon ships, but builds trawlers that can fish, process, preserve, and export their catch in a single journey. Scott also ignores knowledge in the form of aesthetics and design. Cloth may be woven in Sri Lanka, but it is fashioned in Japan. Moreover, Japan invests in R&D in categories considered to be of low-knowledge intensity by the rest of the world, for example, in construction, where Japanese R&D is 1 percent of sales.

Western economies, observes Scott, are still in thrall to Ricardo's theory of natural advantage, by which Britain exchanges wool and cloth from its damp meadowlands in exchange for port wine from the sunnier vineyards of Portugal. But is it really learned advantage that explains even Britain's skill at turning wool to textiles in the nineteenth century, and explains Japan's rise today?[24]

Knowledge intensity is not simply a clever way of getting a premium price for rarer products and educating society in the process. If this were all there was to it, Japan would be getting higher margins for its goods, and of this there is no evidence. The advantages of knowledge intensity are more subtle. The higher the knowledge intensity of goods, the greater are the connections between these and related products, and the faster knowledge circulates. The mastery of, for example, microelectronics or materials science, enables you to supply hundreds of related applications. The knowledge revolution gives the advantage to those with closer social bonds.

The Drive for Market Share

There is perhaps no sharper contrast between Japan and the United States than the emphasis put on a corporation's market share by Japanese culture and that put on profits, earnings-per-share, or return on investment in U.S. culture. While the return earned by the individual shareholder is the quintessence of American and Western individualism, what the corporation has done for the society and its community is captured in the idea of market share and is the quintessence of Japanese communitarianism. [25]

Of course, both are important measures of performance. You would have to be mentally deficient not to grasp that a falling market is going to cripple your profitability before long. Hence, American managers watch market shares carefully. You would also have to be stupid to believe that you can stay in business long-term without profiting. If you counted the number of times the words *team*, *group*, or *close to customer* appear in American journals, you might think Americans were converted to communitarianism. The point we are trying to make is about means and ends. Where gains in market share are a mere means to profitability, the nation remains individualistic. The team is merely a vehicle for the self-interest of individuals. The corporation is a public convenience, abandoned as soon as it proves inconvenient or unprofitable. Where individual profitability is a means to increasing market share, as in Japan, the nation remains communitarian. The prime purpose of business is to benefit society. Profitability is a necessary condition.

Which is the better measure of success, profitability or market share? The advantages of market share, which Japanese newspapers avidly report, are several. Market share measures what has been put into a relationship, while profitability measures what has been taken out. Market share faces outward to the society, while profitability faces inward toward owners. In market share calculations the customers are ends in themselves, strategists like you, with reconcilable aims. In profit calculations customers are means to your own ends, persons to be served only if there is a percentage in it for you. Most customers will understand that before long!

There is also a case for arguing that customers should have priority in any temporal sequence of events. One has to satisfy one's market prior to the realization of profits. Any profits are but a consequence of satisfying customers first. It follows that while profits follow readily upon customer satisfaction, the reverse proposition is less persuasive. Customer satisfaction will not necessarily follow from profits. Indeed, profits can beguile and preoccupy the recipient, who may cash in his chips and shift from production or inventing to consuming.

Market share, or customer satisfaction, is also a quicker signaling system. Any changes in the environment show up first in shifting customer needs, but may start to affect profits only later. Those concerned with profits may realize too late and respond too slowly. Listening to customers' needs can facilitate long-term strategies. In what they call "latent need analysis," Japanese corporations sit down with their customers to project technological advances and recent scientific breakthroughs into the future. Does the customer wish to install sensors in all the main bearings of his machinery, given the catastrophic impact when these bearings fail? If it will take three years to develop such sensors to the required specifications, would the customer want them? Such deliberations look several years ahead, while profitability is usually concerned with the present quarterly reports.[26]

Market share is also a better gateway to learning. The more the volume throughput and the greater the variety of customer needs that are satisfied, the faster the organization learns to improve quality and lower its costs. A narrow, yet profitable, niche gives few such opportunities. Those who would win a learning race need the largest possible share of the market from which to learn.

Market share strategies are, of course, extremely dangerous where all competitors use them. You can bankrupt each other in short order and create a market in which no one is making a living. Such a situation is, however, more feared by individualistic profit-oriented cultures like America than by communitarian customer-benefiting cultures. Market share strategies really pay off when your competitor is trying to maximize profits, because the cost squeeze causes profits to disappear for the U.S. corporation, but market share to increase for the Japanese corporation, as each tries to match each other's price cuts. The former will see itself

---

Box 8-4

How the Japanese Won the Battle for VCRs

The videocassette recorder was first developed by Ampex in the United States and shortly thereafter by RCA and Philips of Eindhoven in the Netherlands. But as with most breakthrough products, these were seen as high-margin niche products for industrial and professional application in broadcasting studios. The strategy was to reap the rewards of innovation before others caught up, and the product was priced at over $1,500 to maximize profits.

The Japanese strategy was to look for a massively enlarged market of ordinary consumers. Thus companies like Victor, Sharp, and Sony-Betamax aimed for the consumer electronics market and a price below $500 (now below $250). What was needed was *kaizen*, the development and refinement of a low-cost reliable product. The authors of *Made in America* comment:

> One key factor in Japanese success was superior engineering. Another was the willingness to invest heavily in both product development and process development for more than two decades while cash returns were low and growing only very slowly. American industry proved much less ready to do this. Over the same period many American firms were actually retreating from consumer-electronics markets, progressively ceding products and functions to foreign competitors and diversifying into less risky and more profitable businesses such as car rentals and financial services, unrelated to their original line of work. . . . We think we have detected a systematic unwillingness or inability of U.S. companies to "stick to their knitting" and maintain technological leadership after the first big returns have been captured. They thereby allow longer-winded companies, most notably Japanese firms, to take over technological preeminence and market share. This is a particularly disturbing phenomenon.

There was a sad sequel. Ampex, who had pioneered the product but had failed to commercialize it for consumers, now finds it niche market for sophisticated studio equipment eroding, as Japanese competitors, using the cost savings from their high-volume business, systematically underprice it. It is more strategically effective to go for broadened markets first and then mop up the high-margin niches, than to go for profitable niches initially.

Source: Made in America: Regaining the Productive Edge, MIT Commission on Industrial Productivity. Cambridge, Mass.: MIT Press, 1989.

as failing according to its prime value of profit maximization, while the latter sees itself as succeeding according to its prime value of satisfying more customers. Hence, Americans are more likely to withdraw, and the Japanese to stay in.

A market share strategy is also more resilient than a profit-maximizing one, since with the former you have the larger number of customers on your side, with a genuine interest in your survival. If things start to go wrong customers can tell you in great detail when, why, and how long you have to set matters right. Since you thought first of them when you were riding high, they will think first of you when things start to go awry and give you ample opportunity to redeem yourself.

Going for market share and using the increased volume to reduce costs and prices is also a strategy that discourages other entrants to the market. They see your large share, low costs, and slim margins and let you alone. In contrast, profit-maximizing strategies attract competitors who, seeking to share the easy pickings, rush in to supply lower-cost variants of your premium product. Within a few years, even innovative Western corporations see their margins eroding, and this trend is increasing. Recent examples include what has happened to mobile phones and medical imaging technologies.

This trend leads to a recognizable pattern of events that has repeated itself across industries. American companies innovate and seek high profit margins as a reward for their creativity. Yet their seasons in the sun grow shorter, since as markets mature the Japanese strike back with massive market-expanding price cuts and *kaizen* (refinements) to the original product, with many customized variations.

It is probably the case that most American corporations cannot afford "suicidal" fights for market share, with profits at best postponed and at worst vanished. Equity shareholders will not support them. Pension fund managers want their dividends this quarter. Because high-knowledge-intensity products are not seen as inherently more valuable to the community, they are not seen as worth sacrificing profits for. Americans lack a strategic calculus against which profits might be traded off. The result is that they increasingly profit in areas where the Japanese permit this, areas of low societal significance. North American and British economies lack the industrial banking sectors of Japan, Germany, France, Sweden, and Holland, who might support their customers in a long, profit-starved contest. For, while you can trade off profitability for increased market share, it is rarely as effective to trade off market share against increased profitability. The retreat into profitable niches is too often the beginning of the end. These strategies met and fought it out in the market for VCRs, when RCA and Philips confronted Victor, Sharp, Sony, et al. The victory of the market expanders over the profit maximizers is described in Box 8-4.

The *Kaisha* as a Community

Several commentators have observed that the *kaisha*, or Japanese corporation, is based on the model of a community, while the model of the corporation inherited from Anglo-American tradition is of a legal-contractual arrangement between individual shareholders and the corporation also conceived of as an "individual." It follows that U.S. corporations are owned legally by those who are not members of the corporate community, who have rights over that community, including the right to sell to someone who will break it up and divest its assets.[27]

Although both individuals and communities learn, communities learn in ways additional to the learning of each member as a person. We know what is contained within our heads, but the person is not the only "container." Knowledge accumulates massively within the corporation as a community in its libraries, software, research laboratories, reports, and shared social experience. The culture of the corporation is a knowledge carrier. Consider a group of persons who meet as strangers but then settle down to work successfully as a group. There is the knowledge that each has gained from his or her journey through life and the knowledge each has gained about other group members and the challenges they have faced together. It is this latter knowledge about who-plays-what-role-best-in-team-relations that becomes the property of a community and can be successfully deployed and refined only when the community stays together. Break up the group and "Bob's creative relationship with Andy" is gone forever, as is their developing mutuality. All knowledge about social relationships in particular groups are dependent on those groups surviving and relationships remaining stable over time. Hence, the dilemma we posed in Chapter 3, and whose results were reported in Table 3-3, concerning the length of time employees planned to stay with a company, assumes major importance. Without stable relationships, social knowledge about the mutual capacities of members of a culture cannot accumulate. With stable relationships, the cultures of corporations learn to meet challenges and grow from strength to strength.

Community-type relationships are not confined to the *kaisha* but may join the whole cluster of bank, company, customers, suppliers, partners, and cross-shareholders. Generally speaking, investment policies can be no wiser than the quality of information shared. In-depth knowledge by a lender-shareholder with a stake in your development is generally superior to that revealed by annual reports to shareholders.

While Western shareholders are often ignorant of the companies in which their shares are held, may not hold those shares for long, and may employ a fund manager, there is still a legal right to dispose of one's property or say how it should be run. Those owning a sufficient number of shares can throw their weight about, remove the CEO, sell, merge, or take the company over.

We are not clear as to what extent these rights exist in Japan, but they are very rarely exercised. It is unacceptable for outside individuals to exercise controlling powers over ongoing communities. For this reason, shareholders are not permitted to interfere in the day-to-day running of the corporation, save as communities of customers, suppliers, or investors making their concerns known. Hostile takeovers are almost unheard of. In any event, shares in major export companies are usually held for growth and appreciation rather than for dividends, another factor allowing the *kaisha* to wait out its foreign rivals in a profit squeeze.

Much of this applies to the strategic core of Japanese industry, its export champions. Surrounding this core is a broad periphery of equity trading, much of it seriously collapsed of late, with speculative bubbles and a rash of bad debts. Soaring land values, now much depressed, and the relatively marginal position of the Japanese equity holder have added to the volatility of the markets. Much to its regret, Japan bowed to American pressure to deregulate its financial markets and has suffered as a consequence. Yet this only emphasizes what Japanese executives value, community, stability, and endurance, as well as what they find unattractive and perilous, the speculative fever of loose money and personal enrichment. The volatility at the periphery only consolidates the stability at the core. Many flies buzz around the Japanese economy's wealth, but they are not *of* it. They are attracted by its success and may not survive the summer. Their fate reinforces community and renews the determination to forgo profits where necessary. The priorities of Wall Street and the City of London are quite different. The shareholders they represent will not agree to forgo profits, even temporarily, and will abandon en masse those corporations who do not keep up payments, often starving key technologies in the process.[28] Business in this view exists not primarily for the sake of employees serving customers, but for what individual owners can extract. James C. Abegglen and George Stalk, of the Boston Consulting Group's Tokyo office, point out that factional strife in Western societies often uses the corporation as a mere means to individual gain:

> The company becomes a vehicle for profit optimization or, at worst, profit maximization. . . . Not surprisingly, then, lower-ranking employees, especially as represented by their trade unions, also seek to optimize and, in fact, seek to maximize their share of current earnings. In this process, the company becomes an organization external to the interests of its members, to be used to further their earnings advantage to the maximum.[29]

This instrumental attitude to the corporation fails to evoke as deep commitments and as close personal ties as does working for a community with a mission to serve customers. This is because customers are encountered face-to-face and share your enthusiasm for expanding the values of the product for each of you. There are natural bonds of interest and affection between a community of suppliers and a community of users. In the case of complex products, these will typically extend the nervous systems of makers and customers alike. These are connections to grow with.

In contrast, the alleged bond between corporation and shareholders is a legal fiction, while American commentators have themselves poured scorn on "the myth of shareholder democracy."[30] At the most, disgruntled shareholders can get some publicity. They are easily and routinely outvoted by proxies, persons not even present but prepared to maximize profits, no matter what anyone has to say.

The attempt to refurbish the shareholder-company relationship into a sacred trust typically fails to impress employees. Shareholders are widely scattered and anonymous and may hold their shares only briefly and for speculative reasons. Many, if not most, shareholders do not even know in what companies their funds are invested, since they have left that decision to insurance companies, pension funds, unit trusts, and a variety of professional investors. In the absence of such knowledge, why should they care? Shareholders are typically faceless aggregates until one or more of them tries to take you over or "greenmail" you.

In such circumstances, pious utterances about "working for shareholders" and "representing them" in the corporation, strike most employees with a less than lyrical note. Top managers claiming to act for shareholders is generally experiences as a power tactic by those resisting wage claims.[31] Its moral appeal brings only modified lumps to their throats. Employee enthusiasm for dedicating their lives to anonymous lenders of money is somewhat muted, whereas it is possible to derive a genuine pride from the fact that your air bags stop several hundred children a year from being hurled against windshields. As your market share expands you find yourself working for your community, your society and your nation. Your work is a gift to your culture, as opposed to a means to pay returns to someone unknown to you.

The M-form Organization and the Keiretsu

Strategies that challenge close communities to fight for increased market shares are also valuable in encouraging corporations "to stick to their knitting" and increase the skeins of learning around their key technologies and distinctive competencies.[32] By getting larger and larger shares of the market for, say, fax machines or copiers, your stakes in those technologies increase. But profit-maximizing strategies will frequently divert you. Faced by a Japanese competitor who has taken the profit out of copiers, video recorders, or fax machines, American companies will diversify into more profitable fields—film, finance, or insurance—even where these are unrelated to their core competence, and thereby lose their "technological integrity."[33]

Bill Ouchi, the Japanese-American academic, has, in a book of the same name, called Japan *The M-form Society* because of the preference of its corporations to form multidivisional companies around a technological core. They typically share in the research, development, and manufacture of, for instance, microelectronic components and then use multiple divisions to reach various markets. Matsushita, for example, has divisions of consumer electronics, industrial equipment, business machines, home appliances, lighting equipment, system products (e.g., broadcasting), and electronic components.[34] This shared technological base makes possible what Ouchi calls a clan culture, a tightly knit group of electronics enthusiasts.[35] Relationships in such a group are very close, subtle, intimate, and long-term, as befits the communication of highly complex knowledge. This central "learning core" feeds numerous applications. Well-known Japanese M-forms include Honda, Hitachi, Nippon Electric, Toshiba, Sharp, Sony, Fujitsu, Matsushita, and Mitsubishi.

Western corporations also have their M-forms—IBM, Philips, ICI, DEC, Apple, etc.—but an even more common type is the H-form (holding company), better known as a conglomerate. This structure is very much the creature of individualized profit maximization; examples include ITT, Hanson Trust, Baldwin United, the Continentals Group, RCA, Sears Roebuck, Federal Industries, etc. The MIT Commission on Industrial Productivity has traced the collapse of the American machine tool industry to its ownership by major conglomerates.[36] The units in such portfolios do not share any common technological or informational core of learning, but rather compete with all other units for the investment funds held by the holding company, thus creating an "internal market" that allows each unit to succeed or fail by dint of its own efforts. Ouchi describes the culture of H-form as a market, with the exception of headquarters itself, which is a bureaucracy, judging each of its business units according to abstract legal and performance indicators, such as return on investment and earnings per share.

While information both codified and personal flows easily throughout the clan culture of the M-form, only "thin" codified information, mostly numbers, is the currency of the market culture of the H-form. Wishing to be left alone, each unit typically issues only that information about itself that is legally mandated. Moreover, the units within the H-form have in common only rules and money.[37] Inevitably, lawyers and accountants rise to the top while the expertise of engineers and marketers is strictly local.[38] The H-form rarely has a vision—save making money—since no other generalizations can be made about two hundred businesses in different fields. No logic of communal ethic binds them. Each seeks to outbid others for investment funds.

Oliver Williamson, the Yale economist, has argued that M-forms have lower transaction costs than H-forms.[39] Exchanging superficial information is expensive. Communicating in-depth about shared enthusiasms is cheaper. Opportunistic behaviors, bluff, deception, "liar's poker," and insider dealing are costs to the community, despite enriching individual malefactors. Authentic and sharing behaviors benefit the whole society.

Williamson's view would seem to be supported by the fact that businesses of lower knowledge intensity are more usually found in H-form organizations, while electronics, space, defense, and telecommunications are dominated by M-forms. It follows then that the M-form, Japan's preferred organization structure, is better adapted to a knowledge-intensifying strategy.[40]

But Japan's major corporations have an additional communal advantage. Most of them belonging to a *keiretsu* or "economic grouping," organized around banks or trading companies.[41] These are based on traditional trading companies, or *zaibatsu*, part of the mercantilist stage of economic development, suppressed but not eliminated by the American postwar occupation. Several of these groupings are centuries old. Not only does the bank own shares in all the members of the *keiretsu*, but each member has extensive cross-holdings of other members' shares.

Where organized around a trading company, the *Keiretsu* imports raw materials at the lowest cost, to the members' advantage. Unlike conglomerates, *keiretsus* are designed on principles of reciprocity and complementarity. Typical of these is the Sumitomo Group. Others include Mitsui, Mitsubishi, Sanwa, Fuyo, and Dai Ichi Kangyo. The Sumitomo Group has sales of over $400 billion, nearly four times the size of General Motors. These groups make joint approaches to government, to universities, and to foreign countries. They set up joint information and research agencies, e.g., the Mitsubishi Communications Study Committee, the Japan Society (located in New York and funded by Sumitomo), the Mitsui Information Systems Council, and the Fuyo Information Center.

A mystery to many Westerners is why these groupings do not collude as did American nineteenth-century trusts and as monopoly or oligopoly suppliers still do. One reason is that members are not maximizing the self-interest of each business unit, but combining together to capture market share, a strategy that may require "the front line" company, say, Mazda, to offer the lowest prices and highest quality available. Companies in a *keiretsu* buy from and supply each other, but they know from market intelligence what comparable prices and qualities are on the outside, and they demand from each other standards better than, or equal to, those available in the marketplace. If a company, although given fair warnings, cannot meet those standards, it will probably be reorganized. In the meantime, supplies will be obtained from outside the *keiretsu*, until the situation is remedied. Multiple pressures are exerted on underperformers.

Because they can pool and move their funds within the group, the company that faces off against its American competitors usually has the resources of the whole group to call on. Resources move toward any unit engaging foreigners, so it isn't Mazda versus Chrysler, as much as Chrysler versus the available resources of the Sumitomo group acting *through* Mazda. It is also impossible for Americans to discover what Mazda's "real costs" are, as opposed to the prices at which it is being supplied by member companies, who may be seeking to give it an advantage. Just as Japanese consumers seem willing to help their corporation by paying more for domestic products than foreigners pay in countries to which these products are exported, so members of a *keiretsu* may be willing to earn less profit in order to help their exporting members. This is in the interests of the national community and of the *keiretsu* as a whole. The logics of community seek constantly to better markets. The *keiretsu*, drawing on all its massive resources, will also fight for technologies regarded as strategically crucial to the future. Pushing Americans out of consumer electronics and photovoltaic cells, for example, means that Japan also gains the many derivatives extending into the future. Each *keiretsu* is a microcosm of the larger economy, a whole within the whole. As in the "diamond sutra," each jewel in the bracelet has facets that reflect the entire bracelet, yet each is also a separate stone.

Cooperative Technologies: The Tools That Make the Tools

Why do M forms and *keiretsu* members fight so long and so fiercely for certain technologies, often making huge demands on the resources of the whole group? What makes them so sure that the sacrifice is worthwhile, and why do they not bleed themselves dry in making wrong guesses about what consumers buy?

Among the major criticisms of Japanese practice by American commentators, is the oft-leveled accusation that the Japanese "pick winners" from among their businesses, deciding that, for instance, metal ceramics will be favored by government assistance and secret subsidy, but not some other industry or line of products. This smacks of arbitrariness and favoritism. Worse, the government appears to be abrogating to itself a choice that only markets can make. Granted the quality of graduates from Tokyo University who enter the Japanese civil service, they are still far from being omniscient. No one is so wise before an event, and even if anyone were, it would be unconscionable to bias the outcome of a fair contest. Just as Japan tilts the table in its own domestic contests, it tries perpetually to move the goal posts when competing with Americans, a habit that has convinced at least one commentator of "the Japanese conspiracy."[42]

Were the accusation about "picking winners in advance" true, then presumably Americans would reap the advantage of fair and genuine contests, while Japanese corporations would suffer all the disadvantages and discouragement of contests whose outcomes have been fixed in advance by corrupted umpires. The West would not need to complain, but only watch the mediocrity and political string-pulling spread. But, of course, Japan does not pick winners. It picks teachers, key technologies such as microchips, whose brains will spread most diffusely through the economy. Japanese culture has a logic of community that asks, "Which are the technologies whose contribution to other technologies, to people in general, and to the economic infrastructure as a whole, will do most to develop these?" An economy must be seeded with millions of microchips if the systems utilizing such chips are to find acceptance with customers.

Let us consider briefly six technologies that the Japanese government has targeted: steel, metal ceramics; number-controlled machine tools; electronics, semiconductors and microchips; robots; and pollution-control technology. What do they all have in common? Because Americans tend to view capitalism as something akin to a demolition derby, with rival machines racing around a track disabling one another by calculated collisions, they fail to notice that certain key technologies, let us call them "meta-technologies," i.e., technologies which are about technology in general and contribute significantly to the success of a majority of all other businesses. If your steel is of better quality and lower cost, everything made from steel will benefit, and when America protects specialty steels, as Reagan did, all U.S. businesses that fabricate steel products suffer higher costs.[43] The same logic applies to ceramic metals. Bereft of iron ore and badly polluted, Japan must import the raw materials for steel making. Metal ceramics would not only reduce the need for these imports, they promise a miniaturization of engines and heat-conserving properties which make possible a 200-miles-per-gallon automobile and would render every conventional engine obsolete and fuel inefficient. Thousands of Japanese businesses could then produce engines of a quality that devastated their foreign competitors. Oil import bills could be cut by two-thirds.

A similar logic guides the special emphasis on machine tools. These are the tools that make the tools. Upon the quality of machine tools depends the quality of tooling in Japanese factories generally, and the quality of the components in a product. To have the best machine tools is an inestimable advantage. But number-controlled machine tools have an even greater importance: these are machine tools with an electronic keyboard on which the exact dimensions of the next job of cutting, milling, boring, or lathing is speedily entered. This has the effect of greatly speeding up the process of tool changing, which, in turn, is the heart of flexible manufacturing. With number-controlled machine tools Japanese factories can produce an astonishing variety of goods aimed at small market niches. The cost is comparable to that for long manufacturing runs of the traditional factory, where tool changes took hours or days and raised the costs considerably.[44]

As markets mature, they typically spread into hundreds of subcategories or niches in which buyers demand customized goods, and it is vital to push the economic order quantities as far down as possible—ideally to one—so that every customer gets a product tailored to his or her special needs. Number-controlled machine tools make possible for thousands of companies this entire production and marketing strategy. Honda reportedly makes three varieties of motor scooter for the unmarried Japanese female commuter in her early twenties![45]

Electronics, semiconductors, and microchips are all important to the Japanese for a variety of reasons. They embody miniaturization in a country desperately short of space and even shorter of habitable space. They represent light as opposed to heavy industry and, barring the acid used to etch silicon chips, are relatively nonpolluting. To say that these components are knowledge intensive is an understatement. They literally insert tiny brains into physical products to make these extensions of human purpose. For a culture that has long regarded physical nature as animate and dynamic, microchips enliven the world of manufactured objects. If your Honda automobile is in a crash, semiconductors inflate air bags, unlock doors to that rescuers can reach you, smother the engine in fire-fighting foam, and signal the rescue services. If your car hits water, the windows close automatically and oxygen is released to keep you afloat. No wonder the Japanese call microchips "the rice of industry," feeding competitive advantage into every object with a mind of its own.

Robots are, similarly, tools that make products with the power to revolutionize manufacturing throughout Japan. Two problems slow the installment and use of robots. They are expensive for small or medium-sized producers. They are updated and improved so rapidly that the temptation is always to wait a bit longer for the best, yet even the best is so soon surmounted that you have paid dearly for an already obsolescent robot.[46]

To solve this problem, the Japanese government agreed to buy the output of robot producers and lease robots to manufacturers, replacing these as soon as they were obsolete. While America now has leasing companies entering its markets also, the lead provided by the Japanese government's leasing arrangement led to an accelerated takeoff, so that Japan's robotization still runs far ahead of America's (see Table 8-1).

Table 8-1   Industrial Robots by Country

	1987	1990
Japan	64,600	150,000
United States	13,000	33,000
Germany	6,600	17,700
Italy	2,700	10,300
France	3,380	10,200
United Kingdom	2,623	5,600
Sweden	2,400	5,034
Spain	1,516	3,042
Belgium/Luxembourg	1,860	2,900
Australia	1,300	2,000
Netherlands	930	1,200
Switzerland	850	1,010
Taiwan	750	980
Austria	700	965

European Management Foundation, *Reports on International Competitiveness* (now *IMD Reports*) Geneva: Switzerland

Finally, pollution-control technology is a precondition for the sustainable development of technologies in general. Unless we control pollution, industrialization will lead not to wealth, but "illth." Pollution-control technology "teaches" other technologies how to clean themselves up. Japan, a string of small volcanic islands, is going to reach the limits of sustainable development before other nations with more space.

The Cooperative Mimicry of Markets

Japan, together with Germany, France, Sweden, and Holland (to be discussed in later chapters) all "came from behind." They saw what market forces had done in Britain and the United States, but they wanted a shortcut to the same achievements. The logics of community described in this chapter are not designed as a war against markets, as was communist collectivism. What is happening is far more subtle. These logics are designed to mimic and gradually replace the classical markets of Western economies. They do this by substituting close relationships of mutuality and the skilled processing of complex information for superficial relationships of exchange and competition, with limited information capacity, which characterize behavior in markets.

As Robert Axelrod has argued in *The Evolution of Cooperation*, the development of capitalism is really a function of evolving cooperation, which spreads outward, pushing competition to its own boundaries. In early capitalism, individuals vied with individuals to serve customers. Early in this century competition was largely between companies, within which employees were expected to cooperate. The area of legitimized cooperation was spreading. By late in the century, wealth was not created within individual companies so much as among networks of cooperating companies, known as clusters or value-added chains. A highly developed version of this is the Japanese *keiretsu*.

Members within these clusters cooperate to match or to exceed standards of quality and cost available in the world marketplace. If any member falls beneath these standards, then other members immediately advise him of this discrepancy and he receives information, advice, and assistance from other members, designed to effect urgent improvement. In this way, the competitive standards symbolized by the United States are surpassed by cooperative substitutes forged by Japan. The calculus is that you will learn more quickly and accurately among friends than among contestants, although contestants still represent the benchmarks you aim to surpass.

9

Will the German Model of Capitalism Sweep Europe?

We are all Germans. . . . The whole EEC is obtaining German virtue—low inflation, a strong currency and a good mix of growth and social welfare.
                              Peter Ludlow, Director of the Center for
                              European Policy Studies, Brussels

THE IMPORTANCE of Germany's business culture and the logics of its wealth creation have, suddenly and quite recently, shot to the head of the international agenda. We have seen the Berlin Wall collapse, Germany reunified, Britain isolated eleven-to-one by a German-led majority of EEC nations at Maastricht, and the collapse of the Soviet Union. All these events either strengthen Germany or exemplify her new influence, or both. She is now by far the largest economy in the EEC. As the former German Democratic Republic raises its productivity and living standards, it will be seized upon by formerly Communist states and Soviet republics. IBM has estimated that the computer market in the old GDR *alone* will be worth $20 billion by the year 2000 and has entered a joint venture with the German electronics company, Siemens, to exploit this opportunity.

Of the three cultures of capitalism introduced so far, who can doubt that it is the "German model" that appeals most to the new Europe, rather than American or Japanese models? Indeed, the current development of Europe follows German experience in several respects. Like Europe, the German states first drew together through the customs union (*Zollverein*) with political union coming later, much as the Common Market is now yielding to greater political unity. Germany today exemplifies, within its borders, the federally decentralized structures most EEC members wish to see on a European scale. The hoped-for community bank, free of political pressures will be modeled on the *Bundesbank*. As Britain's marginalization at Maastricht shows, it is the *Soziale Markwirtschaft* (social market), complete with *Wirtschaftswunder* (economic miracle) to which nearly all EEC nations aspire.

The German economic fingerprint is substantially different from those of the United States and Japan. Germany and the United States are both highly universalistic, whereas Japan is particularistic. But on two other values, Germany has more in common with Japan than the United States. Where the United States is analytical, Germany is integrative. Where the United States is individualistic, Germany is communitarian. The combination of strong universalist, integrative, and communitarian values that Germans bring to their processes of wealth creation is manifested in a highly codified economic system in which the state and private enterprise cooperate in developing and regulating business activity to an extent unthinkable in the more individualistic cultures. In Germany many economic decisions are made at the meso-economic level where government, labor groups, financial groups, and industrial groups interact. This is a level of economic activity which barely exists in the United States and Britain, and which provides Germany with a clear competitive advantage.

German-style capitalism is not simply closer geographically to the ex-Communist world, it is also closer psychologically and ideologically. Certainly, Germany is in some peril politically. As the most eastern ramparts of the West, it is upon Germany's borders that a massive wave of refugees could fall, and chaos attendant on the breakup of the Soviet empire could spill over into Germany, triggering serious domestic disorders. The absorption of *Gastarbeiter* (guest workers) and *Ossis* (East Germans) has already caused disturbances.

But if Germany survives the shocks of being so close to the collapse of former communist states, she is also in the best position to extend the equivalent of the "Marshall Plan" to her eastern neighbors. What made the original Marshall Plan so successful was that *former industrial nations* had the cultural know-how to develop fast, given the means and the opportunities. Consider, for example, that West Germany reached her pre-war GNP level as early as 1950, barely five years after the war and two years after currency reform and the establishment of the Deutschmark. The Slavic nations of the former U.S.S.R., along with Hungary, Poland, Czechoslovakia, and the westerly Balkan states, were all developed economies prior to World War II. Their populations, 200 million in all, are mostly well educated and in many cases multilingual. The speed of their economic reconstruction could be breathtaking once it achieves momentum. Germany may now be due for the same kind of economic hegemony achieved by the United States from 1945 to 1965, before the Vietnam War polarized public opinion and set off inflationary trends. Today, the United States, with a deficit in her international balance of trade of $75 billion, is hardly in a position to finance the revival of Eastern Europe or any other region. Having spent $2 trillion on defense during the 1980s, America is seriously overstretched and deep in debt. Seen with the benefit of hindsight, the Evil Empire, against which America armed herself prodigiously, had all the menace of a Halloween costume. In any case, it is Germany who has the trade surpluses today, $20 billion in 1991, after her absorption of the GDR. Earlier trade surpluses ran at around $80 billion. "With that we can do a lot of things," a spokesman for the German Ministry of Economics told Daniel Burstein. The latter comments a shade too combatively: "The power to invest massive sums across borders is the equivalent of yesterday's ability to occupy countries militarily."

Japan, with a surplus of $90 billion is stronger still, but it is Germany who has unmatched influence in *Mitteleuropa*, while the *Drang nach Osten* (drive to the east) is a strategy much rehearsed historically.[1] In the last few months, Daimler-Benz, maker of Mercedes autos, announced a joint venture with Mitsubishi in an alliance designed to optimize electronic and mechanical engineering. One commentator remarked that the maker of the Zero fighter had joined with the maker of the Messerschmitt 109. As Russia and the United States withdraw from Europe, it is Germany who is filling the vacuum. To this end, Volkswagen has invested $3 billion in the takeover and conversion of East Germany's Trabant automobile plants. It has been estimated that former West Germany needs to grow at 1 percent GDP per year, simply to meet demand in her new eastern territories. The incorporation of these territories does not simply increase the supply of indigenous manpower, likened to the United States having a labor pool of several million New

Englanders, well educated and English speaking, but rescues Germany from its demographic squeeze. The ratio of older to working-age Germans was moving in a highly adverse direction before East Germany's much younger population joined the equation. Now 17 million "new" Germans will be requiring household appliances, automatic teller machines, and automobiles, while adding skills to the pool that generally exceed those of *Gastarbeiter* (guest workers).

Above all, Germany is a "good European." In a recent poll for *Süddeutsche Zeitung*, 17 percent of Germans wanted "a European federal state by the year 2000." Germany already contributes 53 percent of all intracommunity exports. The German mark is the de facto leading currency in the European Monetary System against which all other currencies measure their own worth.

Today the newly emancipated nations of the old Soviet empire look to Germany for advice and emulation. Bartold Witte of the German Foreign Ministry explained:

> This is not just because of centuries of cultural and linguistic relationships with Eastern Europe, it is because we Germans have built up a democracy after the catastrophe of totalitarianism. Germany's reformed capitalism offers a third way to those eager to put communism behind them but not prepared to accept the excesses of Anglo-U.S. liberalism.[2]

Germans, it seems, reciprocate this interest; while they still regard America as Germany's best friend, they aspire eastward. Asked by *Süddeutsche Zeitung* which country they sought "an especially good and close relationship" with, 59 percent of Germans said the (then) U.S.S.R., 42 percent said the United States, 36 percent said France, and 12 percent said the United Kingdom.[3]

We would submit, then, that the capitalist culture described in this chapter, taken with the Swedish, Dutch, and French varieties described in Chapters 10, 11, and 13 together constitute the thrust likely to be manifested by a broadened European community. The old Soviet empire, desperately searching for new directions, is likely to choose Germany as its mentor, since it too is "coming from behind," trying to catch up on the developmental potential of educated European cultures. What lessons are there for ex-Communists and the world in Germany's recent rise to major economic power?

Coming from Behind

Germany was late in industrializing, at least seventy-five years behind Britain, and thirty-five to fifty years behind the United States in setting up her first textile mills. Although the German states had begun to unify economically in 1832, the bourgeois revolutions of 1848, successful in much of Europe, failed in Germany. By midcentury, the German states were still largely feudal and backward economically. There had not, outside Prussia, emerged the kind of entrepreneurial class or capital markets that characterized Britain and the United States. The Franco-Prussian War and the defeat of France gave impetus to the creation of the German state, which came into existence in 1871. Thus, from the beginning, industrial power and German nationalism were joined. What business there was served the nation and contributed to its self-assertion.[4] Germany joined the race at the time of the "second" industrial revolution, that of steel and machinery making. Bismarck regarded such industry as crucial to Prussian, and later, German military strength. His policy of "the marriage of iron with rye" was aimed at transporting German agricultural produce by rail to feed his armies and to unite the nation. A desperate shortage of manpower required the mass migration of whole communities. Old feudal bonds were re-created with new masters. Bismarck banned the SPD (Social Democratic Party) when it tried to come to power in the 1870s, but he also blunted the party's appeal by providing one of the earliest forms of worker welfare. Productivity was asked for and given as a pledge to enhance the power of the new nation. In return, workers had their physical needs taken care of. After industrialization, Germany spurted economically, but foundered politically and militarily. She overtook Britain economically in the first decade of the twentieth century, only to face devastating defeat in 1918 and runaway inflation as a result of reparations and the reoccupation of the Rhur. A short recovery ensued before the Great Depression, and then another spurt before World War II and total devastation. Once again Germany came from behind, overtaking Britain in the early 1950s and leading the countries of the Common Market by the end of the decade, during which her economy grew by a massive 8 percent per annum—*Wirtschaftswunder* indeed.[5]

The strategy of "catch up" employed by Japan, Germany, Sweden, Holland, and France is profoundly different from the strategy of "innovate" and early industrialization employed by Britain and the United States. Both strategies are eminently logical, but designed to fit different circumstances. They contrast as follows:

	United Kingdom and United States	Germany and Japan
1. Time factor	Early Industrializers.	Late Industrializers.
2. Development strategy	Innovate across a broad front of entrepreneurship and management.	Catch up in technological sectors seen as the most valuable.
3. Historical role of governments	Generally ignorant of new business developments. Interfere after the fact to "reform" wealth creators, who have adversarial roles to regulators.	Generally informed about strengths of leading economies. Cooperate before the fact to facilitate industrialization, playing a constructive role.
4. Education	Extremely broad and generalist, with stress on pure science and management studies.	More focused on successful technologies and science applied to key sectors.
5. Economics	Divided between *macroeconomics* (the whole economy) and *microeconomics* (the individual firm).	Organized around *mesoeconomics* (the dynamics of particular industries and sectors).
6. Social Policies	Left behind in the leaps to innovate. Government may seek to reimpose social "burdens" on business retroactively.	Included in concerted efforts to industrialize. Government sees social benefits as key to winning popular consent.
7. Labor relations	Typically poor since catch-up countries put pressure on labor costs, leading to attempted wage cutting.	Typically good since catching up starts with lower wages, steadily increased as leading nations are overhauled.
8. Development philosophy	Laissez-faire, free-trade, and Anglo-American empiricism toward what markets demand, eschewing grand designs or "picked winners."	Managed competition, early protection, and teleology—a logic of ends—already accomplished by leading economies. Target key niches, "pick teachers."
9. Transition from feudalism	Slow and largely complete. Industry built on middle-class values of individualism and self-interest.	Rapid and partly unfinished. Industry built on collective concepts of feudal obligations and reciprocities.

	United Kingdom and United States	Germany and Japan
10. Approach to financing industry	Domination by shorter-term equity markets and risk-taking profit-oriented individuals with high uncertainty, limited knowledge, fleeting relations.	Domination by longer-term bank financing and lower-risk industry-oriented institutions with lower uncertainty, deeper knowledge, closer relations.

Germany shows in every respect the profile typical of a successful "late industrializer." The strategy consists of choosing from among the array of industries, applications, and products, those that promise greater national advantage and greater potentials for future development and "reengineering"—in cheaper refinements of the original. Existing industries in Britain and the United States are studied, codified, copied, and improved upon. Because the destination is known—say, a modern automobile industry—bankers, politicians, engineers, educators, and unions cooperate to imitate and then surpass their competitors, long-term. Because shareholders and innovators take fewer risks, they are less well rewarded. Because refinements and improvements need well-trained work forces, these are typically highly skilled and highly paid, with constructive industrial relations and productivity gains controlling inflation.

The central role of banking in this strategy can be judged by the fact that the *Deutsch Bank*, founded in 1870, predates the founding of the German nation[6] a year later. From the beginning of Germany's rise as an economic power, its industrial banks, often acting through industry associations, have been the principal source of financing, providing long-term, low-interest loans for technologies already operational in Britain and the United States. It is the strategy of the fast follower, systemizing the muddle of innovators and avoiding their errors.

Observing how market forces had operated in Britain and the United States, German industrial associations developed a "social mimicry" of this process. For example, patents are one way of rewarding inventors and innovators, but at the same time, patent protection also slows imitation and dissemination of new technology. Germany, and later Japan, shortened or abolished patent protection—something scarcely imaginable in the highly individualistic United States. For example, the VCI (Chemical Industries Association), founded in 1888, arranged for innovating companies to receive special rewards in exchange for the immediate dissemination of new technologies to all members, rather than allowing a period of patent protection. In this way development was accelerated. Banks can also influence the course of industrial development. By taking large minority holdings in several firms in an industry, banks are able to adopt a mesoeconomic, or "whole industry," stance toward economic development. This is a form of nongovernmental, sector-by-sector industrial policy by private institutions standing above interfirm rivalry and looking to the growth of the large industry.[7] Recently, Michael Porter has argued that economic development is less the achievement of single corporations than of clusters, the corporation, its bank, customers, suppliers, unions, and local training institutes. Even competitors are part of this cluster, because they force up standards and develop challenges that the industry as a whole must meet. If Porter is right, then Germany's mesoeconomic approach to the growth of whole industries is substantially vindicated.[8]

It is this knowledge of where they are heading that has made Germans less interested in Anglo-American empiricism, or *Zweckrationalismus*, literally sequential, means-ends rationality. Their preferred ideal is *Zielrationalismus*, reason drawn toward, and converging upon a target or purpose. This permits the confluence of many cooperating institutions upon existing technological achievements. The German existential theologian Paul Tillich made a similar distinction between the "technical reasoning" he saw as dominant in America, and "encompassing reason" which organized values in a synthesis designed for an envisaged end.[9] Clearly, the perilous process of summoning a whole group to converge upon an idealized end is safer if that achievement is already extant in Britain or America. But now Germany and her EEC partners are breaking new ground. The vision of a Federal Europe, of former proud and independent states, has not been accomplished before, and Great Britain, for one, resists being drawn toward this idealized destination. It may appeal to Germans, but the British seek the right to opt out at any point in a sequence of national decisions. The respective preferences are cultural and appeal quite differently to early and late industrializers.

A Rule for Everything

Germans live within universal codes of rules and laws, about which they are very nearly as enthusiastic as are Americans. In the dilemma, first discussed in Chapter 2, that describes a man having a beer with the safety engineer while an accident occurs, the German preferences for the rule of law and truthful witness are not significantly different from those of American managers. Americans are less enthusiastic about legality than Germans when it prevents a close friend from losing money. We posed the following dilemma:

You have just come from a secret meeting of a board of directors of a certain company. You have a close friend who will be ruined unless he can get out of the market before the board's decision becomes known. You happen to be having dinner at your friend's home this evening. What right does your friend have to expect you to tip him off?

The question pits the respondent's legal duty to company confidentiality against the particular claims of friendship. Here is how our national samples replied:

	JP	GER	USA	UK	NL	FR	SWE	SP	IT	SIN
Univer-sal obli-gation	85.9	75.6	74.8	72.2	60.4	54.0	48.8	47.8	47.6	45.8

Here we see the Japanese and Germans as the most adamant that one's legal duty to the company comes before the speculative activities of friends. The Japanese may be particularistic on many moral issues, but not on the obligations individuals owe to the corporation!

Germans have laws of many kinds and at multiple levels. One answer to the question of whether they could ever revert to fascism is, not without the wholesale destruction of existing rules and laws which render the exercise of power over dissenting opinion virtually impossible. Radical decentralization into federal structures divides Germany into sixteen *Länder* or regional parliaments with considerable local authority, including education, the environment, and relationships to industry in their region. The *Länder* are, in turn, obliged to consult with urban, suburban, and rural authorities. Top management is equally beholden to legal representatives of employees, unions, shareholders, the *Land* in which they are located, and their industry association.

In contrast to the Japanese, who see cooperative relations as ideals to which laws and contracts should adapt, Germans follow Americans in specifying in elaborate detail what the law requires. In the civil service in Baden-Württemberg, there is a rule that the head of an office must send a bouquet of flowers to any member of the staff who has been away sick for six weeks!

Instead of the sharp distinction between the public and the private sectors common to English-speaking economies, Germany has numerous intermediate institutions in the public continental law tradition, charged with the task of reconciling public and private interests. These include the *Länder* who often own banks and have minority shareholdings in businesses within their regions. Another semipublic kind of institution are the *Verbände*, or employers' associations, which help to construct the *Handelsgesetzbuch*, or commercial code, appropriate to their sectors. *Verbände* include *Bundesvereinigung der Deutschen Arbeitgeberverbände* (BDA), the major employers association, and the BDI, which coordinates major industries at the federal level. There are also specific associations for different industries, all represented nationally and regionally.

It is this dual conception of universalism, as a framework for free competition at the federal level and as regional experimentation in policies, technologies, and procedures designed to give local businesses an advantage, that has given Germany a stable evolution since 1945. The *Länder* tend to specialize in different ways of developing the economy. Thus, Lothar Späth, Christian Democratic Union Minister President of Baden-Württemberg, has attracted many high-technology businesses to locate in his state by establishing centers of information technology and biotechnology, especially around the Universities of Stuttgart and Ulm. He played an active part in assisting Daimler-Benz in its friendly takeovers of AEG, Dornier, MTU, and MBB, with the state itself purchasing shares. Bavaria is another "sun-belt" southern state, attracting aerospace and robotics, with over 200,000 employees in microelectronics, especially in the region of Nuremberg. The northern states have struck back with twelve new technology institutes in North-Rhine-Westphalia and a major program in Berlin.[10]

A most important extension of rule making is the creation of ever-higher standards which then become universal practice. Michael Porter has argued that so far from regulations being a disadvantage, they can force up standards and result in a national or regional economy solving major problems ahead of its rivals to become world class. He explains:

> The demanding home market is partly manifested by tough product standards, known as DIN (Deutsche Industrie Norm). DIN are consistently among the most stringent of any nation (within Germany their difficulty and level of detail is the subject of many amusing stories). Germany has also promulgated tough standards in terms of product safety. An example is the *Machinenschutzgesetz*, an early rigorous German law to prevent accidents from machine use. German environmental regulations are also today the most stringent in some fields, and spending on the environment is by far the highest in Europe.[11]

Along with Japan's, Germany's power industry now has the toughest clean-air standards in the world, with electricity-generating stations having to spend 15 billion DM on reducing emissions, 20 percent of its capital costs. Will this make German industry hopelessly uncompetitive? Not if other nations eventually adopt these standards, as Germany's influence in the EEC will probably ensure. There was a row in Brussels in 1985 over German insistence that all new cars manufactured in the EEC be fitted with catalytic converters. Jaques Calvet, chairman of Peugeot, described Bonn lawmakers as "a bunch of hysterics," imperiling the whole EEC automobile industry, but the German view prevailed, and guess who manufactures the majority of converters? Collin Randlesome commented as follows on the general issue of German business and the environmental challenge:

> While German companies were never exactly ecstatic about the massive investments they were forced to make to clean up their act, they now realize that this capital expenditure has placed them at a competitive advantage vis-à-vis many of their neighbors in Europe. The issue of the environment will not go away in any of the European countries, and foreign companies will subsequently be obliged to purchase pollution-control equipment, much of which has been researched, designed and made in . . . Germany.[12]

Indeed, the German proclivity to set rigorous standards, without the fierce libertarian litigation common in the United States, may be the cutting edge of its *Strukturpolitik*. Of the two hundred EEC committees that set industrial standards, over half are chaired by Germans, in the light of their superior qualifications. The strategy is clearly to try to universalize those standards already achieved by German industry, as soon as possible after those achievements are recorded. This may leave competitors not merely behind Germany, but beyond the law.

The Labyrinthine Mind

Germans have a reputation for the depth, even the density, of their thinking. Nietzsche put it well:

> The German soul has corridors and interconnecting corridors in it, there are caves, hiding places, dungeons in it; its disorder possesses much of the fascinating and mysterious; the German is acquainted with hidden paths to chaos.[13]

Perhaps the levels of order we described in the previous section are the counterpoint to such convolutions and wild interiors. John Ardagh, the author of *Germany and the Germans*, speaks of the "contrast between the Germans' passion for orderliness and their tendency towards romanticism, irrationality, and extremism." In any event, such hidden recesses and the felt need to hedge these around with multiple levels of order in which one level safeguards against other levels—all makes for cognitive complexity and a truly labyrinthine consciousness.

Bertrand Russell once commented on the psychological experiments on animals undertaken by American and by German researchers. He observed wryly:

> It may generally be said that the animals studied behaved in ways in which the experimenters believed before their investigations began. Nay more, the animals conformed to the national characteristics of their observers. Thus, animals studied by Americans rushed about with an incredible display of bustle and pep, before finally achieving the desired result by accident, while animals studied by Germans sat still and thought before finally evolving the solution out of their inner-consciousness.[14]

Germany has its own unique contribution to the understanding of mind, *gestalt* psychology (the word means an organized configuration or pattern of meaning). It was Franz Brentano (1838–1917) who was the father of phenomenology, a school of philosophy that put the description of conscious experience at the center of human awareness. For Germans, the whole is prior to the part, atoms are but elements in a larger whole. One comprehends by first grasping the whole and then discovering the function of the various parts within the whole.

In Chapter 13 we contrasted two views of the corporation: (1) as a set of functions, tasks, people, machines, and payments, or (2) as a group of related persons working together. Seventy-four percent of American managers preferred the first description, but only 26 percent preferred the latter. Fifty-nine percent of Germans preferred the second description, but only 41 percent preferred the first. Germans and, even more, the Japanese, chose the holistic[15] approach much more often than did Americans. Germans also rejected significantly more often than Americans the notion that profit was the "only real goal of the company." Goals are for them far more complex and qualified. Hence, two of the world's strongest economies are on the synthesis-oriented end of the spectrum.

It is this liking for holistic and orderly systems that has led Germany to concentrate heavily in manufacturing, engineering, and machinery, using a succession of untranslatable words for these subtleties of machine mastery; for example, *Vorsprung durch Technik*, literally "springing upward through strong technology," which is much featured in Audi ads. According to the OECD, Germany retains far more of her strength in manufacturing than do other developed nations. Forty percent of Germany's GDP is in manufacturing, including oil, compared with 39 percent in Japan, 36 percent in the United Kingdom, 31 percent in France, and 28.5 percent in the United States. Had oil been excluded, German and Japanese dominance in manufacturing would have been relatively greater.[16]

This emphasis is intensified by the fact that Germany also specializes in capital goods, most particularly machinery sold to other factories for manufacturing processes. For example, Germany supplies 58 percent of total world exports of reciprocating pumps, 51 percent of printing presses, 43 percent of spinning and reeling machines, 37 percent of rubber and plastics-working machines, 35 percent of combined harvesters and threshers, 34 percent of packaging and bottling machines, 30 percent of vending and weighing machines, 30 percent of metal reaming machines, and so on. The consequence is that enthusiasts for *Machinenbau* get to intensify the enthusiasm and perfectionism of fellow machine buffs, standards within these "clusters" get pushed ever upward, and German quality becomes state-of-the-art for world-class manufacturing.[17]

Strategically, the making of the tools-that-make-the-tools insures that German manufacturers of consumer products, for example, Daimler-Benz, Hoechst, Zeiss, Nixdorf, Bayer, Volkswagen, and BMW, will get the best process technology, usually ahead of their competition. Germany vies with Japan in numerically controlled machine tools and the world revolution toward flexible manufacturing that these have made possible. Germans speak of "fulcrum industries" in their search for a technology that gives leverage to a hundred different industries and acts as a vital element within the labyrinthine mind which seeks to upgrade entire manufacturing processes.

Isaiah Berlin, interpreting Tolstoy, referred to two rival styles of political conception, that of the "hedgehog" and the "fox," countries like Britain and the United States imitate the fox in making sure they "know just one thing" by empirical examination of the data they analyze. Alas for countries like Germany and Russia; they imitate the hedgehog in "trying to know many things" and seeking the grand synthesis where all points converge. Not surprisingly, it is the hedgehog countries that have yielded historically to the temptations of totalitarianism, some phantom whole to which all parts were supposedly subordinate.[18]

Berlin, in his famous essay, *Two Concepts of Liberty*, went further in criticizing the Soviet and German concept of *freedom for*, as contrasted with the Anglo-American concept of *freedom from*.[19] The idea that the state could facilitate freedoms for specific purposes like economic growth or social development had been discredited by historical experience. "Freedom for" was an *ersatz* freedom to do what the state commanded. The test of any genuine freedom had to be that it contradicted at crucial periods the dictates of state authority.

There is some truth to this Cold War penmanship. Arguably, the English and American dictionaries have to borrow such words as *Zeitgeist*, "the spirit of time," and *Weltanschauung*, "world outlook," because few in Great Britain or America ever felt the need for such grandiose conceptions. According to this view, Germans are less "deep" than sunk in the depth of their own cerebral excesses, of which the formidable obscurities of German philosophers is but one further example.

Yet the perils of holistic ways of perceiving can surely not be extended to those phenomena which are genuinely whole, yet describable. The world is full of systems not reducible to their parts without loss of meaning. Manufacturing reprogrammable machines which in turn manufacture increasing varieties of products is a system of interdependent machines that needs to be conceived of in its entirety. Can it be a coincidence that Germans are so good at this? "Freedom for" may under certain circumstances be the voice of the serpent in the garden, but are not incentives offered by *Länder* for bank finance and educational support in their regions surely a legitimate form of nurturance for private enterprise, and not a dastardly plot? What is necessary to successful business is not simply a geographical infrastructure of road, rail, and communication, but a cerebral infrastructure of informational and educational institutes. The German labyrinthine consciousness is well adapted to the modern information age.

Similarly, relationships between workers, unions, employers associations, and managers are systems of genuine, not elaborated complexity. The position of the German economy in the EEC, and now in greater Europe, is of such vast ramifications that only a *gestalt* approach could hope to do it justice. The world may be moving away from the "foxes" and their object-by-object certainties and their belief that freedom lies in confounding state authority.

Germans are people of great moral seriousness, who take their *Kultur* with not a little reverence and have a *Beruf*, a calling, rather than a job. *Kultur* is not generally regarded as an elitist affectation, or something to be indulged by a minority with the taste for it, but as part of the German shared value system and immutable gift to civilization. The *Länder* spend lavishly on culture, four times the per capita expense of Britain and even more than France. The original West Germany alone had more than fifty opera houses, seventy orchestras, more than one hundred theaters, and 1,300 museums. Cities vie with each other to attract the best talent. In Munich, for example, the *Land* spends 250 million DM a year on cultural activities alone. Theaters receive subsidies of four to five times their box-office takings, a policy which puts even the most lavishly presented operas within the reach of all. And theaters are booked year round to an 80 percent capacity or more.[20]

Is this all a financial waste compounded with snobbery and the worship of tradition? Not if you take a holistic view of culture as part of the region's moral, spiritual, and informational infrastructure. Culture might even be seen to "pay" if we knew what to count and what to leave aside. If a family travels to Munich to see a play, are not restaurants, hotels, shops, and transport thereby enriched, together with costume makers, designers, electricians, and musicians? Might business be more inclined to be done there or offices and plants located there? If *Kultur* pervades the whole society as holistic thinkers believe, are there any boundaries it cannot permeate? Given the fact that *Kultur* is to the arts what high tech and knowledge intensity is to engineering, it may pay a society back a dozen times over to subsidize the arts.

The German labyrinthine mind has also been far readier to understand that the human mind does not and cannot exist apart from the environment.[21] The unit of survival is neither the individual nor the group, but the group-which-encultures-a-sustainable-environment. Germany's battle to save her environment has come earlier than most, because the land is densely populated, because German industry has traditionally been "heavy," i.e., steel, coal, coke, chemicals, plastics, rubber, paper, dyestuffs, metal working, and a large concentration in automobiles. The situation is exacerbated by her geographical location, eastward of the industrialized West and close to the largely uncontrolled pollution of the old Eastern Bloc.

Acid rain, mostly originating from beyond her borders, has decimated the pine trees of the Black Forest and other woodlands. The poet Julius Hammer wrote in 1851: *O Wald, O Waldeseinsamkeit wie gleichst du dem deutschen Gemüt* ("O forest, O solitude of the forest, how similar thou art to the German soul"). The quotation amply illustrates the oneness Germans feel between the nature of human beings and their environment. Even privately owned woodlands must be open to the public in a land where the forests belong to all people.[22]

Few nations have succeeded so well in accommodating themselves to pressing environmental issues, so successfully that the Greens, Europe's largest environment party, are now much diminished, having had many of their policies taken over by the mainstream Social Democratic Party and Christian Democratic Union. Energy-saving measures, including a 5 billion DM expenditure on double-glazing subsidies, had reduced Germany's oil imports from 145 million tons to 103 between 1973 and 1984. Germans recycle 42 percent of their waste paper and 50 percent of their glass bottles. It has been estimated that 6.7 percent of GNP is spent on environmental schemes. When the mining town of Rheinbraun was visited by John Ardagh, he found trees planted on the piles of earth, lakes created from the abandoned works, the whole environment redesigned for leisure and recreation.[23] When the rest of the world wakes up to the environmental crisis, Germans will once again be the experts and beneficiaries.

An interesting ramification of German seriousness and their preference for creating value by painstaking methodological preparation is that the German economy has moved more slowly than most toward the sensuous expressions of the consumer society. It is as if they no longer trust impulses and whimsy because these are fleeting and superficial. Germans have been much scolded by American and British scholars for their "backwardness" in this regard. Michael Porter tells them off as follows:

> An area in which Germany has serious weaknesses in terms of related and supporting industries is in the consumer sector. The historical lack of television and radio advertising (the major television channels can show advertising only about 20 minutes a day, with commercials all bunched together and not on Sunday), coupled with the technical orientation of most German managers, means that image marketing skills are poorly developed. . . . It is rare that a German firm succeeds in an industry in which intangible brand images and mass communication are important to competitive success.[24]

It appears not to have occurred to Porter that Germany might be a stronger industrial culture for having escaped the Cola Wars and the Clash of the Underarm Deodorants. For the truth about products extensively advertised on TV is that they represent, for the most part, the trailing edge of technology and art. We can think of no worse fate for a developed economy than that it comes to specialize in those products which are most extensively advertised on TV and radio. That would leave the country with mostly low-skilled work on homogenous consumer staples, which need advertising to distinguish the otherwise indistinguishable and undistinguished. Such a nation would trade in shampoo, detergents, soda pop, aspirin, and candy, rapidly sinking to the bottom of the economic leagues.

That Germany might be greatly benefited by not joining a shouting match about marginal differences does not seem to have occurred to her critics. Contrived impressions based on imagined advantages may prove unexportable to cultures with different associations. If a product is not worth deep thought and has no physical or material value built into it, then it may not have been worth making in the first place. The international learning race may not be accelerated by puffery. For Germans, value must be deeply imbedded in products of solidity and worth. They do not like it when money or its enjoyment becomes separated from worthwhile artifacts, an issue to which we next turn.

A Deep Ambivalence to Money

Germans have had highly disagreeable experiences with money becoming worthless in their pockets within weeks or days of its issue. A visceral dread of inflation is branded into their souls. Suspicion of money, separated from the fabric of culture, began early with Martin Luther's furious denunciation of the sale of indulgences by the Catholic Church. Luther joined with the Church of Rome, however, when it came to the condemnation of usury. The German princes had traditionally to rely on Jewish financiers; Oppenheimer, Werthheimer, Liebmann, Gompers, Ephraim, Itzig, Lehmann, Baruch, and Rothschild were among the most famous families of bankers.

A "villainous" *Finanzrat* (financial adviser) to Prince Karl Alexander of Würtemburg was Süss-Oppenheimer. Arrested in 1738, upon the death of his master "the Jew Süss" was hanged for treason after a rigged trial. The case was remembered with sufficient approval for Veit Harlan to make his notorious anti-Semitic film during the Nazi era. The accusation was always the same, that the hard work of pious Christian men vanished in the alchemy of money and high finance. From Goethe's *Faust* to Wagner's *Ring of the Nibelungen*, "the glint of gold drives men to madness" (see Box 9-1).

Fresh impetus was given to this belief in the aftermath of the Franco-Prussian War. The French were obliged to pay a war indemnity of 5 billion francs, an extraordinarily large sum for those times, which led to

Box 9-1

The Glint of Gold Drives Men to Madness

In Faust II, by J. W. Goethe, Mephistopheles takes Faust to the court of the Emperor, where he bends the ear of the Treasurer and the Chief Steward, persuading them that limitless wealth can be created by the simple expedient of printing money. They later report to the Emperor:

> These did you make, then thousand fold last night
> Conjurers multiplied what you did write:
> And that straightaway the good might come to all
> We stamped at once the series, large and small,
> Tens, twenties, thirties, hundreds all were there
> You cannot think how glad the people were
> Behold your city once half-dead decaying
> Now full of life and joy swarming, playing

Could Goethe have had prevision of Germany's fearful bouts with inflation? Karl Marx was to continue the attack in *Das Kapital*. "Modern society which soon after its birth pulled Plutus by the hair from the bowels of the earth, greets gold as its Holy Grail, as the glittering incarnation of the very principle of life."

In Richard Wagner's *Ring of the Nibelungen* the *Rheingold* is cursed when Alberich, who stole the ring from the Rhine maidens, finds it stolen from himself.

> Let this ring be accursed!
> As its gold gave me power without limit
> Let its spell now bring death to its bearer!
> Let no happy man delight in it
> Let no fortunate soul enjoy its shining gleam
> Let whoever possesses it be consumed with care
> And whoever does not be gnawed with envy . . .
> Let its possessor hoard it without pleasure
> But let it bring the murderer upon him . . .
> Let him long for death, the Ring's Lord
> As the Ring's slave . . .

Rainer Maria Rilke wrote of this passage: "The ore is homesick and it wants to forsake the coins and the wheels that teach it a petty way of living . . . it will return to the veins of the gaping holes that will clamp shut behind it." Gold separated from the context of the living whole spells doom.

Source: The Germans, Gordon A. Craig. London: Penguin Books, 1990, pp. 104–118.

the overheating of the German economy and a speculative bubble which burst, bankrupting several famous companies. The National Liberal Party and their Jewish banking friends Bleichröder and Oppenheimer were blamed for the stock market crash of 1873.[25]

All this paled into insignificance compared with the devastating inflation of 1922–23. The German Imperial government had already gone deeply into debt during World War I. When the French, in *revanche* (revenge) for 1871, obtained reparations of 132 billion marks in gold at the Treaty of Versailles, Germany fell behind in her payments and France occupied the Ruhr. In this process she seized Germany's chief means of repaying her. When German workers in the Ruhr struck against their occupiers, the Weimar Republic tried to pay them by printing money. In June 1922, the official exchange rate was 350 marks to the dollar, by January 1923 it was 7,525 marks, by August 1923 over a million, in October 250 million, in December 4,210,500,000. A newspaper that cost 50,000 marks in the morning would sell its afternoon edition for 100,000 marks. Banknotes used for modest purchases needed a wheelbarrow to deliver. Millions of people with war pensions or with money saved and in war bonds were bankrupt. Only goods, carefully manufactured and designed to last, retained their value, along with the machinery of production itself. You could trust what you had made or what someone else had made. Money itself was worthless, and those who dealt in debased currencies were worse than thieves. Those who had lived profligate lives and had run up debts could now repay these in inflated marks. Those who had worked and saved, buying war bonds when their country was desperate, were now ruined by their fidelity. The moral life of the nation had been turned upside down.[26]

This bitter experience was repeated in less drastic form from 1945 to 1948 in the cigarette-and-nylons economy of the Occupation. Not until the Deutschmark replaced the Reichsmark in 1948 could the recurrent nightmare be finally brought under control. Yet the fears linger, as portrayed in *The Visit*, a play symbolizing the corrupting influence of money on a small community, by the Swiss-German playwright, Frederich Dürrenmatt. Together with Fritz Lang's famous movie *Dr. Mabuse: Der Spieler* (The Gambler) released in 1924, the fear of "Corruption of Pure Money" (see Box 9-2) continues.

The consequences of these traumas upon German business culture are profound. Germany led Europe in making the management of the currency, through the *Bundesbank*, entirely free of political control and interest rate manipulation by the government of the day. German

Box 9-2

The Corruption of Pure Money

In 1922, at the height of the German inflation crisis, Fritz Lang released his now-classic expressionist film, *Dr. Mabuse: Der Spieler*. The word Spieler means both "gambler" and "one who plays," in this case with people's lives and destinies. The film was a conscious symbolist portrait of German life in the merciless grip of runaway money and financial speculators, selling the mark to secure foreign currencies. Mabuse is utterly ruthless in his dealings, hypnotizing his desperate victims and escaping detection by a clever series of impersonations so that, as Lang explained, "Mabuse is everywhere present in society yet unrecognized."

When public prosecutor Dr. Wenk begins to investigate him, Mabuse completes his financial ruin and is about to murder him when the police intervene. But the doctor escapes and is found days later in a lunatic asylum, crazed by his own money and throwing counterfeit banknotes into the air.

Some thirty years later, and after another world war, the theme is taken up again in Dürrenmatt's *The Visit*. An imposing million-airess, complete with black panther and retinue, returns to the small middle-European village she had left as a young woman, pregnant and ostracized. She is Clara Wacher, now Madam Zachanassian. Her child was adopted and died a year later. She met her millionaire husband in a Berlin brothel, returning with him to America. She now symbolizes the power of the dollar in post-war Europe.

She offers the village a gift of a billion marks and they fête her obsequiously, but there is a price. She wants Anton Schill, her seducer, now married with grown children and slated as the next burgermeister, dead. The village is aghast and long speeches are made about morality not being for sale. But Clara is content to wait, accompanied by two blind men, Kobby and Hobby. These had given perjured testimony before the magistrate years ago, claiming to have slept with Clara, so that Anton could deny paternity of their child. He had bribed them with a bottle of schnapps. She had traced them to another country and had them blinded.

Despite the villagers' indignation, they begin almost at once to spend money in anticipation of their bonanza. They also go deeply into debt, borrowing from banks and shops, not least Anton Schill's own shop. Their excuse is that Clara will relent. When she

> doesn't, murmurs against Schill's "disgraceful conduct" grow and
> grow. Finally, the village "tries" him, kills him collectively, and, the
> affluent society having arrived, they climb aboard the express
> train to Rome.
>
> *Source: From Caligari to Hitler: A Psychological History of the German Film*,
> S. Kracauer. Princeton: Princeton Univ. Press, 1947; *The Visit*,
> Friedrich Dürrenmatt. London, Fontana Modern Plays, 1961.

inflation rates, along with the Dutch, have been the lowest in the EEC,
and the Deutschmark has long been among the world's strongest currencies, appreciating in value against all save the yen. When Germany
raised her own interest rates in December 1991, the rest of the world
feared continuing recession. The Germans alone feared inflation. Never
would they risk their currency again.

Today, Germany's horror of loose money is still very much in evidence.
Her financial sector remains small. Her dislike of debt is so strong that
by 1987 credit card use had reached only 2 percent of the population.
Perhaps more serious is the dislike of anything risky or speculative,
including entrepreneurship. Stock market transactions are taxed and
equity ownership by individuals remains small. There is also weakness
in the service side of the economy and a belief that if a product is not
visible and lacks clear physical dimensions, it is not of genuine substance
or seriousness. Laws severely limiting the hours when shops may open
ensure that producing dominates consuming. Profit making is on a
modest scale and little valued as compared with the continuing opportunities to seek technical perfection and fulfill one's service to society
through durable products.

To test the attraction of extrinsic money rewards versus intrinsic
social and interpersonal satisfactions, we posed a dilemma that had to do
with "loose money" to our international samples of managers:

People have different opinions about how employees should be
compensated for working overtime.

Some people think the only reasonable compensation is a monetary
bonus, which should be bigger as more overtime has to be done. This
should be regulated contractually.

Other people think that working necessary overtime belongs to the
job you do and the appreciation the boss will give you is reasonable
compensation in itself. Therefore, overtime does not have to be regulated contractually.

Which of these hypotheses would you support?

The results:

Monetary bonus, increases with over-time	SWE	JP	US	IT	SIN	NL	FR	UK	GER	SP
	87.8	85.9	70.9	58.7	52.5	51.8	45.8	42.6	41.9	32.0

With the exception of Spanish managers, German managers are the strongest advocates of submerging the money motive within the organizational context. Employees should work for the sake of work, not for financial gain. All this further emphasizes that for German managers, money is a means, not an end; a lubricant of industrialization, not a potion in itself; of value in furthering work, but dangerous in itself.

No wonder, then, that the Deutsche Bank, the Dresdner Bank, and the Commerzbank are all triple-A rated by Standard and Poor, being renowned for their fiscal prudence and support of German industries, in many of which they hold minority shares. Money invested long-term in the R&D capacities of technological firms is considered both safer and more worthy than making money from money. At the end of Goeth's *Faust* the protagonist is not damned to hell, as is Christopher Marlowe's Doctor Faustus. Faust is redeemed when he takes the money and the power he has hankered for so long and puts these to the service of mankind by reclaiming fertile land. Angels bear his purified soul to heaven.

Concerns and Social Idealism

When John Ardagh, author of *Germany and the Germans*, interviewed a group of German trade union officials in Stuttgart, he was impressed by their education, their English, their fluency, and their oak-paneled offices, where they offered him brandy and cigars. One of them explained:

> It is true that relationships [with management] have become a little more conflictful nowadays, owing to lower growth and higher unemployment. But basically we still believe that it is by cooperating with management, rather than fighting it, that we stand the best chance of securing better pay and working conditions—and the results prove it. What is more, as we see it, our moral obligation is not just to our own members or other workers, but to German society as a whole, where we must play an active role in upholding democracy and the rule of law. So, if you like, we're part of the establishment and proud of it. We're certainly not revolutionaries: we do not want to overthrow capitalism but to reform it from inside, in a more social direction,

in a social market economy. We have moved beyond the class-war phase where so many French and British unionists are still bogged down, and we believe that workers have an interest in helping their firms remain profitable.[27]

The results do, indeed, prove the effectiveness of this philosophy. German wages, combined with fringe benefits, are the highest in the world, and their productivity is among the highest. They enjoy thirty-nine paid holidays per annum, nearly twice the number in the United States, and IG Metall, their largest union, recently won a 38.5-hour working week. Forty-two percent of the labor force remains unionized. Moreover, unions experiment in management by running their own companies through the principle of *Gemeinwirtschaft*, a nonalienated family-style camaraderie in the workplace, supposedly superior to the more traditional approach. Unions own the Volkfürsorge life insurance company, Neue Heimat (literally, "New Homeland"), the biggest construction company in Europe, and the *Bank für Gemeinwirtschaft*, the fifth largest private bank in the country. However, financial scandals in the 1980s greatly shook the faith of those who believed in the cosier style of union management. The unions remain, however, the part owners and operators of major businesses.

Another characteristic of German culture is a serious intellectual and philosophical interest in communication and consensus. Immanuel Kant taught his categorical imperative, that the individual's behavior toward others should be such that a universal law could be derived from this conduct. This approach offers a potential reconciliation between universal laws and particular situations, the parts of society and the whole, the rights of the individual and obligations owed to the collective. These are the first three dilemmas of our methodology, to which an eighteenth-century German philosopher worked out solutions. The answer to the moral problems of man in society, said Kant, lay in the "resolution of antinomies"—precisely the theme this book has been pursuing.

G. W. F. Hegel, the world's leading idealist philosopher, argued that history could be understood as a dialectical process of contrasting and contending ideas capable of achieving a larger and more truthful whole. It was Karl Marx who claimed a scientific and materialist basis for his own revolutionary dialectics. But well before the collapse of Marxism, the Frankfurt School had removed the historicism and determinism from German dialectical thinking. In their *Dialectics of Enlightenment*[28] Max Horkheimer and Theodore Adorno had critiqued the German enlightenment of Hegel and his followers as fostering a belief in the truth of

absolute wholes, giant, all-embracing organisms, and ultimate syntheses. This belief reached its culmination in fascism. They argued instead
for an inherent uncertainty and open-endedness in the way contrarian
ideas interacted, citing the Uncertainty Principle of the German physi-
cist Werner Karl Heisenberg, who had said, "Physics is conversation."
The way you looked affected what you saw. In *Theorie des Kommunikati-
ven Handelns*,[29] Jürgen Habermas argues for the logical connectivity of
antithetical viewpoints with creative and unpredictable outcomes. The
prevailing view among British and American academics, that dialectics
is finally disgraced, may fail to account for these more dialogical variations with novel combinations resulting. Paul Tillich was one exponent
of this view, and Martin Buber, the Austrian theologian, another. This
book is intended as a minor contribution to this approach.

It is extremely unlikely that the leadership of the Christian Democratic Union, Germany's principal ruling party, pays any attention to the
Frankfurt School. They come from different worlds and different ends
of the political spectrum. It is rather that German culture at all levels
finds unity in opposites. "Chancellor Kohl is a great believer in promoting
the cooperation of labor and business," Rudiger Thiele, one of his
advisors, told Daniel Burstein. "Everyone at these meetings has agreed
that the social dimension of 1992 is just as important as the economic
dimension. If we keep our social peace we will keep our competitiveness."[30]

A major advocate of management and labor as *Sozialpartner* is Reinhard
Mohn, the retired head of Bertelsmann's, reputedly the world's most
successful publishing house, with offices in over thirty countries. There
are very few German books offering advice to managers in general. In
part because German universalism, unlike American, is industry and
technology specific. However, "success through participation" is as close
as Germans come to generalized advice and it clearly enunciates the
doctrine of "socially responsible freedom."[31] The overall quality of a
product can be assured only if the values of all producers are optimized
in its manufacture and distribution. Conflicts in the workplace are
valuable insofar as they mirror the conflicting views of persons who want
to improve the overall performance of the product. People's basic needs
for health and security must be taken care of if constructive conflicts
are to replace destructive conflicts. Above all, "the purpose of business
activity is no longer maximizing profits but making the greatest possible
contribution to society."

Mohn's philosophy is of especial interest because he represents the nonstatist communitarianism that typifies much of German management. A critic of bureaucracy and of government intervention in the private sector, he yet advocates strong social policies within the corporation, a generous, some say "lavish," profit-sharing scheme and employees' control of their own working environment. Yet the aim of social provision is the self-development of each individual employee.

We have already seen that Germans are more likely than American, Dutch, British, Canadian, or Italian managers to cooperate among businesses in the face of international challenges (see Table 3-5). Fifty-nine percent of German managers reject "more competition" as the antidote to collusion. German managers would be less inclined to fire an employee with a fifteen-year satisfactory service record who is no longer performing well. Only 31 percent of German managers would consider this service to the community to be irrelevant, as compared with 77 percent of American managers and 75 percent of Canadian managers. German managers are also more likely to work for "their fellow man" than are Japanese, Swedish, British, Dutch, Canadian, or American managers (see Table 13-3). We put the following dilemma to our samples, which well exemplifies the German preference for participation, interdependence, and mutuality.

There are two ways in which people can work.

One way is to work as an individual on one's own. In this case a person is pretty well his or her own boss, who decides things personally as she or he gets along in the business. Such a person can look out for him- or herself and does not expect others to look out for him or her.

Another way is working in a group in which all work together. Everyone has something to say in the decisions that are made and everyone can count on each other.

Which way of working do you think is usually better?

Table 9-3

His/her own boss	USA	SWE	JP	NL	SP	UK	CAN	FR	GER
	42.1	40.6	40.2	27.7	23.4	23.2	17.6	12.2	12.0

Here we see that Germans reject solo working in favor of the participating group by a majority of 88 percent, while on this question the Japanese are somewhat anomalous. Perhaps the question tapped an unrealized ideal of greater independence. In some respects, German communitarianism is still preindustrial. Asked whether a man whose shop burned down should rely on his family and close relatives or borrow on his own, 36 percent of German managers thought the family should be involved, but only 13 percent of Swedish managers, 20 percent of U.S. managers, and 25 percent of British and Dutch managers.

Germany is famous, or notorious, for *Mitbestimmung* (worker codetermination). The Codetermination Act was passed in 1976, and requires companies with more than 2,000 employees to have supervisory boards (*Aufsichtsrat*) consisting of half workers' representatives and half representatives of the shareholders, with the *Arbeits Direktor,* or personnel manager, on the board to answer questions. Companies with between 500 and 2,000 employees must have supervisory boards with one-third worker representation. Members must be elected, not appointed. The chair, who is usually a shareholder representative, can exercise a casting vote in the case of a tie. Boards do not interfere day-to-day in the running of the company but must approve major decisions, especially those with human resource implications.[32]

In practice, the system obliges managers to confer extensively with employees but does not prevent managers from taking drastic action if the situation warrants it. This accords with the dilemma we administered on whether neighbors in a meeting should vote down a dissenting minority or strive for consensus. The Germans with the Dutch managers were "strivers for consensus" (see Table 11-4). British and Americans preferred to force a vote and win. Unions are also discouraged from unilateral strike action. German labor contracts have been likened to peace treaties with mandatory processes of discussion, authorization, and arbitration before strike action becomes legal.

But the heart of German participation is less at board level than in the *Betriebsrat,* or works council. All companies with more than five members, whether unionized or not, must by law have a council. It is through these councils that German corporations are reminded daily of the impact of group morale and opinion upon productivity, and because these councils are outside the union structure, every German employer has the opportunity to approach his employees directly on specific issues in the workplace.

Like most countries with strong community ethics, Germany is able to spend copiously on improvements to its national infrastructure. Annual expenditure on R&D comprises 67 billion DM, much of this carefully targeted at "fulcrum industries," those with high leverage over the economy as a whole, for example, machines for the production of other products. The old West Germany had 8,400 kilometers of motorway, scheduled to reach 10,000 by the year 2000. The Rhine-Main-Danube canal will soon join the North Sea to the Black Sea. Spending on health care is more than 10 percent of GNP, the highest outside the United States, and provided by a national system of health insurance, covering 90 percent of the population and delivered by competing public and private sources.[33]

As might be expected from American observers, Germany's preference for cooperation comes in for stern criticism. Michael Porter worries that

> . . . in numerous German industries there has been consolidation and a tendency toward high levels of collaboration. . . . Mergers and alliances among leading German competitors, sometimes justified as preparing for a more unified European market, are proliferating. . . . Almost none have been prohibited on antitrust grounds. The threat to German competitive advantage is palpable.[34]

Why? Presumably because the self-interested industrial organization will earn as much as it can for as little effort as possible, unless threatened by another competitor. But that isn't the way of German culture, and American strictures may not apply.

The G-type Personality

Kurt Lewin, the German-born Jewish psychologist fled persecution by the Nazis and emigrated to America in the 1930s. He made a well-known contrast between the differing kinds of "life space" within the U-type American personality and the G-type German personality. Although his observations were prewar, they retain a certain validity.[35] The American, or U-type, personality has a small "private space." It has a large "public space," which is easily accessible. This means that Americans are friendly, outgoing, and easy to meet and know. Few things about them are strictly private. Indeed, you may be regaled at a cocktail party with awful confessions by someone whose name you did not catch!

The German, or G-type, personality has a large, dark, private space and a small outer public space, and even this is relatively inaccessible. This means that Germans are not so easy to get to know. They tend not to confide in strangers, and much more of their life space is considered off-limits to strangers and new acquaintances. They are not very forthcoming, because most important matters are reserved for private friendships. Their casual discourse will be rather formal and distinctly unrevealing.

An American's large public life space tends to be specific, that is, separated into neat compartments. He or she can be one sort of person on the golf links, another in the local bar, a third at work, and yet another at a scientific meeting. Hence, he could be "Charlie" at the golf club, "Chuck" at the bar, "Charlie Smith" or "the boss" at work, and "Professor Charles Smith" at a scientific meeting. The title is specific to the occasion and to whatever subdivision of his public space Smith appears in.

The larger private space of Germans tends to be diffuse, that is, with boundaries that are permeable and nonspecific. The identities of Germans tend not to change so much in different contexts of life. Therefore, the higher status will tend to be used across contexts. Hence, it is "Herr Professor Schmidt" wherever he appears, and his wife is "Frau Professor Schmidt" whether she is at a party, on the street, or in her local shop. Your title is a permanent extension of your personality and is relevant in nearly all situations.[36]

At a superficial level, then, Germans may seem formal, remote, even prickly. You can be a secretary to a boss whose Christian name you have never used and may not even know. Co-workers may have no social relations outside the workplace. Indeed, this is quite common. Germans are also keen seekers of titles (see "Ja, Herr Konsul," Box 9-3).

The other side of the coin is that once you are admitted to a friend's private space you are within it for life, barring a serious quarrel. A distinguished German woman psychologist who had shown friendship to the English author became extremely angry when she learned that he had visited Frankfurt but not tried to see her. She had admitted him to friendship. The barriers were down. He had no inkling of what this had cost her. By his reckoning, they shared a professional enthusiasm only, specific to psychological studies.

Breaking the barrier between the formal and intimate ways of saying "you," *Sie* and *du*, can be an important passage for many Germans. They may seal their new-found intimacy over a drink together. Access to the interiority of another is much prized. Breaking through that barrier uninvited is seen as wicked. Hence in *The Lost Honor of Katharina Blum*, a popular novel and film, a young woman's privacy and life are destroyed by the gutter press. John Ardagh, who has a German wife, explains:

> Germans have two very distinct sides to their nature. On the one hand they are profoundly drawn to the rich interior life, to the world of emotional, idealism, privacy, depth and sensitivity—and friendship belongs to this. On the other hand they are very practical and ambitious.[37]

Box 9-3

"Ja, Herr Konsul"

Germany has been described as "a semiclassless society," with many of its aristocratic families suffering expropriation and severe problems from resistance to, or collaboration with, the Nazis. It is also a society of relative equality of incomes, with a CEO earning 5.8 times the salary of an unskilled worker, compared to 6.5 times in the United Kingdom, 7.5 in France, 7.6 in Italy, and over 12 in the United States, and rising.

Owing, however to the diffuse nature of German life spaces, a title appropriate in one sphere of life becomes appropriate to nearly all. It follows that titles elevate status very broadly and are, therefore, much sought after. The provincialism of German life, with a large number of major cities, makes nationally recognizable distinctions hard to find. Hence, anyone with a doctoral degree is likely to use it and may take offense if addressed as *Herr*. A widow may call herself *Frau Justizrat* (Mrs. Legal Administrator).

Rich businessmen try to obtain honorary consulships from Third World countries, thereby tying themselves into "international circles" in Munich, Stuttgart, Wiesbaden, etc. Thus, two Swabian businessmen "representing" Haiti and Chad may say, "*Ja, Herr Konsul*," to each other at the *Land* president's annual party. They also receive consular license plates and can fix national insignia on the front of their houses. "Of the forty-one consuls in the Stuttgart telephone directory, only five are career diplomats." Some of the rest have paid 50,000 DM for a "fantasy diplomatic life."

The notorious Hans Herman Wenger of Munich sold aristocratic titles and honory degrees from obscure foreign academies—for example, the University of Tegucigalpa. He was himself *der schöne Konsul* from Bolivia. Charged with tax fraud, he fled to one of his best suppliers, Paraguay.

Source: Germany and the Germans, John Ardagh. London: Penguin, 1991, pp. 173–183.

What is of concern to us here is that a great deal of important business may currently be transacted within the diffuse private circles of G-type personalities. We are not claiming that whole companies of employees interact with each other this way, but quite a number of key employees do have such relationships, and these may be necessary to the highly complex forms of communication in environments of accelerating knowledge intensity.

An unusual feature of German business culture is the very large number of small and medium-sized private companies, still run by founders and their families and with an extraordinary record of sophistication and export orientation. These are among the *Mittelstände*, the medium-sized companies at the heart of the economy, which dominate the machine-tool industry and produce 75 percent of the chemical industry's output. What is unusual about these companies is their preference for small, lucrative niches, for example, dough-kneading machines, and their disinterest in growing any larger, that is, beyond the size where people no longer have access to the private spaces of co-workers. For such companies the rich interiority of souls and of machines appear to have merged into a diffuse whole. Again, John Ardagh has given a vivid portrait:

> The typical Swabian factory is still likely to be owned and run by a self-made man or the son of one. He may earn 300,000 DM a year, but he lives very simply, probably works a 70-hour week, knows exactly how to turn a lathe or adjust an engine, and will readily go to the shop floor and discuss details with his workers. He has a close and benevolent contact with them, usually knowing them all by name, and he is anxious to avoid his firm becoming too large for his personal supervision and thus less efficient. His manner tends to be genial but uncouth; for all his creative intelligence he can rarely express himself eloquently; and he has a blithe disregard for showy public relations, believing that sheer quality will win through—as usually it does. [38]

This persisting success of organizations maintained at human scale and *Gemeinwirtschaft* is a testament to this "other side" of German personality, which few outsiders see or appreciate. Wealth is created by the soul's inner riches, by literally thousands of the most private and inaccessible companies in the world.

This helps to explain the extraordinary international popular and critical success of the eleven-part TV series, *Heimat*, literally "Homeland," but closer to a state of mind in which shared intimacies dominate consciousness, the private life space. This was conceived and written by Edgar Reitz and filmed in the rural village of Woppenroth, between the

Rhine and the Moselle. Reitz conceived of it as a response to *Holocaust*, an American series with stereotyped families of Jewish victims and fascist villains. It was a risk to call it *Heimat* at all, since this is a name given to an escapist genre of rural *Schmaltz* much extolled in Nazi propaganda.

What *Heimat* seems to have done is create a sense of continuity in Germany's cultural consciousness, spanning the Weimar period, the Nazi years, and beyond, without excuses or evasion, but acknowledging that the thread of intimate life continued, even through those years of blanked-out horror and numbed recollection. The "inner German" had somehow redeemed the vainglorious goose-stepping "outer German." There was, after all, a connection between innocence and maturity. Germany's present economic miracle and stable, decentralized democracy had its roots in earlier traditions, roots not completely blasted or withered by fascism, but nurtured by an interior mind-space that had survived. The Nazis in *Heimat* invite revulsion, yet they remain relentlessly superficial to the central chain of being. They belong to the brittle veneer of public life, not to the serious communion of souls among the story's chief protagonists, who love and work and strive in spite of them. [39]

Training, Developing, Complexifying

Tom Peters recently observed that "the Germans are training fanatics. They try to improve everyone continuously. Every year more than a million enter three-year training programs which divide their time between vocational training institutes and their job with the company. Relative skills will determine the future of developed high-wage nations. . . . The Japanese, Singaporeans, . . . Germans clearly understand this. We (Americans) don't."

There are two characteristics that distinguish the German approach to training-for-business from those of English-speaking developed economies. First, Germans train virtually everyone for some useful skill, largely avoiding the idea of failure. Indeed, the Germans hate the whole concept of failing (see Box 9-4, "The Revolt of the German Subsidiary"), and will mobilize considerable energies to rid themselves of it. Second, their training for business is relentlessly practical. The minds and hands are trained, not the character, and training is industry specific and technology specific. Germans do not believe that management is a generalizable skill with universal attributes; they believe that the logic

---

Box 9-4

The Revolt of the German Subsidiary

When the AMRO bank of the Netherlands took over a smaller German subsidiary, they instituted a procedure used in the Dutch head office and branches. It consisted of weekly staff meetings at which faults and errors in customer service were collected and discussed, with the purpose of trying to eliminate them. What, with hindsight, might the staff have done differently?

It proved almost impossible to run these meetings in the new German subsidiary. The staff would not admit to any mistakes and, when questioned, believed that identifying such would leave them vulnerable to sanction from superiors and peers. They did not disagree with the goal of improvement, but asked for this to be raised in training sessions apart from their work, and that these improvements then be incorporated into changed procedures.

This is consistent with the Germans' preference for thinking long and hard before they act and achieving as near perfect a result as they can.

Source: Oscar van Weerdenburg, Centre for International Business Studies, Amstelveen, the Netherlands.

---

of wealth creation lies in the complex provision of goods and services and that investing heavily in technology and training is the way to afford high-wage demands. Labor costs are held down by automating low-skilled jobs and boosting output per man-hour. Instead of fighting their unions, German managers have built a high-wage, high-skill economy in which a disciplined work force has not, with some exceptions, demanded wage increases in excess of productivity increases. We will deal with "failure reduction" and "technology orientation" in turn.

Ninety-five percent of German children attend the publicly funded *Grundschule* (general school). Private schools are rare and philosophically idealistic, for example, the Rudolph Steiner schools. From the general school at the age of eleven, children are sent either to a *Gymnasium* (grammar school), a *Realschule* (intermediate school), or a *Hauptschule* (high school), which cater in descending order to the more and less academically gifted. This tripartite division allows children to contrast themselves with their classmates of roughly equal ability. Even so, the possibility of failure looms for *Hauptschule* adolescents of fifteen or so. It is at this point that German business offers them and other schools an astonishing choice of 260 skilled trades and professions, so that they can train to be a *Feinoptiker* (precision optical instrument maker), a *Glaspresser* (glass maker), or any of many other specialists. There were 1.8 million German apprentices in training even before East Germany was absorbed. In a system with such a vast variety of specialized skills, the abilities of one skilled worker relative to another are simply incomparable, so that judgments of "better" or "worse," "success" or "failure" make no sense. Nearly all working-class youth find a niche in which they can contribute usefully and with dignity. A *Hauptschule* teacher from Karlsruhe explained:

> Kids who at fifteen are bored, rebellious, and awkward in school seem to change completely when they become apprentices. I meet them a year later and they are polite, enthusiastic and self-confident.[40]

No wonder that 70 percent of all German employees are occupationally qualified, as compared with 30 percent in Great Britain, and that Germany leads all Europe in vocational training. Much of the remaining German workers are becoming qualified and will achieve such coveted goals as the positions of *Industriemeister, Fachwirte,* and *Fachkaufleute.* Not surprisingly, output per employee is double that of the United Kingdom. There are fears that accumulating wealth is making Germans lazy. *"Wir sind NICHT faul!"* (We are not lazy), stormed a *Bild Zeitung* headline. Probably not, since *faul* means not just "lazy" but "foul, rotten, putrid" and worse!

But we fail to grasp the German's enthusiasm for applied science, especially engineering, unless we realize that they do not distinguish "the arts" from "the sciences" in the manner of the British and North Americans. One unfortunate societal consequence of what C. P. Snow called "the two cultures" is that pure science and pure art pursued by free individualists get to be prized above applied science and crafts, which are weighed down by social obligations to customers. The German, Dutch, and Swedish distinction is between *Wissenschaft,* literally, "knowledgemanship" and *Technik,* "the making and running of things." Not only are the two callings of equal status, but the use of the first to improve the second is regarded as admirable and necessary. Moreover, *Technik* includes everything necessary to make techniques work, including good management. Instead of engaging in endless fights between "technical" and "human" values, German managers seek to unify their organizations around the advance of *Technik,* which includes the necessary human dimensions.

No wonder, then, that of the hundred largest companies quoted on the Frankfurt stock exchange, 54 percent of their board members can use the title *Herr Doktor.* Thirty-six percent of the board's members of all publicly traded German corporations have doctorates. *Weiterbildung,* or management development, is an in-house affair to which academics and other experts are invited as needed to concentrate on the company's productive tasks. Under codetermination rules, those representing workers must be educated by the company in all areas relevant to that representation, so that they receive, in effect, management education. A major problem for U.S. and U.K. firms is that money spent on development or training may be wasted when a competitor poaches our talent pool. Germany gets around this by leveling a trade tax, *Gewerbe-steuer,* on all companies and then providing, at subsidized rates, training courses funded by the *Laender* but inspected and certified by the Chambers of Industry and Commerce. It is these training courses that allow small and medium-sized companies to keep up in the learning race, and many of the teachers are practitioners in the state of the art.

A more recent enthusiasm is for lifelong learning in which 25 percent of the population between the ages of nineteen and sixty-five take part. Because the take-up has been lower among the less skilled, unions are now demanding *Bildungsurlaub* (extra paid holidays for self-improvement). Employers are all for the improvement—but not the holidays, of which there are already too many, they believe. A major learning impetus comes from the smaller companies wherein generations of a family may have worked in the same industry, with sons following, yet surpassing, their fathers as *Technik* develops.

Some Danger Signals

Even in light of the preceding discussion, it cannot be denied that Germany faces problems that could conceivably get the best of her. Already, much of Eastern Europe is knocking on her door. They could knock it down. The potential for turbulence among the new nations of the old Communist bloc could overtax German resources, so that the would-be leader of the EEC's political union becomes preoccupied and is forced to face eastward. Without German leadership, political union in Europe will probably fail.

There are also other sources of concern. Germany has not taken to electronic engineering as easily or quickly as she did to mechanical and chemical engineering, yet electronics are increasingly involved in improving and monitoring the machinery on which German exports are based. While the culture remains strong in computer-aided design, manufacturing, and machining, much of electronics is bought in and the Japanese could, if so minded, squeeze Germany with their superior electronics.

Here the German dislike of high risk taking, of speculative finance, and of failure may retard her capacity to innovate. The problem for all nations who "come from behind" and whose industrial revolution occurred later, is that they lack a culture of innovation. No sooner does Germany hit the front, than the strategy of community consensus about following fast behind pioneer nations begins to break down. It remains to be seen whether the cumulative advance of *Technik*, the sheer volume of R&D spending (2.5 percent of GNP as compared with 1.9 percent for the United States), and the *Max Planck Gesellschaft*, a new group of research institutes, can substitute for, or remedy, the scarcity of creative breakthroughs.

Other problems arise from granting pay raises to strong unions and then, in order to remain competitive, moving into the supply of premium products with high value added, high capital investment and training costs. Only rarely do German companies compete on low costs, since their welfare, wage, and benefit costs are high, as are taxes. This seems to have lowered inward investment and may lead Germany to try to protect the EEC from lower-cost Asian imports, making Europe more of a fortress than a market. Moreover, the Japanese strategy of capturing the low-cost, high-volume end of the market first, and then moving up market to capture valuable niches, may leave German positions outflanked. Already Mercedes and others are suffering from Honda, Toyota, and Nissan upgrades.

Germany is also trapped between liberal laws on those seeking asylum, a noble attempt to bury past race discrimination, and the anger of her own unemployed. The sudden availability of East Germans alongside the *Gastarbeiter* (guest workers), invited in the days of labor scarcity, threatens Germany with a labor surplus and the recurrence of some ugly violence against foreigners.

On the final worry as to whether Germany will suffer a serious recurrence of right-wing authoritarianism, we have only sketchy evidence, most of it reassuring. German managers report that their corporations are among the least hierarchical in our research. Only Dutch and American managers report flatter hierarchies among twenty-four nations measured. Moreover, Germans are among the most likely to dispute with their boss if an order is mistaken (see Box 10-3) and among the most likely to give more authority to the most knowledgeable among them than to the person with the highest rank. Cultures do not easily forgo successful experience, and Germany's postwar federal democracy has been a great success. Let the last words be those of J. G. Fichte, the nineteenth-century German philosopher, in *Letters to the German People*, in which he tried to awaken the ideal of nationhood.

> The natural impulse of man which should be abandoned only in case of real necessity is to find heaven on earth, and to endow his daily work on earth with permanence and eternity; to plant and to cultivate the eternal in the temporal . . . in a fashion visible to the mortal eye itself.

10

Sweden's Social Individualism: Between Raging Horses

TIME WAS when Sweden was celebrated as "the Middle Way," a country successfully mediating between capitalism and socialism. But that was before the collapse of Eastern bloc Communist regimes and the chronic decline of the Soviet Union.[1] Conservative pro-business governments have prevailed for over a decade in the United States, Britain, and Japan, followed by Canada and Holland. Deregulation, free markets, and fiercer competition are the watchwords of the late twentieth century.

This leaves Sweden as a bridge to a collapsing land mass and suggests that the bridge may not have been necessary in the first place, since the values it reached out for are discredited. The collapse of the Swedish Model is now allegedly imminent and is heralded with increased fervor. But that too is nothing new. Rarely has a death been more frequently foretold or a longevity more impatiently resented.

For without intending to annoy us, the long, continuing success of the Swedish economy is a devastating reproach to our conventional wisdom. If business is necessarily a ruthless struggle among self-interested adversaries who neither give nor ask for quarter, how could Sweden, industrializing very late—only a few years before the turn of the century—have left so many economies far behind? It is more than teeth and claws can stand! Humanitarianism, social conscience, equal-

237

ity, egalitarianism, and environmental concern are all what economists call "externalities." And that is a polite term for what are widely seen as values subversive to the economic struggle, to the leanness and meanness necessary to survival. Is it really possible to combine low inflation with low unemployment and keep a labor force in line without threatening it with emiseration?

Sweden is widely regarded as a small, insulated exception to the universal rules of economic struggle, a sheltered haven in a turbulent world, an enclave that cannot hold out much longer against the inexorable forces of the market. But this will hardly do. Sweden must export 40 percent of its manufactured goods. It is, and has been since the late nineteenth century, a world economy highly exposed to trends in international trade. With the exception of "island economies" like Singapore and Hong Kong, Sweden is the most international economy of all.[2] If the world is changing, the Swedes could not help but notice it first. Far from being sheltered, Sweden finds herself "torn as between raging horses of contradiction," to quote August Strindberg.

We happen to agree with many of our Swedish informants who see their economy as faced with challenges necessitating restructuring. We also agree that aspects of the Swedish Model are outdated. But even assuming the worst, that the Swedish economic culture fails to adapt (which we doubt), the extraordinary record of success thus far would still need to be explained. Sweden's century of rapid industrial development is still an astonishing achievement, a successful defiance of orthodoxies on an impressive scale. Nor should the collapse of the Eastern bloc lead us to discredit the values of humanity, brotherhood, and equality which Communists extolled, yet failed conspicuously to fulfill. These values and aspirations remain perhaps more urgent in their frustration. We have much to learn from the way in which Swedish culture has created wealth.

Yet Swedes have themselves a sense of being "on the edge," of being a culture marginal to major world alliances and bodies of opinion. A recent book, *Sweden on the Edge*, edited by Michael Maccoby, reflects the mood.[3] Sweden is on the edge of Europe geographically, and her powerful social democratic welfare state puts her on the "soft" edge of capitalism. Equally, her large international companies narrowly owned by leading Swedish families and banking interests, with few nationalized industries, puts her outside the socialist camp as well. Sweden is on the edge of the EEC, although now negotiating for membership. She has chosen to abandon nuclear power, although alternative forms of domestic energy are not readily available to her. Her long neutrality puts her outside NATO, although a beneficiary of its protection. Finally, she is very heavily unionized (90 percent of manual workers) in an age when unionization seems to be ebbing, when blue-collar work is declining, and "the working class" as we know it may be obsolescent.

Swedish Culture: A Snapshot View

Like other cultures examined here, Sweden is a product of history. A quick view shows Sweden's wealth-creation values:

Universalism	**Particularism**
USA, Sweden, Germany	France, Japan
Analysis	**Integration**
USA, Sweden	France, Japan, Germany
Individualism	**Communitarianism**
USA, Sweden	France, Japan, Germany
Inner-direction	**Outer-direction**
USA, France, Germany	Sweden, Japan
Status by achievement	**Status by ascription**
USA, Sweden, Germany	France, Japan
Equality	**Hierarchy**
USA, Sweden, Germany	France, Japan
Time as sequence	**Synchronized view of time**
Sweden, USA	Japan, France, Germany

Sweden is, on six of our seven dimensions, similar to the United States, although Swedish individualism has a very different quality, as we shall see, and Swedes are emotionally more neutral and outer-directed.

Like the United States, Sweden is a largely Protestant-influenced country, high in universalism, analysis, and individualism, with codified and contractual approaches to morality as voluntary agreements. Swedes are mostly Lutheran in origin, although the culture is highly secularized today, with two-thirds of its citizens "never" going to church and another 29 percent only "occasionally."

Sweden's egalitarianism originates among its yeomen farmers and the absence of feudalism in its history. Yet a harsh climate and a land mass reaching to the Arctic Circle has taught its individualists to cooperate for mutual survival. The *bruk*, a small town growing up around a factory in the countryside, from earliest times paid the salary of the priest and the schoolmaster. Thus Swedish corporations came to see themselves as sustaining the surrounding society. A parliament of "four estates," nobility, clergy, burgers, and peasants, had Swedes of different classes wrangling for power very early in its history. Swedish kings tend to be classified as either "good" or "weak." The good include Gustav Vaga, Gustav Adolph (known as Gustavus Adolphus), Queen Kristina, and Karl X. Gustav. The weak kings who followed facilitated "the Age of Liberty," 1748–1772. Tyrants were fortunately rare.[4]

The seventeenth and eighteenth centuries saw the rise and decline of Sweden's Baltic Empire, an experience that appears to have cooled the culture permanently toward military adventurism. Not since the Treaty of Kiel (1814) ended Sweden's involvement in the Napoleonic Wars has Sweden been at war with anyone, enjoying a peace of nearly two centuries.

Sweden's close relationship with Germany and its heavy reliance on international trade kept her neutral in World War I, a decision vindicated by the appalling loss of life in the trenches. Sweden's small population and extreme vulnerability to Nazi Germany kept her neutral in World War II, surrounded as she was by occupied Norway to the West, occupied Denmark to the South, and Finland, allied to Germany, to the East.

Sweden's very limited manpower resources and her heavy reliance on exports, in a turbulent twentieth century, may be responsible for her outer-directedness. She has been obliged to react with an outraged Lutheran conscience to the world's holocausts, wars, and obscenities. It is this, perhaps, that gives Scandinavian culture its *ångest* and melancholy, unforgettably captured in Ingmar Bergman's *The Seventh Seal* (see Box 10-1).[5]

This is not an isolated example. Much of Swedish literature laments for human anguish, as in August Strindberg's *Dream Play*.

> Oh how I feel for the agony of existence
> So this is to be mortal
> One even misses what one did not value
> One even regrets crimes one did not commit
> One wants to go and one wants to stay
> The twin halves of the heart are wrenched asunder.
> And one is torn as between raging horses
> Of contradiction, irresolution, discord.[6]

The titles of twentieth-century Swedish poetry, literature, and drama speak for themselves. Pär Lagerkvist's "Anguish," "Kaos," and *Evil*

Box 10-1

The Seventh Seal: The Agonized Conscience
of the Helpless Spectator

Antonius Block, the Knight, and his Squire, Jons, return from the Crusades to discover that the Black Death is ravaging Sweden. Is this God's reward for a noble and pious quest? Death personified comes to Block by the seashore. He pleads for time to discover what, if anything, his life meant. Death is unrelenting until the Knight challenges him to chess. While the two meet periodically to pursue their game, the Knight searches desperately for an answer to his question. He goes to confession but his Confessor is Death. He visits an artist, who explains that life is a frenzied dance at the approach of Death. He looks into the eyes of a fourteen-year-old girl condemned to the stake, who claims to have consorted with the Devil, but he sees only pain and terror. He turns to the monk presiding at her execution. It is Death.

Then, for just a few minutes the sunlight breaks through the clouds; the Knight and his Squire befriend a young couple from a traveling theater and their baby son. The couple invite them to share a bowl of wild strawberries and cream on the grass. It is a revelation. Everything the Knight had searched for in his crusading zeal is now here, alive in the small circle of conviviality, in the secular Last Supper of interpersonal communion. And the Knight had left his young bride to search for the Holy Grail!

He plays one last round of chess with Death, during which he knocks over the board. During this diversion, the couple and their child creep away to their caravan and flee the scene. Death replaces the fallen pieces and cheats in the process. The Knight is check mated. He travels on to his home with his companions, where Death comes for all of them as they read from Revelations about the breaking of the seventh seal. The film's closing scene shows the dance of Death across the horizon, but also the tiny caravan with its frail human cargo crossing a desolate landscape beneath a threatening sky.

The story mirrors the anguish of a neutral nation with a spectator seat upon the killing grounds strewn with human debris. Is it enough that one can save a few innocents from the slaughter, as Raoul Wallenberg did in issuing passports to Hungarian Jews? What else can a culture do whose perceptiveness is so much greater than its numbers or its physical powers?

Tales evoke the postwar mood. Vilhelm Moberg's *Ride This Night* is one of many allegories of Nazi monstrosity overwhelming resistance. In *Return to Ithaca,* by the Nobel prize author Eyvind Johnson, Odysseus is utterly sickened by the violence of the Trojan Wars, but like the Knight in *The Seventh Seal,* finds that it also awaits him at home. Similar visions of corruption and despair are found in *Island of the Doomed* by Stig Dagerman and in his *Crimes of the Night* and *Burnt Child.* [7]

In more recent years, Swedish theater has recovered some of its former luster, but has not lost its doom. Peter Weiss, a German emigré, wrote *Marat/de Sade* and *The Investigation*, which is about Auschwitz, while Lars Noren's *The Courage to Kill* and *Night Is the Mother of Day* stir the pot of revulsion and despair.

One reason that Swedes fall readily into melancholia might be their relative lack of emotional expression. Foreigners tend to regard them as "stiff," "shy," and "reserved." "We are dry balls," one Swedish colloquialism puts it. "To be, not be seen" is the family motto of the Wallenberg industrial dynasty. Jean Phillips-Martinsson, the author of *Swedes as Others See Them,* and founder of the Cross Cultural Relations Center in Stockholm, makes much sport of Swedish social inhibitions, among which are the near-obsession with punctuality and sequential time and an embarrassment at social warmth.

The author, not herself Swedish by birth but British, recalls from her early days in Sweden a fierce determination to get people to smile back at her:

> I remember getting on a train in Gothenberg and refusing to let myself get off until someone—anyone—had returned my smile. Their eyes slid away. Why? Were they insulted by me, aggressive to me? I went to the terminus and back. The driver was looking uncomfortable as he shouted, "Terminus!" for the second time. Finally, a little boy returned my compliment—he stuck out his tongue at me. I surrendered and got off. [8]

Of course, none of this touches on the genuine degrees of friendship established within a culture. "Reserve" is in the eyes and the judgment of the foreigner who is accustomed to a more demonstrative style and mistakes softer signals for the absence of any feeling. Sweden was, until recently, a country of low immigration. The change of policy is quite recent, and the culture may not yet have adapted itself to the process of welcoming strangers by the overt friendliness typical of America, which has absorbed immigrants for more than three centuries. In small countries where everyone grows up together the problem is less finding "friends" than avoiding their sheer numbers! Swedish reserve may be a reaction to bumping into acquaintances all the time.

As for Swedish anguish at the agonies of the world, this surely testifies to deep feelings beneath the reserve. As the Greek dramatists taught us, you look on stark tragedy so that you won't go out and do it yourself and add to the miseries of the world. In this, Sweden seems to have been conspicuously successful. Mental anguish is to be preferred to the physical destruction wrought by aggressive optimism.

This chapter seeks to account for the prolonged success of Swedish-style capitalism. We shall also consider whether the changes in the climate of world business are threatening Sweden. Is this culture capable of self-renewal? If there are flaws in her success, how serious are they?

The Ethic of Socially Oriented Individualism

If Swedes are shy and reserved, if they find small talk unsatisfying and "brilliant" conversation not worth the cultivation, then we must ask where they seek solace for the inner anguish to which they are prone. The answer is that they look for it in the work they do, and this work is a bridge back to the love and affection of their fellow workers, in which meaning and fulfillment may be found. For herein may lie one of the most important clues of Sweden's industrial success. More than any other culture examined in this book, Swedes begin with the individual, his or her integrity, uniqueness, freedom, needs, and values, yet insist that the fulfillment and destiny of the individual lies in developing and sustaining others by the gift of his or her own work and energy.

Ingmar Bergman put it best in his introduction to *The Seventh Seal*. Artists in Western civilizations have made a cult of

> . . . the smallest wound or pain as if it were of eternal importance. . . . Thus we finally gather in one large pen, where we stand and bleat about our loneliness without listening to each other. . . .
>
> Thus if I am asked what I would like the general purpose of my films to be, I would reply that I want to be one of the artists in the cathedral on the great plain. I want to make a dragon's head, an angel, a devil—or perhaps a saint out of stone. It does not matter which; it is the sense of satisfaction that counts. Regardless of whether I believe it or not, whether I am a Christian or not, I would play my part in the collective building of the cathedral.[9]

It is when there is no work to talk about that Swedes feel most shy. They hate empty words and regard sales pitches or blandishments not legitimized by the qualities of genuine products as "American" and of doubtful probity.

Insofar as individualism versus social obligations is one of the major existential dilemmas encountered in wealth creation, as in life itself, Swedes would appear to have come closer to a powerful reconciliation than most other cultures examined here. Their very reserve drives them to seek community through work in preference to the conversational arts, in which they are often regarded as deficient. And unlike the Japanese, Swedes are not born into a world of familial obligation to parents and elders. Swedes regard themselves as born free, encouraged by their parents into yeomanlike independence and then choosing whom to benefit through their work and when and how to do this.

Jan Carlzon, president of the Scandinavian Airlines System (SAS), explains how a medieval Swedish morality tale, "Ronia," helped him to turn around his company by emphasizing the risk of creating new relationships.

Ronia loved the son of a family with which her own family had a bitter feud. The other family lived geographically and symbolically on the far side of a deep gorge, separating the two houses. To miss one's footing in crossing this gorge was certain death. Ronia's true love visited her by stealth in her house but was discovered by her father, who seized the young man and imprisoned him, regarding his prisoner as a valuable hostage in the continuing feud. To prove her love, Ronia leapt to the "enemy's" side of the gorge, risking her life to save her relationship to her beloved and to equalize the bargaining power of the two adversaries.

Now that each adversary held the other's child, the breach between them could be negotiated and the lovers united in marriage. This very Scandinavian version of *Romeo and Juliet* replaces tragedy by a sensible, negotiated solution initiated by the young upon their elders. It is a cultural parable of risk taking to achieve equality and fulfillment of desire. Carlzon told it to inspire his staff to reach out to customers, whatever the sense of personal peril.[10]

Trompenaars' dilemmas questionnaire clearly reveals Sweden's dedication to the individual, together with the social use to which freedom is put. In Box 10-2, Question 1, Swedes are shown as preferring to take sole responsibility for repairing fire damage, rather than asking relations for help. They are more self-reliant in this respect than other cultures. Yet, in Question 2, they also desire to be known and accepted by colleagues at work for the persons they really are. They want their work to define them and to win friendship. This is not a sociability that seeks

Box 10-2

Sweden's Social Individualism

1. Following a fire in his shop, should the owner refinance the repairs himself or ask brothers/sisters for help?

Self Reliance

Swe	Austra	UK	NL	USA	Can	Ita	Ger	Fr	Jap	Sin
87.8	80.0	75.4	75.0	72.8	70.0	67.0	64.0	60.6	52.1	37.5

2. Will the best job be done if the people you work with know you personally and accept you, or will it be done if they respect your work, regardless of friendship?

Knowledge and Acceptance of the Person

Swe	Jap	NL	Ita	Ger	Fr	UK	Sin	Austra	USA	Can
56.2	40.9	34.5	33.6	27.1	24.6	24.1	22.5	21.9	18.0	12.5

3. If the boss gives you an order you think is wrong, do you question the order and the boss, or do you do as he says to avoid problems?

Question Your Boss and His Order

NL	Swe	Ger	UK	Fr	Can	Austra	USA	Ita	Jap	Sin
96.0	95.9	95.9	94.1	94.0	93.0	93.0	90.0	81.0	80.0	79.0

4. Should an employee with a record of 15 years satisfactory performance with a company be dismissed because his current performance is unsatisfactory, or should his whole record and the company's responsibility be considered?

Individual's Whole Record

Sin	Swe	Fr	Ita	Ger	Jap	NL	Austra	UK	Can	USA
78.4	74.6	73.8	72.5	69.0	67.0	62.5	59.4	57.5	46.0	43.0

5. For the best results, should people be fitted to the necessary jobs or the jobs adjusted to the people?

Fit Jobs to People

Swe	Can	Ita	Fr	Jap	Sin	Austra	USA	UK	Ger
36.9	35.0	26.1	25.3	21.1	20.0	19.75	15.8	14.0	13.8

to escape personal responsibility, but one that seeks to confirm it. More than other nations, Swedes seek to individualize themselves by what they contribute to the workplace and to colleagues.

They also exceed Americans in their readiness to dispute with their boss if they believe he is wrong. There is no desire here to shelter within the group or to use it for self-protection. "Groupthink" is conspicuously absent. Yet individualistic Swedes lead the managers of all European countries surveyed to save from dismissal an employee with fifteen years satisfactory service who is no longer performing well. The commitment to the person is in the context of his or her whole career with the company.

Ultimately, Swedes are strongly dedicated to the development of the individual. Asked whether individuals should be fitted to the tasks and jobs required by the organization, or that the organization should go to the trouble—and it is considerable—of redesigning jobs to better fit the individual, only Swedish and Canadian managers opted for the latter alternative in any appreciable numbers. For most American managers, freedom is still the making of choices among predefined job slots and not any sustained attempt to make the workplace more fit for people. Recent experiments in major Swedish companies to improve job design include those at Volvo's Kalmar, Uddevalla, and Skövde plants, and at SAS, Ericsson Talecom, IKEA, and BAHCO.[11]

Throughout this book we have identified gains on both dimensions of a dilemma, in this case individuality and effective group functioning, with the maturing of value systems in general. In this respect, Swedish managers are more developed than those of other nations; whether they rush into communion with other colleagues out of dire existential dread or from sheer pleasure at the prospect, matters less than their commitment to finding individual paths to social usefulness.

One of the authors attended a retreat in which the Swedish multinational insurer, Skandia, was working with its British subsidiary. An insurance recession had combined with serious overcapacity in the industry and catastrophic losses from two hurricanes to create very serious problems in the London market. Up until the final evening, Swedish-British interaction had been impeccably technical, neutral, and restrained. But at dinner, the Swedish CEO rose to make a speech. He recalled the musical *Carousel*, where the ghost of Curly sings to the girl carrying his child and abandoned by his suicide. (The same song had been adopted by the British fans of the Liverpool football team.)

The words, he thought, were appropriate to his feelings toward the struggling British subsidiary:

> When you walk through a storm
> Hold your head up high
> And don't be afraid of the dark . . .
> Walk on, walk on with hope in your heart
> And you'll never walk alone.

Americans wrote this song for lovers, and the British fans sang it to their beloved team. But only Swedes, surely, would apply it to the relationship of cross-national work teams in the insurance industry! It suggests something of the deep sublimated affection at the roots of their work ethic.

The Fullest Use of Human Resources

Cultures vary considerably as to whether they consider efficient business as a calling for which only some people are good enough, or whether they see all people as needing to express themselves economically. Is a sizable unemployed residue a salutary lesson in self-help and a goad to the idle, or is it a reproach to society that it failed to include everyone? Sweden inclines to the second of these two sets of contrasting views. Everyone should work. Great efforts should be made to include all. It is grossly inefficient to pay the able-bodied to remain idle—akin to fielding a team with several players sidelined. "Workfare," as opposed to welfare, is the rule in Sweden rather than the exception. We see in Table 10-1 that Sweden leads the league tables of twenty-three major economies in total employment of its population. Fifty-two percent of all Swedes work. This is even more impressive when we realize that 47 percent of Swedish women are at work, which is 20 percent more than in the Netherlands, and only 5 percent less than the figure for men. Finally, Sweden's percentage of those unemployed is lower than every other nation save Switzerland. Sweden also leads the world in employing the handicapped and adapting the physical environment to enable them to participate. Michael Porter points out that strict government regulations about assisting the handicapped have helped to make Sweden a world-class supplier in the field of health and aids to the disabled. It is part of the trend of adapting work to people, rather than people to work,[12] as noted in Box 10-2.

Table 10-1   Sweden's Employment Strengths

Utilization of Female in Work Force, % of Total		Total Employment in Millions as % of Population		Total Unemployment as % of Labor Force	
Sweden	47.23	**Sweden**	52.12	Switzerland	0.72
Finland	45.37	Denmark	50.84	**Sweden**	1.61
Norway	43.11	Switzerland	50.58	Japan	2.51
USA	42.49	Norway	50.33	Korea	2.51
Denmark	42.35	Finland	49.11	Norway	3.25
Canada	40.53	Japan	49.03	Singapore	3.35
New Zealand	40.08	Canada	47.58	Austria	3.58
Portugal	40.07	Singapore	46.74	Finland	4.59
UK	39.69	USA	46.67	USA	5.50
Korea	39.13	UK	45.92	Portugal	5.83
Japan	39.05	New Zealand	45.67	Australia	6.70
Singapore	37.58	Australia	44.49	New Zealand	7.58
Switzerland	37.30	Germany	42.77	Greece	7.74
Australia	36.94	Portugal	41.10	Canada	7.77
France	36.77	Korea	40.20	Germany	7.89
Germany	35.59	France	38.7	UK	7.92
Netherlands	35.13	Belgium/Lux	38.60	Netherlands	8.29
Belgium/Lux	33.73	Austria	36.98	Denmark	8.56
Austria	33.66	Greece	36.44	Belgium/Lux	9.72
Spain	32.60	Italy	36.27	France	9.99
Greece	31.23	Netherlands	32.62	Italy	12.16
Italy	30.03	Ireland	30.82	Ireland	16.72
Ireland	26.63	Spain	30.13	Spain	19.50

Source: IMO Annual Report on International Competitiveness, Geneva 1990.

Sweden also scores very well on three other broad indicators of human welfare. Life expectancy is second only to Japan's, and the highest in Europe. Higher education enrollment is highest in Europe, with American and Canadian scores inflated somewhat by "higher" education facilities that are below the standards of bachelor's degrees, i.e., community and junior colleges. Sweden also scores well on profit sharing and enterprise incentives (see Table 10-2).

Sweden is often accused of high absenteeism rates, by some estimates as high as 17 percent. But most of this is authorized, not unauthorized absence. Swedes can get leave of absence from work for many legitimate reasons: maternity, paternity (often shared equally), military service, education, marriage, home guard, and union work, among others. The extraordinary lengths to which Sweden's managers will go to include

Table 10-2   A Dedication to the Development of Human Resources

Life Expectancy at Birth in Years		Higher Education Percent of 20–24-year-olds in Higher Education in 1990		Enterprise Incentives for Employees (I.e., Profit Sharing) 0 = nonexistent 100 = many	
1. Japan	78.8	USA	59	USA	62.71
2. **Sweden**	77.8	Canada	55	France	60.29
3. Switzerland	77.6	**Sweden**	37	**Sweden**	55.92
4. Netherlands	77.5	Finland	35	Singapore	54.15
5. Norway	77.4	Korea	35	Canada	54.06
6. Canada	77.3	New Zealand	33	UK	51.58
7. Spain	77.3	Netherlands	33	Korea	50.71
8. Australia	76.9	Belgium/Lux	32	Japan	50.24
9. France	76.6	Spain	32	Germany	45.28
10. Greece	76.4	France	30	New Zealand	39.17
11. USA	76.3	Germany	30	Finland	39.17
12. Italy	76.3	Japan	30	Australia	38.78
13. Denmark	76.2	Australia	29	Switzerland	38.68
14. UK	76.0	Denmark	29	Ireland	37.62
15. Germany	75.7	Austria	29	Austria	35.24
16. Finland	75.7	Norway	28	Netherlands	35.11
17. New Zealand	75.6	Italy	25	Denmark	33.49
18. Belgium/Lux	75.5	Greece	24	Norway	33.00
19. Ireland	75.1	Switzerland	23	Belgium/Lux	32.12
20. Austria	75.0	UK	23	Spain	26.60
21. Portugal	74.3	Ireland	22	Portugal	26.15
22. Singapore	73.8	Portugal	13	Greece	25.00
23. Korea	70.6	Singapore	n/a	Italy	24.40

everyone's interests, even in a situation where one-quarter of the work force had to be made redundant, is captured in our interview with Anders Lindstrom, a turnaround specialist, who took BAHCO, a hand-tool company from bankruptcy to high profitability in just four years. Lindstrom had not only employees to deal with, but a small community largely dependent on the plant for its livelihood.

A few months after I took over, the editor-in chief of the local paper came to see me. "We'd like to know what's happening at BAHCO. Our readers are very concerned about the factory. Could I please get in some time?" "You can get in tomorrow," I told him, "and you can talk to anyone."

It was a gamble, because if things do go wrong, publicity confirms this, but if things go right the publicity builds confidence and pride. Besides, these people were working not just for themselves and their families, but for

BAHCO and the whole community. I wanted them to remember this. If the paper wrote up our problems they would also acclaim any solutions, and I wanted everyone to know just how much was at stake.

We needed to communicate the sheer extent of the crisis if we were to justify laying off 26 percent of the work force, which is what we had to do. But no one, I repeat, no one, left us without another job to go to. We had some of our older employees, who knew a lot of people, set up a relocation office. We provided use of the telephone and strong letters of recommendation. In the end, only eight people could not be placed in jobs outside BAHCO, and those we kept with us.

This wasn't charity, it was common sense. We had to have people pull together, trust each other, trust management, and come through the crisis by helping each other. If I had simply dumped those people, no one would have believed me.[13]

Enlightened Leadership

Anders Lindstrom is one example of the quality of Swedish business leaders. Swedish companies, especially the larger ones, are able to draw on some extraordinary qualities of leadership: Peter Gyllenhammar of Volvo, Ingvar Kamprad of IKEA, Percy Barnevik of Asea Brown Boveri, Bjorn Svedberg of L. M. Ericsson, Jan Carlzon of SAS, Allan Larson of the Labor Market Board, Bo Ekman of the aptly named Holen Group, Antonin Johnson of A. Johnson, Curt Nicolin, head of the Employers' Federation, and many others. Swedish leaders are extremely broad in their interests and their education. The vital contribution of business to Swedish society is at the top of their agendas, and this contribution goes far beyond economics.[14]

One important test of leadership is readiness to delegate. No one with an aspiration to lead deliberately abdicates that role. If you delegate, it is because you trust the subordinate to act in your name. Goran Carstedt, now head of IKEA in North America, put well the Swedish approach:

> If you believe in people and their latent capacities, then the more authority you "give away" to them, the more you get back in ideas and initiatives even you did not foresee. We believe in radical decentralization, in pushing authority down to the level where those dealing directly with customers have the freedom to exercise it.

When Carstedt, several years earlier, had taken over the ailing operations of Volvo, France, his first move was not to tell but to ask. He began his efforts with nine regional meetings with the 150 French auto dealers around U-shaped tables. "I made it clear I was the coordinator, not the boss. I said simply, 'I want to know from you what you think should be done and what Volvo can do to help you sell more cars. Tell me what we are doing wrong, what you want from us, and I'll see it is done if I possibly can.' "

Carstedt said of their reaction: "That surprised them. No one had ever taken dealers seriously enough to ask their advice. It was, 'Why don't you do better? Don't think we can't drop you.' Here someone was listening."[15]

Not surprisingly, given this approach, Swedish managers head the league of national economies in willingness to "Delegate Authority," (see Table 10-3). Sweden is ahead of even Japan by six percentage points and

Table 10-3   Swedish Leadership Strengths: The World's Best?

Managerial Initiative Managers Sense of Drive and Responsibility 0 = low 100 = high		Extent to Which Leaders Delegate Authority 0 = low 100 = high		Capacity of Leaders and Corporations to Take a Long-Term View 0 = low 100 = high	
Sweden	72.29	Sweden	75.51	Japan	89.29
USA	73.67	Japan	69.27	Germany	78.61
Japan	72.20	Norway	68.50	Sweden	76.73
Finland	69.58	USA	66.23	Switzerland	75.56
Korea	67.86	Singapore	65.37	Finland	74.17
Netherlands	67.11	Denmark	64.65	Netherlands	68.64
Singapore	66.34	Canada	64.38	Singapore	64.29
Switzerland	65.71	Finland	62.92	Austria	60.00
Belgium/Lux	65.47	Switzerland	62.20	France	59.71
Ireland	64.76	Netherlands	61.33	Ireland	57.67
France	64.64	Australia	61.22	Belgium/Lux	57.58
Austria	62.56	Germany	60.85	Korea	56.43
Denmark	62.79	New Zealand	60.54	Norway	56.00
Italy	62.40	Ireland	59.53	New Zealand	55.14
Australia	62.04	UK	58.95	Italy	54.40
Canada	61.56	Belgium/Lux	54.55	Denmark	53.49
Spain	61.55	Austria	54.29	UK	51.58
New Zealand	59.46	France	53.62	Canada	51.56
Greece	58.50	Italy	46.80	Australia	51.02
UK	58.25	Spain	44.31	Spain	48.20
Norway	54.50	Portugal	42.56	Portugal	42.54
Portugal	49.74	Greece	37.95	USA	40.98
				Greece	40.00

leads the United States by nine and the French by twenty-two points. It was French car dealers to whom Carstedt successfully delegated. A prominent example of delegation was the decision of industrial financiers, headed by the late Marcus Wallenberg, to skip an entire generation in appointing Gyllenhammar to Volvo at the age of thirty-six, Barenevik to Asea at forty-one, and Carlzon to SAS at thirty-nine.[16]

But delegation does not mean that a leader is passive or wants for inspiration and initiative; this is clearly shown by Sweden's top rating in the accompanying data on "Managerial Initiative, Drive, and Responsibility." Consider for example, Goran Carstedt's initiative that eventually succeeded in doubling Volvo's sales in France. He chartered a plane to take all the dealers and their wives to Göteborg, where they visited the Torslanda factory. That evening he gave our prizes to the best dealers and presented the new models.

> The next day we booked our own train and took it through some of the most beautiful parts of the Swedish countryside, passing Skövde where he took them to the engine factory. The place is immaculately clean. The workers are young and attractive—many are women—and it is high-tech, high-touch, and electronics. We then took them up to Old Stockholm to see the sights, and from there to a Viking party where we drank schnapps, wore helmets, ate with our fingers, and threw the debris over our shoulders.
>
> For lunch the next day we gathered in Stockholm City Hall, where Swedish fiddlers in traditional costume and singers of folk music feted the guests. At that point I gave a speech. My French was never too successful, but I think they gave me points for trying. I said, "For two years now I've been trying to explain to you that there is something special about Volvo: our philosophy and values are important to our success. And to understand Volvo, it helps to understand something about Sweden.
>
> So we've invited you on this trip to see our factories, to meet our people, to see our lakes, forests, trees, and houses for yourselves. Now we're here, in the heart of Sweden, in the room where the Nobel dinners are served before the prizes are given, and you have the Nobel menus before you to remind you that this is the place that gives hospitality to the greatest achievements and the finest quality of which all you can be a part."

This is not simply an unusual leadership initiative, it illustrates the sheer extent to which the manufacture and sale of Volvo cars is treated as an expression of the whole Swedish culture, its values, and its people; Volvo and Sweden are inseparable. Goran explained:

> We pioneered the windshield that does not shatter, the crush-resistant car body, and the three-point safety belt, on which we still have patents. These

ideas come not from any analysis of markets but from Swedish and Volvo cultures themselves. I remember taking my kids ice-skating near our home in Paris. There must have been more than a hundred children at the rink. Ours were the only ones in crash helmets. Swedes take care of each other.[17]

Ignoring the advice that Volvo cars were hopelessly dull by French standards and not *pointe*, that they were cerebral cars, something melancholy Scandinavians thought about on long winter evenings, that the French wanted hot, sporty cars sold amid the effervescence of champagne, Goran went on to win media prizes for advertisements about safety! Especially singled out for praise was the ad of a small sleeping girl strapped safely in the back seat of a Volvo. The caption read: "You need to protect the future, especially when the future is behind you."

The culture of Sweden, as expressed through Volvo, was too important to compromise. Behind it were the convictions of a whole people, presented by business statesmen. It is partly for this reason that Swedish leaders excel in taking the "Long-Term view" (see Table 10-3). You do not easily abandon loss-making industries, and there were plenty in the mid and late 1970s, if they say something important about Sweden and her people. Sweden has historically stuck with her "founding industries"—shipbuilding being a notable exception. This has been achieved by continuous high rates of investment, especially in process technologies. Sweden's economic structure is an advantage here. Capital is owned largely by industrial banks and leading families with dynastic aspirations. Business is less a way of making quick returns than of perpetuating their own influence and that of the small country in which they loom large.

The Uses of Equality

Equality is not a value traditionally associated with business. Indeed, *in*equality has more frequently been advocated on its behalf. The "right to manage" needs to be upheld over the demands of labor monopolies. According to classical economists, the movement of resources toward those who compete most successfully and the loss of those resources to the less competitive is a process vital to prosperity. It follows that unequal rewards, commensurate to unequal levels of ability and achievement, are similarly essential. Those who have already accumulated wealth are surely the best qualified to invest it well. Redistributing resources to the improvident could prove diastrous.

What then, can be said for equality, and why would a culture advocating it not pay a very stiff price economically?

Equality, at least in the context of Western cultures, has some distinct advantages, most especially the custom of treating people *as if* they were equals in the process of discovering what they have to contribute to the solution of problems and the completion of the common task. As we will see in Table 13-5, Swedish managers were the least likely to agree with the statement, "It is important for a manager to have at hand precise answers to most of the questions that his subordinates may raise about their work." Only 10 percent of Swedish managers agreed, compared with 66 percent of Italians and 53 percent of French. Moreover, Swedes tend to see their organizational hierarchy as flatter than most other countries.

For Swedes, the information necessary to improving the work process is widely distributed throughout the group. It follows that without the most open lines of communication and the understanding that answers can come from anyone or anywhere, "shy" Swedes are unlikely to speak up. This ethic of equal access to common solutions is well captured in "The Year of the Ideas," part of Anders Lindstrom's success in turning around BAHCO.

Lindstrom announced that there were no stupid ideas, that all companies in the group must collect them, that units with the most usable ideas would be commended, that all generators of ideas would receive an amount commensurate with their realized value, sometimes as much as several months' salary. There would be local heats, semifinals, and finals.

> I remember attending one semifinal. We took the winners to the Royal Academy of Science in Stockholm for lunch. Every winner receives a crystal glass figure engraved with their name and a cheque for Skr10,000 (£1,000). We televise the proceedings and make it available to the whole company, with videotapes for each semifinalist.
>
> On this occasion there were two young girls among the semifinalists. One, I recall, had been working in the ordering department of the pneumatics company. If pumps fail, then clients want replacement parts urgently, and we ship them out for overnight delivery. But because the warehouse closed at 4:00 P.M., this young girl could not ship any parts requested after that time, although she knew where to find them.
>
> She wanted to know—and had asked in vain for years—why she wasn't allowed into the warehouse to fetch the parts. "They don't listen to a girl," she said plaintively. Well, we'd taken notice now, and the warehouse was open as long as the ordering department was. The girl got her £1,000 and

put her crystal ball on her desk so that no one would underestimate her ever again.

We also honor the people who collect the ideas and first confirm them. They are mostly older people, but they are just as proud of "their" winners as if they had thought of it themselves. For the finalists one year there was a three-day holiday in Paris. They were all workers from different factories and had never been to France before.[18]

In the six months following, BAHCO recorded 320 implementable ideas, ten times more than the entire previous year. And we see again how Swedes identify their work with the highest cultural institutions in the land and feel themselves part of these.

Even the most resented aspects of Swedish equality, the power of its trade unions and working class with their alliance with the long-ruling Social Democratic Party, can trigger valuable forms of adaptation. The refusal of young Swedes to take jobs in factories, allied to a very tight labor market for skilled workers, led to unprecedented efforts to improve the quality of working life, keep excused absences to their minimum, and increase the skills repertory of individual workers so they can perform multiple tasks as needed.

The Volvo factory at Kalmar, with its tools ergonomically designed around the expressed needs of workers, is one consequence. Here the assembly line is broken into circular work stations, where teams work flexibly in assembling the whole vehicle, dividing the task according to agreement within the team and constantly experimenting with novel team formations. At the Uddevalla factory, sequential stages have been abandoned together. "Car craftsmen" build the vehicle from A to Z and personally sign the underside of the body to guarantee its quality. Workers are trained to use computers to order, just in time, the needed parts.[19]

Jan Forslin of the Swedish Council of Management and Work-life Issues (F. A. Radet) describes the long-running rivalry between the HQ of Volvo Components and its engine plants at Skövde and Vara, two experimental plants in humanizing the workplace. The engineer-controlled HQ was skeptical of organizational designs that pushed key decisions down to the grass roots. On several occasions the experiments were dubbed failures, partly because of traditional ways of measuring efficiency. Not until someone noticed that a whole level of supervision had been eliminated at the experimental plants, that less staff was needed and salary costs were far lower, did the true advantages of this new way of working emerge.[20]

In highly individualistic cultures, such as Sweden, equality is essential if agreements are not to be imposed by persons pulling rank. A forced decision of this kind will tend to submerge the viewpoints of the losers, not to mention customers. Goran Carstedt found that in his French Volvo subsidiary there was a tendency to write memos which essentially "moved" the responsibility for failure from desk to desk. Goran eventually forbade memos from people sitting close to each other in the same office. Instead, he asked for shared solutions.[21]

Another important value of equality is that it helps individualist cultures serve customers better. Trompenaars' research has found repeatedly that it is sales and marketing departments within organizations that push hardest for more equal relations. They must do this in order to have the customers' demands register within the hierarchy. For it is mostly low level staff who serve customers in person, and customers cannot get good service where these staff members are powerless and subordinated. Goran Carstedt found this among Volvo dealers in France. So long as dealers were treated as second-class citizens by Volvo France, customers would have the status of third-class citizens. The whole direction of influence had to be reversed.[22]

At about this time, Jan Carlzon of SAS was demonstrating the same lesson, not simply to international airline passengers, but to much of the reading public, thanks to his book *Moments of Truth*. This contained a set of principles that helped turn around his company and was later used by British Airways to transform its own fortunes.[23]

Carlzon argued that what really made a difference to customers were 50 million "moments of truth," fifteen-second encounters between passengers and airline staff, which conveyed to those passengers whether or not the company was concerned to serve them. All the schedules, logistics, servicing, and hardware converged on those few moments which could make or break an airline.

The answer was to empower the service staff to help the customer, to make those fifteen seconds a source of satisfaction, not frustration. Simple though this sounds, it required, as at Volvo, a complete reversal of the usual direction of influence. Those helping the customers must be given support and assistance by middle managers supplying resources and removing obstacles. These resources were to be dedicated to customer service goals that top managers had identified. The whole company served to empower its front-line staff, whose discretion was markedly increased in a radically decentralized organization.

Coming through Arlanda Airport, Carlzon noticed that all the signaling systems for determining on what carousel baggage was coming out, were on the blink. Why had not handwritten signs been posted? Because management in Stockholm said it would soon be fixed so the signs were unnecessary—and that was a week ago. "I phoned the appropriate division head," he said. "The manager (in Stockholm) had a choice. He could either take his handsome desk from his spacious office and move it down to the arrivals terminal, where he could witness the problems personally . . . or yield his decision-making power to the frontline people."[24]

Informality and Lagom

When the early Vikings passed around the drinking horn in a circle, there was often a dilemma of drinking too much or too little. To drink too little would deprive you of intoxicating pleasures, but to drink too much could attract the ire of the fearsome warriors who came after you. The answer was to imbibe *lagom*, just the right quantity to satisfy yourself as well as others. Michael Maccoby regards *lagom* as an important quality of Swedish culture, a search for a mean between the individual and society.[25]

Swedes are famous in the circuits of international management for the "soft," "feminine," and informal aspects of their managerial style.[26] Foreigners have trouble discerning that a decision has even been made, but Swedes appear to know that it has. They rely far less than Americans on formal assessment and evaluation instruments, far more on good relationships within the group and an almost invisible (to outsiders) agreement that *lagom* has been achieved, that somewhere between the opinions expressed lies an optimal position. It is the enjoyment of the companionship of the group that draws individuals into a consensus. Swedes are much more likely than most other nations to seek promotion because it brings them into contact with a new and interesting group, than because of private benefits such as income or sense of responsibility. They are also keener than most to advocate an informal bypassing of line authority. Creating consensus from many scattered opinions may require considerable tolerance for uncertainty, and here too, Swedes have been found to score high, a fact that probably contributes to the anguish felt in tragic times.

Because Sweden industrialized fast and late, nearly everyone's great-grandparents were of humble origins. As recently as 1850, 90 percent of the population was agrarian. It seems a matter of pride to have come from yeoman stock or the backwoods in two or three generations. An unusual number of our Swedish friends appear to have inhabited the Arctic Circle until quite recently. To put on airs or to create social distance is greatly disfavored. The naturalness of children is also admired, and it is a criminal offense to administer corporal punishment to your own child. One transcendent reason for working is to create a *folkhem*, literally, "people's home" and a home should be informal and affectionate.

International Heterarchy

According to Gunnar Hedlund of the Stockholm School of Economics, there is good reason for regarding Sweden as the most multinational economy in the world, relative to its size. Exports account for 30 percent of Swedish GNP as opposed to 10 percent in the United States. One in every four people employed in Swedish manufacturing industries works abroad. In Table 10-4 we see that Sweden heads twenty-three of the world's principal economies in the readiness of its companies to enter cross-border relationships, and that Swedish managers also head the league in their willingness to be posted abroad. This may not be entirely a compliment to Sweden, since managers from New Zealand, Ireland, and Australia also like to be posted abroad, and all three of these countries and Sweden fear a "brain drain," that their managers may not wish to return to their homeland.

Sweden excels in language acquisition, with many managers fluent in English, French, and German at a minimum. Swedish multinationals send their "best and brightest" abroad and "this is a condition, at least implicitly, for getting top jobs."

Major Swedish industries have been international virtually from their inception, since the home market was rarely large enough to support them. Alfa-Laval, Aga, Atlas-Copco, BAHCO, Electrolux, Ericsson, Esab, Nobel, Sanduik, SKF, and Swedish Match were all founded between 1860 and 1914, all internationalized within a decade, and all constitute part of the core of "Genius Firms" that, with periodic upgrading, have helped to sustain the Swedish economy ever since. It is said that the third person employed by Esab was its president of international operations.

Swedish international industry has an extraordinary coherence and "integrity" for want of a better word. Swedes have stuck long-term either to resource-based industries that elaborated their natural advantages

Table 10-4   Swedish Internationalism: Advantages and Problems

Extent to Which Companies Enter Cross-Border Relationships 0 = low 100 = high		Extent to Which Managers Are Willing to Accept Postings Abroad 0 = not at all 100 = readily		Extent of "Brain Drain." Do Well-Educated People Want to Return? 0 = to a large extent 100 = to a small extent	
Sweden	77.18	Sweden	72.65	USA	87.54
Switzerland	73.18	New Zealand	71.67	Germany	75.83
Netherlands	71.11	Ireland	68.84	France	74.41
Japan	70.73	Australia	68.57	Japan	74.15
UK	67.37	Netherlands	67.11	Switzerland	73.19
Germany	67.22	Finland	61.25	Korea	63.43
Canada	66.25	Switzerland	60.88	Norway	63.00
Belgium/Lux	66.06	USA	60.33	Italy	56.73
Finland	65.83	Canada	60.31	Netherlands	54.22
New Zealand	65.41	UK	58.95	Canada	53.75
Singapore	64.29	Belgium/Lux	58.79	Portugal	53.33
USA	64.26	Korea	57.86	Australia	51.43
France	60.88	Denmark	57.67	Spain	49.71
Ireland	59.07	Greece	57.50	Finland	49.58
Korea	57.86	Japan	57.07	UK	49.47
Italy	57.60	Germany	55.83	Austria	48.57
Australia	56.73	Portugal	54.87	Belgium/Lux	44.85
Denmark	56.28	Singapore	54.63	Singapore	44.39
Spain	55.64	Austria	48.57	Denmark	42.83
Norway	54.00	France	47.06	Sweden	41.22
Austria	52.30	Norway	44.00	New Zealand	41.08
Portugal	50.77	Italy	42.00	Greece	31.50
Greece	48.72	Spain	41.78	Ireland	26.67

and/or to key technologies used to upgrade and add value to these resources, i.e., fine paper as a development of its timber resources. Gunnar Hedlund notes:

> Profits have been reinvested in geographical expansion within major fields of business rather than used for business or returned to shareholders. (In later decades, the national tax policy has explicitly prevented this from happening.) This means that the identity of firms has been kept relatively intact. Sustained investment on improving products, finding related areas of business, and penetration of new markets has created world leaders within well-defined fields.[27]

Swedish subsidiaries abroad are famous (or infamous) for the autonomy they are accorded and the radical decentralization of the whole group of companies. Hedlund tells of the Australian subsidiary not visited for eight years. Hedlund's research shows that not only do the subsidiaries of Swedish multinationals have higher levels of influence than those of the United States and Japan, but formalized integration in terms of written manuals and set procedures mandated by them are fewer and less extensive. Swedes cohere through sustained personal contacts, job rotation, and networks. Their employees, who are promoted from within, often spend their lifetimes with the same company and share values rather than formal measurement systems and internal markets.

Gunnar Hedlund argues that from Swedish informality there is emerging a new *heterarchical* system, which anticipates a more effective and fully international system.[28]

The concept of heterarchy is borrowed from the work of Jay Ogilvy and refers to *multiple hierarchies whose salience depends on what knowledge is most situationally relevant.*[29] In such a network, first one source of authority predominates and then another, as a new body of expertise arises to meet fresh challenges. An international heterarchy might locate authority in whatever national subsidiary is furthest advanced in any particular area, so that "a Swedish MNC may have a financial center in Brussels, the largest headquarters division in London, an R&D center with group responsibility for certain products in India, a regional unit in Hong Kong with a role of coordinating activities in Asia, and an Italian unit with global responsibility for components."[30] Strategy for these areas of responsibility would originate locally. Within reach is a policy of having each national unit specialize in tasks at which that culture is most adept.

Dedicated to Investment in Quality Engineering

A much more familiar and traditional explanation of Sweden's persistence and prosperity is that the culture accords the highest status to engineers and engineering. The Genius Firms were founded by engineers often applying expertly the discoveries of other lands. The Royal Institute of Technology (KTH) and Chalmers University in Gothenberg are among the most prestigious in Europe. Gothenberg and Upsala, the Harvard and Yale, or Oxbridge, of Sweden are heavily populated by engineers. Of Swedish students graduating from "integrated upper secondary school" (high school) 48 percent go into technical, scientific, and industrial studies, 21 percent go into economics and mercantile studies, and only 15 percent, three-quarters female, go into the arts and social studies. Management is not regarded as a middle-class "profession," but as an opportunity to develop tools useful to society. Sweden remains among the top five world economies in the wide use of robots, computers, and telecommunications. Typically, the greatest gains in input-output ratios come not from personal services, in which Sweden is weak internationally, but through the deployment of more efficient technologies. Countries that accord high status to engineering—Japan, Germany, France, and Holland—tend to have strong economies in manufacturing and industrial goods. Sweden is no exception. Hedlund comments:

> The establishment of prestigious technical universities resembles the German pattern, as does the emphasis on technical education at the craft and worker level. There never was a gentlemanly class of classically educated gentry, as in England. Engineers have always been held in high esteem.[31]

It is, perhaps, part of Sweden's balance between individuality and social concern that their products are very strong in quality and safety, and these seem attentive to the marketing environment and the ecological environment (see Table 10-5). "Shy" Swedes speak through what they make and its impact on the environment. Their dislike of hype and blandishment may be part of a conviction that what they produce should speak for them. This sustained capacity to produce high-quality products is only possible through R&D investment that also exceeds most other economies.

Multiplying Problems

Yet many Swedes are worried by the state of their economy, and not all the signs are positive. The Social Democratic Party has recently lost power, and there is widespread feeling that Sweden is coasting along on the extraordinary records of only a score or more of Genius Firms founded around the turn of the century and constantly upgraded since. There is a curious failure of self-renewal. Where are the "genius firms" of the 1940s, 1950s, 1960s, 1970s, and 1980s? Sweden has grown very few major companies since World War II, and while it has used electronics to improve productivity, it is not a major force in the technologies of the information revolution. While the social democratic consensus appears to have produced a culture capable of adapting, improving, and extending core industries, with the assistance of a

Table 10-5   High-Quality Products with Concern for Customers and the Environment

Product Safety How National Companies Rate 0 = not at all 100 = to great extent		Product Quality 0 = poor 100 = excellent		Extent to Which Countries Protect Environment, Long-term 0 = not at all 100 = to great extent		Extent to Which Countries Are Oriented to Marketing 0 = not at all 100 = to great extent	
Germany	88.06	Japan	92.68	Denmark	79.52	Japan	83.41
Sweden	85.71	Germany	92.50	Sweden	76.73	USA	75.41
Japan	83.41	Switzerland	89.67	Switzerland	74.29	Germany	75.28
Switzerland	80.44	Austria	82.81	Germany	70.0	Sweden	73.88
Denmark	79.07	Belgium/Lux	81.82	Austria	69.52	Singapore	79.05
Austria	76.19	Denmark	80.00	Netherlands	69.33	Netherlands	64.44
Norway	76.00	Sweden	79.59	Finland	69.17	Switzerland	63.30
Canada	73.55	Finland	76.25	New Zealand	68.11	Belgium/Lux	61.82
USA	73.44	Singapore	73.00	Singapore	67.62	Canada	61.25
Netherlands	73.33	Norway	73.00	Norway	67.00	France	58.82
Finland	72.92	Netherlands	72.89	Australia	64.49	Denmark	58.14
Australia	70.20	Canada	68.13	Canada	57.19	UK	57.19
Belgium/Lux	69.09	Korea	60.71	Japan	56.10	Italy	55.60
New Zealand	68.11	Ireland	60.47	USA	56.07	Australia	54.29
Singapore	66.67	USA	59.67	France	53.91	New Zealand	54.05
UK	65.96	New Zealand	59.46	Ireland	52.56	Austria	50.48
France	61.45	Italy	56.00	Portugal	46.67	Ireland	50.48
Ireland	56.28	France	55.94	Belgium/Lux	44.24	Finland	49.58
Korea	50.71	UK	54.39	Korea	43.57	Korea	48.57
Italy	43.60	Australia	51.43	UK	41.75	Greece	48.57
Greece	42.50	Portugal	49.34	Italy	36.00	Spain	45.50
Portugal	42.05	Greece	47.00	Spain	33.98	Norway	38.50
Spain	36.70	Spain	40.97	Greece	29.47	Portugal	37.95

Source: IMD Report on International Competitiveness, 1990.

generally cooperative and flexible labor force, it has not reproduced the genius of earlier generations, and the suspicion that kindness and consensus dulls the sharp edge of creativity continues to haunt the *folkhem*.

An associated concern is that Sweden excels in areas shrinking in size, for example, manufacturing and resource-intensive businesses, such as metals and forest products, while being notably weak in expanding areas, such as services. Sweden may have the world's most constructive relationship between management and a unionized working class, but the basis of this working class, repetitive mass manufacture, is disappearing. The multiskilled, multimachine operators of flexible manufacturing systems are not in much need of protection and have increasingly middle-class attitudes. There is concern lest the offensive solidarity of blue-collar workers change over to a defensive solidarity aimed at preserving the status quo and slowing adaptation to new markets.

Sweden's serious problem is the creation of new business structures, as revealed in Table 10-6. She is last of twenty-three nations surveyed on "Anticipated Net Increase in New Business." She is last again in the expectation that "New Employment Opportunities"—even in established companies—will be generated. Some of this may be due to the "Dominance of Existing Industries," where Sweden again scores poorly.

It is less that large businesses bear small businesses any ill will, than that the whole system has been set up as a bargaining process between big business, big finance, big government, and big unions, and small business has not traditionally been part of this discussion. Ake Beckérus of F. A. Radet found serious obstacles to the growth of small business in

Table 10-6   Swedish Weaknesses: Lack of New and Small Businesses and of Capacity to Create New Jobs

Anticipated Net Increase in New Business over the Next 2 Years 0 = low 100 = high		Dominance of Existing Enterprises Detrimental to New Business 0 = to great extent 100 = not at all		Extent of New Employment Opportunities over Next 3 Years 0 = severe reduction 100 = many	
1. Japan	70.24	USA	67.87	Japan	75.00
2. Spain	67.18	Denmark	66.51	Singapore	74.63
3. Germany	66.94	Portugal	65.13	Ireland	67.80
4. Portugal	66.67	UK	63.51	Austria	66.67
5. Ireland	66.51	Ireland	62.79	Portugal	66.67
6. Singapore	65.71	Belgium/Lux	61.82	Germany	66.57
7. Italy	62.40	Germany	61.39	USA	63.00
8. Korea	61.43	France	60.29	Italy	62.40
9. Austria	60.00	Switzerland	59.75	Denmark	60.47
10. Netherlands	58.67	Netherlands	59.56	Belgium/Lux	60.00
11. France	57.68	Norway	58.50	Netherlands	60.00
12. Belgium/Lux	56.36	Greece	57.95	Australia	59.59
13. Switzerland	54.29	Italy	57.60	Canada	59.03
14. Denmark	52.49	New Zealand	57.30	New Zealand	58.92
15. USA	51.80	Canada	56.25	UK	58.55
16. New Zealand	49.19	Singapore	56.19	Spain	58.43
17. Finland	48.33	**Sweden**	54.17	Switzerland	57.78
18. Canada	48.13	Australia	53.06	France	57.23
19. Norway	47.00	Austria	52.38	Finland	54.58
20. Greece	45.50	Japan	52.50	Korea	54.29
21. UK	45.26	Spain	51.57	Norway	54.00
22. Australia	40.82	Finland	41.67	Greece	52.50
23. **Sweden**	40.0	Korea	40.00	**Sweden**	46.94

recent Swedish political climates, including government regulations beyond the capacities of small firms to meet and public attitudes that were patronizing, hostile, and indifferent.[32] The prevailing opinion appears to be that large businesses serve the culture, while small businesses serve merely their owners. In some ways the very efforts of big business to humanize working conditions may prevent disgruntled employees from starting up on their own.

Although new starts have jumped in recent years and venture capital is now readily available, new business bankruptcies have soared as well and the net gain is meager. The belief of Swedes that the fulfillment of their individuality is found in working to win the affections of group members may impede entrepreneurialism in which the individual must remain, at least for a time, on his or her own. An equally severe disincentive could be the heavy burden of personal income tax, the highest of any major economy and, ironically, higher than corporate taxes.

It is expensive to be on your own! Beckérus found that Swedish entrepreneurs neither hoped nor expected to get rich. They loved the independence and might wish to stay small. Whatever the reasons, something is preventing the growth of acorns into giant oaks, and the long-term consequences could be very serious.

Let the last word be that of Michael Maccoby, editor and contributor to *Sweden at the Edge*:

> Sweden is a living case of what it is possible to achieve when managers take on the challenge of creating a better society as well as more marketable products. To the best Swedish managers, that last statement might sound too idealistic. They would perhaps say, "Only by creating a better society can we succeed in the marketplace."[33]

11

Self-Constructed Lands: The Dutch as God's Apprentices

It is an artificial country. The Dutch made it; it exists because the Dutch preserve it; it shall vanish whenever the Dutch abandon it.

Edmundo Del Amicis (1880)

THERE IS A FAMILIAR SAYING: "God made the world, but the Dutch made Holland." It has made the Dutch reverential toward *kunstwerk*. The word means both a work of art, as in painting or writing, and a product of human ingenuity as opposed to a product of nature. The Netherlands are a triumph of human ingenuity in the face of the forces of nature. *Kunstwerk* includes the arts of engineering, hydraulics, dredging, building, architecture, and planning the environment. Even to call these "artworks" underestimates their role in Dutch society; they are practical responses to centuries of cumulative emergencies, the basic framework and underpinnings of any tolerable cultural existence at all.

Sigmund Freud defined the development of the psyche as the growing capacity of the ego to master the dark and turbulent dynamics of the id, as well as the atrophied prohibitions of the superego. He wrote:

> Where the id was the ego shall be. It is a work of culture—not unlike the draining of the Zuider Zee.

Now the Dutch are not noted enthusiasts for psychoanalysis, which is based on a model of the mind that submerges too much in the dark

265

waters of unconsciousness. The Dutch are busy enough with the "waterwolf" they can see from their windows to bother themselves about any alleged floodings in the basement of the mind, but they would surely agree that the conscious ego must be master of the self and the environment.

Indeed, they are surrounded by physical proofs of that mastery, a flat land, criss-crossed like a chessboard with a rational pattern of canals, polders, barriers, and roadways. As you come in to land at Schiphol Airport, it is instructive to recall that it used to be Lake Haarlem, the scene of a major naval battle in the Eighty Years War against Spain. The triumph of perseverance and willpower over the unruly elements is as firmly anchored in Dutch character as are those long piles driven into the wet earth to support large buildings. As recently as January 31, 1953, a westerly storm tore at the flags celebrating Crown Princess Beatrix's fifteenth birthday. In the ensuing storm, two thousand inhabitants of Zeeland drowned along with innumerable farm animals. It is said that this was the old waterwolf's last visit ever, but the character and language of the Low Countries is indelibly etched by the centuries' long struggle (see Box 11-1, "Some Watery Dutch Aphorisms").

We have argued throughout the section on America, Chapters 2 to 5, that the Calvinist conception of the saint as God's earthly agent, justified through works performed in this life, helped to lay the foundations of capitalism. The seventeenth-century Netherlands were natural candidates for such a creed. If Calvinism had not already been promulgated, it would have had to have been invented to justify Dutch survival. Not to toil prodigiously on earthworks was not simply a threat to your soul, but an invitation to drowning. Early visitors to the Netherlands claimed to know of a prisoner's cell in which the occupant accused of idleness had to bail water incessantly to avoid death. Its existence was never established. More likely it symbolized the predicament of Dutch people in general: work or the sea will claim you and everything you own.[1]

And this work was holy, a duty to God, your fellow man, and society. Jan Leeghwater (the name means literally "empty water") was a shoeless seventeenth-century pioneer of land reclamation and a traveling expert on drainage. He wrote: "The draining of the lakes is one of the most necessary, most profitable and most holy works in Holland."[2]

But there are anomalies in the portrait of the Dutch as standard-bearers of the Puritan ethic. In fact, there are marginally more Catholics, especially in the south of Holland; and Protestants, Catholics, and secularists constitute roughly each one-third of the nation's population.

Box 11-1

Some Dutch Aphorisms

"Do not go over one-night's ice." (Be cautious.)

"When the calves dance on the ice." (It will never happen.)

"He is as healthy as a fish."

"He got there with his heels over the canal." (He just made it.)

"The water has almost reached the top of the dike." (He is close to tears.)

"That doesn't put sods on the dike." (Doesn't help.)

"To go straight through the sea." (To be honest.)

"In times of storm one gets to know one's crew."

"He has been hit by a windmill." (He is nutty.)

"To come home with a wet sail." (To stagger drunkenly—ships used to wet their sails for tacking.)

"Getting old cows from the ditch." (Dwelling too much on the past.)

"Getting your sheep on dry land." (Succeeding in business.)

"To help someone from the shore into the ditch." (To make things worse.)

"Catch cholera!" (Cholera is a disease of polluted water or food.)

Source: Of Dutch Ways, Helen Colijn. New York: Harper & Row, 1984. ("Knowing the Netherlands," briefing paper, Royal Tropical Institute, Amsterdam, 1989.)

Moreover, Holland was slow to move from mercantilism to industrialization, being still predominantly agricultural until late in the nineteenth century after a century of decline, which included French occupation. Yet Amsterdam remained a major financial center.

Today there is every reason for taking the Netherlands very seriously indeed as an instructive prototype of advanced capitalism. With a positive trade balance of $7.4 billion and a positive current account balance of $11.3 billion, the Netherlands is the EEC's second strongest performer. Her inflation rate, just below 4 percent, is among the lowest. Her GNP continued to grow through the recession of 1990–92 at about 2 percent, while the United States, Canada, Belgium, Italy, and Spain showed negative growth. Her current unemployment is 4 percent, the lowest in the EEC, although the Handicapped Act (WAO) removes a number of people from the pool. All this was achieved despite the highest social spending in the EEC, which allegedly tempts citizens to idleness. With an average life expectancy of 77.5 years, the Netherlands is fourth in the world, surpassed only by Japan, Sweden, and Switzerland.

Surveys rate her third in willingness to enter cross-border relationships (see Table 10-4), sixth in the capacity of its corporations to think long-term, and sixth in the reputation for drive and initiative among its managers (see Table 10-3). On three of these last four measures she leads the EEC.

Moreover, the Netherlands industrialized late, as did Germany and Japan. Still largely agricultural until World War II, her industry and ports were devastated by the war. Her extraordinary postwar recovery under Willem Drees, the socialist premier from 1945 to 1948, however ideologically unorthodox, showed an industrial discipline of wage increases earned from heightened productivity that made Holland the envy of Europe. Her economic miracle was second only to Germany's, to whom her economy was closely tied, and whose economic miracle was greatly to her benefit.

But the Netherlands has never been a "planned society" in the ideological sense of the state "commanding" the economy. For the Dutch, planning is "the best conceivable adjustment of space and society to each other" and "an instrument for giving everyone a voice." Governments do not subjugate as much as they orchestrate. Holland's extraordinary postwar growth owed much to Jan Tinbergen and the *Centraal Planbureau*, who strove masterfully to depoliticize economic and social indicators, so that the *Sociaal Economische Raad* (Social Economic Council), in which management and workers were equally represented, was able to raise the country's competitive position by measurements that both sides trusted.[3] The postwar Dutch political climate was characterized by a "harmony model."

Although the Netherlands departs somewhat from the proposition that the Puritan ethic was the springboard of early industrialization, the country closely resembles the American and British profiles on the seven dimensions introduced in Chapter 1. Dutch managers are on most questions more *universalistic* than particularistic, more atomistic/specific than holistic/diffuse, more individualistic than communitarian, marginally external in their locus of control (as befits a country invaded by foreign armies and the sea), more achievement than ascription oriented, much more egalitarian than hierarchical, and more sequential than synchronous in their orientation to time. Only in rejecting an innerdirectiveness that has never been their cultural experience do they differ much from Anglo-Saxon attitudes on these seven dimensions.

The historical contributions of the Dutch to American culture comes as no surprise. Peter Stuyvesant, the founder of New York; Henrik Hudson, the explorer; three presidents, Martin Van Buren, Theodore and Franklin D. Roosevelt; Cornelius Vanderbilt, the industrialist; Fritz Roethlisberger of the Human Relations School of Management; and many others. The British and Americans are also among the preferred partners of the Dutch. Royal Dutch Shell is an Anglo-Dutch enterprise with extensive American holdings. Unilever is also owned jointly by the Dutch and British, while Philips, although Dutch owned, operates widely in Britain and the United States. In contrast, Franco-Dutch partnerships are relatively rare, as are those with Southern Europe.

Does this mean that Dutch management culture differs little from Anglo-American profiles? Not at all. That one difference in orientation appears to be extremely significant. A number of the dilemmas on our questionnaire and on those designed by others do reveal crucial differences, which we consider in this chapter.

Bluntness, Defiance, and Equality

The reader may recall the third question in Box 10-2: "If the boss gives you an order you think is wrong, do you question the order and the boss, or do you do as he says to avoid problems?" We saw that Swedes were unusually defiant, but they were exceeded in this by only one nation, the Dutch, 96 percent of whose managers would tell a mistaken boss to his face where to get off.

In seeking reasons for this readiness to speak out and speak plainly, we must remember that the Dutch are more egalitarian and less hierarchical than any culture in our survey. The Dutch see their organizational pyramids as flatter than those described by all other nations, including the United States (see Box 5-1). The Dutch distrust anyone who shows off or draws attention to him- or herself. Only once have we seen a Dutch CEO seriously angry with the director of his British subsidiary company, and even then he barely betrayed his anger. The cause of the dispute was the subsidiary's annual report. The Dutch CEO had received a proof copy for his approval before printing. It contained six quarter-page photographs of the English director engaged in various knighthood-earning activities. The telephone communication was very brief: "I have your report. I would like one photograph of you.

One, small, photograph *only*. . . . Goodbye."⁴ (He then replaced the receiver.)

Dutch policemen have been known to remove their hats before confronting a squatter: "Because I would like to be on par with him." Nor is it done to sit in the back of a taxi rather than beside the driver. When the English author sits in the back, the driver knows he is foreign. Wealthier Dutch also like to remove the metal letters from their automobiles that reveal that they have purchased the most expensive Mercedes or BMW in the range. To have a fine car, yet disguise its ultimate distinction, is a gesture towards equality.

The Dutch have a saying: *Doe maar gewoon, dan doe je al gek genoeg* ("Act normally and you will be conspicuous enough"). Indeed, no one is permitted to rise too high—no political party, no religion, no industry, and, certainly, no individual. Shell and Unilever are both carefully structured so that neither the British nor the Dutch can dominate. All actions of the Dutch crown must be consented to by Parliament, and the monarch herself gives an example of reserve rather than grandeur. William Z. Shetter explains:

> The Dutch monarchy can be abolished at any time by an Act of Parliament, but it remains firmly established because of the consent that supports it which has been proved repeatedly. The Dutch people are not monarchists at heart, but republicans who come close to believing everyone should be his own sovereign. It is only the high regard for the house of Oranje Nassau and its role in Dutch history that supports the monarchy. There can be little doubt that if the family were to die out, a republican form of government would be declared immediately.⁵

While there is considerable public affection for the House of Orange, this stems from its historical services to the Dutch nation: a catalyst for the defiance of Spain in the seventeenth century, a sovereign voice in exile during World War II, and a principle of continuity as coalition partners haggle to form governments.

It is as a symbol of sovereign imperturbability, middle-class stolidity, and dependability that the Dutch royal family is taken to the hearts of the nation. Angry demonstrators against housing shortages and policies toward Germany swirled around the wedding of Princess Beatrix and Prince Claus in 1966 amid smoke bombs. The couple remained calm amid the storm, self-controlled amid indulgence. They were less monarchs than banners for the burgers and the bourgeoisie. In a less happy incident, Prince Bernhard accepted considerable monies from the Lockheed Corporation. Full responsibility was at once accepted by the government and the Council of Ministers. The Prince was publicly reprimanded and resigned all business and military functions.

A source of flexible authority is that Dutch managers see a person's knowledge as justifying his or her authority at work, so that influence shifts with expertise. Eighty-six percent would make the most knowledgeable person the head of a task group, even where a manager of greater seniority or formal authority was available. If knowledge is the source of authority in undertaking a specific task, and the Dutch also lean toward analysis, then it logically follows that a mistaken order erodes a leader's authority and must be corrected by his more knowledgeable subordinate.

Dutch managers also endorse, by a decisive 82 percent, that the purpose of an organization is not so much to show "who has authority over whom," but to "allocate and coordinate functions." Hence the role of authority is not to exercise power over people or force them to do your bidding—attributes repellent to many Dutch managers—but to make sure that functions are properly organized to achieve the agreed-upon purposes of the business.

It is within the purposefully organized enterprise that many Dutch managers seem to find freedom to agree and personal discretion to discharge their tasks free of close supervision. Our questionnaire posed to samples of international managers the dilemma below:

There are people who believe the work of a department can best be done if the individual members and the company agree on objectives, and it is then left to the individual to decide how to attain these goals.

Other people believe the work of a department can best be done if the manager sets the objectives and also directs the members of the department in completing the various tasks that need to be done.

Dutch managers were exceeded by only the pristine rationality of the French in preferring the first of these alternatives. The scores were as follows:

Table 11-1

	FRA	NL	JP	GER	USA	UK	SP	SIN	SWE	IT
Freedom within earlier agreed objectives	88.0	81.4	76.0	72.9	70.5	67.0	65.5	60.0	56.6	52.1

What appears to be happening here is that managers from the Netherlands identify highly organized activity with the protection of their own integrity and liberty. So long as their organizations have their consent, they will work conscientiously to advance the purposes of the company, but defiance follows quickly and forcefully whenever the organization is seen to breech an agreement or act foolishly. In the years both authors worked in Royal Dutch Shell there were several occasions, perhaps a half dozen, in which planned training exercises or presentations by visiting speakers were brought to a halt at lunchtime or at the coffee break and the activities discontinued thereafter. It was nearly always the Dutch managers who halted the proceedings. This was not what they had agreed to. The speaker's theme was without relevance or practicality and a waste of their time. They wished to be otherwise employed. Visiting speakers closed down without ceremony included a conservative economist, knighted on the recommendation of Mrs. Thatcher, and a distinguished Freudian writer and psychoanalyst. At a meeting on cross-cultural management at Lyon, a Dutch member of the audience rose to his feet two-thirds of the way through the session to confront the imposing performance of the French presenter: "This is billed as a workshop," he objected. "So far you have done all the work; when do the rest of us get a word in edgeways?" The audience stirred uneasily. "Dutch," murmured the man behind me. Yet this was not rude by intention. For the Dutch to speak plainly is a matter of respect, even affection. They have an expression: *Maak van je hart geen moordkuil* ("Do not make a hole in the body of your heart"). Alone in Europe they scorn diplomatic language as a false coin. The Dutch author remembers his French mother being amazed and indignant when a Dutch doctor was so blunt as to tell her that her condition, although not fatal, was incurable.

Lives Lived In Separate Compartments and Radically Decentralized

In another important respect, Dutch managers exceed any other group in our sample. We posed the following situation:

An employee at work will shortly marry. Should the organization take chief responsibility for throwing a party for work colleagues, or should those friends at work do it, as a strictly private initiative?

This is hardly a loaded question, one might think, not an issue on which preferences would be vehement. After all, an organization usually has more spare cash than do employees of marriageable age. But as we see in

Table 11-2 the Dutch do not want the work organization in their private affairs, even in a benign role.

Table 11-2 Marriage celebration is the responsibility of:

The employees as private celebrants	NL	SWE	GER	SP	IT	JP	FRA	USA	SIN	UK
	91.2	90.2	88.0	81.7	80.0	77.4	76.2	72.0	60.0	57.7

Why might the Dutch be so much more vehement on this subject than others? Partly, perhaps, because they are members of multiple organizations, including the family, and they identify their liberty and safety as citizens with what has been called a "pluriform culture," or multiple memberships in working, sporting, religious, neighborhood, and family groups.[6] No wonder, then, that they reject overwhelmingly the suggestion that the corporation should have any responsibility in helping to find employees housing, and this despite a chronic housing shortage in which the resources of the corporation might be useful. Eighty-two percent of Dutch managers would reject such help, despite the advantage it might give them, while 91 percent would reject the suggestion that the size of one's family should be of any concern to one's organizational paymaster. Such findings suggest that individuals in this culture use a principle of strong separation between organizations catering to different spheres of their lives, with special emphasis on the separation of public and private, work and recreational spheres. The spread of diverse memberships prevents any one organization from capturing their allegiance.

Indeed, Dutch management is a byword for decentralization. Shell, Unilever, and Philips are renowned for having given each country in which their operations are located high degrees of local autonomy and national coloration. The typical Dutch corporate form is the multinational, as opposed to the global or international form. The distinction is made by Bartlett and Ghoshal in *Managing Across Borders*. Multinationals are the most decentralized. Global organizations are the most centralized, and international ties between Dutch multinationals work best where styles of detergent and laundry use vary considerably from country to country. This also works well for gasoline retailing and distribution, but not so well for electronics, where Philips has been losing out to Japans R&D-driven globalism. The authors report difficulties Philips has had in adopting more centralized strategies.[7]

There is one more issue that divides the Dutch from many other nations. They value deeds above words, and specific acts of assistance far more than expressions of emotions or friendship. For example, we asked the following question:

Here are four general types of people. Which one would you most like to resemble?

(a) A person who is *esteemed* by others and takes a continuous interest in human welfare in general

(b) A person who is *enjoyed* by others and takes his joys and sorrows as they come, from day to day

(c) A person who is *loved* by others and takes a continuous interest in the personal welfare of all those who are dear to him

(d) A person who is *approved* by others and attends to his affairs conscientiously from day to day

The Dutch managers preferred approval of their specific acts and behaviors. Enjoyment is too convivial for them, love too demonstrative, esteem too broad. What this question taps is the Analytic–Integrative dimension, cross-coordinated with Neutral versus Affective styles of relating (see Fig. 11-1). Various cultures scored as follows:

Figure 11-1

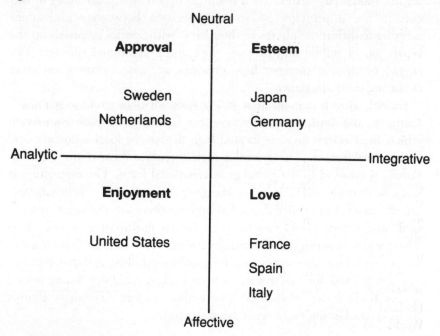

Dutch neutrality of affect probably comes from the very high density of the population, more than 100,000 people per square kilometer, the highest in Europe. The population is small, 14.5 million. The people you grew up with and know well are rarely far away, since two and a half hours of driving south or east will usually put you in Belgium, France, or Germany. What is scarce, therefore, is privacy. If you were to walk around glad-handing, there would be even more people under your feet; hence the Dutch saying, "Being too nice makes you your neighbor's fool."

What one needs from neighbors are specific and reliable acts of help and assistance in emergencies; hence the saying, "When in need, one learns to know one's friends." When the sea, or the Spanish or the Germans are coming for the whole neighborhood, then the lack of a finger in the dike, the neglect by a single person of his or her duty, can mean a flood or a firing squad. What you require of your neighbors is less love or conviviality than that they conscientiously live up to their responsibilities. Dutch preferences are for what makes their contrived and crowded habitations livable. In this precarious, man-made ecosystem everyone must play his part. A Dutch etiquette book, *Hoe Hoort Het Eigenlijk* ("Now What's the Right Way to Do It?") now in its seventeenth edition, reminds its readers:

> Making violent gestures is still considered vulgar and talking with the hands is still impolite. Well-bred people gesture as little as possible, and if they do it is done gracefully and harmoniously. . . .
>
> Greeting someone with a hug is also something that isn't done. In public we should use nothing more than words to communicate with, words which are not normally amplified by gestures. We don't use gestures of revulsion, horror, satisfaction or surprise. That is the way things are done, and that is in keeping with our national temperament, because we don't wear our hearts on our sleeves.[8]

The English author's own surprise on first encountering Dutch audiences is that they clap for about six seconds and then stop in a strangely peremptory silence. He still feels he must have bombed. It makes a change from addressing Californians, some of whom assure you after you have finished speaking that your words changed the course of their lives.

None of this means that the Dutch are emotionally crippled. Indeed, restrained emotional expression may be channeled into good deeds. Holland is among the most generous nations in assisting the Third World. It is one of the very few not listed at all by Amnesty International for oppressive governmental or police activities. Homegrown terrorism is scarce to nonexistent—although in the 1970s some Dutch children were hijacked on a train by South Moluccan immigrants, a group not at that time integrated into Dutch society and to whom promises had been broken. Indeed, despite their reluctance to emote, the Dutch are overwhelmingly "feminine" or tender-minded in their cultural attitudes.

Beyond Sex-Role Stereotypes

Geert Hofstede, a Dutch academic who has done major work studies on cross-cultural dimensions, employed a series of questions originally administered by IBM to managers at all national sites. He isolated several questions indicative of "feminity" and "masculinity"—not terms we would have chosen, although these provide insight into the incorporation of "feminine" values by Dutch managers. The distinctions were as follows:[9]

Feminine	Masculine
Men and women both assertive and nurturant	Assertiveness for men, nurturance for women
Equality of sexes	Men dominant
Quality of life focus	Perfomance focus
Work to live	Live to work
People and environment most important	Things and money most important
Interdependence ideal	Independence ideal
Service	Ambition
Sympathy for underdog	Liking for achiever
Unisex, androgyny	Manliness

We introduce Hofstede's dimension because the Dutch are startlingly different from their British, American, and German friends on this measure (see Table 11-3).

With the exception of Sweden (and Norway), the Netherlands are the most nurturant and socially responsive of nations. A major concern held by the Dutch about European political union is that the Germans may pressure them to abandon their highly liberal and permissive policies towards drugs, delinquency, penology, alcoholism, euthanasia, and the mentally abnormal and handicapped. The Netherlands are convinced,

Table 11-3   Scores on "Femininity"

Sweden	95
The Netherlands	86
Spain	58
France	57
Singapore	52
Canada	48
Australia	39
United States	38
United Kingdom	34
Germany	34
Italy	30
Japan	5

for example, that without their campaign to supply sterile needles to drug addicts, the AIDS epidemic could have become considerably worse. They fear the more "masculine" and punitive approach taken by the Germans, which they believe will criminalize those in need of help and prevent them from cooperating with authorities.

Paradoxically, Dutch women have not made as much progress in employment as elsewhere in Europe, so that more "feminine" values of equality and nurturance among mostly male managers does not appear to have worked to their benefit. Only 35.13 percent of Dutch females are in the work force (see Table 10-1) as compared with 47.2 percent in Sweden, 42.5 percent in the United States, 40.5 percent in Canada, 39.6 percent in the United Kingdom, 39.0 percent in Japan, 37.7 percent in France, and 35.6 percent in Germany. The issue here may be intense house-pride and cleanliness, of which Unilever is probably an offspring and beneficiary. The Dutch are homebodies, and delight in one's home is captured in the word *gezellig* or *gezelligheid,* meaning literally, "pleasant, cosy, and entertaining." "Why don't you come over for an evening of *gezellig* talk?" is a popular invitation. Compliments about the furniture and the house by visitors are greatly prized. It is likely, then, that some women prefer to preside over the home than try to make it in the workplace.

We now turn to the historical roots of the phenomena we have noted, to see how these cultural preferences might have been formed initially.

The Historical Antecedents

There is a clue to the roots of Dutch culture in the official title of the country, *Koninkrijk der Nederlanden*, "the Kingdom of the Netherlands," or *de Lage Landen*, "the Low Countries." The Kingdom may be singular, but the Lands are plural. In fact, for centuries they were literally separated by shifting bodies of water so that lands and seas appeared and disappeared. If we are searching for an explanation of the characteristics we have noted—decentralization, multiple organizations, a strong emphasis on specific acts of duty and assistance, a refusal to be dominated, a strong dislike of affectation, status seeking, or display, an insistence upon knowing and consenting to the purposes of an organization in which each person plays a key part, an instant defiance of those who challenge this order of things, and the compartmentalization of life into many "watertight" compartments—then Dutch history gives us reasons aplenty.

Firstly, and obviously, it is each small community, each "polder-land" that needs to defend itself at a moment's notice from encroaching waters. Only a decentralized system, with the highest levels of quick-acting local responsiveness and initiative, can survive in such circumstances. While it takes organization beyond the level of local communities to build coherent defenses against the sea, such action is at the behest of each community, coordinates the initiatives of each community, and requires of all participants that each does his or her duty to all concerned and is fully informed of the total plan. If any group is left out and its defenses insufficiently prepared, all may suffer through the neglect of the least and for the least. Water is a great equalizer, submerging all impartially. The very flatness of the land means that those who preen themselves achieve an illusory stature. Let them be judged by their works, not their sentiments, by their tangible contributions in keeping the common enemy at bay.

In much of Europe in the sixteenth and seventeenth centuries, the age of monarchy and the nation state was in the ascendant. Britain had grown powerful under the Tudors, Francis I had begun the process of building up the magnificence of the French monarchy and had challenged Spanish power in Italy, while Spain, enriched by gold and silver from her South American colonies, had reached the zenith of her power by late in the sixteenth century. When Charles V, king of Spain and Holy Roman Emperor, retired to a monastery in 1556, he was succeeded by Philip II. The Netherlands were at that time his farthest-flung possessions, very near the margins of political control.

The historical experience of the Netherlands was very different. Under the Dukes of Burgundy during the fifteenth century, they had been subject not to a feudal hierarchy, but one of the earliest examples of a rationalized civil service charged with taxation and local administration. When at the end of the fifteenth century these lands passed to the Habsburgs, Charles V, who came from Gent in the Burgundian Netherlands, left his lands in the charge of *stadhouders*, local military and judicial authorities, who acted as the agents of the emperor during his absence in Spain. One of these, the *stadhouder* of Holland, Zeeland, and Utrecht, was Prince William of Orange (1533–1584). Although not a king, he was very much the first among equals as far as other *stadhouders* were concerned. As his nickname, William the Silent, attests, he was not much given to drawing attention to himself.

In the meantime, the religious ideas of the Reformation had come early to the Netherlands. Her busy seaports at Antwerp and Amsterdam were the crossroads not only of trade but of new ideas. Desiderius Erasmus (1469–1536), the illegitimate son of a priest, was no Protestant, but his pleas for tolerance, understanding, liberality, pacificism, and the relative nature of moral absolutes, made him into a Dutch cultural hero (see Box 11-2, "The Prototype Netherlander"). His views were remarkably contemporaneous. He not only helped nurture the ground that was to produce Holland's Golden Age, but represented the very antithesis of Spanish Catholic orthodoxy and its inquisitorial assault on its enemies. The independence required for trading, the administrative and geographical islands of defense against the sea, the highly decentralized political structure run by local dignitaries, not Spanish conquerors, all combined against the overextended reach of Spanish power. Skilled on the water, the *watergeuzen*, or "sea beggars," harassed Spanish shipping and kept enclaves of resistance supplied. The word *geuzen*, first used by the Spanish in contempt, became a banner of Dutch egalitarianism. It was to be used to defy the French, and yet again by the early Dutch Resistance against the Nazis. When Walter Laqueur, the American commentator, referred slightingly to "Hollanditis," an alleged European disease of having to consult too many constituencies, the Dutch once again put the word on their banners of protest.

In 1568, William, with an army raised in Germany, engaged Spanish troops under the notoriously brutal Duke of Alva. It was less the Dutch

Box 11-2

The Prototype Netherlander

Desiderius Erasmus (1469–1536) was the quintessential Dutchman. The country that took Erasmus of Rotterdam to its heart appears to have inherited many of his admired characteristics, which are surprisingly modern and combine the disciplined habits of the North with a more Burgundian love of life.

The bastard son of a priest and his housekeeper, he never lost his concern for the marginal and the outcast. He was himself ordained priest in the Augustian monastery of Steyn and devoted himself to the Greek and Roman classics and their influence of the early Fathers of the Church. Following the tradition of Christian humanism, he pleaded with the Church to reform itself and turn from ceremony and superstition to the Bible and charitable works. An advocate of moral relativism, mutual understanding, pacificism, and harmony, he refused to side with the Protestant Reformation in its violation of Catholicism, urging instead a dialogue that respected the humanity of both parties.

He translated the Bible into Greek and some passages into several local vernaculars, so that its message could be spread. "Do you think the Scriptures are fit only for the perfumed?" he asked. Using the new printing presses, he was able to publish and disseminate *In Praise of Folly, The Adages, Colloquies,* and other works. He wrote with style and wit, while giving practical or allegorical advice on the problems of everyday living.

Erasmus seemed especially well disposed toward women and toward youth in general. He urged the education of adolescent girls, so that their future husbands "would rejoice in a partnership on an intellectual level." He may have been thinking of Sir Thomas More's daughter, Margaret. Erasmus and More were close friends. *Econium Moriae* can also be translated *In Praise of More,* and it was a joke between them. In this book "Folly," or *Moriae,* is a female who personifies youth, vitality, happiness, and freedom for care. Folly's role in life is to qualify hierarchy and authority by leavening these with vivacity. Folly is attended by Self-love, Pleasure, Flattery, and Sound Sleep, who combine to keep merry company.

Erasmus had many Dutch characteristics: an obsession with cleanliness, a playfulness with ideas, a dislike of strong emotions, a strong sense of realism and practicality, a pronounced international and itinerant bent, and a concern with the peaceful reconciling of disputes.

as individuals, than the entire local administration led by the Prince of Orange, including the dense network of Calvinist consistencies, that arose to resist the Spanish. For the Dutch, survival throughout the Eighty Years War owed everything to locally controlled organizations. This strength has served them repeatedly since. The Nazi governor was immediately dubbed "the New Alva." The Dutch civil service was forced to obey him, but dense levels of organization in every sphere of Dutch life helped to keep the occupiers at bay. The Dutch, unlike the Americans and the British, would never try to undermine their own trade union structure, which struck with sometimes devastating effectiveness against German occupation forces. In 1941 there was a general strike by dock workers, not for better wages, but against the sustained persecution of Dutch Jews. Queen Wilhelmina added the words *Heldhaftig, Vastberaden, Barmhartig* (Heroic, Resolute, Merciful") to Amsterdam's coat of arms in honor of the strike. "The Dockworker," a statue by Mari Andriessen stands in Amsterdam as a commemoration to their sacrifice.[10]

No wonder that the Dutch judge neighborliness by specific acts of assistance, not emotional reassurance. In the bitter *Hongerwinter* ("hunger winter") of 1944, with the urban population starved and frozen, the farmers either gave to the *honger trekkers* or they didn't. Nor despite the dramatic protests of the 1960s would the Dutch turn on their own students. Recent memories were too vivid. In 1943, on pain of closing the entire university system, Dutch students were ordered to make a pledge of loyalty to the German Reich. Eighty-six percent refused. The universities closed. The students hid or were conscripted and transported into labor gangs.

Dutch newspapers and journals still have a rebellious tinge, perhaps because the war years radicalized them or because they began as underground journals. Their names speak (spoke) of their origins. *Het Vrije Volk* ("The Free People"), *Vrij Nederland* ("The Free Netherlands"), *Het Parool* ("The Watchword"), *Trouw* ("Faithfulness"), *Het Vaderland* ("The Fatherland"). Only the conservative *Telegraaf* appeared throughout the occupation. The Dutch have had a surfeit of illegitimate and oppressive authority. Repeatedly they have used a defiance based on organizations-in-depth to frustrate its aims.

On September 18, 1944, thirty thousand Dutch railway workers struck, paralyzing German transport throughout the region. Holland expected to be liberated in weeks. It took eight more months to liberate the whole country, and defiant railway workers were forced to join an estimated 200,000 *onderduikers*, or underdivers, hiding out in the dense labyrinth of Dutch underground and front organizations. These printed no fewer than sixty liberation newspapers, forged thousands of food coupons and false identity papers for those in hiding, and mounted guerrilla attacks upon the occupiers.

The Reconciliation of Individualism with Community

In chapter after chapter we have shown that different cultures of business have all had to address the "impossible" question of what their individuals owe to their communities, and what their communities owe to their individuals. In Goethe's *Faust*, Mephistopheles takes Faust to a high mountain to be tempted by earthly kingdoms. Faust proposes that the water be pushed back to reclaim the land. This is part of his devilish quest for power over divine creation, and is a clear reference to Holland. But if survival means that human dispensation challenges the divine, what is the price to be paid?[11]

The story of the Flying Dutchman is Holland's own version of the Faust story. It retells an ancient myth, the point of which is that *hubris* and excesses of individual prowess can be atoned for and redeemed only

---

Box 11-3

The Flying Faust

The "Flying Dutchman" is Holland's Faust story, adapted to the struggle with the sea. Captain van Straaten has decided to defy the sea and, deaf to the entreaties of his friends and family, sets sail into the teeth of a storm. He finds himself alone at the helm of his ship when a huge wave sweeps his crew overboard. As the ship begins to founder, he calls upon the help of the Devil, who saves his ship and his life but dooms him to sail the seas forever, in the midst of storms, within sight of land, but never set foot ashore. There is one exception: he can go ashore one night every seven years and search for a woman's love that will lift the curse. At last, one night, off the coast of Scotland, he lands, and the daughter of a fisherman who has long dreamed of his coming, runs after him to the quay side as he tries to reboard his ship, and casts herself into the sea to save him. The curse is lifted.

by the antithetical principle, that of community and loving self-sacrifice. Captain Van Straaten, defier of the sea, calls upon the assistance of the Devil during a storm and is doomed to sail forever in perpetual storms, within sight of land, or until his curse is lifted by a woman's loving sacrifice. See "The Flying Faust," Box 11-3. To avoid the situation in which the exponents of both principles—individuality and community—perish in dramatic point and counterpoint, how can a culture reconcile the individuality of its members with the disciplined community necessary to survival?

We have already considered two tentative answers. The individual must know in advance and give his or her consent to the purpose pursued by the organization. The individual is involved in multiple organizations, no one of which is permitted to influence more than a part of the person's life. But there are several other ways in which the Dutch mediate between individuality and community, which in several cases distinguish them sharply from Britain or America. It is to a discussion of these that we now turn.

Extensive Efforts to Negotiate Among Principled Positions

One of the items in our questionnaire that contrasted at least two ways of being "democratic" was "Extensive efforts to negotiate among principled positions." A situation was described where the street in the respondent's neighborhood was about to be closed to all traffic because of a government-sponsored project. The neighbors who are divided on this issue have the right to choose a delegate to confer with the project leaders and represent the views of the neighborhood. How should this delegate be chosen?

"It is better that all people meet and discuss things until almost everyone agrees on the same person."

"It is better that all people meet, names be put up, a vote be taken, and then the person who gets the majority of votes sent, even if there are several people who are still against this person."

What this question measures is *consensual* versus *adversarial* democracy. Does the community go the extra mile and take the time to try to find a candidate acceptable to nearly all, or does a majority seek to defeat a minority? It is on this issue that the Dutch managers differ most sharply with Anglo-Saxon colleagues. The results are shown in Table 11-4.

Table 11-4   Democracy entails . . .

	JP	GER	NL	FRA	UK	AUS	SWE	SP	USA	IT
Extended discussions and widest agreement	84.6	69.0	66.0	61.9	58.7	53.4	41.0	39.4	37.7	35.3

This question, although not ostensibly about business, could be a very important clue to the continuing industrial strength of Japan, Germany, the Netherlands, and France, as compared with the difficulties of the English-speaking nations. Both Britain and the United States, with their first-past-the-post electoral systems, are able to vote their minorities into relative impotence, and what starts as persuasion ends in victory for one party and defeat for the other, with words as weapons. The Christian Democratic Alliance, the largest of the Netherlands' twenty-five political parties, currently winning about a third of the vote, is obliged to rule in a coalition with at least one other party and sometimes two or three. Currently the CDA shares power with the PvdA (*Partij van de Arbeid*), or Labor Party. In this way, the ruling coalition combines not simply advocates of workers with managers, but religious with secular parties, all working out programs acceptable to their constituencies. The Christian Democratic Alliance is itself a fusion of the original KVP (Catholic People's Party); the ARP, the (Calvinist) Anti-Revolutionary Party; and the CHU, Christian Historical Union, based on the moderate Dutch Reformed Church. The three merged in 1977, suggesting that Dutch society is engaged in an extended process of negotiating principled differences. It has taken as much as eighteen months to agree on the composition of a cabinet among coalition parties, but the Dutch persist in taking infinite pains to accommodate minority views.[12]

It is hardly a coincidence that in the four nations who see democracy as entailing wide agreements, trades unions are still influential, while the United States and Britain have them on the run. For whatever the costs to the civic culture of simply voting down minority opinions, the cost to the industrial culture is very high indeed. You do not make high-quality products with sizable pockets of malcontents within an organization. "Losers," whether employees or customers, must be minimized if the resulting disharmony is not to cripple the culture's capacity to create wealth. While it is difficult to estimate the costs of consigning defeated electoral minorities to the sidelines, they probably show up in crime, addiction, and other measures of alienation. Yet the costs of working with an alienated workforce are known to be high. Holland's high productivity and stable unionized work forces speak for themselves.

Negotiating Between Zuilen or Pillars

The "pillarization," or *verzuiling*, of Dutch society is much commented on and is unprecedented among the developed nations of the world. Instead of the usual social strata: upper class, middle class, lower class, the Netherlands seems far more concerned with ideological blocs or pillars. These include (1) Roman Catholic; (2) Orthodox Reformed (Calvinist); (3) Reformed, including Lutherans and moderate Protestants; (4) Socialist; (5) Humanist, General, and Non-Church.

These blocs run broadcasting and television, the primary and secondary education system, union and professional organizations, their own newspapers, and even leisure organizations, so that one can, for example, hike, cycle, or skate exclusively with Orthodox Reformed companions. It is clear what perpetuates this system. The government doles out money for schools and broadcasting to various blocs in proportion to the numbers of their persuasion that can be identified and assembled, so that education and programming are publicly funded but doctrinally organized.[13]

The historical origins of this arrangement are unclear, but can be guessed at. The long struggle of the Netherlands for independence was fought in the name of religious toleration, and the area continued to act as a magnet for refugees from harsher religious climates. Since the United Provinces came together for mutual protection rather than to celebrate like-mindedness, the notion of a "league of minorities," joined in mutual toleration, lived on.

The actual origin of *verzuiling* (pillarization) was the schools issue of 1857. The mostly small-business and working-class constituency of the *Gereformeerde kerk* (the Orthodox Reformed Church) joined with the minority of Catholics in demanding, in the name of social equality, government recognition of and subsidy for their own religious schools. Their motto was "*In het isolement is onze kracht*," "In isolation is our strength." Despite the isolation of each "pillar" all combined to support with their loyalty the edifice of the state, along with the rights of each other to their own shares of the public purse. As "polder land" (parcels of walled land reclaimed from the sea) are developed, each *zuil* receives its allotment of land. This curious juxtaposition of differentiation with integration is unique to the Netherlands.

It may account for the readiness with which the Dutch seem to tolerate behaviors proscribed in other lands, so long as these occur in designated places apart from the rest of society. Brothels are licensed and medically inspected. Rotterdam has a place set aside for pickups and sexual assignments by automobile, with specially secluded parking spaces, walled off from those just passing by. For several years the Hippies congregating in Amsterdam were accommodated in parks and allowed to bed down beside war memorials. Gays congregate in well-recognized places. There seems to be a compartment for everyone, with videos on sale at Schiphol Airport thoughtfully segregated by a variety of sexual tastes. Pillarization also allows the Dutch to rejoice in the use of titles within their zuil, while being egalitarian outside. There is much use of *Prof*, *Dr*, *Ir* (Engineer), and even *Drs*, (candidate for doctorate or master's degree).

But the other side of the pillarization process is that the Dutch who grow up in a *zuil* may rarely have encountered anyone close to them with differing ideology. The terminated training sessions at Shell, mentioned earlier, may be partly the result of this encapsulation. For the Dutch can be principled to the point of preachiness. The word *hokjesgeest* refers to a national state of mind which encourages the moral domination of subdivisions. With 70 percent of all publicly funded schools at secondary and primary levels being *bijzonder* (specially organized along usually religious lines), it can be hard in some areas to educate children without doctrinal presuppositions. Complaints are heard about the expense and duplication of such schools. Most parents are now more concerned with academic performance, yet here the *bijzonder* schools do slightly better on average.

There is wide agreement that pillarization is blurring its once classic outlines. The three confessional parties have joined the Christian Democratic Alliance. Once sectarian, the trade unions are now either in a Christian or Socialist federation, which often ally. *Verzuiling* is probably responsible for the stable yet accommodating style of Dutch democracy with its twenty-five political parties chosen by proportional representation. Your *zuil* reinforces your principles for long, hard bouts of bargaining. In many respects these pillars are microcosms of negotiations among EEC partners in which the Dutch are often mediators, as they were during the seventeenth century. The Christian influence on conservative forces makes compassion and social concern the aim of many parties, instead of polarizing "tough" economics against a "tender" social dimension, which is the rule in English-speaking democracies. In Holland many class and left-right issues are resolved within parties, rather than splitting the whole culture into adversarial halves.

The tender-mindedness or "femininity" noted earlier is probably shaped by relationships within the *zuil*, coupled with the logic of universalism. If you seek support and understanding for co-religionists and close members of your community, can you logically deny it to others? High social expenditures are partly the result of "pillars" competing in helping their own and in general high-mindedness. Since forms of caring evolved by one religious group should be available to all, there is a "ratchet effect" in which no one knowingly "undercares." There may also be a tendency to confine principled positions to your *zuil* and negotiate flexibly beyond it. Dutch universities are nearly all of equal status, but the same cannot be said for student clubs within the universities. Here the secret insignia of special statuses emerge.

Although the Dutch are avid negotiators, eager and skilled at speaking other people's languages, almost to the exclusion of their own cultural preferences, they remain highly Analytic in their thinking. Perhaps years of living in the same *zuil* as other people leads them to believe that sharp disagreements are (1) necessary to make life tolerable and (2) can always be healed later because one lives close to the other person. In any event, there is a Dutch tendency that has been satirized by the phrase "I think you are an idiot but don't take it personally." The Dutch tend to separate negative judgments about things they dislike from the people who produce these things. According to this view, if a reasonable person does a stupid thing, one should not confuse that thing with the person, nor should that person feel slighted by criticism of his or her product (see Box 11-4, "The Italians Walked Out").

An Individualism Not for Power or Display but for Contribution

We have seen that the Dutch do not encourage showing off or scintillating conversation. Sir William Temple, writing in the seventeenth century observed, "Though these people are naturally cold and heavy, may not be ingenious enough to furnish a pleasant or agreeable conversation, yet they want not for plain, downright sense to understand and do their business both public and private."[14]

A common accusation is that the Dutch are bourgeois to the core. They have a word, *burgerlijk*, which has more negative connotations than *bourgeois*, including narrow-mindedness and conformity. What does

---

Box 11-4

The Italians Walked Out

A joint Dutch and Italian team were working on the design and building of a bridge. The Italians contributed a very aesthetic design. The Dutch engineers ran it through their computer-aided design software and agreed that the plan was structurally unsound. It would not stand up for very long to the stresses specified in the contract.

They therefore reported back to their Italian counterparts that "the design is crazy." They began to elaborate, but the Italians were conferring with each other, repeating the translated phrase in shocked voices. Then they rose as one and walked out of the room. For Italians, the design and its designers were a diffuse whole; to attack one was to attack both. In the Dutch view, intelligent people make mistakes all the time. You must distinguish product from producer.

---

seem to happen is that individual strivings and ambitions are swiftly and thoroughly transformed through socially ordered activity, rather than expressed in ways that vaunt the individual. A famous satirical short story called *"De woonwagen"* ("The House Trailer") by Gerrit Krol tells of a middle-class community formed around some gypsies living in a converted bus on an empty lot. The suburbanites, scandalized by these free spirits in their midst, immediately form a *Belangenvereniging*, a "Society to Represent the Interests of . . ." that writes articles on proper living and hygiene, which it then distributes door-to-door. The society must, of course, respect the rights of all minorities, which makes it difficult to achieve the purposes for which the society was originally founded. A major restraining force on individually offensive behaviors is the *aktie*, roughly, an action group, except that the word denotes highly organized activity used to civilly demonstrate an issue. A Dutch telephone directory may have several numbers under *aktie: Aktie Argentinië, Aktie Stop de munitietrein*, etc.[15]

There is perhaps no better illustration of the socialization of individualism than the national supermarathon skating competition, the *Elfstedentocht*, "the tour of eleven towns," supposedly held in Friesland annually, but in practice, only if the ice on lakes and canals is sufficiently firm. Although the winners are announced, the prime emphasis is on completing the course and standing up to the 200 kilometers of ice in an all-day race that begins and ends in darkness. Some 18,000 skaters follow in the wake of the competitors, trying to complete the course and having documents stamped along the route as proof of their progress! Ninety percent of Dutch television sets were tuned into the most recent festival, with Parliament going into recess to watch the finish. "All of life is an Elfstedentocht," enthused one newspaper. Anthropologists have variously described the festival as "symbolic of the nation's life" and of "deep religious significance." Much is made of a small village on the route called *Bartlehiem*, or Bethlehem. The winner is described as *nieuwe ijsheilige*, "the new saint of the ice." Admired behaviors in a winner include their acting as a windbreak for others skating behind, pacing a group and in turn being paced by another leader, joining the choreographed rhythms of groups on the ice who pull and lever each other along, and sharing refreshments.

The 1954 winner was publicly criticized for not helping others along the route. In 1956, the five skaters in the lead, as they approached the finish line, locked arms and crossed the line together to overwhelming national applause.[16] The Dutch certainly believe in individual excellence, but of the kind that enriches rather than contrasts with the wider social context. Competition between religious and secular groupings to enrich that context has given the Netherlands what is probably the most generous and expensive welfare system in Europe, with a worryingly high ratio of recipients to workers.

Engineering as a Prototype of Science for Social Utility

If we had to choose just one social indicator that explained and predicted the relative industrial effectiveness of national cultures, it would be the status which that culture attributed to its engineers and the extent to which their achievements were regarded as important. The Netherlands was made and is sustained by engineers. The country does not really have a Harvard or a Yale, an Oxford or a Cambridge, preferring its major educational centers to be relative equals. But the nearest the Netherlands comes to a supreme educational institution is Delft, a school of engineering and architecture.

Nearly all major Dutch corporations are engineering based. Royal Dutch Shell is based on chemical, petroleum, construction, and geological engineering, and the Exploration and Production function in Shell, based in The Hague and predominantly manned by Dutch engineers, is where the company has historically made most of its profits.

Unilever is similarly based on chemical detergents, foods, and cleaning agents, while Akzo and DSM are major employers of chemical engineers. Another major Dutch niche in international markets is the construction of harbors and the sea barriers, of which Royal Volker Stevin is one major example. We found that this activity was so prestigious in Dutch society that companies were doing it for quite minuscule profits. The building of sea defenses was its own reward. Philips has a prominent world position in electronic engineering, especially consumer electronics, digital switching, and lighting. Its prowess is maintained by the nearby technological university in Eindhoven.

The prestige of knowledge applied to commerce is not confined to engineering. The Sprenger Institute, the Agricultural University of Wageningen, and the Aalsmeer Research Station have been cited as largely responsible for Holland's competitive advantage in cut flowers and their fast distribution.[17] The whole concept of knowledge becoming more valued as it connects producers to consumers, the head to the hands, and the individual to society is foreign to Anglo-Saxon thought patterns, but pleases the "earthy" Dutch. It helps also to account for their successes in biotechnology.

Despite considerable contemporary advice on "getting close to customers," the emerging shape of successful European and Asian capitalism is that they are closer to manufacturing and production. This direction is not taken primarily for extrinsic rewards such as profits or wages, although clearly neither managers nor companies can do without these in the longer term. However, Holland's 60 percent top income tax bracket would kill enterprise were it motivated primarily by money rewards. The reason for working is largely that society gives its approval to certain activities and that its members feel that excellence in these technologies is a value of intrinsic worth. As they say at Shell, the "Calvinist conscience" of its engineers propels the corporation through "technology push."

What we see in modern international competition are technologies developing so rapidly and achieving such complexity that only nations totally dedicated to knowledge-intensive learning races can hope to stay ahead. Recently, the Ministry of Education and Sciences has been advocating "horizontal technologies," for example, biotechnology, microelectronics and materials science, on the grounds that these impact across the whole economy. A new category of "strategic research" has been developed to link pure with applied studies. Government grants have been used to stimulate information technology in education, research dissemination, and marketing, with an emphasis on the private sector. Major initiatives, include a broad-band system of optic fibers for telecommunications, a move clearly designed to help Philips become a world-class competitor in digital switching and related fields.

On Bourgeois Aestheticism

Holland has another notable distinction. It is one of the few cultures in which a major renaissance of the arts and the presiding image of beauty arose unashamedly from middle-class origins. The Golden Age of Dutch arts and letters in the seventeenth century grew out of the triumph of the merchant class against the empire of Spain. The idea that high culture requires of necessity a royal house, a leisure class with delicate sensibilities, the patronage of popes, princes, kings, and the landed aristocracy gains no credence whatever from Dutch history.

However true it might have been for France, Britain, and Italy, that the bourgeoisie were uncouth philistines whose money-grabbing preoccupations blinded them to beauty, it cannot be said of Holland.

The art of the Golden Age is a mirror held up to nature, full of the finely observed details of everyday life: Frans Hals' pictures of ordinary people, their vivid expressions caught as if by a snapshot, Rembrandt's etching *The Ratkiller*, Brueghel's depiction of peasants dancing in a graceful composition. Here for the first time was the texture of everyday life—kitchens, parlors, courtyards, humble tasks, even children having their behinds wiped. Great art no longer required elevated themes, baroque figures, or romantic interpretations to lift them above reality. Beauty was fused with the mundane, the familiar, the routine, and the commercial. It was possible to have good taste, to buy and sell art, to paint for appreciative audiences in a marketplace, rather than in only the parlors of a leisure class.

It is hard to estimate the benefits to Dutch culture of not having business polarized with beauty, or commercial activities with aestheticism, for the Myth of the Ugly Businessman haunts many Western cultures, along with the conviction that if you are practical you must be a bore, and if you desire to create wealth your mind must be empty of finer things. But for the Dutch, as we have seen, *kunstwerk* embraces everything necessary for survival and for the appreciation of living.

Playful Expressions of Conflict and Protest

The Dutch also have the distinction of being the most protest-prone of developed nations, yet the least likely to resort to violence.

How does one protest without losing one's own temper or provoking official violence? The world has watched peaceful protests and civil rights demonstrations disintegrate into murderous scenes in the United States, Great Britain, Northern Ireland (especially), France, Italy, and Germany. Have the Dutch alone developed the secret of high levels of protest activity with low levels of social trauma?

Some major restraining influences have already been touched on. There is a seeming need to form an *aktie* and formulate its principles. The Dutch word *vergadering* implies an official style of conducting meetings, close to Robert's Rules of Order in English-speaking discourse, but far more extensive. In formal meetings, speakers nearly always address the leader as *Meneer de Voorzitter*, "Mr Chairman."

Younger people in Holland get impatient with such rituals, and it is not unknown for intensely socialized groups to excite each other to violence. So what are the additional restraints? Johan Huizinga, the Dutch historian, in 1938 wrote *Homo Ludens: A Study of the Play Element in Culture*, arguing that play is a form of experimentation and learning, an act performed at a level "above" day-to-day discourse and, therefore, capable of being adopted if relevant and ignored if not. Play can be mock-confrontational in that it challenges the ideas of the status quo, but being satirical and sportive, it is not a serious attempt to unseat those in authority, but a colorful way of making your point.[18]

It is important to grasp that to show suffering in simulation may be a crucial way of avoiding suffering in fact. The purpose of classic Greek drama was to get the audience to laugh at the absurd antics of civil life or weep at their tragic consequences and thereby to avoid enacting them in reality. Drama is a culture's "early warning system": "Go this way, and the consequences will be what we dramatized."

The Netherlands has a rich history of drama used to teach moral lessons. In the *abele spelen* of the twelfth century, we find Europe's first secular dramas, especially the six *cluyten*, or comedies, broad social satires on the foibles of the time. Erasmus, in *The Praise of Folly*, makes a similar case for our capacity to learn from foolishness. In the Golden Age, literary guilds, or "Chambers of Rhetoric," created moral plays for public edification, and the famous, if short-lived, Netherlands Academy founded by Samuel Coster in 1617 used plays especially written for the curriculum.[19]

No wonder, then, that Dutch protests are rarely far from *ludiek;* the word means "playful," referring to the way adults, rather than children play. Amsterdam in the 1960s saw *Anti-Smoke Sorcerers* and the *Medicine Men of the Western Asphalt Jungle*. There were more serious movements too, but rarely without a sense of humor. Dolle Mina's "Mad Minnies" demanded greater equality for women and parity with other European countries. The anti-nuclear movement opposed NATO missiles stationed in Holland and was heavily supported by the Reformed Church.

Another endemic issue attracting protest is housing. In the 1980s, the *Krakers* (squatters) declared *kraakdag* (squatting day) and seized empty buildings owned by speculators. The *Loesje* movement, based on the moral protest expressed in the graffiti of an Arnhem high-school girl is a more recent happening. There is even official instruction on protest from IPEC (*Instituut voor Politieke Educatie en Communicatie*), a foundation for public education in citizenship. It is as if the Dutch, shy about any personal exhibitionism, readily seized the chance for *aktie* for public welfare, as one of the few legitimate areas of personal expression.

The creation of dramatic scenes and stories has found its way into Dutch business in a number of ways. Shell has pioneered the scenario method of planning,[20] in which two or three alternative scenarios of the future are set out as coherent stories. This not only appeals to Dutch *ludiek* but is a major way of mediating potential conflicts about business strategies appropriate to the future. If you cannot agree on what is going to happen to your industry, then you will not agree on how to engage that future. The use of scenarios allows contingency planning for up to three possible environments, allowing diversity of viewpoint to make the corporation more flexible, more robust in its plans, and quicker to respond to envisaged potentials. It is of particular note that a scenario team from the Dutch government is preparing a major exercise on the alternative futures for the EEC.

Under its planning coordinator, Arie de Geus, Shell took major steps toward the simulation of situations faced by the oil industry. Trying to tell other senior managers how they "ought" to plan gave way to computer modeling of key situations they faced so that problems could be solved in "play" before being tackled in reality. The role of planning was to model the issues, not to provide the answers. De Geus wrote "Planning as Learning" in the *Harvard Business Review*, arguing that the effectiveness of modern corporations was a function of the speed with which they learned, not only about their core technologies but about the shifts in their environment. Modeling such changes was the key to "learning how to learn."[21] A major initiative of Dutch business and government is the *Informatica-universiteit*, a two-year university-level course in information sciences with an enrollment of 3,000 students. A major thrust in its activities is toward simulation and modeling.

A Fascination with Paradox

The final element in the capacity of Dutch culture to reconcile opposed conceptions, most especially of the individual and the community, grows from their fascination with paradox. The Duke de Baena, a Spaniard, wrote *The Dutch Puzzle* (1966), pointing out that the Netherlands is a nation of paradoxes. The Dutch love independence, yet burden themselves with elaborate conventions. They are a monarchy but think and behave like republicans. They are thrifty yet generous, blunt yet caring, protesting yet tolerant, squeezed into narrow "pillars" yet international and multilingual. They possess both the puritanism of Calvin and the sensuousness of Jan Steen.[22]

But the Dutch go further to embrace the whole idea of paradox and dilemma. Erasmus wrote much of the "relativization" of moral perspectives. Taken together and combined, they formed, he believed, a larger truth. Frits Haselhoff, a professor of business at the University of Groningen, has written extensively on the dilemmas of business policy and strategy. The Dutch author of this book conceived of the crux of national culture as different ways of mediating the dilemmas of existence. When the British author wrote "The Dilemmas of Planning" in *Shell Guides to Planning, No. 3*, it became an underground classic and, although confidential and restricted, was widely circulated and leaked and described by two Dutch newspapers. His work was championed within Shell largely, if not entirely, by Dutch managers, most particularly Arie de Geus, Cornelis van der Heijden, and Jaap Leemhuis. Requests to speak or consult on the subject of dilemma have come from most major Dutch corporations, including Shell, Philips, AKZO, DSM, Unilever, and KLM. It is clearly an issue at the center of national consciousness in a land of principled positions and upraised fingers of admonition.

The work of M. C. Escher, the Dutch engraver, is a fascinating visual exploration of relative and paradoxical points of view, which ceaselessly challenge the models of reality stored within the human brain with images that contradict them: staircases that ascend downward, dragons that devour themselves, hands that draw hands that draw, infinite

---

Box 11-5

A Paradox of Morality

M. C. Escher is celebrated for his engravings. He called an arrangement of devils and angels, white on black and black on white, *Circle Limit IV*. It contains all the playfulness, irony, paradox, and mock-combativeness we have detected in Dutch culture. Here "the Last Battle," that between good and evil, is satirized in a way Erasmus would surely have approved. Angels and Devils are not live beings or forces struggling for our souls but contrasting evaluations chosen by human beings to signify what they like and dislike. Moreover, each needs the other as light needs the dark in which to shine more brightly, and deviltry needs white angels in order to menace us more darkly.

The human race has the doubtful genius of terrifying itself with its own values system and escalating contrasts until they tear us apart. Or, as Franklin Roosevelt put it, when the Great Depression was in danger of dividing Americans irreparably: "The only thing we have to fear is fear itself." One Dutch manager said, in response to our showing a slide of this picture, "He's teasing us. . . . For 'good?' and 'evil?' read 'erring?' and 'correcting?' That's how we learn."

---

regressions, living eyes who see that the seer will die, and reversible patterns of figure and ground. Especially notable is his playfulness and sense of humour (see Box 11-5, "A Paradox of Morality," in which Escher reveals the essential interdependence of our ideas of good and evil.[23])

Let the last word be that of Frans Kusters, author of *Het Milde Systeem* (The Kind System).

> The answer lies in "relativizing," a word that refers to the Dutch instinct for seeing matters whether personal or social with an ironic eye that declines to take anything with full earnestness. Not so much a theme, as an attitude that pervades nearly all Dutch writing.[24]

12

Britannia Rules the Airwaves

Words, words, words, I'm so sick of words
I get words all day long
From him now from you
Is that all you blighters can do?
　　　Eliza Doolittle in *My Fair Lady*

The economists you see on television making their forecasts nearly all see the economy as a complicated machine, built by engineers. You pull a lever here and you see the effects follow through in more efficient working. But, in reality, the economy is far more complex than even this. It is run by human beings and is more like a large organism. You prod it and sometimes it jumps this way and then, for its own reasons, jumps that way. It's not an engineering or machine problem. . . .

Economics has really obscured rather than clarified the fundamental problem of British economy by seeming to be able to give a specific solution, by pulling a specific lever, or set of levers. This has obscured the longer-term decline of our industry and the longer-term decline of our labor force which politicians should have been addressing thirty to forty years ago. If we survey our European competitors, who have turned up far fewer economists than Britain, these have succeeded in doing far better than the UK.

　　　　　　　Professor Paul Omerod, Henley Centre
　　　　　　　for Forecasting on "Pandora's Box,"
　　　　　　　BBC 2, 14 November, 1992

AS THIS CHAPTER IS COMPLETED and this book goes to press, the United Kingdom faces, yet again, the latest in a long series of economic crises. This time it is the enforced withdrawal from the Exchange Rate Mechanism, a free fall of the pound against the German mark, a 17 percent fall even against the dollar, and the deepest, longest, most stubborn recession since the Great Depression of the 1930s. What is increasingly looking like an "English-speakers' sickness" grips the United Kingdom worse than Canada, Australia, and New Zealand, although all these economies are also in trouble. We now have to face the fact that economic growth is inversely proportionate to the influence of economists and the number of M.B.A.s being graduated annually.[1] The two countries that began the Industrial Revolution, Britain and the United States, and to which the whole developed world has traditionally looked to as pathfinders, have been turning in consistently substandard performances.

It takes brave authorship even to address Great Britain's long and anguished struggle against an economic decline, generally thought to have begun in the second half of the nineteenth century. It takes fortitude, because the British, however uncompetitive they are at actually running corporations and making products, are fiercely competitive and verbally moralistic at talking about it.

To hazard an opinion about British economic decline is to be assailed at once with so formidable an array of analyses, expressed with such marvellous lucidity, that one is left impressed yet bewildered that such ideological and rhetorical convictions have failed for one hundred and forty years to halt the national economic subsidence. If only British commentators could sell their rhetoric, if only the cut and thrust of debate and the art of devastating rejoinder could somehow be sold abroad to ease the huge deficit in the international balance of payments, the nation might be rich indeed. And nowhere is the contest fiercer than in the "What's Wrong with Britain" leagues. The sheer numbers with diagnoses, many of which pin the blame squarely on rival commentators, bring to mind the curse that Dean Swift called down upon an enemy: "I sentence you to be preached to death by wild curates."

In our travels, we have rarely encountered a culture so thoroughly briefed on economic, industrial, and financial affairs by press, television, and radio. Since the English language is in general use throughout the economically developed world, it is Britons and Americans who get to report events, define issues, shape agendas, and take an ascendant role in discussions, armed with their native tongue. Such verbal initiatives are, in Britain's case, far, far beyond the actual economic or military capacities referred to. It is a curiously unreal existence of symbols without substance, and talk without walk. Since 1979 when Mrs. Thatcher came to power, Britain has been personifying the Free World, celebrating markets and championing free trade, while steadily losing effectiveness within these.

We do not imply that this talk is cheap or empty. On the contrary, it is for the most part very impressively delivered and endorsed by an ennobled or knighted professorate who at key moments in their careers said things that politicians wished to hear. *The Economist, The Financial Times*, Reuters and business programs on the BBC and ITN represent standards of professionalism and sophistication which are of world class. The mystery we seek to solve is why, in an age of information, is Britain's mastery of verbal and numerical complexity nowhere near matched by actual economic performance? Whence the winning words and losing businesses? We address this problem at the outset because it seems to us that the very eloquence of Britain's self-assertions are impeding change. A nation too busy propounding economic doctrines to notice that they are not working, and which behaves as if it "knew better," even about the reasons it is doing worse, is very hard to influence.[2] As when Mrs. Thatcher spoke, it was hard to get a small word in edgeways.

Within Britain, much of the talents appear to have been siphoned off into a culture of commentary of journalists and pundits, a kind of groaning Greek chorus on the edges of the stage, bewailing the folly of the actors. Commentators are individuals referred to as the "chattering classes," usually by that class itself. People would rather look on and arbitrate socially about who is "in" and "out" of fashion, than actually participate in the economy, much as they would rather consult to business than be within it.

No wonder, then, that in a recent survey by the Henley Forecasting Centre on mutual perceptions among leading economies, Britain was voted the least Successful, only moderately Hard-working or Helpful, yet the second most Arrogant, the most Humorous, and by far the most Boring![3]

The British also behave as the unelected arbiters of world economic issues, handing out bouquets and brickbats to other nations for their approximation to capitalist ideals. Hence, *The Financial Times* and *The Economist* recently congratulated Sweden on having rid itself of its Social Democratic government, which has ruled almost continuously since

1932. The Swedes were assured that now their economy would improve. But GDP per person in Sweden is $29,770, according to *The World in 1992*, an *Economist* report, as compared with $17,700 in the United Kingdom. Swedes are $12,000 per head better off, or nearly 25 percent richer. At what stage might a note of humility or even curiosity creep into British pronouncements? All the six other wealth creators examined in this book outdistance Britain easily. We are in danger of forgetting just how badly Britain fares (see Table 12-1).

Table 12-1

	GDP per capita (1991)	Growth 1991–92 average %	Inflation 1991–92 average %
Japan	$30,007	+5.5	2.8
Sweden	$29,770	−0.8	6.0
Germany	$25,500	+3.7	3.7
United States	$23,720	+1.7	3.8
France	$22,900	+4.4	3.1
Netherlands	$19,400	+3.6	3.3
United Kingdom	$17,710	−2.6	4.8

Britain's GDP per capita is also below that of Switzerland, $35,810; Finland, $29,700; Norway, $28,200; Denmark, $26,150; Canada, $23,870; Belgium, $21,280; Italy, $20,300; and Australia, $18,080. She has continued to lose comparative advantage during the fourteen years of Conservative government from 1979 to 1993. Current polls reveal that fewer than 10 percent of Britons accept the thesis that the Thatcher years saw an "economic miracle," or that the country's economic decline has been halted. With a 2.6 percent negative growth from 1991 to September 1992, the decade 1981–91 is no better than the decade 1971–81.

Britain's Business Culture: A Snapshot View

Most of the data from our dilemmas questionnaire have by this time been presented, although there is one more recent research study on polarized thinking. Here we shall merely summarize the comparative placements (see Fig. 12-1).

The managers in our U.K. sample are preponderantly Universalist, Analytic, Individualist, Inner-directed, Achievement oriented, Egalitarian (moderately), and Sequential. However, it is in the qualities of

Figure 12-1

Universalism	**Particularism**
USA, Britain, Germany, Sweden	France, Japan
Analysis	**Integration**
USA, Britain, Netherlands, Sweden	France, Germany, Japan
Individualism	**Communitarianism**
USA, Britain, Netherlands, Sweden	Germany, France, Japan
Inner-direction	**Outer-direction**
USA, Britain, Germany	Sweden, Netherlands, France, Japan
Status by achievement	**Status by ascription**
USA, Britain, Sweden, Germany, Netherlands, Japan	France
Equality	**Hierarchy**
USA, Germany, Britain, Netherlands, Sweden	France, Japan
Time as sequence	**Synchronized view of time**
USA, Sweden, Netherlands, Britain, Germany	France, Japan

British individualism and analysis, and in the way the traits combine, that we shall find most of our clues to the current malaise. In contrast to American managers, U.K. managers were rather more moderate in their allegiances, but otherwise differed very little from English-speaking developed cultures generally, for example, Canada and Australia. On the other hand, managers as a group are not particularly influential in Britain, and what they think may be less important than the views of captains of industry, economists, politicians, financial analysts, bankers, pundits, journalists, or even consumers. For British managers, as we have seen, come in nineteenth out of twenty-two in international surveys of "Initiative and Drive," fifteenth in the capacity to delegate authority, and seventeenth in the ability to take a long-term view (see Table 10-3). British managers over forty-five years old are also very poorly educated, and only 35 percent have a college degree. Yet those talking about British industry and those buying its goods enjoy considerably more prestige and confidence than those actually running industries. These constitute the market and, since the Thatcher revolution, what markets demand is deemed to be all the direction and social purpose that British society requires.

But there is a catch here. Markets are not independent of culture, and market forces, like weather systems, have prevailing winds and known currents. To "leave it to market forces" in the hallowed tradition of classical economics is not, as we have seen, to submit to an impersonal mechanism of allocation, but rather to the forces of British culture. Laissez faire is equivalent to the injunction "let British·culture be." Are the British seeking to adjust their economy to follow a cultural pattern that is deeply subversive of the very economic development they seek? This will be the theme of this chapter.

A Commanding Social Presence

In a previous book, the English author noted:

> If there was one abiding theme in my upbringing—one idea that held all others in its thrall—it was the necessity for a commanding social presence. To be a gentleman, or to become one of the many modernistic transformations of a gentleman, was to command the attention of others with grace, style, wit, eloquence, self-possession and infinite subtlety. There were many other values, of course, intelligence, affection, wealth, but these were mere resources to be pulled into center stage on cue. The purpose of life was that stage itself, a scenario where ultimate ideas and great passions would play themselves out around me. And I was curiously dismissive of all those subjects which did not lend themselves to social fluency, i.e., science, technology, industry, and similar subjects known to make people conversationally dull. I expected such people to work *behind* the stage.[4]

This pattern of values helps partly to explain what the British do well and what they do badly. For example, the British excel at TV and radio programs, at advertising and PR, in theaters, musical plays, and dramas, in services that stress personal relationships with fiduciary elements, for example, legal services, insurance, money management, and banking, and at up-market retailing. There is a festive or party atmosphere to many such products: scotch, beer, cider, cigarettes, tea, biscuits, pastry, confectionary, chocolates, and jams. A matching set of products adorn the person and the social settings where persons meet, i.e., high-quality knitwear, woollens, tailoring, fashion and accessories, and expensive furniture, carpets, porcelain, china, ceramics, antiques, silverware, jewelry, and gold. The coffee tables are strewn with quality journalism, printed information, and illustrated books—everything, in short, that might be displayed or discussed in a well-appointed drawing room. The British produce goods for circles of affability and for arenas of self-presentation: Lipton's tea, Kipling's cakes, Schweppes tonic water, Gilbert's gin, Jaguar cars, Ronson lighters, Harvey's sherry, and delicacies from Fortnum and Mason.

The prestige of various professions has to do with rights to public display. At the top of the list come royalty, the "dignified" rather than the "efficient" part of government, followed by earls, dukes, courtiers, politicians, judges, barristers, actors, and media personalities. The license to exhibit oneself publicly is the key to social standing. It was the English-born anthropologist, Gregory Bateson, later married to Margaret Mead, who pointed out the major difference between American and British households. In America, exhibitionism comes from children, with the parents constituting the audience. In Britain, parents exhibit themselves before the audience of their children. Self-display was far too important and grave a matter to be left to children. Trapped as audiences before the ludicrous exhibitions of their elders, the British have developed a strong line of satire as in "Beyond the Fringe," "Private Eye," and "Fawlty Towers." Even the Queen is not spared. Yet the satirists are themselves but the new turn on a revolving stage, impatient to replace the targets of their mirth. A largely arts-educated elite remains in power in Britain, because verbal articulation is the currency of competition, the race is to the suavest. In part, it was this that the Thatcher revolution tried to attack, but with every fresh failure, the articulators came back as hindsight beat foresight.

One of the major targets of the Thatcher era was the ethos of the gentleman and the insider. Henri Taine, in his *Notes sur Angleterre*, observed:

> At the bottom of their hearts [the English] believe, or are tempted to believe, that a manufacturer, a merchant, a monied man, obliged to think all day about gain . . . is not a gentleman.[5]

According to the proponents of the Thatcher revolution, gentlemen were "wet," lacking the idealized determination and ruthlessness of the job-creating, risk-defying entrepreneurs who had earlier made Britain great and had then invigorated the United States. Mrs. Thatcher, herself a Grantham grocer's daughter, stood for the upwardly mobile middle-class elements within the Conservative party, the antiestablishment outsiders, those who seized opportunity rather than standing on privileges. The earlier Conservative party of Anthony Eden, Douglas Hume, and Harold Macmillan was still patrician and squirearchical. Edward Heath, the Conservative leader whom Mrs. Thatcher replaced, was considered only a hesitant transition to bourgeois conservatism. With his departure, Britain could at long last complete its transition to an out-and-out meritocracy, where ambition and achievement ruled.

The Conservative party had not been the traditional business party. Until the mid-1920s, the interests of industry were represented by the old Liberal party of Lloyd George. When the electorate polarized between Conservative and Labour parties, businessmen were forced to seek help from Conservatives, but they were late-comers and only marginally respectable.[6] Moreover, industry, as such, was rarely represented in the House of Commons, since workers voted in greater numbers in industrial areas for Labour politicians.

Part of the ethos of the Conservative squirearchy was a semifeudal concern for their tenants and estate workers. The Conservative parties of the 1950s and 1960s were drawn into the Keynsian consensus and the welfare state because gentlemen, having been given privileges and land at birth, owed social obligations to the less fortunate and to public service. For Thatcherites, the Civil Service especially was sodden with gentility, and the humiliation of the Conservative party at the hands of miners and trade union militants, during the 1970s, had been made possible by the "wetness" of those in power. Mrs. Thatcher bought in Ian Macregor, an American, to fight the miners on behalf of the National Coal Board. Her watchwords were TINA (There Is No Alternative) and "The Lady's Not for Turning." She was a "conviction politician" who made a virtue of being unswerving in her determination. She was a woman telling men that they hardly qualified in manliness. British gentrification staggered from resolute blows of her handbag.

But is Britain not surely better off for the demolition job on this effete posturing of the "Oxfam liberal" with his upper-middle-class compassion? And has not the residual leisure class, with its hunting, shooting, and fishing ethos, been further consigned to history? Did not Mrs. Thatcher, at long last, hold Britain's nose to the grindstone of economic survival, substituting the classless model of American capitalism for the mishmash of failing consensus? Why, then, has the British economy fallen further and harder into recession than any other developed nation? So serious is the current turn-down that British companies are frantically cutting their investment in future productivity.

The problem lies in substituting an admittedly spurious gentility, symbolized by Harold MacMillan's self-deprecating gestures, for the drive by flamboyant outsiders to acquire power and money. What connects these two types is the psychology of expressive individualism. In both, whether the desire is to become gentrified or to gain money and power, the quest for a commanding social presence is similar. Admittedly, the styles differ. The gentleman is idealized as civilized, urbane, impressive, subtle, and socially pleasing, yet wary of being seen to exert himself. The outsider-acquisitor is driving, clever, dynamic, blunt, and tenacious, while unafraid of hard work. Yet both parade before the British media, strutting on the national stage and claiming for their own personalities the lion's share of credit for collective efforts, and both turn whole organizations, even large lumps of economic infrastructure, into hostages of their personal whims and judgments.

Of course, the deep recession in which this book is being completed exposes the hyped personalities of business. We might expect some "mighty" operators to fall, but the sheer extent of the wipeout, the near total casualty rate of those the British public were told were great and good, staggers credulity. It is almost as if any businesspersons with more than six column inches in the national press were doomed from the outset. They last about as long as fireworks streaking into the sky, and with them collapse the hopes and livelihoods of thousands of men and women. Consider just a few of these colorful personalities: Peter Clowes, the investment chief sentenced to ten years for robbing small investors of an estimated £18 million; Ernest Saunders, the Guinness chief executive, sentenced to five years for illegal share-support schemes in his takeover of Distillers (the sentence was then reduced on appeal to two and a half years); Jack Lyons, stripped of his knighthood in the same scandal, which also included Gerald Ronson.

Robert Maxwell, known colloquially as "the bouncing cheque," appropriated the pension funds of his *Mirror* employees, diverting them to his private companies, after making an in-house video for employees featuring animated bags of money being jealously guarded by their heroic proprietor.

Other high-flyers have seen their fortunes crash. Asil Nadir of Polly Peck is accused of perpetrating one of the biggest frauds in English commercial history. Roger Levitt of The Levitt Group pleaded guilty to breaches of FIMBRA after the collapse of his £40 million empire. Almost every month brings new revelations of once-powerful figures tumbling from their pedestals. The British nation pays many times over for these episodes. There is the fraud itself, then there is the cost of the trial, estimated at $35 million for the Blue Arrow takeover trial, and, of course, the cost to victims, the public, and national reputation. There is evidence that the legal system is breaking down, with juries and defendants unable to tolerate the hundred day trials.

The list of corruption, failure, and venality could be extended indefinitely.[7] But the source of this greed and corruption is clearly the overblown estimate of what flamboyant individualists bring to an organization.

Of course, British entrepreneurs have from the beginning been outsiders. Of one hundred leading lights in Ashton's *History of the Industrial Revolution*, 50 percent were nonconformists and a large minority so marginal that their beliefs are not known, only their machines. So, why could not Mrs. Thatcher get history to repeat itself? Why is Britain now twenty-first of twenty-three nations in "Anticipated Net Increase in New Business" (see Table 10-6)? Wasn't it for new businesses that hundreds of older ones were permitted to founder? Why was not Britain engulfed in waves of innovation, rather than scandal and fraud? Why did not the lean and mean legions shake Great Britain out of its gentrified stupor and reconstitute its industrial backbone?

On the basis of our eleven previous chapters, we can begin to answer this question. We have seen that the ethos of competitive individualism, persons displaying themselves with the purpose of beating other individuals, is negatively correlated with economic development. We found no exceptions to this trend. Whether such individuals are tough and businesslike or tender and gentrified may, therefore, be irrelevant. Moreover, persons directed from within, by resolute moral convictions, are ill adapted to kaleidoscopic world changes. The "conviction leader," of whatever gifts, cannot for long sustain an organization or country by feats of "brilliant" manipulation.

There is simply too much going on, too many responses that have to be made and lessons to be learned. Mental arteries harden. The need for self-justification exhausts. The world moves on. There is, of course, now as always a need for resourceful individuals. The question remains, how best are these developed, by extolling and exaggerating the influence of the leader in the organization, or by managing the community in such a way that its individual members develop? Japan, Germany, Holland, Sweden, and France prefer the latter sequence, and it seems to be working better for them.

There is considerable historical evidence that individualism was the way in which capitalism began, and continues to be necessary to entrepreneurialism. But capitalism, in its organizational stage, would appear to require different cultural emphases. In retrospect, Thatcherism set out to emulate the American model of capitalism shortly after the time when that model began to seriously underperform. Britain might indeed have been wise to imitate America, but much earlier in her economic history. As it was, the mutual admiration society formed by Ronald Reagan and Mrs. Thatcher appears to have blinded both nations to shifting patterns of world competitive advantage in a world no longer responding to this culture.[8]

And the collapse of the gentlemanly ethos may even have done harm. At least gentlemen had powerful reasons not to cheat, lie, and rob. They were members of a club. Their word was their bond. In the City, where an instant verbal promise could gain or lose millions and paperwork ran days behind transactions, the rules of clubland were vital to the effective conduct of business. A gentleman has more to lose than money, and only because of this can he be trusted, in the absence of precise regulations, to act honorably and with an intuitive sense of what constitutes "good form." In the San Francisco earthquake of 1906, it was Lloyd's and the insurers backed by the wealth and reputation of Lloyd's Names, who paid promptly and in full, while several American insurers defaulted. Today Lloyd's faces a series of crises that may be terminal (see Box 12-1, "Gentlemen of England Now Abashed"). The trappings of gentrification merely permitted the new breed of ruthless operators to escape detection, as desperate expedients were tried by the remainder to "avoid scandal."[9]

Arguably the erstwhile gentlemen had a group ethic, an Old-Boy Network of those with whom he went to school and college. For years this prevented abuse. But the internationalization of the money markets, widening use of the English language, means that even those expelled from the society can settle in Florida or the Virgin Islands and join the ranks of the lengthening Rogues Gallery of British business people living abroad.

A Preference for Consuming

Another problem about individualism and the residues of the gentleman ethos is that those with a commanding social presence are preponderantly consumers. Consuming leaves far greater room for idiosyncratic tastes and postures than does producing, which must typically involve a cohesive group working on a product, not necessarily of their choosing but to which they are jointly committed long-term. In comparison, a

---

Box 12-1

Gentlemen of England Now Abashed

Lloyd's of London is less an insurance company than a market-place and society. Founded in 1688 in Edward Lloyd's coffee house, it was a place where shippers congregated with merchants who would underwrite their cargoes. It is unique in offering unlimited liability backed up by its Names, wealthy persons willing to put up money and accept liability for its losses to the last earring or cuff link. Today, over half of Lloyd's Names are embroiled in disputes with the society over false accounting, misrepresentation, and mismanagement.

The first sign that something was seriously wrong came in 1981, when the Ruling Committee of Lloyd's launched an investigation of the Oakley-Bourne syndicate to which Names had been referred, although knowledge of its malpractice was widespread. The syndicate was closed, but the Committee declined to publish the report, not even to the Names involved, whose losses continued mounting by the year. The case reached the courts in 1988, where the Names were given access to the report. A civil suit is pending. Lloyd's is pleading that it had no duty of care or attention to its Names under the law at that time.

Ian Hay Davidson, made Lloyd's first-ever chief executive officer in 1983, told reporters: "There were three problems: first, extensive corruption; second, the rule-book was like something from a gentleman's club, and provided no explicit protection for investors, and the culture of the place was such that it was difficult to achieve effective, independent self-regulation."

The problem centered around "baby syndicates," special small syndicates of six or seven insiders into which the most profitable business was channeled, leaving the "outside Names" to take the major risks and bear the losses. A spate of scandals led to a succession of underwriters forced to leave Lloyd's: Peter Cameron Webb, now in exile in Miami; Christopher Moran; Sir Peter Green, who had himself expelled Moran, was fined £33,000 for channeling his Names' money through the Cayman Islands without telling them. The expulsion of Ian Posgate for siphoning off his Names' money overseas followed, together with that of Alexander Howden. The rabbits were very much in charge of the lettuce. As Ian Hay Davidson explained, "I said we must go through the apples one by one and throw out those that were rotten, but the problem was the barrel itself." Davidson settled a tax-evasion scam involving 92 percent of Lloyd's underwriters with the Inland Revenue for £45 million. No one was imprisoned.

But the Society is also in deep financial trouble. Marine Insurance, once all its business, has declined. Lloyd's moved into catastrophe insurance, then came Hurricane Hugo, the Gulf War, and the Piper Alpha oil-rig disaster, among others. The habit of laying off big risks within the Society meant that Lloyd's reinsured Lloyd's in a spiral of commissions to insiders, thus intensifying losses to £15 billion. Lloyd's was also heavily into America, where the crisis of asbestosis was accelerating. This is a worldwide problem, but owing to American litigiousness, an insurance disaster in the United States, with 20,000 cases pending. Some already settled at over $1 million each.

Because Names include powerful people, including politicians, Lloyd's is in deep trouble. Accusations of "structural rottenness" have been made by a group of MPs. After years of paying themselves from profits, 150 underwriters have put themselves on fixed salaries of over £100,000, while 6,000 nonworking Names face losses of £90,000 each.

Sources: "Lloyd's in Trouble," Fulcrum Production, Channel 4 TV; *The Independent,* 13 January 1992.

consumer, especially of the expensive up-market goods in which Britain tends to specialize, is able to seek and achieve quite rare combinations of personal effects. The quintessential British and American individualist has, since the cultural revolutions of the 1960s, personified the values of consuming, not producing. As the English author wrote in *Gentlemen and Tradesmen,*

> Because Top People have traditionally consumed with style, but have rarely consented to produce material goods for sale, the entire British economy is skewed toward consumption. Status tends to increase in direct proportion to one's proximity to sophisticated consumers, and to decrease as one approaches crude producers. A few years ago, *Punch* had a cartoon which satirized the nursery story of the Little Red Hen. No one would help the Little Red Hen to obtain raw materials . . . to manufacture or warehouse them. But when it came to advertising and PR, the cat, the dog, and the mouse clamored to do this and, of course, they were willing to consume! You will find Sloane Rangers (upper-middle-class women) aplenty selling gloves or perfume at Harrods, who would not be seen dead in a factory, unless it was to annoy Mummy or win a bet. Finished goods are associated in Britain

with finished and refined people, who may even have gone to finishing school. Raw products in nonrural settings are associated with raw and unrefined people.

In the sixties, *Time* magazine voted London the swingingest city in the world. The British knew how to have a good time. Earlier, the magazine *Queen* had boasted:

> BOOM for brokers, decorators, dress designers
> BOOM for cars, champagne, art treasures
> BOOM for lavish living[10]

And so it has been every few years since that time. Britain's consumers run amok with enthusiasm as the Maudlin Boom was followed by the Barber Boom, followed by the Lawson Boom. On each occasion, inflation got out of hand, unleashed by too much money chasing too few goods, and by the opportunities to pass on higher costs to consumers and fatten profits during booms. On each occasion, demand had to be throttled back, stalling the development of the economy and deepening the next recession. Also on each occasion, the sudden strengthening of consumer demand sucked in imports, which replaced less nimble domestic suppliers, precipitating an adverse flow in the international balance of trade. Britain's incurable addiction to inflation, which only recession can control, is a result of both its consumption preferences and the ease with which higher prices are administered. Unlike the United States, Britain is too small to be genuinely competitive. Tacit agreements to raise prices are rife among supposed "competitors." Individual self-interest means earning more for doing less wherever this looks feasible. Where Britain would be today without the windfall of North Sea oil revenues is an awkward question. She might at best have been forced to rethink her entire economic philosophy.

The sociologist Daniel Bell, in *The Contradictions of Capitalism*, argues that the self-expressive mode of modernism and consumptionism has been metaphorically devouring the economizing mode of productive enterprise.[11] Time was when the cultures of capitalist societies largely supported their economizing modes, and we have seen this survival in Japan, Germany, Sweden, and Holland. Here the purpose of life for many managers is still to accomplish prodigies of complex work. This was true of Britain and America so long as capitalism was still satisfying basic human needs for sustenance.

But when capitalism through its own success had met such needs, the market was expanded to include wants, along with fashions, whims, and fantasies, many of them stimulated by advertising. Expanding production needed a voracious and expansive appetite for consuming to keep it going. The credit card and the TV commercial joined in urging us to present enjoyment and later payment. This, argues Bell, was the true significance of the 1960s cultural revolution. It represented a massive shift from the economizing to the self-expressive modes, from the ascetic, disciplined, prudent "joyless" values of production to the easy, spontaneous, impulsive, joyful values of consumption.

The problem is exacerbated by the fact that most impulse purchases and theatrically presented temptations are not forms of manufacture or distribution that challenge the intelligence or develop learning. They have about them the moral seriousness of Schweppes tonic water, traditionally advertised by clever little fantasies of "Schweppeshire" written by the late Stephen Potter, great fun, but not the infrastructure of an advanced economy. So long as the nation strives to consume what it seems reluctant to manufacture, the consumer appetite will feed on what remains of the productive infrastructure. As the Cambridge economists Robert Bacon and Walter Eltis pointed out in 1978, Britain suffers from too few producers relative to other occupations.[12] With the slump of the early 1980s, their numbers were further thinned and, although Britain achieved sizable gains in productivity, the achievement was illusionary. All but the most efficient manufacturers had been allowed to go under. The remainder were leaner and had shed labor. The producers are even fewer now, the structure of the economy more lopsided than ever.

Unfortunately, Britain's relatively efficient retailing sector is of no help in redressing this balance and may be regarded as part of the bias toward consumption. The beguilement of advertising, PR, and merchandising are as favorable to foreign goods as to domestic ones, making British markets easier to penetrate than foreign ones. Walter Eltis, until recently with the National Economic Development Council, believes that Britain's effectiveness at retailing widens the trade gap.[13]

Moreover, the individualist consumer in search of ways of making his or her personality more distinctive, will tend to favor exotic products from distant climes. For Britons, products from France, Italy, Switzerland, and Scandinavia are more personally distinctive than goods shipped from Crewe, Huddersfield, Stoke, or Birmingham. Phrases like "The Black Country" tell of the dismal cultural reputation of Britain's industrial centers.

A lopsided propensity to consume-in-gracious-settings, or if the setting is unaffordable simply to consume, helps to explain why Britons have consistently paid themselves more than their productivity increases justified. Persistent devaluations of the pound sterling, or letting it float downward, and persistently high interest rates to help shore up its value in world markets has been the result. Managers have historically yielded to high wage demands, relying on further devaluation to make their exports affordable again. Attempts to instill discipline in wage bargaining via income policies collapsed in 1979, with unions openly defying the Labour government they had helped to elect. Today, with Britain driven from the European Monetary System, the pound has once more been devalued and the cycle is about to start again.

A society that values consuming above producing is prey to social envy. There are always some people having a better time than you, fawned upon by the media, preening themselves in public and receiving worshipful attentions, not for work or sacrifice on behalf of the common enterprise, but for seeming to enjoy themselves more than others. Thus, Sir Ralph Halpern, head of The Burton Group, the retail tailor, led a much-publicized sex life in which his mistress regaled the tabloids with reports of his performance during office interludes and escapades. Like so many British stellar performers, he is no longer there, and The Burton Group itself, the mere stage on which he performed, was left in the doldrums. The rancour and sourness of Britain's class war has long puzzled foreigners. A clue may lie in the nature of British competition, which ceaselessly compares the enviability of life-styles, leaving a sullen residue of losers.

Money as Empirical Data and Commerce Decontaminated

The British attitude toward money is complex and contrasts most strongly with German attitudes. We saw that money by itself repelled many Germans. The evil glint of Rhinegold reminded them of traumatic years of inflation and merciless speculation. Yet money invested was thereby transformed into solid, long-lasting products that people needed, ensuring cultural stability and social worth. The British tend to reverse this process. They admire the extraction of money from large and mature organizations and from lumpy artifacts so that it can be wafted around the world's airwaves in a matter of minutes. Money's lack of visible substance is what recommends it. Money is commerce decontaminated, as Alistair Mant has argued. The smoke and debris of the factory, the grimy hands and noisy machines are purified and distilled into a clean row of figures on white paper, or digits on a screen, which gentlemen or the new acquisitors can handle with clean shirt cuffs and mental acumen.[14]

There are several cultural biases working in tandem here. To work with universal symbols of wealth (money) is regarded as superior to dealing with the particular things or objects themselves. Hence, checks and money orders are considered superior to cash and cash superior to manufactured objects, every level on the abstraction ladder being identified with levels on the status ladder.

But there is a second bias operating. Monies are empirical data to which a corporation and its products can be reduced. It is part of the analytical and atomistic bias that truth and precision are found in breaking down complex organizations and systems to their constituent pieces, hence, financial analysis the Analyzing—Integrating dilemma with the British favoring the former. Money and profitability are elegant distillations of what a corporation and its products are "really worth." The reduction of all the mess and complexity of wealth creation into precise figures and formulas is the reason Britain so admires accountants, financiers, and economists. These are the cultural "high priests" of the purifying process. Politicians and civil servants actually believe they are dealing with industry when they pull fiscal and economic levers.

The preference for money is also influenced by the preference for Individualism over Communitarianism. There are few things an individual can do on his or her own to manufacture products. The task is collective. But individuals *can* swing deals, take over companies, account "creatively" for the proceeds, play the market, avoid taxes, shuffle assets, and generally engage in paper entrepreneurialism. The City of London remains a haven for the independent manipulator of abstract symbols, the market makers, the dealers, the brokers, and the financial analysts who look on their chosen industry from afar and through statistical instruments.

Michael Porter has conceived of capitalist nations passing through several sequential stages of development. These are, in turn, factor driven, investment driven, innovation driven, and wealth or money driven (see Fig. 12-2).[15]

The dot on each line of Fig. 12-2 represents the postwar starting point, and the tip of the arrow the point now reached. Porter sees Japan as innovation driven; Sweden as not really succeeding at innovation and falling back on its investment strategies; Germany as being innovation driven since 1948, but refusing to enter the wealth or money zone; and the United States and the United Kingdom as either close to or well into the money-driven phase. Porter sees this phase as the accompaniment of economic decline and believes Britain, under Mrs. Thatcher, was trying to retreat to the innovative phase, but with doubtful success; hence the question mark. He notes:

> The wealth-driven stage, if it occurs, will eventually lead to a slow decline in economic prosperity. It may be decades before aggregate data reflect the underlying loss of competitive advantage. . . . In fact, in the transition from innovation to wealth driven, company profitability and the standard of living may still be *rising,* as companies harvest (underinvest in) market positions, and as managers and employees obtain wage increases that begin moving ahead of productivity improvements. [16]

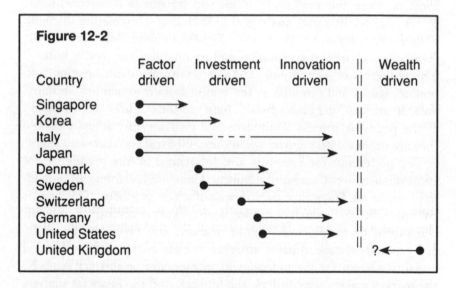

Figure 12-2

Country	Factor driven	Investment driven	Innovation driven	‖	Wealth driven
Singapore	●——→			‖	
Korea	●————→			‖	
Italy	●————————————→			‖	
Japan	●————————————→			‖	
Denmark		●——→		‖	
Sweden		●——→		‖	
Switzerland		●————————→		‖	
Germany		●————————→		‖	
United States		●————————→		‖	
United Kingdom				‖	?←——●

Why should money-driven capitalism lead to decline? Porter gives us few clues. But among reasons already adduced in Chapters 2 to 7 are that "working for the benefit of shareholders," people whom the employees rarely see and do not know, is neither meaningful nor inspiring, while making challenging products for known customers is often both. Money orientation propels to the top of the organization those trained in accountancy and law, not in advanced technology capable of generating world-class projects. Orientation to profits and harvesting these makes British industry less willing to cut prices and compete with the Japanese for market share. This is not in the interests of short-term institutional shareholders seeking maximum yields for pension funds. Nor, by the same logic, is there a willingness to invest long-term in human and technological resources, of which the money men know little, having abstracted their statistics from the distasteful mess of industry to hone their calculations.

The logic of "following the highest returns" by businesses within the portfolio of a company is not the path to greater learning and knowledge intensification for the vast majority of employees. For employees to learn, products must be joined to products by the knowledge, discipline, and technology required to make and distribute them. Thus, fifty products joined by electronic engineering and mutually informing, can develop from a coherent body of knowledge. But a credit card company, a car rental organization and a bakery have no logic that joins them except finance, and each is isolated from the other and is driven to deliver more money to the conglomerate HQ in a contest for available funds. It is an energetic system, a lean and sometimes mean one, but also mentally impoverishing and narrowing. It ill-prepares the participants for the Learning Race.[17]

Britain has a long and dismal record of commercial failure at the point at which great individualist inventors handed over their breakthroughs to organizations for development and manufacture. In the early postwar years, it was government bureaucrats who largely dropped the ball. More recently, the anticipated returns have not been quick or safe enough to satisfy the City. Consider: Sir Frank Whittle invented the jet engine in 1939, at age twenty-two, but because it was given to a car manufacturer (Rover) and steam turbine company (BTH) to manufacture by the Department of Defense, Heinkel created the first fighter jet in 1944. The British *gave* Whittle's drawings to the United States government.

Penicillin was invented by Sir Alexander Fleming, but British drug companies were uninterested! The Rockefeller family put up the money for further development and MERCK, in America, obtained the patent. "One does not patent medical discoveries," the British medical establishment opined. It was bad form.

By 1948, Manchester University had created the world's first working computer, or "electronic brain." This time the National Research Development Council backed it and tried to cajole British industry into developing it. Ferranti tried, lost money, and sold its license to IBM. Anyway, Vincent Ferranti did not like *developing* products. He liked *inventing* them and regularly sold embryo businesses to other countries, including high-voltage alternating cables, switch gears, and computers. He complained that developing products "wasn't fun."

Sir Christopher Cockerell invented the hovercraft, and Professor Eric Laithwaite, the hover-train. Derisory amounts of money were invested in the first, while British Rail, at that time in thrall to the Advanced Passenger Train which later failed, dismissed the hover-train with vehemence. To this day, the bureaucrats concerned congratulate themselves for saving money. "The markets did not want them." But markets respond to developments, not inventions. The market is not an impersonal arbiter "out there" in an Analytical Universe. The market is our own vision and the response thereto. Both might have changed the history of transportation forever.

EMI's Sir Godfrey Hounsfied, who invented the CT body scanner and won a Nobel prize for the company, failed to interest any British hospitals and had to visit the United States before orders came pouring in. EMI lost millions marketing their product against a reengineered competitor from America's General Electric. When Thorn took over EMI, it closed down the CT operations.

Far more important, and ranked with the discovery of x-rays, is the MR (magnetic resonance) scanner developed by EMI just at the time Thorn acquired it. Thorn was quite uninterested in developing this technology after the CT debacle, and it was offered to GE and GEC. The former promised to manufacture in Britain, but the latter, being British, won after political intervention. GEC moved manufacturing to the United States and, being "the world's smallest x-ray company," produced disappointing results.

Britain's Elliott Automation also pioneered the microchip in the 1960s, but was forced to sell to GEC after the cancelation of defense contracts. GEC shut down development. Professor George Gray invented the liquid crystal display. The Grace Company took it up, but STC failed. The British share of a billion-dollar market is now minuscule. A ferroelectric display also invented by Gray was sold to Japan, by Thorn-EMI, who could not raise the money to develop it. A British lead in gate-arrays, a system by which microchips talk to each other, was abandoned by Ferranti as "too big a risk to be involved in . . . our investors expect 20 percent return and up." The opportunity was seized by LSI Logic, a U.S. company, who raised its capital in Japan and manufactured there.

It is a matter of supreme irony that Britain has awarded peerages to Lord Hanson and Lord White as personifying the new spirit of Thatcherite enterprise, when they are, in fact, "the Lords of Decline" (see Box 12-2). They have amply demonstrated the capacity to enrich shareholders by transferring to them the rights and rewards of other stakeholders, customers, employees, pensioners, the government, and the community. One problem with an economy in decline is that the assets stripped and the corporations disintegrated are worth seemingly more in their bits and pieces than in their integrity and wholeness. There is thus an ever-profitable market in disaggregation and disintegration. The question that remains to be answered is whether the very process of taking to pieces and selling off does not so damage the morale of those concerned that economic underperformance is thereby perpetuated, and whether Britain's Atomistic/Specific cultural bias leads her to a chronic surfeit of takeovers, shake-ups, and reductions-to-money of every human system on which acquisitors can lay their hands. For there is no evidence at all that Hanson Trust has actually grown the corporations it has taken over. Scott-Malden, a conglomerate's analyst for BZW, looked at all Hanson acquisitions since 1982. He concluded, "Ongoing organic growth is problematic. There is little evidence of internal growth, and what there is is less than its peers'."[18]

The problem, then, is not that Britain as an economy has been unprofitable or has failed to generate money, but rather that this money has been generated in a way that excludes other elements necessary to economic development. The *Sunday Times* of 22 April 1990 highlighted the performance of the fifty largest companies in Europe, out of a total sample of the largest two hundred. The headline proclaimed: "New survey shows that British companies are outperforming continental rivals."

> The results contradict all the accepted wisdom about the British economy. How can a country which has 28 of the top 50 European companies be in such a parlous state? Even P-E International consultants (the authors of the survey) were perplexed. It double-checked and triple-checked the figures.

The survey showed that on "margin," pre-tax profit as a percentage of sales, British companies, Glaxo, RTZ, British Telecom, and Guiness held four of the first five places. British companies, including Tarmac, Beechman, Great Universal Stores, Hanson, BTR, and British Steel held ten of the first fifteen places. Of the top fifty European companies, the British held twenty-eight of the most profitable. The others were relatively nowhere. France had eight in the top fifty performers, Finland four, the Netherlands three, Switzerland two, Germany two, Belgium, Ireland, and Sweden one each. "The trouble with companies on the Continent is 'they don't make their assets sweat,' " said Sir Eric Fountain, chairman of Tarmac. Since he took over Tarmac in 1979,

Box 12-2

The Lords of Decline

Two Yorkshire businessmen, James Hanson and George White, were extolled throughout the '80s as paragons of British business and were awarded peerages. Starting 1964, Hanson Trust is now an $11 billion conglomerate operating in Britain and the U.S.A. Lord Hanson unashamedly puts shareholders first, "I'm very fond of them," he explained. "First come the shareholders, then customers, and then workers like myself." He was especially admired as the scourge of complacent managers.

His tactics are as follows: (a) take over a dozy company, preferably another conglomerate with high head office expenses and valuable real estate; (b) sell off the real estate plus any businesses in highly competitive markets *to* those competitors; (c) sell also any complex businesses or those needing heavy investment; (d) keep "low-tech" businesses with large market shares, e.g., bricks, coal, cement, cigarettes, and flashlight batteries; (e) milk these businesses for cash by cutting labor and rationalizing and setting tough targets for their managers. Perform or you go.

A typical example of a Hanson acquisition was Ever Ready, with a large oligopolist's share of the British and South African flashlight battery market. Within weeks he had closed the Advanced Projects group, then he closed the Central Laboratory. Next he withdrew from the U.S.A. and Hong Kong, then sold the German and Italian plants plus a major R&D component to his major competitor, Duracell. He thereby recovered virtually all the costs of his original purchase and had free assets. Profits surged, but European market share fell from 60% to 10%. No wonder Duracell had paid so well. Ever Ready was no longer a serious international player but Hanson shareholders were enriched. In the meantime, the work force had been halved. As the managing director of Imperial Tobacco, another Hanson acquisition put it, "We are profitably managing the decline of our industry."

The money pouring in for Hanson shareholders comes from numerous sources, but *not* the growth of the industries in his care. It comes from selling the business units of acquired conglomerates to specialists in that technology who manage them more effectively, from closing factories (three of Imperial Tobacco's five), from shedding labor, from "pension holidays" and appropriating surpluses in pension funds, from avoiding stamp duty on purchases by shuffling assets internationally, by tax avoidance (not evasion) through the use of twenty-six Panamanian companies, and through "dealing profits" generally. Hanson does invest short-term but demands a three-year payback.

If Hanson Trust is a microcosm of the British economy, it is not difficult to understand the overall decline, the selection of "low-tech" products, the selling off of market share, the retreat from Europe and Asia, the cutting into the muscle of organizations and selling this to competitors, the search for market shares large enough to administer higher prices. It reads like a catalog of Britain's ills.

Source: "The Hanson File," Channel 4 Television, January 1991.

profits have risen 1,400 percent from £26 million to £393 million in 1989.

In two other measures used in the *Sunday Times* survey, ROTA (Return on Total Assets) and Added Value (revenue less purchases per currency of unit of pay), British companies also triumphed and have extracted more value from their employees for less commensurate pay than their Continental rivals. The article is dismissive of European performance. They are less profitable because they are less competitive. "British managers find that when they take over Continental companies, local managers do not have the same drive to make profits."

What is completely ignored is that profitability, what companies extract from their organizations and give to individual shareholders, may not be an adequate measure of economic development or corporate success. What we may be seeing is the Analytic-Specific cultural bias, "What matters are units I can count up," and the Individualistic bias "What matters most is what individuals gain."

Despite waxing fat in profits from 1984 to 1989, much of the money then extracted from British corporations was not reinvested. Come a recession, profit maximizers seeing no gain for themselves, underinvest chronically, which helps to explain why Britain, America, and other English-speaking countries shoot farther up in booms, but crash farther and deeper in recessions.

Nonetheless, PE International's survey points out some interesting features. Britain's strength is in pharmaceuticals—Glaxo Beecham, ICI; in private-sector near-monopolies—British Telecom, British Steel; in conglomerates—Hanson Trust, BTR, BAT Industries; and in retailing and food—Great Universal Stores, Marks and Spencer, Kingfisher, Sears, Boots, Allied Lyons, Associated British Foods, Guinness, and Cadbury-Schweppes. This accounts for the higher overall profits. Margins in pharmaceuticals are traditionally high. Retail margins are a matter of tacit agreement among retailers and are culturally conditioned. There have been fierce complaints about the markups in British supermarkets, compared to those on the Continent, and a foreign invasion is pending.

There has been similar indignation about the exactions by Britain's newly privatized public monopolies. British Telecom makes £101 per second and announced a 22.6 percent rate of return in November 1991, higher than any other telecommunications company in the United States, Europe, or Japan. Its total profits then stood at £1.61 billion. We have to ask whether the British economy as a whole might be better served by lower infrastructure costs than high private monopoly profits. So much cheaper is the American telecommunications market that it is now 40 percent cheaper for a subscribing company to route its international calls through International Discount Telecommunications in New York than to dial direct via British Telecom.

Finally, the profits of BAT, BTR, Hanson, and other conglomerates are swelled by some of the methods discussed in Box 12-2. The major casualty of high-profit orientation is probably the product itself, market share, and the willingness to "follow" an advancing technology until you are the undisputed world leader. Britain comes in only nineteenth of twenty-three nations in "estimated product quality" (see Table 10-5). The path to such world predominance is often quite unprofitable for several years, and outside chemicals, Britain appears to have generally abandoned such quests.

Aggregated Individuals and Remote Controllers

Another unsolved issue that exacerbates Britain's economic decline is the failure of social consensus over an extended period. Britain has failed to join workers with managers, government with industry, educators with business, to agree on minimum necessary conditions for the formation of a development economy that puts the growth of people and technology ahead of divisive private agendas.

Again, the cultural origins are clear: a preference for analysis and reductionism over potentially unifying visions of the whole, fragments the way people think, while a preference for the individual over the community and its superordinate goals fragments the social world. This is so severe that Mrs. Thatcher recently questioned whether society could be said to exist at all, and she insisted on renaming the Social Science Research Council on the grounds that the social sciences were subversive of free economic choice and too many Marxists called themselves sociologists.

But it is when a world of bits and pieces, inhabited by aggregated individuals, is remotely controlled by general principles of alleged universality that the society as a whole becomes extremely difficult to organize or to manage. The United States finds itself with similar cultural preferences and similar problems. As capitalism increases in complexity, the "remotely controlled aggregates" start to break down, their energy sapped by divisive conflicts.

Thomas Hobbes and, later, John Locke started the process of trying to apply the natural science of Galilei to the political system. Man is conceived of as selfish yet rational. To avoid the war of all against all, men consent to create Leviathan, a sovereign who is the sum of individual strivings. Hobbes argued that the sovereign so formed, being the choice of individuals, ruled only with their consent. There are close parallels between this thinking and the modern view of markets as sovereign, especially the internal markets of conglomerate corporations, which are miniature Hobbesian systems.[19]

Conglomerates are typically run by a system of financial controls. Each unit tries to maximize profits independent of all other units, in an attempt to win more investment pounds from HQ. Managers are rewarded for achieving and surpassing targets. There is no overall strategic plan among units in the portfolio, no communal relationship or shared vision, and no objective that transcends the profiting of individual units. They are miniatures of the British economy as a whole.

Units in a conglomerate are, of course, "remotely controlled" by financial levers and incentives. Remote control is also the traditional habit of British governments. They prefer to sit above the commercial fray, pulling levers, dangling rewards and applying sanctions. This helps to explain the phenomenon noted at the outset of this Chapter, that the British know all about the malfunctioning of their economy and will talk rings around any discomforting theses, while hardly being engaged in any real business at all. The rule is not "hands on" but "hands off." The British, after a late start, are now avid exponents of business schools, starting with London and Manchester; even the cloisters of Oxford and Cambridge now teach management, along with Ashfield,

Cranfield, Aston, Henley, Warwick, and many others. Yet the urge to climb the abstraction ladder away from, and above, business remains very strong.

It is a form of crude "natural science," after Hobbes, applied to self-seeking aggregates of rational actors maximizing utilitarian satisfaction in the tradition of Jeremy Bentham and John Stuart Mill. The paradigm is mechanical, with an expert as the "cause" trying to create an "effect" by the arms-length manipulation of levers that supply and withhold rational motivators. For this is the idealized role of economics in British society. Having created the world's first industrial revolution, the British contributed economists of the rank of Adam Smith, David Ricardo, Alfred Marshall, and John Maynard Keynes to explain to the world what had been achieved. The nation remains in thrall to the idea that all business people are really the "objects" of a science known only to a secretive elite of civil servants, politicians, and economists. Up to the mid-1970s, many thought that the economy could be planned, or that at least demand could be managed by fiscal and monetary levers and state expenditures, when from the onset of stagflation, and the humiliation of having to beg from the International Monetary Fund, a new economic orthodoxy arose. Monetarists taught that inflation, Britain's ancient enemy, could be controlled by controlling the money supply through raising interest rates to choke off overheating of the economy. Mrs. Thatcher came to power on the crest of this new orthodoxy.

The authors lack sufficient economic training to critique monetarism on its own terms, but its cultural and psychological appeals are obvious, so that Britons might be expected to buy it because of the cultural values entailed as opposed to its practical effectiveness. It was a technical and universalistic answer of quite extraordinarily analytic precision and specificity—suspiciously so. Money supply figures controlled inflation. Interest rates controlled the money supply. Individualists could have a fine old Hobbesian contest of all-against-all, with politicians the referees and ringmasters, while contestants reallocated resources. And it was all done by numbers! Through it all is revealed an extraordinary ignorance about, and disinterest in, "the Real Economy," as it is now being called to distinguish those losing their jobs and going bankrupt from the official figures and Treasury Models. Monetarism was supposed to usher in a new dawn for aggressive business achievers, but, in fact, the role assigned to industry was that of performing rats in a scientist's experiment. "Rational expectations theory" held that contestants fighting each other for rewards would do so with greater fierceness and determination if the government never changed its mind and kept "the Game" consistent, while breaking union power. Hence, extraordinary pride was taken in cognitive rigidity and a refusal to change the rules of the contest, "U-turn if you want to, but the Lady's not for turning" is one of the few surviving specimens of Mrs. Thatcher's wit. Stranger, stronger, less recent was the aversion expressed by John Maynard Keynes for the "foul" activities of business:

> Economic development arises out of nothing so much as avarice, . . . usury and precaution, none of them genuine virtues. . . . Yet these must continue for a little longer to be our gods, since only they can lead us out of the tunnel of economic necessity. . . . For the time being, then, we should pretend to ourselves and everyone that fair is foul, and foul is fair, for foul is useful and fair is not.[20]

Given such attitudes by Britain's foremost economic mandarin and civil servant, it should come as no surprise that attempts to intervene in the economy, whether on the demand side or on the supply side, have met with so little success over the years. One rarely succeeds in enlisting the cooperation of someone one disdains.

Hence, there is no legitimation, much less tradition, for those representing the government, unions, or employers' groups to curb their respective rights by joining together in consensual policies designed to develop the whole economy, any more than there is legitimacy for pooling sovereignty with Europe. Encounters between government and industry are legal-rational, with civil servants claiming to be mere instruments of the sovereign will of ministers, who brook no interference. They are literally "servants" without personal discretion or flexibility. Of course, televised satires like "Yes, Minister" make short work of this pretense. Interpretations of procedure by Sir Humphrey tie his minister in knots and serve Sir Humphrey's interests, but this is the "joke." The consequence is that shared, voluntary, discretionary, problem-solving partnerships between government, industry, unions, and educators, aimed at developing the economy, have never been achieved. The market has been resurrected as the Remote Controller par excellence. David Marquand has eloquently stated the issues at stake:

For the central premise on which the whole market-liberal system is built is that choices which the market registers are made by separate, sovereign, atomistic individuals of the reductionist model and that these individuals pursue their own private goods for themselves. If that premise goes, the rest of the system goes too. The competitive market is no longer by definition the most efficient mechanism for allocating resources; and state intervention or producer-group pressures which "distort" the market are no longer by definition harmful. . . . If it is false—if the sovereign, freely-choosing consumer and the national, profit-maximizing entrepreneur are myths; if choices market actors make are, in reality, shaped by a vast array of factors, including ambition for power and status, resentment against being pushed around, the influence of friends and work-mates, the constant drip, drip, drip of the advertising industry, respect for the moral code of one's society and even an unwillingness to change old habits; if, in short, the preferences the market registers are socially as well as individually determined—then there is no reason to believe the diagnosis or to take the cure it implies. *The very notion of timeless, spaceless economic laws, holding good in all societies at all periods of history, becomes untenable. So does the notion that the task of the economic policy maker is simply to ensure that these laws are allowed to operate.* (Emphasis added.)[21]

It is important to realize that British politicians from rival parties do not talk *to* each other as interdependent agents within an economy, save on a few committees and on parliamentary procedural issues. For the most part, they debate, talking *at* each other or to the audience of their constituency, scoring debating points, before going on to win predictable "victories," secured by the overall majority of the party in power. The myth being enacted is of the rhetorical defeat of opposition parties.

We should appreciate what a major advance this system was when instituted over three hundred years ago. Instead of attacking the member opposite with a sword, you used words instead and "won" when the division bells sounded. The government and opposition still sit at opposite sides of a divide *two sword lengths apart*, originally to deter a lunge across the aisle. Prime Minister's question time well symbolizes the thrust and parry from which anything approaching dialogue is entirely absent, with each contestant being cheered on by the jungle noises of supporters and the Speaker crying "Ordah! Ordah!" as if her voice were recorded.

Why does Britain, and to a lesser extent, America, find it so hard to achieve consensus, and how does one mediate changes necessary to economic adjustment? The answer may lie in what Mancur Olson calls "common-interest organizations."[22] These groups exist to distort the market in favor of their members. They include trade unions, lawyers, monopolies, privatized utilities, Lloyd's of London and doctors in the

National Health Service. "All professions," wrote Bernard Shaw, "are a conspiracy against the laity."

Britain's problem, Olson says, is two hundred years of relative peace and stability, in which these slow-growing organizations finally become thick as weeds and start to choke the economy with their assumptions of scarcity and needs to win. But Sweden has also been peaceful and is full of common-interest organizations. One difference, Olson suggests, is the "encompassing" nature of common-interest groups in Scandinavia. We interpret this to suggest that Japanese, Swedish, and other European interest groups are more inclined to conceive Integratively and Holistically with common aims and visions, are more valuing of Community with the wider society, are more prepared to be Outer-directed by others' influences, and are willing to think Long-term and Synchronously. We have seen that all the stronger economies described in this book have these inclinations. Britain and the United States have opposite preferences.

The reckoning is at its most severe in manufacturing, an enterprise in which common-interest groups from different social classes must work together. For all the Thatcher years, 1979 to 1991, British manufacturing grew only 4.9 percent, as compared with Japan's 60.4 percent, 33.3 percent in Germany, and 26.6 percent in the United States.[23] So long as the underlying economy continues to underperform, it does not matter what politicians do or say. At best, they can choose who goes under first, or which "horn" of the dilemma, inflation or unemployment, is magnified.

David Marquand has summarized this situation by dubbing Britain "the Unprincipled Society." What this culture lacks is any vision, superordinate goal, or higher calling that might enable its fragmented interest groups to cohere around an issue greater than the private advancement of their members. No wonder, then, that Britain stood alone against eleven other nations at the EEC Maastricht summit in its opposition to the Social Charter, a charter predicated on principled mutual understandings between management and labor (see Box 12-3, "Too Much for Britain"). What is lost is the economy and politics of mutual discovery and education with participants willing to listen and to learn together. Unfortunately, this learning approach ill befits the colorful British character because "its style is humdrum, not heroic; collegial, not charismatic; consensual, not ideological; conversational, not declaratory."[24] It seems somehow unworthy of the political heirs of Churchill, accustomed to rolling oratory.[25]

The Educational Deficit and the Trap of Ideology

We have seen that the British have a love affair with words, that they prefer to talk *about* something rather than to do it, that posture or form means more than practice, that profit figures extracted from a corporation mean more than the corporation itself, that received economic axioms about markets are more interesting and more admired than what is happening on the ground in the real territory of mixed motives and messy industrialism.

But the penalties for going to the top of the abstraction ladder and staying there are far more extensive than this. What words and numbers do is to draw attention to differences between quality and quantity. A verbal or numerical "map" differs from the real "territory" by highlighting those particular differences in which the mapmakers and users are most interested. Hence, relief maps reveal differences in the height of the ground. Other maps show ocean depths, currents, geological substrata, or tourist attractions. There is an inherent tendency to highlight

---

Box 12-3

**Too Much for Britain
The EEC's Social Charter**

"High Noon for One Nation Against Eleven," thundered *The Sunday Times*, warning of a shoot-out at the Maastricht summit of the EEC. When Britain refused to sign the Charter, opted out of monetary union, and got the dreaded F-word (federalism) removed from the treaty, *The Daily Mail* headlined "Major 3, the French 0," revealing that, for its editors at least, the EEC was a football match. So, what is the Social Charter? Its twelve principles are set out below.

1. Freedom of movement throughout the community, with equal treatment in access to employment working conditions and social protection.
2. Freedom to choose and engage in an occupation which shall be fairly remunerated.
3. Improvement of living and working conditions, especially for part-time and temporary workers, and rights to weekly rest periods and annual paid leave.

4. Right to adequate social protection.
5. Right to freedom of association and collective bargaining.
6. Right of access to lifelong vocational training without discrimination on grounds of nationality.
7. Right to equal treatment for men and women, especially in access to employment, pay, working conditions, education and training, and career development.
8. Right to information, consultation, and participation for employees, particularly in conditions of technological change, restructuring, redundancies, and for trans-frontier workers.
9. Right to health protection and safety in the workplace, including training, information consultation, and participation for employees.
10. Rights for children and adolescents, including minimum working age.
11. Right for the elderly to have a decent standard of living on retirement.
12. Right for people with disabilities to programs to help them in social and professional life.

Note that the Charter does not harmonize wage rates, specify a European-wide minimum wage, or conflict with any of Britain's strike-curbing trade union legislation. Britain's objection is to the rights offered to part-time workers, currently being employed in great numbers to dilute union power and far cheaper, since they are not entitled to paid leave, sick pay, pensions, or National Insurance contributions. But the nub of Britain's hostility is to worker participation and worker councils for employees in excess of a thousand members. Such participation is already widespread, as we have seen, in Germany, Holland, Sweden, and Japan. Despite the fact that workers would only have to be consulted, and could always be overruled, the prospect of any real relationships seems to strike fear into British politicians and managers alike. But then Britain finds the whole cultural style of the European Community unacceptable, the idea that individual sovereign rights can be joined, that a whole vision of the future of Europe can draw you toward the future, that outer-directed influences are legitimate, that the attribution of greatness and power to Europe can and should be self-fulfilling, that you must commit yourself to long-term relationships. Such thinking is Franco-German, and hence foreign.

differences rather than commonalities, and polarities rather than continua. For unless a culture keeps dipping down from abstract ideas to concrete realities, the strata of ideas will lose touch with the underlying strata of realities. Ideas begin to contend furiously with ideas, because these have lost their common reference points. No one says, "Let us stop arguing and *try* it." Gradually, the *polarized* structure of language and the hundreds of invidious distinctions take over from the *integrated* nature of the real world in which cultures cohere and pursue common purposes. Britain is caught in this trap of ideology, which mistakes the structure of reality for the structure of a debate or argument.

The problem is that the clash of ideas has high entertainment value. Each advocate of a polarized position comes on like King Arthur in the shining armor of righteousness. Television's definition of fairness is to let each tilt three times at the other, using sharpened sound-bites to score points with viewers. The moral issues are forever being restated but never resolved, since their statement is entertaining and structured like crystals of clarity, while the resolutions are painstaking, diluted, and dull. Besides, the resolution belongs to the less-favored ends of our seven cultural dimensions.

A constant theme running through this book, and here repeated as summation, is that *wealth creation is a function of the resolution of dilemmas facing a national economy.* Britain's peculiar difficulty is that it enjoys the *Point Counter Point* of "intelligent" discourse, as satirized by Aldous Huxley in his book of that title.[26] The consequence is a culture bristling with false dichotomies and distinctions invented for no better purpose than putting another group or person down and claiming the status of unassailable truth. Nor is there any prospect of these ideological jousts ending, since the answers lying between polarized positions remain invisible.

There is, for example, the lethal distinction between "pure" science and "pure" art, drawn attention to by C. P. Snow in *The Two Cultures*. The English anthropologist Edmund Leach commented:

> The more closely the scientist interests himself in matters of direct human relevance, the lower his social status. The real scum of the earth are the engineers and sociologists. . . . Good science is pure science, and must on no account be contaminated with real life.[27]

The main victims are engineers and, of course, manufacturing, hopelessly trapped between "clean" heads and "dirty" hands and doomed to social utility and the necessity of having to descend the abstraction ladder to discover whether ideas actually work. The result is low status and one of the poorest composition levels in Europe. Ian Glover, in a compensation report to the Department of Industry noted:

> The other three countries [France, Germany, and Sweden] have not, for example, encouraged an undue proportion of their best brains to be directed into scientific research, in the mistaken belief that natural science is the key to technical development in manufacturing. Continental engineering has not had to shelter under the wing of natural science in higher education. It has not had to fish in the wrong pool of talent because of factors associated with academic snobbery and early specialization at the secondary level. Moreover, Continentals do not classify, in semiliterate fashion, engineers as scientists of a type. They are widely understood to be performing a more important function than the scientist, one that offers more personal fulfillment because it is closer to men's traditional central preoccupations.[28]

Nor do European nations choose their engineers from students less than promising in physics and mathematics as the British tend to do, advising second-rate students to apply their knowledge to a mere vocation. The failure of Britain's pioneers of engineering in the nineteenth century to get their genius properly codified and taught in schools has cost the culture dearly. Until the late 1960s, engineers and accountants were the *only* professionally qualified members of British management. That, as accountants and M.B.A.s have now largely taken over from engineers, explains why profit extraction dominates technological contribution. The accountant purifies, the engineer adulterates.

Britain also suffers from ideological splits between business enterprise and education. Mrs. Thatcher hated the intelligentsia because they, in turn, looked down on her provincial commercialism. During the 1980s, Britain had the rare distinction of actually cutting expenses on university education in the face of the greatest knowledge explosion in the history of economic development. Mrs. Thatcher did not receive an honorary degree. But the problem is much, much older. C. P. Snow commented on the Industrial Revolution:

> Almost none of the talent, almost none of the imaginative energy, went back into the revolution which was producing the wealth. The traditional culture became more abstracted from it as it became more wealthy. . . . The academics had nothing to do with the industrial revolution; as Corrie, the old Master of Jesus, said about trains running into Cambridge on Sunday, "It is equally displeasing to God and to myself."[29]

The choice between education *or* business enterprise is no choice at all. Britain can develop only if her products are crammed full with the latest knowledge. The whole argument between educational attainment and "mere" vocations is a poisonous polarization, death by a thousand cutting remarks.

But if Britain's higher education has failed to engender capability, this is dwarfed by a far more pervasive failure, that of not educating the bulk of its population in necessary skills of literacy and numeracy required by work environments. The result has been periodic skill shortages—even in the midst of recessions—the bidding up of scarce skills, and the abandonment of attempts to increase the knowledge intensity of products because no one can be found to do the work. Employers are notoriously reluctant to train manpower themselves, because other employers will poach them.

Britain now has a low-wage, low-skill work force and is increasingly competing with newly industrializing countries. Just about the only exception to this laissez-faire drift toward relative ignorance is Britain's high-tech defense and aircraft industry. Alas, the end of the Cold War and the surplus of cheap East bloc weaponry leaves skilled employees with nowhere to go and the defense sector sinking.

There are two major educational problems accounting for this failure. First, an elite private educational system educates up to European standards, but covers only about 8 percent of the population, none of them manual workers; yet this has been enough to lull middle-class politicians into doing nothing drastic in a situation where their own children are taken care of. The second problem is a seventy-year-old ideological dispute about traditional versus progressive education. Once again, neither side is right. Rather, it is the dispute itself that splits the integrity necessary to genuine learning. Education is both "poured into" children by adults from the outside and "led out" (*educatus*) from the innate structure of their minds. Real damage is done by setting these two processes against each other and creating an impossible choice wherein the child loses both ways (see "The Perils of False Concreteness," Box 12-4).

It is obviously undesirable to produce drilled, docile automatons who know nothing or say nothing that has not been received from a teacher. But it is equally fallacious and somewhat more tempting to believe the child will open like a flower to the sunlight at a time of his or her own choosing, that competition must be avoided lest the gifted child discourages others with his or her gifts. Once polarized, these positions have all

Box 12-4

The Perils of False Concreteness

Four British cultural biases cause the two sides of the conflict to throw rocks of rectitude at one another. The *Universalistic* bias convinces each side that this is an ultimate issue. The *Analytic* bias treats values as engraved objects and "rocks." The *Individualistic* bias sees such "rocks" as the weapons of individual conviction, and the *Sequential* or short-term bias makes people believe that in a single "slice of time" you cannot be both, excellent and equal.

The Möbius strip, so-called after the German mathematical topologist August Ferdinand Möbius, is our attempt to visualize an alternative German, Dutch, or Japanese view. Excelling and equalizing are *Integrative* processes patterning whole communities and are essentially *Synchronous*, with one *Particular* aspect to the fore and then other, over the long term, in which a variety of excellences are judged equally to discover the one of most situational relevance.

Box 12-5

'Two Sailors Attempting to Steady a Boat That Was Steady to Begin With'

This illustrates the Trap of ideology from which even the most logically minded person cannot escape, where that logic is based on individual rationality. Each "sailor" standing in a masted boat is forced to compensate for the extremity of the other's posture as each leans farther to the right or to the left. He or she *must* do so if the "ship of state," or corporation, is not to capsize in the direction he or she most dreads; hence each is obliged to perpetuate an extreme stance. Only a *logic of the whole relationship*, an agreement by each to move by degrees closer to the mast, can end this impasse. If a culture lacks such a logic, it is trapped.

the destructiveness of half-truths which excite each other to do battle. The truth is, rather, that freedom lies just beyond discipline. Master a language and you are free to use it creatively. But discipline also lies just beyond freedom. Act freely and the consequences must discipline your future conduct. A half-century of polemics championing this or that side of the wholeness of learning is a colossal waste of time, yet even intelligent people find themselves trapped in this dispute by the one-dimensionality of advocates. One feels driven to "make up for" their biases. Box 12-5, "Two Sailors Trying to Steady a Boat That Was Steady to Begin With," discusses the dynamics of ideological entrapment which are very real indeed.[30] Having "beaten" the teachers in a series of strikes in the 1980s, the country faces the prospect of teaching its children with a beaten profession, with only 17 percent of primary school teachers supporting Major's government, down from 65 percent in 1979. Teaching has been politicized.[31]

Other destructive ideological disputes pit excellence against equality, the individual against the group, the private against the public sector, the City against Industry, the market against social concerns, planning against freedom, British sovereignty against European union, and gentlemen against tradesmen. The British have a high old time debating such issues as the economy comes apart in the process. What is lost is a culture with so many varieties of excellence that they must, of course, be treated equally; groups that develop and nurture individuals; a public sector facilitative of private sector innovation; a City that gives long-term, low-interest loans to the key technologies of the future; a market created *from* social needs; scenario planning that allows one to choose from visualized alternative futures; a European union built on British cultural experience; and gentlemen with sensibility and honesty to be the world's best traders. The cost, for example, of treating government like one more common-interest organization on the make is a chronic weakening of Britain's infrastructure, with traffic jams costing an estimated $4 billion a year and the worst train service in Europe.

Does Britain's Polarized Thinking Harm Its Managers?

We recently tested the proposition that British managers have trouble reconciling polarities, even when these are not political or ideological. The test took the form of using six of our dilemmas to measure the values of managers about their task of selling microprocessors to customers. The questions asked were not about universals and particulars, analysis and synthesis per se, but about whether the managers believed in the "universal microchip" that every customer wanted, or the "particular microchip" tailored to customers' needs; whether quality was best improved by "perfecting parts and components," or by helping the customers' "whole system solutions to work." Hence all dilemmas were embedded in the day-to-day work of British, German, Swedish, French, and Italian sales engineers working in Europe for a U.S.-based parent company.

Respondents were asked to rate their U.S. parent, their present practice, and their idealized values on the grid (page 333).

The vertical axis on the left measured either Universalism, Analysis-to-parts, Individualism, Inner-directedness, Achieved Status, or Sequential time orientation. The horizontal axis at the bottom measured either Particularism, Synthesis into wholes, Group orientation, Outer-directedness, Ascribed Status, or Synchronized time orientation. The results confirmed those already cited in this book. All European sales forces, including the British, wished to move away from the vertical axes most

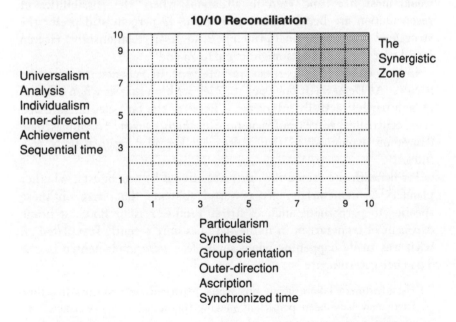

10/10 Reconciliation

The Synergistic Zone

Universalism
Analysis
Individualism
Inner-direction
Achievement
Sequential time

Particularism
Synthesis
Group orientation
Outer-direction
Ascription
Synchronized time

preferred by the U.S. parent, toward the horizontal axes. However, the British were *least* pronounced in this desire, i.e., most like Americans. The Germans were *most* concerned to move rightward, followed closely by the Swedes, French, and Italians.

But the most crucial question was about what managers *ideally* sought. Did they wish to reconcile dilemmas so that short-term and long-term achievement and ascription, parts and wholes, were resolved in a more valuable combination, or did they see conflicting polarities without end? We counted the percentages of managers from different nations who sought to reconcile high levels of attainment on *both* axes. They qualified if they scored anywhere between 7/7 and 7/10 on the grid, or any combinations within the Synergistic Zone. Here is how the different nations scored:

% Choosing Reconciliation
88% Germans
84% Swedish
75% French
70% Italians
51% British

Even where British managers are set free to imagine the solution they would most like, and even in situations where the possibilities of reconciliation are being urged upon them, 49 percent still prefer the struggle of principle against principle in adversary relationships. Heaven forbid that the arguments might come to an end!

In any event, it is perilous to intervene in vehemently polarized debates. As Dean Swift once put it: "Hell hath no fury as when a friend of both parties tactfully intervenes." Between the far poles of opinionation, centrifugal forces pull potential mediators apart. Dilemmas have dangerous dynamics, so that cultures take sides against their own integrity.

For beneath the "scientific" theories offered by economists, whether planners or monetarists, are powerful subtexts that seize on these theories to perpetuate ancient strife. Professor Alan Budd, a prime exponent of monetarism in its heyday, has only recently speculated on what was really happening when such ideas were implemented by the Thatcher government:

> The nightmare I have about this whole experience runs rather like this. There may have been politicians making the actual policy decisions who never believed for a moment that this was the best way to bring down inflation. They did see it as a very good way to revive unemployment and so reduce the strength of the working class. Did they help us stage a "crisis of capitalism" to recreate a reserve army of labor so that industry could make higher profits?[32]

Economics or Culture?

We therefore leave our readers with the disturbing thought that economic theories, however wise they might be in themselves, are probably vitiated in their intended impacts by the underlying cultural and political dynamics of those who use them to clobber those they believe are enemies. Lord Keynes warned us that our entire intellectual framework could be due for drastic revision. He wrote:

> The ideas of economists and political philosophers, both when they are right and when they are wrong, are more powerful than is commonly understood. Indeed the world is ruled by little else. Practical men, who believe themselves to be quite exempt from any intellectual influences, are usually the slaves of some defunct economist. Madmen in authority, who hear voices in the air, are distilling their frenzy from some academic scribbler of a few years back.[33]

Perhaps so, but perhaps the real answer lies within ourselves and our own cultures. We turn to "scientism" because we dream of a weapon that will make all our adversaries behave in ways we can predict and control. We need them to resemble the dead objects of physics, and so we fatally underestimate their humanity. In our fierce adversarialism, we dream of a universal that will bring order. But the deeper problem is that we, in the English-speaking economies, are still at war with each other, fighting for scraps of wealth in a scarcity contrived by our own beliefs. Value can be created only by many of us working together to create syntheses from which all wealth derives.

It never was unemployment *or* inflation, as first the British left and then the British right pretended. Japan and Germany have kept inflation *and* unemployment low. It becomes either/or because ideologists champion one horn of the dilemma over the other, so that, in the words of Chancellor Norman Lamont, unemployment is "a price well worth paying" to keep inflation low. But in the real world "beneath" the rhetoric, one horn is as lethally wounding as the other. As of now, Britons refuse to spend, traumatized by the prospect of job loss, fearful that their bosses will call a "fire drill" and then lock them out of the building, tossing their personal possessions from the window, as the police recently reported City firms doing. This was not so much "the unacceptable face of capitalism," as Edward Heath once put it, but the unacceptable ass.

In the depth of its current despair, British economists have not given up, but are busy refurbishing the Dismal Science. The latest theory is Goodhart's Law, so-called after Professor Philip Goodhart. He explained it on television as follows:

If ever a government decides to rely on any particular statistical relationship as a basis of policy, as soon as this happens, this relationship will fall apart, and that is just what has happened.[34]

That is exactly what we would expect if the world of wealth creation consisted of dilemmas, but its inhabitants insisted these were not horns, but handles or levers they could use to control others.

13

Crisis and Contradiction: Exceptional France

A STORY told in a French subsidiary of a Dutch multinational explains that the headquarters in Holland has staged a contest for all French employees. First prize is a weekend in The Hague . . . third prize, ten days.

France is different, as the French frequently remind us. They are part of NATO politically but are military independent. American jets were forbidden to cross France when bombing Libya. When, in the early 1980s, most Western economies moved decisively toward monetarism and the belief in the free market, France moved in the opposite direction, electing a socialist president and prime minister, extolling centralized planning, and attempting to stimulate its economy through deficit financing.

France is a fascinating country for English-speaking cultures to study, especially if they are willing to question, even to confound, their own basic assumptions. Indeed, France defies easy categorization. It requires a sense of irony, for which the French are famed, to make sense of seemingly contradictory traits. How is it that this secular, republican, and frequently anticlerical state remains 80 percent Roman Catholic, at least nominally? Despite a fiercely insurgent history, with successive uprisings from below, unleashed in the name of equality and fraternity, France remains one of the most hierarchical and least egalitarian of

Western democracies. Can any centralized state have been challenged and replaced so frequently and yet have remained so powerful and centralized? A passionate belief in personal liberty vies with a cultural enthralment with great leaders who have periodically saved France and/or plunged her into disaster.

A Snapshot View of the Seven Dimensions

On most of the seven cultural continua introduced in Chapter 2, France is on the opposite side of the English-speakers, the United States, the United Kingdom, and Canada. This may be the product of historical antipathies, which continues in current tensions in the EEC and over French Canada. For example, on the dilemmas which pitted Universalism against Particularism, France averaged well toward the Particularist end. The scores are combined below.

Table 13-1

Upholding Universal Obligations	USA	GER	NL	AUS	CAN	UK	BEL	JP	SIN	IT	FRA
	94.5	92.0	87.0	86.5	86.0	83.0	62.0	61.0	60.0	51.5	50.0

France is the most Particularistic country in our sample. Does this mean that France is lawless? On the contrary, France is highly regulated centrally in a great number of ways, and half its managers would, in any case, uphold their universal obligation. How, then, do we account for those who seek to get their friends out of difficulty?

In French management, authority is highly personalized. It is therefore unacceptable to those in authority not to have powers of interpretation over rules. What the French call "Système D" is the art of bending rules without breaking them. It means, literally, to "unravel or disentangle" (*débrouiller*) or, more scatologically, *démerdre*. Behind every formal system is a set of informal contacts, to be used when necessary. *Pistonner*, the art of machination, or pulling strings, is also admired, as is *la combine*, the scheme or connection. Any foreigner hoping to be well informed needs to locate the "pistons" that activate or deactivate the rules.[1]

Using inside influence is not considered shameful or unfair, since it qualifies the rules according to the human purposes those rules are supposed to serve. Hence, the French get their hostages out of Lebanon by private deals far more readily than the British, Americans, or Germans, who believe that "the rule of law" must not be bent by subversive elements. France has also extracted its agents from New Zealand following the sabotage of *The Rainbow Warrior* with what many nations regarded as a lack of scruples. From the French point of view, the liberalization of its own particular agents came well ahead of any allegiance to embryonic laws of international behavior.

The qualification of rules by personalities makes at least some regulations less arbitrary and inappropriate. It is as if the very denseness and proliferation of regulations were designed to empower those who can get around these on behalf of particular friends and contracts.

French management has never been as beholden to universal laws as to the correct employment of principles. Henri Fayol, dean of France's business thinkers wrote:

> For preference I shall adopt the word *principles* while dissociating it from any suggestion of rigidity. . . . Principles are flexible and capable of adaptation to every need. A change in the state of affairs can be responsible for a change of rules which had been engendered by that state. . . . I call this "the law of situation."[2]

This has echoes of Baron Montesquieu's *Spirit of the Laws* (1748), where "animating principles" were to be found.

The problems associated with French "flexibility" are obvious. Principles are used by insiders against outsiders. Rules bent by powerful personalities are used to maintain their power. Such words as *cabale* and *entre nous* speak of exclusive advantages won by *la combine*. Talented newcomers are treated with contempt as *arrivistes* (go-getters) and *nouveaux riches*, terms of greater opprobrium within French contexts. On the other hand, the French are quicker to realize that the law can be an ass and that concrete human beings often suffer from abstractions.

Perhaps the most inspiring example of particularistic love renewing the meaning of a universalist law is "The Case of the Lying Bishop" in Victor Hugo's classic story of redemption (see Box 13-1).

The French are also at the Holistic end of the Analyzing-Integrating continuum, while English-speaking nations tend to be at the Specific end. If we combine the dilemma that asks whether a corporation is a system of tasks and functions or a web of social relations with the dilemma of Profit versus stakeholders' well-being, then French preference for holism becomes clear.

Table 13-2 Analyzing vs. Integrating

Corporation reducible to functions, tasks, profits	USA	CAN	SWE	NL	IT	UK	GER	FRA	SIN	JP
	55.0	52.6	46.0	43.5	42.0	34.5	33.5	26.4	25.0	18.5

Box 13-1

Particularism and the Redemption of Jean Valjean: "The Case of the Lying Bishop"

In Victor Hugo's *les Misérables*, now in the form of a popular musical, Jean Valjean stole a loaf of bread and broke a window. He was condemned to nineteen years on a chain gang. Eventually paroled, he must wear his yellow ticket-of-leave on his jacket and is driven from town to town, refused a job and detested by their citizens. But the Bishop of Digne gives him supper and a bed for the night and sits up late with him to hear the story of his life.

After the Bishop has retired, Jean snatches the silver from the table and runs into the night. He is seen with silver in his pockets by local townspeople, who call the constables. They bring him back to the Bishop, and fling him to the ground, arrest him, daring him to repeat his lie that the silver was a gift. But the Bishop interrupts:

> That is right!
> But my friend you left so early
> It has surely slipped your mind
> You forgot I gave these also
> Would you leave the best behind?

He gives Jean two valuable candlesticks, thanks the constabulary, and dismisses them. Then he turns to Jean.

> But remember this, my brother,
> See in this a higher plan.
> You must use this precious silver
> To become an honest man.
> By the witness of the martyrs,
> By the passion and the blood,
> God has raised you out of darkness,
> I have bought your soul for God

The Bishop, faced by a dilemma between universalism and particularism, has used a *particular* act of kindness and deceit to restore Valjean to a condition in which *universal* "higher plan" can appeal to him and guide his life.

It is easy to sneer at this "sentimental," "Roman Catholic," and "extravagant" act of charity. Should silver be distributed free to convicts? Ha ha! But that misses the whole point. The gift was not intended as a universal answer to the crime problem, but as a *particular* act of love toward one man whom the Bishop judged would respond. *There may be no universal answer to crime*

> *without particular acts of concern aimed at particular people.*
> There are 2.7 serious crimes per 100,000 people per annum in
> Japan, 86.7 in France, and 225.15 in the United States. The
> comprehension of codes is of no avail without the particulars,
> unique instances in which persons sustain persons.

French holism fills the language with masterful totalities of impressions: *panache, recherche, ambiance, éminence, chic, formidable, finesse, élan vital, mystique, joie de vivre,* and *je ne sais quoi.* Not surprisingly, sociology, the study of man in the social context, tends to be stronger in France than psychology. Indeed, the Father of Sociology is generally regarded as August Comte (1798–1857), author of *Plan for the Scientific Works Necessary for the Reorganization of Society.* Emile Durkheim (1858–1917) advocated *solidarisme* as the antidote to suicide.[3] Persons were suicidal in inverse proportion to the frequency with which they socialized with intimates. Today, Michel Crozier is France's foremost expert on bureaucracy.[4]

In philosophy, the positioning of rather vague if impressive wholes, was also notable. Montesquieu, as we have seen, saw whole institutions as governed by "animating principles" lying beneath the laws. Jean-Jacques Rousseau (1712–1778) commended the *l'Ingénu,* the Noble Savage, because he alone has enjoyed the organic unity with all nature. A whole people, Rousseau argued, could develop "a general will" which became sovereign, with contrary opinions "canceling each other out." Strongly influenced by Rousseau was the philosophical evolutionist, Henri Bergson (1859–1900), who championed the *élan vital,* or "vital impulse." Living matter could be distinguished from dead materials by the vitality that gave it organization and structure. When a creature died, its organization failed, not its ingredients. New organization was responsible for creative evolution.[5]

A French-trained business theorist, and a student of Henri Bergson, was Mary Parker Follett, who taught in the United States before World War II. Her views, although swamped at the time by the influence of Frederick Winslow Taylor, are unmistakably French and remarkably pertinent to contemporary managerial issues. She wrote:

> I believe we shall soon think of the leader as one who can organize the
> experience of the group. . . . It is by organizing experience that we transform
> experience into power. The task of the chief executive is to articulate the

integrated unity which his business aims to be. . . . The ablest administrators do not merely draw logical conclusions from the array of facts . . . they have a vision of the future.[6]

Vision comes easily to the holistically operating mind, while those with an analyzing bias admit, like ex-President Bush, as not being "good at the vision thing." His difficulty clearly stems from believing that vision is a thing. In fact, vision is organized perception, or phenomenology, a philosophy identified with Merleau-Ponty.[7] It is in men like Jean Monnet and Jacques Delors that a vision of what Europe has become and could become found its origins. Vision is an imagined pattern of possibilities to which whole nations can be drawn. The secret is to generate enthusiasm and momentum. "It is the bicycle theory," an aide of Delors explained. "Right now we must know where we are going. If we stop pedaling and start thinking about our direction we shall fall off." "We must think in terms of power," Delors added. "I want for Europe the possibility to play a world role. This is my ultimate goal."[8]

Power is not an end in itself, but a means of radiating culture. Fundamental to the French vision for Europe is a passionate belief in the superiority of French culture. De Gaulle was uninhibited in his enthusiasm for an ideal that could not be falsified, because tawdry episodes only strengthened the need for it:

All my life, I have had a certain idea about France. In my heart . . . as well as in my mind, France is like a princess of fairy tales. . . . Should it occur that mediocrity marks its gesture, I will experience it as an absurd anomaly, imputable to the mistakes of the French people, not to the genius of the country. . . . France cannot be France without grandeur.[9]

This statement clearly illustrates the thought patterns of French holism. Ideals are constructed from the high points of a nation's history and have nothing to do with the mere aggregation of experience. The whole is not simply more than the sum of the parts, but relegates and excludes all moments of mediocrity. France, like Camelot, is a synthesis of shining moments.

The authors encountered an entertaining example of Shell Française "revolutionizing" the procedures by which their Shell employees were supposed to be evaluated by supervisors for promotion. The Anglo-Dutch personnel function of Shell International has decreed the use of the (American) Hays Method for evaluation and selection of candidates for promotion. This puts universal rules of job description and employee selection ahead of particular preferences, and detailed checklists with "atoms" of evaluation ahead of whole and intuitive judgments. But the French operating company had simply turned these criteria upside down in a "revolution of the cycle". They first chose who they wanted to promote on intuitive grounds, then ordered them to fill in the evaluation forms!

Earlier, we used our "snail" or spiral diagrams to show that some cultures go to the point first and then spiral outward, while others circle around first before coming to the point by indirection. The French resemble the Japanese in the limited respect that they like to elaborate a whole scene, create a friendly context or ambience, and only later come to the point. They need to discover whether they can trust you and how you behave when not fixated by the possibilities of personal gain. Hence, French managers may drive visitors to distraction by discussing lunch menus during a meeting and supplying more historical context and background than was ever wanted, much less asked for. The Dutch author came across an article on inflation in a French journal that began with Aristotle and made its contemporary observations last. French writing is "flowery" and "overelaborated" by English-speaking standards. A sophisticated negotiator knows that no Frenchman can digest a new business proposal until dessert or, *entre la poire et le fromage*. The French need plenty of contextual information about the other party before they decide. French management was recently described in the *Harvard Business Review* as less a set of techniques than "a state of mind."

The French with their communitarian bent, are also quite opposite from the individualistic Americans, Dutch, Swedish, and British managers. It is not that the French conform to mass opinions, but that major political changes in France have rarely been achieved, if ever, without some powerful social group demanding them. French ruling elites have yielded only to the *force majeure* of organized communities. The harder and the longer insurgent groups had to struggle, the more glorious and elevated became the social ideals that kept them struggling. As the chorus of student revolutionaries sing in *les Misérables*,

> Do you hear the people sing?
> Singing the song of angry men
> It is the music of a people
> Who will not be slaves again
> When the beating of your heart
> Echoes the beating of the drums
> There's a life about to start when
> tomorrow comes!

The poignant part of Victor Hugo's story is that these young men died for their ideal of the People. But the people left these students at the barricades alone to face National Guard.

But do these refrains extend to French managers? We believe they do. One of our questions posed the following dilemma.

Two people were discussing contrasting ways to improve the quality of life. One said, "It is obvious that if one has as much freedom as possible and the maximum opportunity to develop oneself, the quality of one's life will improve as a result."

Another said, "If the individual is continually taking care of his fellow men, then the quality of life for all of us will improve, even if it obstructs individual freedom and individual development."

The scores were as follows:

Table 13-3

As much freedom as possible	CAN	USA	SP	NL	UK	SWE	JP	IT	GER	SIN	FRA
	80.0	78.2	70.2	69.9	67.8	61.1	59.7	55.0	53.3	51.2	45.1

It is clear that French managers still feel drawn to serve their "fellow man" rather than their own freedom, despite the fact that no other country sampled gives majority allegiance to mankind. Henri Fayol made the "subordination of individual interests to the general interest" one of his General Principles of Management:

> This principle calls to mind the fact that in a business the interest of one employee or group of employees should not prevail over that of the concern, that the interest of the home should come before that of its members and that the interest of the State should have pride of place over that of one citizen or group of citizens, [since] ignorance, ambition, selfishness, laziness, weakness and all human passions tend to cause the general interest to be lost sight of in favor of individual interest. [10]

Like Rousseau before him, Fayol seems not to doubt that this general interest or will can be discerned. Among his other principles are Unity of Command, Centralization, and *Esprit de corps*. The organization is referred to as the *corps social*, literally, "the body corporate," a biological metaphor reminiscent of Bergson. "Union is strength . . . harmony is vital," Fayol insists.

Jacques Calvet, head of PSA (Peugeot) put himself deliberately in counterpoint to America. "What was good for General Motors, was good for the U.S.A.? Well, I consider what is good for France is good for

Peugeot." In French management it is the *cadre*, originally the key group of officers necessary to the training of the whole unit, in which prestige is invested. The word is widely used for senior managers trained together at the *hautes écoles*. Different levels of command and authority are also attributed to the echelon (literally, steps on a ladder) to which the individual belongs. Lifetime employment is the rule for well-educated managers. Promotion is from within. Underperforming managers are less likely to be fired than "parked" *voies de garage*, in railroad sidings.

But the French tend also to be inner-directed. This gives their group orientation a very different character from Japanese and Singaporean communitarianism, which is directed from the outside. French culture tends to be driven by the conviction that the group will, by searching the consciences of its members, be ignited by a shared purpose and common conviction. The "general will" manifests itself by spontaneous combustion. This led us to conclude that the organizing metaphor for French management was "the Barricade," a combination of Communitarianism and an Internal Locus of Control (see Box 5-2).

This has clear antecedents in French history (to be discussed shortly) and helps to account for the tendencies of fiercely determined groups to collide in mutual opposition, for example, French farmers assailing trucks of imported British lambs. French bureaucracy also tends to create barriers between different echelons or strata. It was Mary Parker Follet who pointed out that "taking orders" from a superior was potentially shaming to the dignity of the subordinate.[11]

By separating the strata within the corporation, such orders do not have to be given face-to-face, and the sense of honor is preserved. Many of the gaping fissures in French bureaucracy are preserved by this need to depersonalize the subordination. The gaps go some way to preserving *liberté*, while *égalité* and *fraternité* are maintained *within* the encapsulated groups.

We saw in the dilemma of Achieved versus Ascribed status that French managers were tightly clustered at the ascriptive end. This does not mean that the French are uninterested in achievement, but they consider that the time to compete strongly is when you are at school or college. Depending on how well you do, you will be assigned to a *cadre* or *échelon*, which has higher or lower status ascribed to it. This enables a centralist and *dirigiste* government (the word means steering or directing the economy) to deploy persons' known qualities to fulfill national objectives.

French managers are unusually hierarchical, in part a legacy of the ordering of their companies according to the rationality of educational attainment and, in part, because strong leadership is needed to resolve internecine rivalries. This hierarchical tendency is frequently mocked by the French themselves: "Why is the national symbol of France the cock? Because it goes on crowing even with its legs in shit."

But the most unusual characteristic of the French is their orientation to time. Alone among our national samples, the French see the past as more prominent than the present or the future. Is this because the luster of French history shines more brightly than the status quo, Charlemagne, Henry VI, Le Roi Soleil, the Enlightenment, the Revolution, the Empire of Napoleon, *la belle époque*, General de Gaulle, and *trente glorieuse* (thirty years of economic growth)?

Possibly so, but another clue is found when we notice that the French are among the most synchronous of all our samples and the most synchronous in Europe. This means that the French tend to see everything through the historical lens of the past. The present and the future are integral to the past. They are but additional blossoms in the unfolding flower of France. French articles and essays tend to move from historical contexts to present issues. The Dutch author, on visiting Thomson's, the French electronic and electrical giant, found pamphlets on "Thomson in the Seventies." Believing he had been given outdated material by mistake, he asked to exchange it, only to be told it was right off the press! Thompson's record in the 1970s was crucial to its standing today. One of the reasons the French are particularly uncomfortable conversing in English, and will avoid it if they can, is that they feel stripped of their culture and context and must think of present and future without the fullest deployment of the rich historical context shared among French people.

French Culture as a Product of History

If France seems so different to outsiders, it is because her history has also been different from that of other states. The absolute powers of reigning monarchs, the *ancien régime*, survived much longer in France than in much of the rest of Europe and North America. The pattern in Holland, Scandinavia, Britain, and the English-speaking world was one of incremental changes and gradualist reforms, bringing the middle classes to power. But in France this pressure was successfully resisted for so long that it was dammed up and finally burst through in violent revolution in 1789.

This long-surviving royal power made France a byword for splendor and grandeur, with the considerable wealth of the country lavished on its court and aristocracy. The French monarchy was the most magnificent and the most admired in Europe, so much so that French was the language of diplomacy and was spoken in most of the courts in Europe—in the case of the Russian Tzars, until 1917! No other royal house had so successfully patronized the arts, dined so sumptuously, dressed so elaborately, built on such a scale, and contributed so much to world culture. "The Sun King," Louis XIV, and the palace built at Versailles personified such grandeur.

The influence of this period in French culture remains profound. France still excels at *haute couture, haute cuisine,* elegance, poise, sophisticated conversation, *savoir faire* and *savoir vivre.* The justification of a leisured aristocracy was that it had the culture to live life to the full, together with the resources that would be wasted on the vulgar mob lacking the taste or refinement. The authority of the ruling class was essentially mysterious, an infinite sensibility, an affinity with beauty and the five senses. "To know how to live," wrote Montaigne, "is all my calling and my art." The end of the nineteenth century witnessed *la belle époque.* "Inevitably Paris beckoned," wrote Henry Adams. "Scores of artists—sculptors, painters, poets and dramatists, workers in gems and metals, designers in stuffs and furniture—hundreds of chemists, physicists, philosophers, physicians and historians were at work, a thousand times as actively as ever before, and the mass and originality of their products would have swamped any previous age as it nearly swamped its own."[12]

France retains much of this sensibility as a competitive advantage over other cultures in wines, fashions, perfume, gourmet foods, cosmetics, bags, scarves, etc. Such companies as L'Oréal, Yves Saint Laurent, Christian Dior, Hermès, Vuitton, LVMH, and Romane Conti carry on this tradition. A royal and aristocratic culture built on the appreciation of the finer arts would tend to be particularistic, diffuse, and oriented to its own social group, whose elaborate contexts were designed to mystify foreigners, adventurers, and the bourgeoisie. Status was attributed by birth and family, in a steeply hierarchical order held together by familial and, hence, synchronous bonds.

Upheaval and Insurrection

But why would not several revolutions against these elites push their values to opposite extremes? It is hard to say, but revolutions frequently abort the very changes they advocate. Revolutionaries may finish up with the very opposite of their intentions, terror instead of fraternity and a new authority as autocratic as the one that was opposed. As Pierre Vergniaud put it, "There was reason to fear that the Revolution, like Saturn, might devour in turn each one of her children." In any event, the First Republic replaced the monarchy with the imperial glory of Napoleon I, as depicted in paintings by Jacques Louis David. Grandeur, panoply, and hierarchy survived.

This is not to deny that the revolutions of 1789, 1830, and 1848 significantly altered French culture. *Plus ça change, plus c'est la même chose*, "everything changes but remains the same." Hierarchy and status by attribution survived, but the rationale was different. Now Reason was at the helm of society, and civil engineers of the *école des ponts et chaussées* were embodiments of the Enlightenment and received *titres de noblesse* from the Empire.

The revolutions also gave the French culture its unusual combination of group orientation with an internal locus of control appealing to each person's conscience, especially the *contestaire* (one who challenges established order). These are the natural consequences of resistance to gradual reform, which results in pressures for social change building and building until, one day, the outraged internal conscience of each person explodes in a spontaneous group revolt, accompanied by high levels of synchronous thought. What is experienced is a "general will" toward change, with near unanimity in the reasons for it. The "myth of revolution" is that the people share a spontaneous, synchronous, collective sense of rightness, as indeed they do when repeatedly frustrated by a small elite. *Solidarisme* is thus an important value for the French.

Modern French society often reenacts revolutionary fervor in ritualized forms. This occurred not simply in the bicentenary celebration in the summer of 1989, but in demonstrations and rebellions—the French student revolt of 1968, the demonstrations by a million people against admitting Roman Catholic curriculum to public education, the huge recent demonstrations by secondary school students, and the recent rampages through Paris by the residents of the *banlieue* (suburbs).

Social changes have come to French culture through sudden discontinuities. The First Republic was born in the 1789 revolution, and the

Second Republic by the 1848 revolution. The Third Republic was founded on the defeat of French forces in the Franco-Prussian war and overthrow of Napoleon III, while the Fourth Republic came to an end in the aftermath of World War II and the collaboration of the Vichy government with Hitler. In 1958, de Gaulle returned to power to settle the war in Algiers and the revolt of white settlers. This ushered in the Fifth Republic, and de Gaulle resigned in the aftermath of the French Student Revolt. Today there is once more talk of *"crise."* Political change in France is dramatic, conflictful, sudden, and painful, and the French, more than any other culture, find beauty in tragedy. "I love the majesty of human suffering," wrote Alfred de Vigny.

France witnessed the world's foremost bourgeois revolution, as opposed to later proletarian revolutions in Russia and China. Enacted in the name of Reason, it gave permanent prestige to middle-class professions: engineering, science, law, civil administration, and medicine, and to the scholastic qualifications required for these. Business has enjoyed far less esteem until the last few years. But fewer died in the French Revolution's six years than in one week of the Paris Commune of 1871. Here also died a major attempt to decentralize the nation, and its agony sowed bitter dissension between left and right.

The status of the intellectual in France, of the writer using ideas as levers for change (*idée-force*), is perhaps the highest in the world. Again, there is a history of heroic interventions with Emile Zola's *J'Accuse*, indicting the government for the persecution and false imprisonment of Captain Dreyfus, and Henri Alleg's *Gangrène* and *la Question*, exposing the use of torture in Algeria against those suspected of terrorism. These *causes célèbres* and many others were triggered by writers. Even today, the French boast what is perhaps the world's only TV literary talk show with a mass audience, "Apostrophe." The tendency to deduce moral action from first principles leads to both sides regarding themselves as "reasonable," so that conflicts become difficult to reconcile.

Yet the ability to think and to reason, especially in oppressive circumstances, fills the French with admiration. They despise philosophy that makes things look easy and automatically self-rectifying; witness Dr. Pangloss in Voltaire's *Candide*, an indirect attack on Leibnitz. Blaise Pascal probably put it best:

> Man is only a reed, the feeblest reed in nature, but he is a thinking reed. There is no need for the entire universe to arm itself in order to annihilate him: a vapour, a drop of water suffices to kill him. But were the universe to

crush him, man would be yet more noble than that which slays him; because he knows that he dies, and the advantage the universe has over him; of this the universe knows nothing. Thus all our dignity lies in thought. By thought we must raise ourselves. Let us strive to think well—therein lies the principle of morality.[13]

The intellectual, as opposed to intelligent person of science, thinks about turbulent and passionate issues of politics and morality. It follows that the acme of intellectuality is to look on horrors and not be shaken in one's powers or reasoning or in reaching inexorable conclusions. This affects management as well. Jean Louis Barsoux and Peter Lawrence note that French managers see their work as an intellectual challenge, requiring remorseless application of brainpower.[14] An old joke has one civil servant telling another, "That's fine in practice but it will never work in theory." The most coveted jobs in French corporations tend to be the most intellectual ones: planning, research and development, and strategy.

Consensus vs. Contradiction

This entire book has been written around the concept of dilemma. One recognizes dilemmas or contradictions and sets forth to reconcile them. But the readiness to perceive dilemmas and the willingness and skills of reconciliation are themselves at variance between different national cultures. Japanese managers, mentioned earlier, tend to see the world of wealth creation as consisting of complementarities to be harmonized. The United States and English-speaking democracies tend to see individual goals that balance out. The French tend to see stubborn contradictions among the aims of social groups, which lead to periodic outbursts if not negotiated.

All such views are realistic "maps" of the way the world works, with their characteristic insights and blind spots, and each accords with some of the cultural experiences of the countries that believe in them, yet also represents an idealization of what is considered best. The Japanese have not always enjoyed harmony, however, and Americans have not always let competing goals find their own equilibrium, and the French have not always seethed with suppressed energies that burst out in vivacious enthusiasms and new dawns of liberation.

France's focus on contradictions is partly the result of the combination of two trends we have already noted:

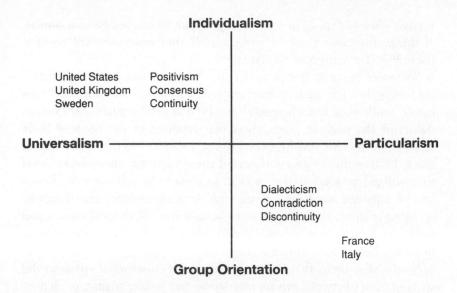

Cultures that believe that individuals have the capacity to discover universally verifiable facts will tend to deduce that a consensus can be formed around such positivistic data. Progress and continuity consist in discovering and agreeing on more and more, in an incremental process of accruing knowledge. This typifies the United States, the United Kingdom, Sweden, and Holland, which are located at the top left of the quadrant above.

Cultures that believe that groups form particular interests, and that these groups inevitably pursue the ideas that best symbolize those interests, tend to cluster at the lower right quadrant. The logic of these contending particularities tends to be dialectical, with different goals in contradiction with each other, with contretemps and struggles ensuing, in which first thesis and then antithesis predominates. Progress is less continuous than discontinuous, with the suppressed ideas storming back to regain the initiative. French management culture tends to be influenced in this respect by the wider political and intellectual currents.

The French tend to see ideas struggling against ideas, the heart with its own reasons divided against the head. It is "incessant movement of contradictions," to borrow a favorite phrase from Albert Camus. *L'Homme Révolté* is fully alive only when his mind rebels fiercely against the social oppression surrounding him, and only when, like Dr. Rieux in *La Peste*, he saves the few he can amid catastrophe. "I rebel, therefore

I exist," wrote Camus in a variation of René Descartes' famous phrase, "I think, therefore I am." Camus argued that inner-directed revolt is the origin of a true group solidarity.[15]

"We were never so free as under the Nazis," wrote Jean Paul Sartre. Seen superficially, such statements seem perverse. Did not the Nazis coerce millions of French people? For French intellectuals and existentialists of the postwar years, there was freedom in the revolt of their minds against what had happened to their society. To feel that contrast was to be free. In the long darkness of the occupation, many Frenchmen were obliged, at least on the surface, to seem to be collaborating, hence mental rage and ideological revolt took on a significance that English-speaking cultures typically miss. To be in a state of contradicting social reality with one's own personal reality was to be as free as was possible in a truly horrendous situation.[16]

No wonder, then, that French existentialists discovered virtue in the sheer contrast between private conviction and public stigma, or shame. The blind pianist, said Sartre, was magnificent because his brilliant playing was counterpointed by his blindness. Saint Genet was a "saint" because he was raised as a thief in a sadomasochistic homosexual gang, and yet transcended his condition to express profound ideas.

It is not simply society and the individual that are at odds. Human relationships are, according to Sartre, a struggle between "being-for-itself" (*pour-soi*), the fluidity of our personal sense of existence, and "being-in-itself" (*en-soi*), ourselves as objects located on the periphery of the other's viewpoint. We yearn to be free, yet are ceaselessly frozen and objectified by the gaze of other people. In *Huis Clos*, meaning, roughly translated, "vicious circle," Sartre portrayed Hell in the style of a perpetual group confrontation in which the *pour-soi* of malefactors is negated by the hostile gaze of others, fixing them *en-soi* as contemptible objects. "Hell is other people," one of the victims explains. She finds herself forever negated by other's reification of her being, tortured by the perpetual contradictions between her personal aspirations and their knowledge of her crimes.[17] While for Americans such confrontations are deemed therapeutic, the French are less optimistic. It is somehow quintessentially French that its leading philosopher, Jacques Derrida, would search for a theory of irony, the collision of language with reality, and it was Claude Lévi-Strauss, the French anthropologist, who anticipated us in claiming that dilemmas among binary concepts lie at the basis of culture.

Even couples and lovers are expected by the French to be continually at odds, their needling badinage being evidence of their underlying affection, while American couples are expected to be mutually supportive and loving. The anthropologist Raymonde Carroll has wittily described the contrasts (see Box 13-2).

Hence for long periods of French history and cultural experience, popular anger has built up against despised domestic regimes, or patriotic fury has simmered against first Prussian and later Nazi overlords. French freedoms are the product of these tensions, hammered ceaselessly on the anvil of oppression and forced to act *contre coeur*, "against the heart," in killing each other or enduring occupation. It is for such reasons that the French culture is often skeptical of American-style consensus models, in which managers "overcome misunderstandings" and errors of communication. Gilles Amado, Claude Faucheux, and André Laurent comment:

> For French organizational psychologists, contradictions will always dominate both within each human being and within organizations. Consequently the individual-organizational relationship will necessarily be problematic. [18]

So, far from the organization facilitating the individual development of its members, it could instead "represent the embodiment of alienation." For these three authors "efficiency" and the perfecting of instruments can lead as logically to Auschwitz as to personal growth. It would depend on what the different groups wanted. Again, such viewpoints are based on French experience. An entire society can be organized to repress Algerian independence or to collaborate with the Nazis. No wonder, then, that French managers question the "neutrality" or organizational development and that unions such as the Confédération Générale de Travail (CGT) are hostile to Management by Objectives, denounced as antidemocratic in *Le Peuple*. The article questioned the whole assumption that workers and managers had objectives in common, or that agreeing to objectives suggested by managers could ever be more than manipulation. [19]

It is partly for this reason that the French sociologist Michel Crozier has referred to France as *The Stalled Society*, with power structures pitted against each other. Change has most frequently come from outside the organization, e.g., from government initiatives, social movements, and new legislation. In this atmosphere of struggle Crozier detected hidden games and the use of information for power purposes, rather

Box 13-2

The Couple in France and in the United States

In France, "being a couple" precedes the separate existences of each party. If an American woman asks a French man to telephone or notify her before coming around to see her, that is an infringement of the spontaneity of their relationship. Each should be free to see the other on impulse—or refuse on impulse. Their affective relationship comes before the schedule of either party.

When a couple voluntarily joins a larger group of friends, the wishes of that group precede the preferences of the couple. Group members will talk to, dance, or play with the unfamiliar partner to test to see if they like him or her. They will not acknowledge the exclusiveness of the couple's relationship. Any signs of private intimacy between the couple are regarded as antisocial: "Hey, why don't you two go home?" Yet if the same couple is among strangers, they may feel free to express their intimacies in ways that Americans find shocking.

Americans are also shocked by "attacking" behaviors between French couples in which they poke fun at each other, contradict each other, and have "violent" disagreements, showing exasperation—all before friends. By teasing each other publicly they are showing, paradoxically, how strong their bond is: "And despite all this, I love him." "We are free to be ourselves with one another." Affection, for the French, does not equal harmony (*de la haine à l'amour il n'y a qu'un pas*—"from hate to love the distance is only one step"). Rather, affection is shown by the strength of positive *or* negative feelings. Harmony may constitute a hypocritical disguise for indifference. "True" feelings are not contained.

American couples will, typically, signal their special bonding in the midst of a larger group, which will respect their greater intimacy. They will exhibit an "ideal relationship" in public by confirming the warm feelings they have for each other. They will not argue, contradict each other or "make a scene." This would embarrass the group: "Hey, you guys!" Couples will, of course, give negative feedback in private, but will otherwise show unity against the world. Agreement is seen by Americans as the basis of intimacy, and conflict or disagreement as a threat.

For Americans, each partner should encourage and support the development of the other's "ideal self." To behave as if these virtues were about to flower is to help elicit the warmth, strength,

and understanding which one trusts is latent. Affection presup-
poses harmony. Passion can threaten harmony. Surprises tend
to be feared. To anticipate and to meet the other's needs is
admired conduct.

In summary, the French view is dialectical love-hate, passion-
exasperation, up-down, contrasting moods that make a relationship intense and exciting. The American view is the perfection of
ideals, with love and harmony vanquishing anger and conflict.
The French regard American behavior as "naive," "hypocritical,"
and "sentimental." The Americans see French behavior as "dis-
loyal," "negative," and "overemotional."

Source: Cultural Misunderstandings, Raymonde Carroll. Chicago: University of
Chicago Press, 1987.

than the enlightenment of all the organization's members.[20] French
researchers generally regard "obvious data" used by Americans as naive.
Canvassing individual attitudes does alter the social determination of
such data, or reveal what employees, freed of mystification and false
consciousness, might decide for themselves were they unthwarted by
social institutions. In an analysis of T-group encounters, Lappasade
detected "a hidden authoritarian order," implicit in fee schedules. The
process only *seemed* to be open and developmental. Hence, for the
French, sociology is really prior to psychology. They prefer "institutional
analysis," "sociopsychoanalysis," "sociological intervention," and "strategic analysis" (a group's power-expanding strategy).[21]

Is all this unduly cynical and pessimistic? Only if progress by separated individuals is your ideal, not if you take a tough and realistic view
of the inertia of social and political systems to being changed, or regard
wrestling with contradictions as a heroic virtue. The French believe that
there are profound differences in group interest between different
classes, estates, organizations, and bureaucracies. These conflicts will
either tear the social fabric or must be negotiated. Thus, when André
Laurent asked managers from ten countries to agree or disagree with the
proposition, "The manager of tomorrow will be, in the main, a negotiator," the results were as seen in Table 13-4.[22]

To some extent the French belief in a social order of antagonism that
is self-perpetuating and self-fulfilling.

The contradiction of revolutions leading to both life and death, honor
and shame, victory and defeat, is caught up in the community galvanized

Table 13-4

Agreed:
"The manager of tomorrow will be, in the main, a negotiator."

France	86
Belgium	84
Netherlands	71
Italy	66
Sweden	66
Denmark	63
United Kingdom	61
Germany	52
United States	50
Switzerland	41

by personal convictions. It is a volatile mix, ready at any moment to explode, brilliantly conveyed in the film *The Wages of Fear,* where class antagonism is symbolized with a tale of transporting gelignite. Indeed, French films are probably the most widely publicized evidence available of the national taste for irony and contradiction (see Box 13-3).

Box 13-3

Contradiction and Irony in French Cinema

In *The Wages of Fear,* an oil company hires some down-and-out laborers to transport two trucks full of gelignite by road to a burning oil well, where it is hoped to blast the fire out. The exploitative relationship between the company and its truckers is mirrored by the exploitative relationship between one of the protagonists and his girlfriend. He pushes her off the moving truck, while she pleads with him not to risk his life. It is mirrored again by the two truckers, one of whom throws a brick into his companion's face, after both have agreed to drop their missiles. One truck gets through, and the fire is extinguished. The cocka-hoop driver returns home to celebrate with his companions and his girl, but crashes his empty truck and dies.

The Return of Martin Guerre is a historical footnote from sixteenth-century France. A young married man with a baby son deserts his family, joining a band of passing soldiers. His grieving parents die within the year. Eight years later "Martin Guerre" returns, greatly changed. He is now literate, upright, and a devoted husband and father to his wife and his son, and they have two more children. He charms the whole village, but then quarrels with his uncle in demanding the profits from the cultivation of his land during his absence. Persistent rumors that "Martin" is an imposter are doing the round and are beginning to be taken seriously by Uncle Guerre, but denied hotly by "Martin Guerre's" wife, his sisters, and the parish priest.

However, Uncle Guerre is influential and persists in his accusations. "Martin Guerre" is exonerated by one inquiry and is about to be acquitted a second time, when the real Martin Guerre enters the court. He and the imposter were soldiers together and Martin had described to his friend in detail the village and the relatives he had deserted. His friend had taken his place.

Who *was* the "real Martin"—the imposter, who loved Martin's family and nourished them, or the husband who deserted them? And who was the real fraud? The only "Martin" ever loved by the entire village is hanged in the village square for theft and defiling "the holy bonds of matrimony," irony indeed.

In *Jean de Florette,* based on a popular novel by Marcel Pagnol, an urban idealist brings his wife and small daughter, Manon, to farm the land he has inherited in Provence. The land is coveted by two neighbors, an older farmer, M. Soubeyran and his nephew, Ugolin Gallinette. The old Soubeyran more or less "adopts" Gallinette as a son, regretting very much that he was apparently never able to have sons of his own. Gallinette wants the land in order to cultivate carnations. Both conspire to block the well, whose whereabouts they discovered accidentally and without which Jean de Florette's land is waterless and useless. Jean de Florette persists against all odds but has to give up during a long draught. In a last-ditch effort, dynamiting the place of a possible well, a stone strikes him and he dies. His wife and daughter leave after virtually signing away their heavily mortgaged property to the two conspirators. When the "Soubeyrans" gleefully unblock the well, they are being watched by Jean de Florette's daughter, Manon.

In *Manon des Sources,* the sequel to *Jean de Florette,* Manon decides to return and stay near her father's land. She has become the local shepherdess and has grown into a beautiful young woman. In pursuit of a stray goat in the mountains above the village, Manon discovers the main well which supplies the water for the whole area, including the village fountain. In the meantime, Gallinette, now growing carnations on her father's land, has watched her secretly and has fallen in love with her. He tries to court her, and Manon now takes her revenge. She blocks the main well, threatening the crops of all the farms in the vicinity. The villagers, all aware of the injustice done to Jean de Florette, but having kept quiet out of either fear or indifference, now see the loss of their water as God's punishment for their quiet collusion, and they confront Gallinette. Accused by the village and spurned by Manon, he kills himself. Manon, in love with the schoolteacher and accepting him as her husband, is persuaded by him to unblock the well. Old Soubeyran finds out that Jean de Florette was, in fact, his only son and Manon is, therefore, his granddaughter. He has destroyed his own and only progeny.

In *Sundays and Cybele,* an invalided pilot from the Algerian war, haunted by the vision of a child in the sights of his machine gun, meets and befriends a little girl, abandoned by her father at a Catholic orphanage. He takes her out every Sunday, posing as a relative. Their strange friendship warms. She desperately needs a parent. He needs to give life to the little girl to atone for the life he took. In the last scene, the girl and the pilot are celebrating Christmas, and she has put her real name, "Cybele," within a silver ball as a present for him on the tree (the nuns insist on calling her "Françoise" because *Cybele* is "pagan"). He is just reaching for the present when the police break in and shoot him, having discovered his imposture. Asked to identify herself, Cybele cries forlornly, "I have no name. I have no name!"

These are not isolated examples of the exquisite ironies in which the French seem to rejoice, despite their being tragedies, which would certainly doom their appeal to Americans.

Similar themes are found in *Les Diaboliques, Le Petit Soldat, Les Enfants du Paradis, Les Liaisons Dangereuses,* and *Cyrano de Bergerac,* where true love wears an outsize nose.

An Instrumental View of Organizational Structure vs. Sociopolitical, Power-diffusing View

The dominant American attitude, as we have seen, is that the organization is an instrument for accomplishing key tasks. The contrasting French view is that organizations exist to confer upon their members social and political power, so that they have sufficient influence and authority to get the whole job done. These two views are, once again, a combination of the opposing cultural traits highlighted at the beginning of this chapter.

The United States, the United Kingdom, Canada, Sweden, and the Netherlands are analytical and oriented to the achieving individual. They seek to match people to tasks, qualifications to roles, managers to objectives, achievements to rewards, and quantifiable merit to incremental advances in status. The organization (from *organon*, meaning "instrument") is seen as an instrument for the achieving of specific tasks. The managers' authorities derive from the jobs with whose execution they have been entrusted and lapse when they act outside these jobs.[23]

France, Italy, and Japan tend to be diffuse in their criteria for judging performance and to attribute status to members on the grounds of age, education, affiliation, gender, and professional qualifications. What counts are contacts and relationships, hence the diffuse criteria for judging managerial worth. The organization is conceived of as a sociopolitical power center diffusing knowledge, influence, and authority in multiple forms and directions. To these power centers status has been attributed by the organization, and/or by government for carefully calculated reasons.

Hence the French government attributes status to its railway transport infrastructure on the grounds that this constitutes a sizable competitive advantage in a Europe where France is increasingly a strategic crossroads. It seems determined via Mintel to "wire" the French nation, doubling the number of telephone subscribers in the 1980s, and keeping Alcatel the world's second-largest manufacturer of telecommunications equipment as a world-class competitor, to promote Aerospatiale, SNECMA, Dassault, and Thomson's Electronics, while resisting the influence of Shell and Exxon with its homegrown Elf and Total. Renault and Peugeot are among the "national champions" to which patriotic status is attributed.

The rational calculations for this industrial policy seem to resemble those of Japan, although they have clearer historical origins in the glories of seventeenth-century France.

The rationale goes back to *Colbertism*, a name derived from Jean-Baptiste Colbert, Louis XIV's brilliant minister of commerce and finance. Colbert personified the high tide of mercantilism, the national policy of spreading trade abroad under state protection. The original theory was that an excess of exports over imports increased the power of the nation in the world. As Colbert himself put it, "The trading companies are the weapons of the king, and the industries of France his reserves." Modern industrial policies put heavy emphasis on using high professional qualifications to generate wealth in sectors with the greatest knowledge intensity, which will then generate sufficient profits to further upgrade the nation's knowledge infrastructure. It has all the hallmarks of a supra-intelligent General Will administered by centralized *dirigiste* governments in which the French rejoice. Only in France could a public housing project be named "Antigone," after the daughter of Oedipus, and look like imperial Rome.[24]

However, French industrial policy has been nowhere nearly as skillful or successful as Japan's. French companies remain small by world standards, and there is a continuing loss of market share in the manufacturing sector. Protecting French electronics and automobiles against Japanese competition has left French manufacturers with large domestic shares of the market, but much smaller European and world shares. Generally speaking, the French argument for protectionism is that domestic companies can use the breathing space to become world-class competitors, but this does not seem to have happened. While the promotion of knowledge-intensive products is immaculately reasonable—they should, all considered, produce higher rents—it is, in practice, very hard to consider everything, and even a superlatively educated administrative elite may have trouble with variables that surface after they have qualified for their jobs. For reality is messy. The strengths of real companies are uneven and full of happenstance. The Anglo-American empiricist tradition that leaves companies free to seize their own opportunities and eschews national plans has some virtue, too.

Perhaps because business does not yet enjoy the prestige of professions and civil administrators in French culture, their governments, especially socialist governments, appear to have listened to business leaders less well than Japanese bureaucrats. The pro-business liberals were in power when France fell to German occupation in 1940, and the French have never fully trusted their business interests since. Successful industrial policy needs harmony, not dialectic.

Is there evidence that French managers share these cultural preferences? André Laurent of INSEAD tested the proposition that the U.S. and northwest European managers had instrumental views of their organizations, while the French and Italians had sociopolitical, power-centered views of influence diffusion, by asking the questions that appear in Table 13-5.[25]

We see the diffuse nature of multiple relationships in question 1 (Table 13-5), where the manager is supposed to have precise answers to most of the questions posed by subordinates. In a subsequent study, using the same question, Japan scored 75 percent, Indonesia 63 percent,

Table 13-5

1. Agreement (%):
"It is important for a manager to have at hand precise answers to most of the questions that his subordinates may raise about their work."

Italy	66
France	53
Germany	46
Belgium	44
Switzerland	38
United Kingdom	27
Denmark	23
United States	18
Sweden	10

2. Agreement (%):
"Most managers seem more motivated by obtaining power than by achieving objectives."

Italy	63
France	56
Switzerland	51
Sweden	42
United States	36
United Kingdom	32
Germany	29
Netherlands	26
Denmark	25

3. Agreement (%):
"Through their professional activity, managers play an important political role in society."

France	76
Italy	74
Switzerland	65
Sweden	54
United States	52
Germany	47
Netherlands	45
United Kingdom	40
Denmark	32

France and Italy 59 percent, and Sweden and the United States 16 percent. Laurent comments that in the Japanese case subordinates take care not to raise questions which their superiors lack the knowledge to answer. The idea that leaders "know" may be more a convention than a reality.

Under such a system leaders radiate powers in multiple dimensions, and this is not forfeited when they temporarily cease to occupy a job slot or step outside their expertise. Power is a semipermanent possession attributed to members of a particular group, hence French and Italian managers can legitimately seek power, as in question 2. Unlike their counterparts in the United States and northwestern Europe, these managers see no necessary separation between person and instrument, business and politics, and powers are not limited to specified tasks; thus French, Italian, and Swiss managers feel themselves very much a part of national power centers (question 3).

Hence, the French tend to see power as a finite resource. If A, or group A, has more, then B, or group B, must have less. While Americans and northwest Europeans see a chance for the whole organization to improve the effectiveness of the instruments they share, in a consensus on improved tools, the French would be more likely to vie between groups for relative powers of influence. Thus American power is *through* others, while French and Italian powers is largely *over* others, with the consequences for hierarchical authority, which we examine next.

These differences between instrumental and sociopolitical views lead the French to be largely perplexed by the Americans' enthusiasm for Organizational Development. The mutual miscomprehension is epitomized in Box 13-4, which also helps to summarize the instrumental versus sociopolitical divergence. For Americans, to "develop an organization" is to improve an instrument shareable by all. For the French to "develop an organization" is to increase the power and knowledge of certain groups at the expense of others. "Instruments" so called turn out to be the interests of an elite or faction.

Organizations as Umpires vs. Organizations as Systems of Rational Authority

France remains one of the most hierarchical cultures in Europe, immeasurably stirred by grandeur and the charisma of great leaders: Jeanne d'Arc, Henry IV, Louis XIV, Napoleon I, Maréchal Pétain, Charles de

Box 13-4

Organizational Development

"Works" according to U.S. culture, because . . .	"Does not work" according to French culture, because . . .
The growth of individuals and the corporate instrument they share are compatible.	The growth of individuals is largely incompatible with what corporations seek.
Where miscommunications and misunderstandings between individuals are confronted, better understandings can be forged.	Where miscommunication and misunderstandings are analyzed, they will expose fundamental contradictions between sociopolitical goals.
If individuals are authentic, open and trusting, common need will be revealed.	If individuals are genuinely open, they will grasp the social bases of their conflicts.
Truth, love, and trust are genuine ideals, capable of reconciling all members of an organization around the optimal utilization of instruments.	"Truth, love, and trust" are mystifications used to disguise the aims of an autocracy seeking to manipulate more easily naive subordinates.
An organization consists of the voluntary efforts of its freely contracting members.	An organization is a loose assemblage of conflicting group interests struggling with each other.
The French view is unnecessarily cynical, adversarial and theoretical, carrying the weight of past political baggage.	The American view is unnecessarily naive, idealistic, and psychological. It is a-historical, superficial, and amounts to "false consciousness."

Source: *"Organizational Change and Cultural Realities: Franco-American Contrasts,"* Gilles Amado, Claude Faucheux, and André Laurent, in *L'Individu dans l'Organisation: les Dimensions Oubliées,* (J. F. Chanlat, ed., Quebec: Presses de l'Université Laval, Collection Sciences de l'Administration, 1990.

Gaulle. Great leaders are, in part, a consequence of the cultural combinations already discussed. A culture of upheaval and discontinuous change will throw up great crises with great leaders to match. A culture caught in the throes of violent contradictions, needs visionary leaders to cut through the knots and to integrate rival factions. A culture based on sociopolitical power centers tends to magnify the stature and the failings of leaders. As the *crise* of the Algerian war grew, de Gaulle demanded and received not simply a mandate to clean up the mess, but a new Republic, designed around his personality. *"L'état, c'est moi,"* Louis XIV is supposed to have once said. De Gaulle remade the state to his specifications. French leaders have even been treated with breathless respect in their *folies de grandeur*. Luigi Barzini expressed it well in *The Europeans*:

> The French long to be unified and pacified, by force if necessary, led to harmony, saved from ruin, and made prosperous by one man, a man who can enforce law and order, bridge the gap between mediocre reality and their national dream.[26]

While Americans see organizations as the promoters of contests in which many managers have equal opportunities to achieve, the French perceive a hierarchy of attributed qualifications designed as a force for rational change in the world.

When André Laurent asked managers in a U.S.-based multinational what was the most important ingredient in their own success, American managers mentioned "ambition and drive" to a greater extent than British, Dutch, or German managers. But of most interest was the item chosen by French managers in the same company. "Being labeled as having high potential" was for them the strongest influence; in other words, the probable place in the hierarchy attributed to them by the organization.[27]

For Americans, the organization is the promoter of fair contests in which those with ambition and drive deservedly win and, in doing so, promote the interests of the organization and its customers. Were the contest not equal and individual achievements not fairly weighed, the organization would suffer. For the French the very structure of the organization is a competitive weapon with a chain of command already in place. It remains for those to whom status has been attributed to act out its rationale in practice, for the engineer from the *Haute Ecole Polytechnique* to do the outstanding work for which he is prequalified. The group's top leaders are propelled by the faith of their subordinates.

Le Chef, le Patron, le Seigneur, "Monsieur le Directeur," senior qualified engineers, often use *tu* instead of *vous* when talking down to a mere *technicien*. This was, until recently, the habitual form of address for servants, a mixture of familiarity and subordination. "To be an engineer in France," explained a manager with Saint Gobain, "doesn't mean you can fix a machine. It implies something about social standing, about outlook, about professional self-esteem and national pride."[28]

The elitist nature of management in large French companies can be noted from the great number of overlapping board memberships. Jean-Marc Vernes, head of the Compagnie Industrielle, sits on the boards of twenty-six other companies. Ambroise Roux, head of Générale Occidentale has seats on the boards of CGE and nine other companies. Between them, such members can usually fend off takeover bids, and shareholders have little influence. Voting is very rare and is seen as an insult to, or lack of confidence in, *le président*. The consequences for French management are not seemingly beneficial. France is nineteenth out of twenty-four developed economies surveyed by IMD on its "willingness to delegate authority to subordinates," and the failure of French leaders to keep their subordinates informed is much remarked upon.[29]

When André Laurent asked questions to groups of managers from different cultures about the importance and function of hierarchy in their organizations, he obtained the results summarized in Table 13-6.

"That everyone knows who has authority over whom" seems to be much more important to French and Italian managers than to American, German, or Swiss managers. Sixty-four percent of French managers see "an authority crisis" in organizations, but only 22 percent of American managers. Finally, the matrix organization, wherein one leader represents the specialty or discipline, while another represents the totality of the project to be worked upon, confronts Belgian, French, and Italian managers with more problems than it does Swedish or American managers. Divided authority seems less a threat to running fair contests than to organized systems of rationality. Laurent summarizes the conclusions of his research:

> For the French . . . the achievement of objectives is secondary to the acquisition of power. For Americans . . . goal attainment has primacy over the aspiration to attain power.[30]

Table 13-6

Agreed (%):
"The main reason for having a hierarchical structure is that everyone knows who has authority over whom."

Italy	50
France	45
United Kingdom	38
Netherlands	38
Belgium	36
Sweden	26
Switzerland	24
Germany	24
United States	18

Agreed (%):
"Today there seems to be an authority crisis in organizations."

Italy	69
France	64
Belgium	64
Sweden	46
United Kingdom	44
Denmark	40
Netherlands	38
Switzerland	29
Germany	26
United States	22

Agreed (%):
"An organizational structure in which certain subordinates have two direct bosses should be avoided at all costs."

Belgium	84
France	83
Italy	81
Germany	79
Switzerland	76
United Kingdom	74
Netherlands	60
Sweden	54
United States	54

Detached/Impersonal Stance vs. Personalist and Familial Relationshps

The French are more affective than Americans and northwestern Europeans, displaying both more emotion and more simultaneous activities involving all the senses. Their business lunches of more than ninety minutes are half as long again as American lunches, and more business is transacted over lunch, as if wine and food were stimulants to judgment rather than instrumental to rest and recuperation.

The hierarchical nature of French companies needs to be qualified by the closer and more personal nature of superior-subordinate relationships. In this respect the French resemble the Japanese, to whom the group is considered closer to a family than to an instrument. One advantage of attributing to senior persons an almost unassailable status and seniority is that they may be less threatened by, and more nurturant to, subordinates, who are not going to overtake or replace them by doing better in some contest.

What makes for American detachment is both the idea that the world is governed by universal laws and objective, specific data, and that the best way of discovering what is instrumentally the most efficient is to detach yourself emotionally from the issue, not taking sides between contestants. Facts are unaffected by our wishes. What "works best" is demonstrable if you avoid emotional bias.

Detachment refers not simply to relationships between people, but between values and spheres of action. The American boss, who is chief when in his office, is not necessarily foremost in the parking lot, in the bar, in the dining room, or on the commuter train. His authority is task-specific. Nor is he responsible for the welfare of his employees outside their salary contracts. But the French boss is likely to be deferred to widely and to feel keenly a personal responsibility, not just to subordinates but also to their families and dependents. The anthropologist Edward T. Hall recorded the following in an interview with a French company president from the provinces:

I felt responsible for them to be happy. I needed good administration and reasonable profits, but just as a means. I knew everyone and used to spend time in the workers' houses to share contact.

When sales were slackening and inventories rising, I used to think, "This means my people are going to work thirty-two hours weekly instead of forty. This means Robert will not be able to finish the small house he is building before winter. This means Jacqueline, who lives twelve miles away, will not be able to come to work at 5:00 A.M. in her small car and will have to ride her bike in the frosty mornings. . . . This means that Maurice will not be able to afford his son's studies in Paris." Then I used to snatch up the sample case and dash to Paris to fight like a lion for the customers, to earn Robert's new house, to pour gasoline into Jacqueline's Renault . . . and to allow Maurice's son to get educated. When I came back with a full basket of orders, I felt with pleasure the *finalité* of my job. I never lived such happy years.[31]

But, as in most things French, there is another side. The same manager subsequently found himself in a rational, Paris-based bureaucracy in which he learned to fill quotas, count profits, and never traveled to the plant. "I betrayed my 'children,' " he lamented.

> When I appear in God's Court, I imagine this dialogue will take place:
> "Daniel, what did you do on earth with the life I gave you?"
> "Oh! Father God, I was extremely efficient! I mean, I made profits. I respected my schedules and pre-costs and never missed my appointments. My quotas . . ."
> "Well, Daniel, do you think I gave you life to fulfill quotas?"[32]

André Laurent asked samples of American and French managers, "In order to maintain his authority, is it important for a manager to be able to keep a certain distance vis-à-vis his subordinates?" Fifty percent of U.S. managers agreed with this statement, but only 28 percent of French managers. For such reasons it is grossly unfair to accuse the French of *authoritarianism*. This term refers to people who dominate and so lose contact with subordinates. But French managers are actually closer to their "children" than American managers, their attributed status permitting them to feel parental-type concern without undermining their own positions. It is some Americans at least who feel they must maintain distance, since "the contest" is about getting ahead and staying there.

Capitalism *Contre* Capitalism: The French Fire the First Salvo

Perhaps it was inevitable that a Frenchman, Michel Albert, should be the first to pick up on the secret war between different versions of capitalism. The French are alert to conflicts, contradictions, and controversy, and anything likely to discomfort Anglo-Saxons will probably register with them earlier rather than later. Nor are they shy about confrontation. Albert's *Capitalisme Contre Capitalisme* was published in September 1991 and is already a best-seller in France.[33]

"Communism is defeated," argues Albert. Capitalism is not simply victorious, but lacks serious competitors, and in its triumphalism has become dangerous, making hostages of our future. Yet an internecine war has started, all the fiercer for being secret, like a schism between chapels. On one side is neo-American capitalism, typical of the English-speaking economies; on the other, in "Rhenish capitalism," presumably Holland, Germany, France, and Switzerland, although France is not, in his view, a full member, and he is urging it to engage more fully. He regards Japan as following the Rhenish flow, but for Asian reasons. Neo-American capitalism is individualistic, short-term, and has a trading ethos. Rhenish capitalism is communitarism, long-term and with a technological ethos. The first works by seduction; the second, by performance. An inexorable war is on, which Rhenish capitalism will win. France must side with Rhenish capitalism if the future of its children, its old people, and its poor are to be preserved—so must the EEC.

Capitalism has been thrice victorious. In forcing back the state under Reagan and Thatcher, in collapsing communism, and in the Gulf War. But now capitalism is about to split. It will do so in response to ten issues, or questions:

1. Should immigration be encouraged?

Pro-immigration countries, such as the United States and the United Kingdom, admit foreign labor to control the market price of indigenous labor, continuously held down by this influx, which is seen as a cost advantage. In contrast, Germany and Japan maintain a homogenous, harmonious national labor force whose growing prosperity is seen as elevating the entire economy. France, with her dangerously insurgent minorities, must decide which policy to pursue.

2. The causes of poverty

Under neo-American capitalism, poverty entails failure, idleness, and disgrace. The poor are culpable. To try to help them is to be exploited by their chronic dependence. In Rhenish capitalism, poverty is the consequence of the economy having to adapt to the disadvantage of those in dying industries. They must be trained, empowered, and assisted to make the transition.

3. Does social security aid economic development?

In neo-American capitalism, a social "safety net" subverts independence and industry. It attracts the lazy and fosters irresponsibility. From the Benelux countries to Scandinavia and down the Rhine and Danube to Austria, social security is seen as an aid to economic progress and a way of socializing the dislocations of economic development so that no organized groups will resist progress.

4. The role of salary differentials

In neo-American capitalism, the capacity to offer higher salaries to key persons is a major lever of economic effectiveness. Pay must be approximate to performance, rewards to contributions. Since the Thatcher-Reagan conservative revolutions, increased differentials have been seen as progress. On this issue, France has sided with the English-speakers. Yet Germany, Austria, Switzerland, Scandinavia, and Japan have tried to limit differentials in favor of consensual relationships and intrinsic work satisfactions.

5. Should taxes stimulate debt or savings?

Neo-American capitalism promotes "grasshopper" societies, where people "leap" for wealth and make or break in a single bound. Their fiscal policies favor *debt*. The more you borrow, the better your tax treatment. In Germany, Japan, and other "ant" societies, taxes favor *saving*. The results are clear. Germans and Japanese save at twice the rate of Britons and Americans, whose rates are falling, and whose consumer spending must be financed by German and Japanese funds.

6. Are we in favor of more regulations and functionaries, or fewer regulations and more lawyers engaging in more litigation?

Albert argues that the rule of law cannot be evaded. If you seek to avoid being regulated up front, you'll only be litigated ex post facto. Neo-American capitalism opts for the litigious society, Rhenish capitalism for the regulated one. In America, lawyering is a commercial business that feeds off litigation. Deregulation has led to massive frauds, followed by feasts of litigiousness. The Japanese are ashamed to dispute publicly. Germans actively seek rules to live by.

7. The bank or the stock market?

The decline of neo-American capitalism has been accompanied by a massive switch to equity financing, away from bank financing. In 1970, 80 percent of corporate funds still came from American banks. By 1990, only 20 percent. Rhenish capitalism, including Japan's, have maintained high levels of bank financing, long-term, committed, and well informed about the client company.

8. Should power be distributed mainly to shareholders or to managers, employees, customers, and the public?

Here again, neo-American capitalism favors the first option; Rhenish capitalism, the second.

9. What is the role of the enterprise in the education and development of professional people?

"As little as possible," is the neo-American answer, since this imposes high costs on the revenue stream to shareholders. It is a very risky investment in mobile labor markets. In Rhenish and Japanese capitalism, social harmony and low turnover assures that training and education accrue to the benefit of the corporation.

10. The role of insurance

For neo-American capitalists, insurance is simply an activity of the market, a choice by individuals for varying levels of security. For Rhenish capitalism, it is a way for communities to socialize risks so that members are encouraged to accept new challenges to replace those now insured against and venture into the future courageously.

France, in Albert's view, belongs to neither of these camps. Her communitarianism is overcentralized. Her government is too *dirigiste* rather than facilitative of corporate initiatives. She suffers from "centralized Jacobinism," with the residues of Marxist baggage. Her strong military tradition leads to the top-down issuance of orders to lower echelons, while the private sector has been subordinated too long to the public. France missed the conservative revolution that rolled back the state. She needs to combine this process with a more decentralized Rhenish capitalism.

Summary and Illustration: Jacques Delors and Conflicts in the EEC

Let us summarize the arguments in this chapter and illustrate their consequences by examining the tensions between Jacques Delors, French president of the Commission of the European Economic Community, and the objections leveled against his policies by Mrs. Thatcher, John Major, and the British government. At stake are two contrasting approaches to the future of the European Community, in which Britain closely reflects the English-speaking and American views of how wealth is created, while Delors is busy putting French-style policies at the helm of the whole community. We will illumine the dispute by considering six of the eight dimensions on which France differs most from the United States and Britain, adding in the contrasts discovered by André Laurent. British government objections to Jacques Delors are largely taken from *Business Life*, the British Airways journal.[34]

1. UNIVERSALISM ───────────────────── PARTICULARISM

For Britain, the EEC is but one more set of trading nations to be covered by the universal laws of classical economics, or capitalism as American and British conservatives currently conceive of it. The most important aspect of the EEC is the Single Market and the abolition of tariff barriers, which will make that market more efficient. In such an event, Britain would not have to choose between Europe and her special relationships to the countries she once colonized; rather, Europe would become a better member of GATT and contribute to an expanding system of free trade.

Yet, to Britain's dismay, Jacques Delors appears to regard the EEC as a particular case, a distinctive continent with unique traditions and unprecedented forms of philosophical enlightenment to which he, a philosophy graduate, seems keen to contribute. He appears to regard Europe, in the manner of France, as a cultural ideal with, in British judgment, near mystical qualities. For Michael Howard, British Employment Secretary, the EC's approach is "narrowly inward-looking."

2. ANALYZING ───────────────────── INTEGRATING
(low-context)   (high-context)

Nothing is stranger to the British than the elaborate, diffuse, and all-encompassing vision of Europe which Delors seeks to proclaim and gain agreement upon, appearing to believe that all nations should be drawn toward this overarching principle. *Business Life* complains:

> Delors' style, though, has never been popular in the United Kingdom. . . .
> His approach is typical of the idealistic continental politician, focusing on
> the final goal, and tends to gloss over details.

British politicians prefer to deal incrementally with small specifics, empirically testing each step and ready to pull back if any prove erroneous. They see the community as specifically economic and competitive, not as intervening diffusely in the social, political, environmental, and fiscal affairs of sovereign states. They would not appreciate the judgment of John du Monceau, head of Accor, who described 1992 as "a rendezvous with history."

3. INDIVIDUALISM ───────────────────── GROUP ORIENTATION

Jacques Delors is a Catholic ex-trade unionist and a socialist, intellectual critic of "unfettered capitalism." For the British this all reeks of communitarianism, of "socialism by the back Delors," as Mrs. Thatcher put it with her uneasy wit. For radical individualists and classical liberals, "society" is nothing but the individuals who constitute it, who, by consuming and voting, register their own preferences. When in 1988 Delors addressed Britain's Trades Union Congress on the subject of the social charter, Mrs. Thatcher was reported as believing "that it was the face of the unacceptable future consorting with the unacceptable past." For what had she broken Arthur Scargill and the miners' strike?

For much of French public opinion, minimum-wage laws, health and safety regulations in the workplace, tax credits for training and educating employees, restrictions on hours worked and giving employment rights to part-time workers, severance payments and guarantees commensurate to the proportion of time they work—all benefit employees directly and employers indirectly, since the latter must then invest more in the machinery and the training each worker brings to bear on the task. More consumer purchasing power is unleashed by decent provision. For the British government, this is gross interference in the rights of employers to compete fairly using Britain's lower wage costs. The Community is attempting to interfere with market forces that favor low-cost producers and allow those who have fallen behind to benefit from their austerity and catch up again.

For the British, the acceptable part of the misnamed "social charter" includes equal opportunities, the internationalization of qualifications so that these are comparable, freedom of movement, the right to set up business anywhere in the EC, and some health and safety standards. For the French, "unfair competition" consists of British manufacturers working their employees long hours and denying them rights, which might push down costs short-term, but would harm industry long-term. Indeed, all Europe has a stake in the welfare and education of its workers.

When we combined individualism with universalism, this resulted in the gradually evolving consensus on positive evidences of success. This is Britain's notion of how Europe should evolve, but Jacques Delors has proved himself the master of dialectic and the tireless negotiator among contradictory views.

> He is an intensely intellectual man, who relishes arguments [who] . . . made weekends with commissioners . . . into exciting and stimulating events. Delors himself admitted that he relished "stirring up doctrinal debate" in the Community. . . . He is irrepressibly argumentative and some would say pushy.[35]

And much of this was achieved by placing Reason at the center of the Commission's deliberations in quintessentially French fashion. A highly centralized *dirigisme* had come into its own. Delors "exploited the right of the Commission to bring forward proposals to a greater extent than any of his predecessors." The Single European Act, the Social Charter, the Central Bank, the Single Currency and Political Union were all "brought forward" and enshrined in the Delors Plan.

4. STATUS THROUGH ACHIEVEMENT — STATUS THROUGH ATTRIBUTION
It is one of Britain's complaints against Delors that "he has fought only one election in his life" and stayed in the French Assembly for only two years before becoming finance minister in 1981. It is alleged, perhaps unfairly, that his appointment to the presidency of the European Commission was a mere token for being passed over as prime minister. In any event, he is now one of the powerful figures in Europe because he was appointed and had status attributed to him. He is, in Britain's eyes, an "unelected bureaucrat," or a "failed politician," in the words of Nicholas Ridley, forced to resign from Mrs. Thatcher's cabinet for his anti-European rhetoric.

Let us recall that a combination of status by achievement and high analysis leads to the view of the Single Market, or similar organizations, as an instrument for achieving tasks. That is Britain's view of the Community as an enlarged market mechanism. But the French view involves combining status by attribution with a diffuse approach to a multidimensional community, which culminates in a sociopolitical power center for the spreading of influence. This would appear to be precisely Delors' strategy.

> [He] has single-handedly turned the once quietly diplomatic post of president of the European Commission into an international power base . . . and is now one of the most powerful political figures in Europe with a guaranteed seat at nearly every major international gathering.[36]

In fury at Delors' power tactics, Rupert Murdoch's *Sun* newspaper urged Britons to turn in unison toward "Frogland" and shout "Up yours, Delors," accompanied by appropriate gestures. It was not Britain's finest hour. But Delors was to outlast even Mrs. Thatcher.

5. EQUALITY ————————————————————— HIERARCHY
One of the major sources of British complaint against Jacques Delors is that he "appears driven by a mystical self-confidence to develop the cohesion and power of Europe." "That aloof iciness which his colleagues find so off-putting has given him an aura of authority." "Because he behaves like their equal when he meets President Bush or President

Gorbachev, they treat him as if he is." This is élan and panache in the approved French style. With his habit of leaving meetings abruptly to attend chapel, he leaves his colleagues muttering, "The Delors is my shepherd."

Thus, while the British see the EEC as the potential promoter of fair contests among national members, Delors sees it through French cultural lenses as a rational system of hierarchical authority with himself as the apex.

> His mind is now turned to what he calls "the democratic deficit." In particular he wants the Commission President to have real powers, including the right to veto commissioners and change their portfolios. . . . A few years ago, ministers would have laughed at Delors' recent suggestion that "ten years hence, 80 percent of our economic legislation and perhaps even our fiscal and social legislation as well will be of Community origin."[37]

The laughter seems to have died.

Finally, we must add that cultural characteristics appear to persist long-term, even where managers cooperate cross-culturally. In longitudinal studies, British and French management students, educated together at INSEAD in Fontainbleu, near Paris, became more distinctly British and French culturally as the course progressed. Eurocrats in Brussels, after eighteen years of collaborative, international work, became more distinctively national in their views. Laurent found the same was true in a major multinational corporation.[38] What appears to be happening is that cross-cultural interaction reminds members of various nations of the differences between one set of cultural views and another, and this seems to lead to a slight intensification of cultural traits, perhaps to protect and confirm these and so maintain identity.

Afterword

WE NEVER REALLY ESCAPE from the culture that trained us. Both the British and Dutch authors are American-trained, and this book despite its reservations about American-style capitalism is American to the core. We share the American Dream of a New World, although ours is beyond even the American Way of organizing business. Our dream is of a world culture in which all paths lead to a shareable integrity. The vision is American because it would constitute a new kind of world order created by cross-cultural communication. Admittedly this differs from America's current universalism, but it draws upon American cultural aspiration toward such orders and the confidence that they exist and can be found. There may be a "science" of wealth creation after all.

We have tried to show that although all cultures are different in the values to which they give priority, they are all addressing the same human condition and are bound to discover in one another elements they may have underemphasised or overlooked in their own struggles to create value.

Implicit in these pages has been a consistent approach to how wealth is actually created by everyone, everywhere. Whether they start with particular customers or with universal demands, both approaches must be fine-tuned and developed together. You cannot create viable and valuable wholes unless you also have the skill to deconstruct these into their fine details. No person can grow in individuality without the support of a community, and no community can long survive without the allegiance of its individuals.

We are not just speaking of balances or golden means, but of virtuous cycles or helices in which sensitivity to the outer world strengthens one's inner direction, where carefully synchronized processes learn to move faster and faster in a "dance" that becomes a "race." It is not

377

wrong to favor status through achievement. It is incomplete. Because the human value of some achievements greatly outstrips that of others, and this realization has an electrifying impact on achievement itself. For beyond separate values lies a harmony among values, a synergy between equality and the sponsorship of those who decree the contest initially. Here lies the integrity of created wealth and value.

Bibliography

Abeggden, James C., and George Stalk, Jr. *Kaisha: The Japanese Corporation*. New York: Basic Books, 1985.

Agren, Lars, and Forslin, Jan. "The Volvo Truck Company," *Sweden at the Edge*, Michael Maccoby, ed., Pennsylvania: University of Pennsylvania Press, 1991.

Aizawa, Susumu. "Japan's High Technology Agenda," *High Technology*, August 1985.

Albert, Michel. *Capitalism Contre Capitalism*. Paris: Edition de Seuil, 1991.

Algulin, Ingemar. *A History of Swedish Literature*. Stockholm: The Swedish Inst., 1989.

Amado, Gilles, Claude Fachucheux, and André Laurent. "Organisational Development and Change," *American Review of Psychology*, 33, 1982.

Ardagh, John. *Germany and the Germans*. London: Penguin Books, 1991.

Argyris, Chris. *Inner Contradictions of Rigorous Research*. New York: Academic Press, 1980.

Argyris, Chris. "Skilled Incompetence," *Harvard Business Review*, September/October 1986.

Argyris, Chris. *Strategy, Change and Defensive Routines*. Boston: Pitman, 1983.

Argyris, Chris, with R. Putman and D. M. Smith, *Action Science*. San Francisco: Jossey-Bass, 1985.

Argyris, Chris, and Donald A. Schon. *Organizational Learning: A Theory of Action Perspective*. Reading: Addison-Wesley, 1978.

Argyris, Chris, and Donald A. Schon. "Reciprocal Integrity," presented at the Symposium on Functioning of Executive Integrity, Case Western Reserve, October 1986 (mimeo).

Argyris, Chris and Donald A. Schon. "Rigor or Relevance? Normal Science and Action Science Compared," Harvard University and MIT, September 1988 (mimeo).

Axelrod, Robert. *The Evolution of Cooperation.* New York: Basic Books, 1984.

Bacon, Robert and Walter Eltis. *Too Few Producers.* London: Macmillan, 1978.

Baden-Fuller, Charles, and John M. Stopford. *Rejuvenating the Mature Business.* London: Routledge, 1992.

Bakan, David. *The Duality of Human Existence.* Boston: Beacon, 1971.

Barsoux, Jean Louis, and Peter Lawrence. *Management in France.* London: Cassell, 1990.

Bartlett, Christopher A., and Sumantra Ghoshal. *Managing Across Borders.* Boston: Harvard Business School Press, 1991.

Bartlett, Donald L., and James B. Steele. *What Went Wrong?* Kansas City: Andrews & McMeel, 1992.

Belbin, Meredith R. *Management Teams.* London: Heinemann, 1981.

Bell, Daniel. *The Coming of Post-Industrial Society.* New York: Basic Books, 1976.

Bell, Daniel. *The Contradictions of Capitalism.* New York: Basic Books, 1978.

Bellah, Robert N. *Tokugawa Religion—The Cultural Roots of Modern Japan.* New York: Free Press, 1985.

Bellah, Robert N., et al. *Habits of the Heart.* Berkeley: University of California Press, 1985.

Bergson, Henri. *Durée et Simultanéité.* Paris: Alcan, 1922.

Berlin, Isaish. *The Hedgehog and the Fox.* New York: Mentor, 1965.

Berlin, Isaiah. *Two Concepts of Liberty.* Oxford: Clarendon, 1958.

Boisot, Max. *Information and Organisation.* London: Fontana, 1987.

Boisot, Max, and John Child. "The Iron Law of Fiefs and the Problem of Governance in Chinese Economic Reforms," *Administrative Science Quarterly,* No. 33, pp. 507–27, 1988.

Booker, Christopher. *The Neophiliacs.* London: Fontana, 1970.

Brockway, George M. *The End of Economic Man.* New York: HarperCollins, 1991.

Burstein, Daniel. *Euroquake.* New York: Simon and Schuster, 1991.

Butterfield, Herbert. *History and Human Relations.* London: Collins, 1951.

Camplin, Jamie. *The Rise of the Plutocrats.* London: Constable, 1978.

Camus, Albert. *The Rebel.* New York: Vintage, 1956.

Carlson, Jan. *Moments of Truth.* New York: Harper and Row, 1986.

Carrol, Raymonde. *Cultural Misunderstandings.* Chicago: University of Chicago Press, 1987.

Chandler, Alfred. *The Visible Hand.* Cambridge, Mass.: Harvard University Press, 1977.

Childs, Marquis. *Sweden: The Middle Way.* New Haven: Yale University Press, 1936.

Choate, Pat. *Agents of Influence.* New York: Simon and Schuster, 1990.

Christopher, Robert C. *The Japanese Mind*. London: Pan Books, 1984.

Cohen, Stephen, and John Zysman. *Manufacturing Matters*. New York: Basic Books, 1987.

Colijn, Helen. *Of Dutch Ways*. New York: Harper and Row, 1984.

Cooper, Joseph. *How to Get More Done in Less Time*. New York: Doubleday, 1971.

Cottle, Tom J. "The Location of Experience: A Manifest Time Orientation," *Acta Psychologica*, 28, 1968, pp. 129–149.

Craig, Gordon A. *The Germans*. London: Penguin, 1991.

Crozier, Michel. *The Bureaucratic Phenomenon*. Chicago: University Chicago Press, 1964.

Crozier, Michel. *The Stalled Society*. New York: Viking, 1973.

Crutchfield, R. S. "Conformity and Character," *American Psychologist*, 10, 1955.

Daalder, H., and P. Mair. *West European Party Systems*. London: Sage, 1983.

Dagenais, James G. *Models of Man*. The Hague: Martinus Nijhoff, 1972.

Daniels, William R. *Group Power II: A Manager's Guide to Conducting Regular Meetings*. San Diego: University Associates, 1990.

Davidson, Marshall. *France*. New York: American Heritage Publishing, 1971.

Deal, Terence E., and Allan A. Kennedy. *Corporate Cultures: The Rites and Rituals of Corporate Life*. Reading: Addison-Wesley, 1982.

De Baena, Duke. *The Dutch Puzzle*. The Hague: Boucher, 1966.

De Geus, Arie P. "Planning as Learning," *Harvard Business Review*, March/April 1988.

Dertouzas, Michael L., Richard K. Lester, and Robert M. Solow. *Made in America: Regaining the Productive Edge*. Cambridge, Mass.: MIT Press, 1989.

Dobb, Maurice. *Studies in the Development of Capitalism*. London: George Routledge, 1947.

Doi, Takeo. *The Anatomy of Dependence*. New York: Kondansha/Harper, 1976.

Dore, Ronald. *Taking Japan Seriously*. Stanford: Stanford University Press, 1987.

Dudley, Nigel. "Jack the Lad," *Business Life*, February 1991.

Durkheim, Emile. *The Division of Labour in Society*. New York: Harper and Row, 1964.

Eatwell, John. *Whatever Happened to Britain*. London: BBC/Gerald Duckworth, 1982.

Eatwell, John, and Milgate Murray, eds. *Keynes' Economics and the Theory of Value and Distribution*. London: Macmillan, 1978.

Emerson, Ralph Waldo. "Freedom," *Poems*. William Heinemann, 1927.

Fayol, Henri. *General Industrial Management*. London: Pitman, 1949.

Follette, Mary Parker. *Freedom and Coordination: Lectures in Business Organization.* New York: Garland, 1987.

Fores, Michael, and Ian Glover eds. *Manufacturing and Management.* London: HMSO, 1978.

Forslin, Jan. "Volvo Components: From Sweatshop to Playground." *Sweden at the Edge,* Michael Maccoby, ed. Philadelphia: University of Pennsylvania Press, 1991.

Friedman, Milton, and Rose Friedman. *Free to Choose.* New York: AVON, 1981.

Fromm, Erich. *Man for Himself.* New York: Holt, Rinehart and Winston, 1947.

Garratt, Bob. *The Learning Organization.* London: Fontana, 1987.

Garratt, Bob. *Learning to Lead.* London: Fontana, 1990.

Gazzaniga, Michael S. "The Split Brain in Man," *Scientific American,* January 1964.

Glover, Ian. "Executive Career Patterns," *Manufacturing and Management,* Fores, Michael, and Ian Glover, eds. London: HMSO, 1978.

Goold, Michael, and Andrew Campbell. *Strategic Styles.* Oxford: Basil Blackwell, 1988.

Gordon, Colin. "The Business Culture of France," *Business Cultures of Europe,* Collin Randlesome, ed. Oxford: Heinemann, 1990.

Gouldner, Alvin. "Metaphysical Pathos and the Theory of Bureaucracy," *American Political Science Review,* 49, 1955, pp. 496–507.

Gurvitch, G. *The Spectrum of Social Time.* Reidel, Dordrecht, 1964.

Halberstam, David. *The Reckoning.* New York: AVON, 1988.

Hall, Edward T. *The Cultures of France and Germany.* New York: Intercultural Press, 1989.

Hall, Edward T. *Dance of Life: The Other Dimension of Time.* New York: Anchor, Doubleday, 1983.

Hall, Edward T. *Hidden Differences: Doing Business with the Japanese.* New York: Doubleday, 1987.

Hall, Edward T. *The Silent Language.* New York: Doubleday, 1959.

Hamel, Gary, and C. K. Prahalad. "Strategic Intent," *Harvard Business Review,* May–June, 1989.

Hampden-Turner, Charles M. "Approaching Dilemmas," *Shell Guides to Planning,* No. 3, 1985.

Hampden-Turner, Charles M. *Charting the Corporate Mind: From Dilemma to Strategy.* Oxford: Basil Blackwell, 1990.

Hampden-Turner, Charles M. *Creating Corporate Culture.* Reading: Addison-Wesley, 1992.

Hampden-Turner, Charles M. *Gentlemen and Tradesmen: The Values of Economic Catastrophe.* London: Routledge and Kegan Paul, 1983.

Hampden-Turner, Charles M. *Maps of the Mind*. New York: Macmillan, 1981.

Hampden-Turner, Charles M. *Radical Man: Towards a Theory of Psychosocial Development*. London: Duckworth, 1973.

Handy, Charles. *The Age of Unreason*. London: Century-Hutchinson, 1989.

Handy, Charles. *The Gods of Management*. London: Souvenir Press, 1978.

Harrison, Roger. "*Start-up: The Care and Feeding of Infant Systems*," *Organizational Dynamics*, September 1981.

Harrison, Roger. "Understanding Your Organization's Character," *Harvard Business Review*, May–June, 1972.

Haselhoff, Fritz.*Ondernemingsstrategie, een dilemma; de moderne ondernemingsorganisatie in het spanningsveld van doelmatigheid, overleving en zingeving*, Alphen aan de Rijn: Samson, 1977.

Hedley, Barry. "Strategy and the Business Portfolio," *Long-Range Planning*, February 1977, p. 10.

Hedlund, Gunnar. "Managing International Business," *Sweden at the Edge*, Michael Maccoby, ed. Philadelphia: University of Pennsylvania Press, 1991.

Hedlund, Gunnar, and D. Rolander. "Action in Heterarchies: New Approaches to Managing the MNC," *Managing the Global Firm*, G. Hedlund, C. Bartlett, and Y. Doz, eds. London: Routledge, 1990.

Heilbroner, Robert. *The Worldly Philosophers*. New York: Simon and Schuster, 1980.

Heyne, Paul. *The Economic Way of Thinking*. Chicago: Science Research Associates, 1983.

Hoffman, Stanley. *In Search of France*. Cambridge, Mass: Harvard University Press, 1963.

Hofstede, Geert. *Cultures and Organizations: Software of the Mind*. New York: McGraw-Hill, 1991.

Hofstede, Geert. *Cultures' Consequences*. Beverly Hills: Sage, 1980.

Holstein, William J. *The Japanese Power Game: What It Means for Americans*. New York: Charles Scribner and Sons, 1990.

Huizinga, Johan. *Homo Ludens: A Study of the Play Element in Culture*. Boston: Beacon, 1970.

Inzerilli, George, and André Laurent. "Managerial Views of Organization Structure in France and the USA," *International Studies of Management and Organization*, Vol. XIII, No. 1–2, 1983.

Ishihara, Shintaro. *The Japan that Can Say "No."* Congressional Record, November 14, 1989; also New York: Kubansha/Kappa-Holmes, 1989.

Ishinomori, Shotaro. *Japan Inc*. Berkeley: University of California Press, 1988.

Jacobs, Michael T. *Short-term America*. Boston: Harvard Business School Press, 1991.

James, William. *Essays in Pragmatism.* New York: Haffner Publishing, 1949.

Jaques, Elliott. *The Form of Time.* New York: Crane Russak, 1982.

Jaques, Elliott. *Free Enterprise, Fair Employment.* New York: Crane Russak, 1982.

Jaques, Elliott. *A General Theory of Bureaucracy.* London: Heinemann, 1976.

Jay, Martin. *The Dialectical Imagination.* London: Heinemann, 1972.

Johnson, Chalmers. *MITI and the Japanese Miracle.* Stanford: Stanford University Press, 1982.

Jonsson, Berth. "Production Philosophy at Volvo," *Sweden at the Edge,* Michael Maccoby, ed. Philadelphia: University of Pennsylvania Press, 1991.

Kaplan, Abraham. *The Conduct of Inquiry.* Scranton, Penn.: Chandler, 1964.

Keynes, John Maynard. "Economic Possibilities for Our Grandchildren," *Essays in Persuasion.* Cambridge: Cambridge University Press, 1930.

Kluckhohn F., and F. L. Strodtbeck. *Variations in Value Orientations.* Westport: Greenwood Press, 1961.

Koestler, Arthur. *The Act of Creation.* New York: Macmillan, 1964.

Koestler, Arthur, with J. R. Smythies. *Beyond Reductionism: New Perspectives on the Life Sciences.* Boston: Beacon, 1969.

Laing, Ronald. *The Divided Self.* New York: Penguin, 1965.

Laurent, André. "Cross-Cultural Management for Pan-European Companies." *Europe 1992 and Beyond,* Spyros Makridakis, ed. San Francisco: Jossey-Bass, 1991.

Laurent, André. "The Cross-Cultural Puzzle of International Human Resource Management," *Human Resource Management,* Vol. 25, No. 1, 1986.

Laurent, André. "The Cultural Diversity of Western Conceptions of Management," *International Studies of Management and Organization,* Vol. XIII, No. 1–2. M. E. Sharpe Inc., 1983.

Lawler, Edward E. *High Involvement Management.* San Francisco: Jossey-Bass, 1986.

Lawrence, Paul R., and Jay W. Lorsch. *Organization and Environment.* Boston: Harvard Division of Research, 1967.

Leach, Edmund. *Runaway World?* London: BBC, 1968.

Lebra, Takie Sugiyama. *Japanese Patterns of Behaviour.* Honolulu: University Press of Hawaii, 1976.

Lesieur, Frederick C. *The Scanlon Plan.* Cambridge: MIT Press, 1958.

Lewin, Kurt. *Field Theory and Social Science.* New York: Harper and Row, 1951.

Linton, Ralph. *The Study of Man.* Englewood Cliffs: Prentice-Hall, 1965.

Lipset, Seymour Martin. *First New Nation.* London: Heinemann, 1964.

Lodge, George C. *The American Disease.* New York: Knopf, 1984.

Lodge, George C., and Ezra F. Vogel, eds. *Ideology and National Competitiveness*. Boston: Harvard Business School Press, 1987.

Lux, Kenneth. *Adam Smith's Mistake*. Boston: Shambhala, 1990.

McClelland, David. *The Achieving Society*. Princeton: Van Nostrand, 1961.

Maccoby, Michael, ed. *Sweden at the Edge*. Philadelphia: University of Pennsylvania Press, 1991.

McCormick, Janice. "Ideological Divisions and Global Reality." in *Ideology and National Competitiveness*, George C. Lodge and Ezra F. Vogel, eds., 1988.

McGregor, Douglas. *The Human Side of the Enterprise*. New York: McGraw-Hill, 1960.

McNeil, Elton B. *The Nature of Human Conflict*. Englewood Cliffs: Prentice-Hall, 1965.

Magaziner, Ira, and Mark Pantinkin. *The Silent War*. New York: Random House, 1989.

Makridakis, Spyros, ed. *Europe 1992 and Beyond*. San Francisco: Jossey-Bass, 1990.

Mant, Alistair. *The Rise and Fall of the British Manager*. London: Macmillan, 1977.

March, Robert M. *The Japanese Negotiator*. Tokyo/New York: Kondanshi Int., 1988.

Marquand, David. *The Unprincipled Society: New Demands, Old Politics*. London: Fontana, 1980.

Maruyama, Magorah. "Epistemological Sources of New Business Problems in the International Environment." *Human Systems Management*, 9, 1989.

Maruyama, Magorah. "New Mindscapes for Future Business Policy and Management." *Technological Forecasting and Social Change*, 21, 1982.

Maruyama, Magorah. "The Second Cybernetics," *American Scientist*, 51, 1963.

Maslow, Abraham. *Motivation and Personality*. New York: Harper and Row, 1954.

Matson, Floyd. *The Broken Image*. New York: George Braziller, 1964.

May, Rollo. *Freedom and Destiny*. New York: Norton, 1981.

Melville, Herman. Moby Dick.

Merleau-Ponty, Maurice. *The Phenomenology of Perception*. New York: Humanities Press, 1962.

Michael, Donald N. *On Learning to Plan and Planning to Learn*. San Francisco: Jossey-Bass, 1973.

Mintzberg, Henry. "The Manager's Job: Folklore or Fact?" *Harvard Business Review*, July/August 1976.

Mintzberg, Henry. "Planning on the Left Side, Managing on the Right." *Harvard Business Review*, July/August 1976.

Mintzberg, Henry. "Crafting Strategy." *Harvard Business Review*, March/April 1987, pp. 66–75.

Mintzberg, Henry. "Opening Up the Definition of Strategy." *The Strategy Process*, J. M. Quinn, H. Mintzberg, and R. M. James, eds. Englewood Cliffs: Prentice-Hall, 1987.

Mitroff, Iain. *Business NOT as Usual*. San Francisco: Jossey-Bass, 1987.

Morgan, Gareth. *Images of Organization*. Beverly Hills: Sage, 1986.

Morgan, Gareth. *Riding the Waves of Change*. San Francisco: Jossey-Bass, 1988.

Morita, Akio. *Made in Japan*. New York: Signet, 1986.

Nock, S. L., and P. H. Rossi, "Achievement vs. Ascription in the Attribution of Family Social Status." *American Journal of Sociology*, Vol. 84, No. 3, 1978.

Nonaka, Ikujiru. "Towards Middle-up-down Management." *Sloan Management Review*, Spring 1988.

Ogilvy, Jay. *Many Dimensional Man*. New York: Oxford University Press, 1977.

Ogilvy, Jay. *Social Issues and Trends: The Maturation of America*. Menlo Park, Ca.: VALS, SRI International, 1984.

Ohno, Taiichi. *Toyota Production Systems*. Cambridge, Mass.: Productivity Press, 1978.

Olsen, Mancur. *The Rise and Decline of Nations*. New Haven: Yale University Press, 1982.

Orstein, Robert. *The Psychology of Consciousness*. San Francisco: W. H. Freeman, 1973.

Ouchi, William. *The M-form Society*. Reading: Addison-Wesley, 1986.

Ouchi, William. *Theory Z: How American Business Can Meet the Japanese Challenge*. Reading: Addison-Wesley, 1981.

Ozbekhan, H. "Planning and Human Action," *Systems in Theory and Practice*. P. A. Weiss, ed. New York: Haffner, 1971.

Pascal, Blaise. *Pascale's Pensées or Thoughts on Religion*. Mount Vernon: Peter Pauper Press, 1946.

Pascale, Richard T. "Perspectives in Strategy: The Real Story Behind Honda's Success," *California Management Review*, XXVI, No. 3, 1984.

Pascale, R. T., and A. G. Athos, *The Art of Japanese Management*. New York: Simon and Schuster, 1981.

Parsons, Talcott, and Edward A. Shils. *Towards a General Theory of Action*. Cambridge, Mass.: Harvard University Press, 1951.

Peters, T., and R. H. Waterman. *In Search of Excellence*. New York: Harper and Row, 1982.

Porter, Michael E. The Competitive Advantage of Nations. New York: Free Press, 1990.

Porter, Michael E. *Competitive Strategy: Techniques for Analyzing Industries and Competitors*. New York: Free Press, 1980.

Prestowitz, Clyde V. *Trading Places*. New York: Basic Books, 1989.

Pribram, Karl. *Languages of the Brain*. Englewood Cliffs: Prentice-Hall, 1971.

Prigogine, Ilya. *Order out of Chaos*. New York: Bantam, 1984.

Pugh, Derek S. *Organization Theory*. London: Penguin Books, 1983.

Quinn, James B. "Logical Incrementalism." *Sloan Management Review*, 20, Fall 1978.

Quinn, James B., Henry Mintzberg, and Robert M. James. *The Strategy Process*. Englewood Cliffs: Prentice-Hall, 1988.

Randlesome, Collin, ed. *Business Cultures of Europe*. London: Heinemann, 1990.

Reich, Robert B. *The Next American Frontier*. New York: Times Books, 1983.

Reich, Robert B. *Tales of a New America*. New York: Times Books, 1987.

Reich, Robert B. *The Work of Nations*. New York: Alfred Knopf, 1991.

Reich, Robert B., and John D. Donahue. *New Deals: The Chrysler Revival and the American System*. New York: Viking and Penguin, 1985.

Reich, Robert B., and Eric D. Mankin. "Joint Ventures with Japan Give Away America's Future," *Harvard Business Review*, March–April, 1986.

Robbins, Lionel. *An Essay on the Nature and Significance of Economic Science*. London: Macmillan, 1946.

Roethlisberger, Fritz, and William Dixon. *Management and the Worker*. Cambridge, Mass.: Harvard University Press, 1937.

Rosenberg, Morris. *Society and the Adolescent Self Image*. Princeton: Princeton University Press, 1965.

Rotter, J. B. "Generalized Experiences of Internal vs. External Control of Reinforcement," *Psychological Monographs*, 609, 1966.

Russell, Bertrand. *Unpopular Essays*. London: Constable, 1951.

Sampson, Anthony. *The New Anatomy of Britain*. London: Hodder and Stoughton, 1971.

Sanford, Nevitt, and Craig Comstock. *Sanctions for Evil*. San Francisco: Jossey-Bass, 1971.

Sartre, Jean-Paul. *No Exit and Three Other Plays*. New York: Vintage, 1955.

Sartre, Jean-Paul. *Saint Genet*. New York: George Braziller, 1963.

Schein, Edgar H. *Organization, Culture and Leadership*. San Francisco: Jossey-Bass, 1985.

Scott, Bruce R., and Lodge, George C., eds. *American Competitiveness*. Boston: Harvard Business School Press, 1985.

Sculley, John. *Odyssey: From Pepsi to Apple*. New York: Harper and Row, 1987.

Senge, Peter M. *The Fifth Discipline*. New York: Doubleday, 1990.

Sennett, Richard, and John Cobb. *The Hidden Injuries of Class*. New York: Alfred Knopf, 1973.

Shetter, William Z. *The Netherlands in Perspective*. Leiden: Martinus Nijhoff, 1987.

Skinner, B. F. *Beyond Freedom and Dignity*. New York: Random House, 1964.

Snow, C. P. *The Two Cultures*. Cambridge: Cambridge University Press, 1961.

Sperry, Roger W. "The Great Cerebral Commissure," *Scientific American*, January 1964.

Stouffer, S. A., and J. Toby. "Role Conflict and Personality," *American Journal of Sociology*, Vol. 1, No. 5, 1951.

Tatsuno, Sheridan M. *Created in Japan*. New York: Harper and Row, 1990.

Taylor, Frederick Winslow. *The Principles of Scientific Management*. New York: N. W. Norton, 1947.

Thompson, George. Aeschylus and Athens. New York: Haskell, 1940.

Thoreau, Henry David. *Walden Economy*. New York: NAL, 1956.

Thurow, Lester C. *Head to Head: The Coming Economic Battle Among Japan, Europe and America*. New York: William Morrow, 1992.

Thurow, Lester C. *The Zero Sum Society*. New York: McGraw-Hill, 1980.

Thurow, Lester C. *The Zero Sum Solution*. New York: Simon and Schuster, 1985.

Thurow, Lester C., ed. *The Management Challenge, Japanese Views*. Cambridge, Mass.: MIT Press, 1985.

Toffler, Alvin. *Future Shock*. New York: Bantam, 1970.

Toffler, Alvin. The Third Wave. New York: Bantam, 1976.

Toffler, Alvin. Introduction to *Order Out of Chaos* by Prigogine Ilya. New York: Bantam, 1984.

Trompenaars, Fons. "The Organization of Meaning and the Meaning of Organization." Dissertation, The Wharton School, Pennsylvania, 1981.

Trompenaars, Fons. *Riding the Waves of Culture*. London: Economist Books, 1993.

Vogel, Ezra. *Comeback: Building the Resurgence of American Business*. New York: Simon and Schuster, 1985.

Vogel, Ezra. *Japan as No. 1*. New York: Harper and Collins.

Wack, Pierre. "Scenarios: Uncharted Waters Ahead," *Harvard Business Review*, March–April, 1988.

Watzlawick, Paul, J. H. Beavin, and D. Jackson. *The Pragmatics of Human Communication*. New York: W. W. Norton, 1967.

Webber, Ross A. *Time Is Money*. New York: Free Press, 1990.

Weber, Max. *The Protestant Ethic and the Spirit of Capitalism*. London: Macmillan, 1930.

Weisskopf, Walter. *Alienation and Economics*. New York: Dutton, 1971.
Whyte, William H. *The Organization Man*. New York: Simon and Schuster, 1956.
Williamson, Oliver E. "Transaction-Cost Economics: Governing Economic Exchanges," *Journal of Law and Economics*, 22, 1979.

Notes

CHAPTER 1   Seven Ways of Wealth Creation

1. *Head to Head: The Coming Economic Battle Among Japan, Europe, and America*, Lester Thurow. New York: William Morrow, 1992.

2. The issues are well discussed in *Studies in the Development of Capitalism*, Maurice Dobb. London: George Routledge, 1947.

3. *Creating Corporate Culture*, Charles Hampden-Turner. Reading, Mass.: Addison-Wesley, 1992, Chapter 1.

4. The distinction between "the logic of discovery" and "reconstructed logic" is made by Abraham Kaplan in *The Conduct of Inquiry* (Scranton, Pa.: Chandler, 1964).

5. *Alienation and Economics*, Walter Weisskopf. New York: Dutton, 1971.

6. *The Economic Institution of Capitalism*, Oliver E. Williamson. New York: Free Press, 1985.

7. "The Meaning of Organization and the Organization of Meaning," Alfons Trompenaars. Ph.D. diss., Wharton School, 1982. See also *Man's Search for Meaning*, Rollo May (New York: Norton, 1961).

8. *Charting the Corporate Mind*, Charles Hampden-Turner. New York: Free Press, 1990, pp. 7–14.

9. The idea that the health and effectiveness of a society was a function of the "synergy" found between the individual and community is usually credited to Ruth Benedict. She was widely cited by Abraham Maslow in "Synergy in Society and the Individual," *Journal of Individual Psychology*, vol. 20, 1964.

10. *Toward a General Theory of Action*, Talcott Parsons and Edward Shils (Cambridge: Harvard Univ. Press, 1951).

11. The difference between "specific" and "diffuse" modes of relating was first pointed out by Kurt Lewin in *Field Theory and Social Science* (New York: Harper & Row, 1951). Since then analyzing versus synthesizing modes have been attributed to operations of the left and right brain hemispheres. See "The Great Cerebral Commissure," R. W. Sperry. *Scientific American*, January 1964.

12. Originally "individualism versus collectivism." See *The Division of Labor in Society*, Emile Durkheim (New York: Harper & Row, 1960); also *Community and Society*, Ferdinand Tonnies (New York: Harper & Row, 1957).

13. The planner's view that "dominant man" wrests control from nature is critiqued in "Planning and Human Action" by H. Ozbekhan in *Systems in Theory and Practice*, P. A. Weiss ed. (New York: Haffner, 1971, pp. 123–230). We use a scale measuring internal versus external loci of control devised by J. B. Rotter; see "Generalized Experiences of Internal vs. External Control of Reinforcement," *Psychological Monographs* (609) 1966, pp. 1–28.

14. Our view of time is taken from T. J. Cottle, "The Location of Experience: A Manifest Time Orientation," *Acta Psychologica* (28) 1968, pp. 129–149. See also *The Spectrum of Social Time*, G. Gurvitch, Reidel, and Dordrecht (1964). See also *The Form of Time*, Elliot Jaques (New York: Crane Russak, 1982).

15. This is a central plank of "modernization theory," which used to insist that achievement was crucial to development and the ascribing of status an impediment. See for example "Achievement vs. Ascription in the Attribution of Family Social Status" by S. L. Nock and P. H. Rossi in *American Journal of Sociology* 84 (3) 1978, pp. 565–590. The distinction was originally made by Ralph Linton in *The Study of Man* (Englewood Cliffs: Prentice-Hall, 1965; original 1936).

16. This and our other six distinctions can also be found in the anthropological literature on relative values. See especially *Variations in Value Orientations*, F. Kluckhohn and F. L. Strodtbeck (Conn: Greenwood Press, 1961).

17. In all, the results of thirty-four dilemmas presented in this book are taken from a questionnaire with seventy items. Some of these were designed to discriminate between nations not discussed here. Others did not discriminate. Some 15,000 managers were involved among the nations sampled here. The Centre for International Business Studies in Amstelveen has results coming in continually from fifty-four nations in its data base.

18. See for example, *The American Disease*, George C. Lodge (New York: Alfred Knopf, 1984), and *Gentlemen and Tradesmen: The Values of Economic Catastrophe*, Charles Hampden-Turner (London: Routledge and Kegan Paul, 1984).

19. *The Visible Hand*. Cambridge, Mass: Harvard Univ. Press, 1977.

20. This is an abiding theme in conflict resolution literature, where adversaries have a "mirror image" of each other's supposed vices. See *The Nature of Human Conflict*, Elton B. McNeil ed. (Englewood Cliffs, N.J.: Prentice-Hall, 1965, pp. 45–64).

CHAPTER 2 Codifiers-in-Chief, Analyzers Extraordinary

1. For the idea that the American government is viewed as a "referee," see *American Competitiveness*, Bruce R. Scott and George C. Lodge, eds. (Boston: Harvard Business School Press, 1985), pp. 105–106.

2. See *Toward a General Theory of Action*, Talcott Parsons and E. A. Shils (Cambridge: Harvard Univ. Press, 1961).

3. The point is in "Role Conflict and Personality," S. A. Stouffer and J. Toby, *American Journal of Sociology* 1:VI–5 (1951), pp. 395–406.

4. *Walden Economy*, Henry David Thoreau. New York: NAL, 1956. See "Conclusion."

5. For a description of melting-pot rituals see Robert Bellah, "Evil and the American Ethos," in *Sanctions for Evil*, Nevitt Sanford and Craig Comstock, eds. (San Francisco: Jossey-Bass, 1971).

6. Of the many discussions of this issue we prefer *The First New Nation*, Seymour Martin Lipset (London: Heinemann, 1964).

7. *The M-Form Organization*, William Ouchi. Reading, Mass: Addison Wesley, 1981.

8. The idea of ritual cleansing is from *The Rise and the Fall of the British Manager*, Alistair Mant (London: Macmillan, 1977), pp. 6–7.

9. "Crafting Corporate Strategy," in *The Strategy Process*, Henry Mintzberg and James Brian Quinn, eds. Englewood Cliffs, N.J.: Prentice-Hall, 1991, pp. 105–113. Also in *Harvard Business Review*, March/April 1987.

10. *The Strategy Process*, pp. 371–375.

11. *The Strategy Process*, p. 419.

12. *The Strategy Process*, p. 246.

13. "Strategy and the Business Portfolio," Barry Hedley, in *Long Range Planning*, February 1977, p. 10.

14. *In Search of Excellence*, Tom Peters and Robert H. Waterman. New York: Harper & Row, 1982, Chapter 1.

15. New York: McGraw-Hill, 1960.

16. New York: Signet Classic, 1961.

17. New York: Random House, 1964.

18. The best popular treatment of this theme is by Robert Ornstein in *The Psychology of Consciousness* (San Francisco: W. H. Freeman, 1973). See also Isaiah Berlin, *The Hedgehog and the Fox* (New York: Mentor, 1965).

19. *In Search of Excellence*.

20. These two metaphors are prominently featured in *Images of Organization*, Gareth Morgan (Beverly Hills, Calif.: Sage, 1986).

21. *Beyond Reductionism: New Perspectives on the Life Sciences*, Arthur Koestler and J. R. Smythies, eds. Boston: Beacon, 1969.

22. *The Competitive Advantage of Nations*, Michael E. Porter. New York: Free Press, 1990.

23. *Odyssey: From Pepsi to Apple*, John Sculley. New York: Harper & Row, 1987, pp. 328–355.

24. *The Japanese Negotiator*, Robert M. March. Tokyo/New York: Kondanshi International, 1988, pp. 15–32.

25. "The Tables Turned," *Poems of William Wordsworth*. London: Longman, 1948.

26. *History and Human Relations*, Herbert Butterfield. London: Collins, 1951.

27. *Images of Organization*, pp. 19–71.

28. *Odyssey*, pp. 154–199.

29. *The Next American Frontier*, Robert B. Reich. New York: Times-Mirror, 1983, pp. 201–228.

30. Ibid., p. 121.

31. "National Strategies the Key to International Competition" in *American Competitiveness*, pp. 71–143.

32. This is very well explained in *High Involvement Management*, Ed Lawler (San Francisco: Jossey-Bass, 1986).

33. "Metaphysical Pathos and the Theory of Bureaucracy," Alvin Gouldner, in *American Political Science Review* (49) 1955.

34. *Images of Organization*, p. 21.

35. *Free to Choose*, Milton and Rose Friedman. New York: NAL, 1981.

CHAPTER 3   The Triumphant Individual Within

1. *Habits of the Heart*, Robert Belluh et al. (Berkeley: California University Press, 1985), p. 182.

2. *The Revolution of the Saints*, Michael Walzer. Cambridge: Harvard University Press, 1965, p. 18.

3. *The Duality of Human Existence*, David Bakan. Boston: Beacon, 1971, p. 44.

4. *Essays of Ralph Waldo Emerson*. New York: Harper & Row, 1947.

5. "Freedom" in *Poems*, Ralph Waldo Emerson. London: William Heinemann, 1927, p. 62.

6. *Moby Dick*. New York: Rinehart and Co., 1948, p. 461.

7. *Habits of the Heart*, p. 146.

8. Ibid.

9. "I Have a Dream." Speech delivered at Lincoln Memorial in Washington, 28 August 1963, in *Testament of Hope: The Essential Writings of Martin Luther King*, James Washinton, ed. New York: Harper & Row, 1986.

10. *The Wordly Philosophers*, Robert Heilbroner. New York: Simon and Schuster, 1980.

11. *An Inquiry into the Wealth of Nations*, Adam Smith, p. 651.

12. Ibid., p. 423.

13. The two quotations by Adam Smith and the one by Junius Morgan are cited in *Adam Smith's Mistake*, Kenneth Lux (Boston: Shambhala, 1990), pp. 78–79, 88–89.

14. May 24, 1991, *USA Today* Business Section.

15. *Tales of a New America*, Robert B. Reich. New York: Times-Mirror, 1987.

16. *Society and the Adolescent Self-image*, Morris Rosenberg. Princeton: Princeton Univ. Press, 1965. The backgrounds of those who refuse to conform in psychological experiments in which the subject believes him/ herself is isolated has also been described in "Conformity and Character," R. S. Crutchfield, *American Psychologist* (10) 1955.

17. *The Scanlon Plan*, Frederick C. Lesieur. Cambridge: MIT Press, 1958.

18. W. H. Whyte. New York: Simon and Schuster, 1956.

19. "Planning as Learning." March/April 1988.

20. *The Economic Way of Thinking*, Paula Heyne. Chicago: Science Research Associates, 1983, p. 277.

21. New York: The Free Press, 1990.

22. Personal communication with Geert Hofstede.

23. "Invictus," *Poems of the Empire*. London: Faber and Faber, 1938.

24. *Man for Himself*. New York: Holt, Rinehart & Winston, 1947.

25. New Haven: Yale Univ. Press, 1950.

26. Harmondsworth, Middlesex: Penguin Plays, 1982.

27. *Management Teams*. London: Heinemann, 1981.

28. "Understanding your Organization's Character," Roger Harrison, in *Harvard Business Review*, May–June 1972.

29. *Tales of a New America*, pp. 119–120.

30. Ibid., p. 122.

31. Ibid., pp. 118–119.

32. *Made in America*, MIT Commission on Productivity, Michael L. Dertouzas et al. eds. Cambridge: MIT Press, 1989, pp. 217–231.

33. "America's Toughest Bosses," *Fortune*, 27 February 1989.

34. *The Comparative Advantages of Nations*, pp. 148–152.

35. New York: Basic Books, p. 9.

36. "The General Theory of Gridlock," Chapter 11 in *Tales of a New America*, pp. 130–146.

CHAPTER 4   When You're Racing with the Clock

1. *Short-Term America*, Michael T. Jacobs. Boston: Harvard Business School Press, 1991, pp. 18–19, 194–196.

2. "The Location of Experience: A Manifest Time Orientation," in *Acta Psychologica*, 1968, p. 28.

3. *Oxford Book Verse*. Oxford: Oxford University Press, 1961, p. 216.

4. A very plausible account of F. W. Taylor's work as a specific response to America's industrial situation in the 1920s and 1930s is given by Robert B. Reich in *The Next American Frontier* (New York: Times Books, 1987), pp. 62–64.

5. *The Poems of Rudyard Kipling*. London: Longmans, 1948.

6. For example, see *How to Get More Done in Less Time*, Joseph Cooper (New York: Doubleday, 1971); *Time Is Money*, Ross A. Webber (New York: Free Press, 1990); and, of course, *The Principles of Scientific Management*, F. W. Taylor (New York: N. W. Norton, 1947).

7. *Short-Term America*, pp. 1–29; also *Made in America*, pp. 53–67, 143–146; and *Trading Places*, Clyde W. Prestowitz, Jr. New York: Basic Books, 1989, pp. 363–364.

8. *Made in America*, pp. 59–62.

9. *The Fifth Discipline*, Peter Senge. New York: Doubleday, 1990, p. 154.

10. Ibid.

11. *The Next American Frontier*, pp. 140–173.

CHAPTER 5   Level Playing Fields

1. *Odyssey: From Pepsi to Apple*, pp. 25–52.

2. Quoted in *The Rise of the Plutocrats*, Jamie Camplin (London: Constable, 1978), p. 168.

3. *The Achieving Society*, David C. McClelland. Princeton: Van Nostrand, 1961. This book argues essentially for the universality of "achievement motivation" and its superiority to the need to affiliate or exercise power as far as economic development is concerned. Having assumed the polar structure of these traits, McClelland naturally finds them an interesting example of cultural presuppositions shaping the data collected.

4. "The Meaning of Organization and the Organization of Meaning", Fons Trompenaars, includes the entire scale; for more information contact: the Center for International Business Studies, Amsterdamseweg 498, 1181 BW Amstelveen, the Netherlands.

5. *Theory and Practice*, Chris Argyris and Donald Schon. San Francisco: Jossey-Bass, 1982; also *Strategy, Change and Defensive Routines*, Chris Argyris. Marshfield, Mass: Pitman, 1985.

6. New York: Alfred Knopf, 1973.

7. *Integrating the Individual and the Organization*, Chris Argyris. New York: John Wiley, 1965.

8. The argument is made by Ezra Vogel in *Comeback* (New York: Simon and Schuster, 1985) and Chalmers Johnson in *MITI and the Japanese Miracle* (Stanford: Stanford Univ. Press, 1982).

9. See *Organization and Environment*, Paul Lawrence and Jay Korsch, (Cambridge: Harvard Business School Press, 1965).

10. See *Mintzberg on Management*, New York: Free Press, 1990

11. A phenomenon much commented on by neo-conservatives writing in *The Public Interest*, see especially "The Crisis in Economic Theory," September 1981.

12. Beverly Hills: Sago, 1986, pp. 19–76.

13. For stern lectures to America on her surfeit of lawyers, see *The Japanese Mind*, Robert C. Christopher (London: Pan, 1984), pp. 148–151.

CHAPTER 6   Harmonious Patterns of Particulars

1. Here and elsewhere we are heavily indebted to Edward T. Hall and Mildred T. Hall in *Hidden Differences: Doing Business with the Japanese* (New York: Doubleday, 1987) and *Japanese Patterns of Behavior,* Takie Sugiyama Lebra (Honolulu: Univ. of Hawaii Press, 1976).

2. *Japan as Number 1: Lessons for America*, Ezra Vogel. Cambridge: Harvard Univ. Press, 1979.

3. *Made in Japan*, New York: Signet, 1986, p. 283.

4. Ibid., p. 285.

5. A point made in the now-classic study *Organization and Environment*, P. R. Lawrence and J. W. Lorsch (Boston: Harvard Business School Division of Research, 1967).

6. Ibid., See also quotes in "The Matsushita Example," Chapter 2, *The Art of Japanese Management*, Richard T. Pascale and Anthony G. Athos (New York: Simon and Schuster, 1981).

7. For a fuller account see "Map 3: The Yin and the Yang" in *Maps of the Mind*, Charles M. Hampden-Turner (New York: Macmillan, 1981).

8. Ibid., pp. 104–107.

9. Ibid., pp. 86–89.

10. *The Japanese Power Game*. New York: Charles Scribner's Sons, 1990) pp. 27–28.

11. *The Enigma of Japanese Power*. New York: Alfred A. Knopf, 1989, p. 241.

12. Ibid., p. 240.

13. *Essays in Pragmatism*, New York: Haffner Publishing Co., 1949, p. 83.

14. *The Japanese Power Game*, p. 29.

15. New York: Simon and Schuster, 1991, pp. 1–14.

16. "New Mindscapes for Future Business Policy and Management," *Technological Forecasting and Social Change* 21 (1982), pp. 53–76.

17. Ibid., p. 64.

18. Karl Pribram, brain-researcher. Personal communication, September 1984.

19. "New Mindscapes for Future Business Policy and Management," pp. 63–65.

20. *Steps to an Ecology of Mind*, Gregory Bateson. New York: Ballantine, 1972.

21. "New Mindscapes for Future Business Policy and Management," p. 55. See also "Heterogenetics and Morphogenetics," Magorah Maruyama, in *Theoretical Sociology* 5 (1978), pp. 75–96.

22. *Order out of Chaos*, Ilya Prigogine. New York: Bantam, 1984. See especially Foreword by Alvin Toffler, pp. xi–xxvii.

23. "The Split Brain in Man," Michael S. Gazzaniga, in *Scientific American*, January 1964, pp. 60–72.

24. *Languages of the Brain*. Englewood Cliffs: Prentice-Hall, 1971.

25. *Toyota Production System*, Taiichi Ohno. Cambridge, Mass: Productivity Press, 1978, pp. 17–21.

26. Ibid., pp. 40–43.

27. Personal communication with Ray Stata of Analog Devices, who uses the method. See also *Created in Japan*, Sheridan M. Tatsuno (New York: Harper & Row, 1990), pp. 104–106.

28. Quoted at the International Conference of Personnel Management, Istanbul, Turkey, July 23, 1990, by Roger Smith (reference not given).

29. That most Asian managers prefer less codified forms of communication was reported by Max Boisot in *Information and Organization* (London: Fontana, 1987), pp. 23–27.

30. See *Inner Contradictions of Rigorous Research*, Chris Argyris (London: Academic Press, 1980).

31. *The Conduct of Inquiry*, Abraham Kaplan. Scranton, Penn: Chandler, 1964, p. 45.

32. Quoted in *Created in Japan*, p. 45.

33. The point is well put in *Made in America*, Michael L. Dertouzos, p. 132.

34. "Epistemological Sources of New Business Problems in the International Environment," Magorah Maruyama, in *Human Systems Management* 8 (1989), pp. 71–80.

35. "New Mindscapes for Future Business Policy and Management," pp. 82–84.

36. Toyota Production System, pp. 14–18.

37. *Competitive Strategy*. New York: The Free Press, 1980, pp. 34–46.

38. See *Charting the Corporate Mind*, Charles M. Hampden-Turner (New York: The Free Press, 1990), Chapter 1.

39. *Alienation and Economics*, Walter Weisskopf, pp. 16–17, 79–85. See

also *The End of Economic Man*, George P. Brockway (New York: Harper-Collins, 1991), pp. 8–20.

40. *Alienation and Economics*, pp. 89–115.

41. *Charting the Corporate Mind*, p. 9.

42. *The Japanese Negotiator*, pp. 69–70, 76–80.

43. Described in *The Japanese Negotiator*, pp. 100–101.

44. *The Japanese Negotiator*, pp. 210–218.

45. "Transaction-Cost Economics: Governing Economic Exchanges," Oliver E. Williamson, in *Journal of Law and Economics* 22 (1979), pp. 233–261.

46. There are discrepancies between this and passages quoted in the *Congressional Record*, 15 November 1989. Akio Morita's name was attached, then removed.

47. *The Japanese Negotiator*, p. 46.

48. *The Art of Japanese Management*, p. 276.

49. *Made in Japan*, pp. 292–293.

50. Ibid., p. 216.

51. "The Second Cybernetics," Magorah Maruyama, in *American Scientist* 51 (1963), pp. 164–179, 250–256.

52. "New Mindscapes for Future Business Policy and Management."

53. *Theory Z*. Reading, Mass.: Addison Wesley, 1981. See also *The M-form Society*, William Ouchi (Reading, Mass.: Addison Wesley, 1986), p. 1976.

54. "Epistemological Sources of New Business Problems in the International Environment", Magorah Maruyama, pp.73–74.

55. *The Competitive Advantage of Nations*, Michael E. Porter (New York: Free Press, 1990), pp. 164–165.

56. *Made in Japan*, pp. 225–226.

57. See *The Broken Image*, Floyd Matson. New York: George Braziller, 1964.

58. *The Japanese Power Game*, p. 72.

59. Ibid., p. 27.

60. *Aeschylus and Athens*, George Thompson. New York: Haskell, 1940.

61. *Made in Japan*, p. 226.

62. *The Work of Nations*, Robert B. Reich (New York: Alfred Knopf 1991), pp. 154–157.

63. See *Taking Japan Seriously*, Ronald Dore (Stanford: Stanford University Press, 1987), Chapter 1.

64. For the image of the corporation as an organism, see *Images of Organization*, Gareth Morgan (Beverly Hills: Sage, 1986), pp. 39–76; and *Kaisha: The Japanese Corporation*, James C. Abeggden and George Stalk (New York: Basic Books, 1985), pp. 181–213.

65. *American Competitiveness,* Bruce R. Scott and George C. Lodge, eds. (Boston: Harvard Business School Press, 1985), pp. 71–143.

66. *The Theory of Social and Economic Organization.* New York: The Free Press, 1947.

CHAPTER 7   On Synchrony, Hierarchy, and Time

1. *Japan as Number 1,* Ezra Vogel (European Management Forum, 1989), pp. 158–183.

2. *Creating Corporate Culture,* C. M. Hampden-Turner, p. 115.

3. *Scientific American,* 261, 4 (1989), pp. 19–24.

4. James C. Abeggden and George R. Stalk, Jr., *Kaisha.* p. 62.

5. Arthur Koestler, *The Act of Creation.* New York: Macmillan, 1964.

6. "Japan's Technology Agenda," Susumu Aizawa, in *High Technology,* August 1985, pp. 11–15.

7. "Epistemological Sources of New Business Problems," Magorah Maruyama, in p. 74. See also "The New Logic of Japan's Younger Generations," *Technological Forecasting and Social Change* 28 (1985), pp. 351–364, and "Mindscapes in Multicultural Management," *Asia-Pacific Journal of Management* 2 (1985), pp. 124–149.

8. *Created in Japan,* Tatsuno, Sheridan M. (New York: Harper & Row, 1990), pp. 65–66.

9. New York: Bantam, 1980.

10. Magorah Maruyama, "The Second Cybernetics . . ." pp. 164–179.

11. Richard T. Pascale, "Perspectives in Strategy: The Real Story Behind Honda's Success" in *California Management Review* 26, 3 (1984), pp. 47–72.

12. *The M-form Society,* William Ouchi (Reading: Addison-Wesley, 1986). pp. 26–31.

13. *Free Enterprise, Fair Employment.* New York: Crane Russak, 1982.

14. "Toward Middle-up-Down Management" in *Sloan Management Review* (Spring 1988), p. 14.

15. *Made in Japan,* Akio Morita, (New York: Signet, 1986), p. 179.

16. *Hidden Differences,* Edward T. Hall and Mildred R. Hall (New York: Doubleday, 1987), pp. 54–56. The source of most Western accounts of Japanese intimate relationships is *The Anatomy of Dependence,* Takeo Doi (New York: Kondansha/Harper), 1976.

17. "Mindscapes: How to understand specific situations in multicultural management" in *Asia-Pacific Journal of Management* 2, 125 (1985).

18. Ibid., pp. 23–25.

19. Japan Inc., Shotaro/Shinomori. Berkeley: University of California Press, 1988, p. 291.

CHAPTER 8   The Logics of Community

1. *Cultures and Organizations,* Geert Hofstede. New York: McGraw-Hill, 1991, pp. 49–78, 128–130.

2. Boston: Harvard Business Press, 1986, pp. 306–309.

3. *Patterns of Japanese Behavior,* T. S. Lebra (Honolulu, Hawaii: University Press of Hawaii, 1976), p. 167.

4. *USA Today,* 24 March, 1991, Leisure Section p. 1.

5. See *Riding the Waves of Culture,* Alfons Trompenaars (London: Economist Books, 1993), pp. 92–98.

6. Hidden Differences, Edward T. Hall and Mildred Hall (New York: Doubleday, 1987), pp. 44–48, 54–60.

7. New York: Doubleday, 1990.

8. *Made in Japan,* Akio Morita (New York: Signet, 1986), p. 166.

9. Ibid., p. 167.

10. *Kaisha,* James C. Abeggden and George Stalk, Jr. (New York: Basic Books, 1985), pp. 190–193.

11. *Created in Japan,* (New York: Harper & Row, 1990), pp. 52–53.

12. Ibid., p. 54.

13. *Charting the Corporate Mind,* Charles M. Hampden-Turner (Oxford: Basil Blackwell, 1990), pp. 62–63.

14. *An Essay on the Nature and Significance of Economic Science.* London: Macmillan, 1946, p. 95. Quoted in *Economics and Alienation,* Walter A. Weisskopf (New York: Dutton, 1971), p. 90.

15. *Charting the Corporate Mind,* pp. 178–184.

16. *Social Issues and Trends: The Maturation of America,* Jay Ogilvy. Menlo Park, Calif.: N VALS. SRI International, 1984.

17. *American Competitiveness,* Bruce R. Scott (Boston: Harvard Business School Press, 1985), pp. 27–34.

18. *Tales of a New America,* Robert B. Reich (New York: Times Books, 1987), pp. 86–87.

19. "Joint Ventures with Japan Give Away America's Future" (with Eric D. Mankin), *Harvard Business Review,* March–April 1986.

20. Ibid.

21. *American Competitiveness,* pp. 91–143.

22. *The Next American Frontier,* Robert B. Reich (New York: Times Books, 1983), pp. 173–229.

23. *American Competitiveness,* pp. 77–90.

24. Ibid., pp. 73–77.

25. *Trading Places,* Clyde V. Prestowitz (New York: Basic Books, 1989), pp. 307, 323.

26. *Creating Corporate Culture,* C. M. Hampden-Turner (Reading, Mass.: Addison-Wesley, 1992), pp. 122–123.

27. "Whose Company Is It?" James Abeggden and George R. Stalk, Jr., in *Kaisha* (New York: Basic Books, 1985), pp. 181–213.

28. *Short-term America*, Michael T. Jacobs (Boston: Harvard Business School, 1991), pp. 33–34. See also *The American Disease*, George C. Lodge (New York: Knopf, 1984), pp. 50–51, 288–289.

29. *Kaisha*, James G. Abbegden and George R. Stalk, (New York: Basic Books, 1985), p. 184.

30. *The Organization Man*, W. H. Whyte. New York: Simon and Schuster, 1956, Chapter 12.

31. "Strategic Intent," Gary Hamel and C. K. Prahalad, in *Harvard Business Review*, May–June 1989.

32. *Tales of a New America*, p. 71.

33. Ibid.

34. *The M-form Society*, William Ouchi (Reading: Addison-Wesley, 1986), p. 42.

35. Ibid., p. 46.

36. *Made in America*, Michael L. Dertouzos et al. (Cambridge, Mass: MIT Press, 1984), pp. 232–234.

37. *The M-form Society*, p. 63.

38. *The Next American Frontier*, p. 144.

39. *Markets and Hierarchies*, New York: Free Press, 1975. pp. 40–46.

40. *The M-form Society*, p. 31.

41. *Trading Places*, pp. 293–294.

42. See "Green Tea and Dirty Tricks," Chapter 2, in *The Japanese Conspiracy* (London: NEL, 1983).

43. Ibid.

44. *MITI and the Japanese Miracle*, Chalmers Johnson (Stanford: Stanford Univ. Press, 1982), pp. 133, 226.

45. *Created in Japan*, pp. 250–251.

46. *Kaisha*, pp. 140–142.

CHAPTER 9   Will the German Model of Capitalism Sweep Europe?

1. *Euroquake*, Daniel Burstein. New York: Simon and Schuster, 1991, p. 200.

2. Ibid., p. 206.

3. *Germany and the Germans*, John Ardagh. London: Penguin Books, 1991, p. 572.

4. "Germany: Competing Communitarianisms," Christopher S. Allen, in *Ideology and National Competitiveness*, George C. Lodge and Ezra F. Vogel, eds. Boston: Harvard Business School Press, 1987, pp. 81–85.

5. *Germany and the Germans*, p. 11.

6. *Ideology and National Competitiveness*, p. 87.

7. Ibid., p. 92.

8. *The Competitive Advantage of Nations*, Michael Porter (New York: Free Press, 1990), pp. 356–369.

9. *The Courage to Be*. New Haven: Yale Univ. Press, 1959.

10. *Germany and the Germans*, p. 112.

11. *The Competitive Advantage of Nations*, p. 373.

12. *Business Cultures of Europe*, Collin Randlesome et al., eds London: Heinemann, 1990, p. 46.

13. Quoted in *Germany and the Germans*, p. 148.

14. *Unpopular Essays*. London: Constable, 1951, p. 66.

15. The peculiarly German contribution to the social sciences is discussed in *Models of Man*, James G. Dagenais. The Hague: Nijhoff, 1972.

16. *Business Cultures of Europe*, pp. 9–14.

17. *The Competitive Advantage of Nations*, p. 372.

18. *The Hedgehog and the Fox*. New York: Mentor, 1965.

19. Oxford: Clarendon Press, 1958.

20. *Germany and the Germans*, pp. 314–316.

21. A point famously made by Friedrich Engels in *Private Property and the State*, 1884.

22. Quoted in *Germany and the Germans*, p. 148.

23. Ibid., p. 147.

24. *The Competitive Advantage of Nations*, p. 355.

25. *The Germans*, Gordon A. Craig. London: Penguin Books, 1991, pp. 14–116.

26. Ibid., p. 117.

27. *Germany and the Germans*, p. 125.

28. For English-speakers, the most accessible account of the Frankfurt School is *The Dialectical Imagination*, Martin Jay (London: Heinemann, 1972).

29. Ibid.

30. *Euroquake*, p. 189.

31. Ibid.

32. *Germany and the Germans*, pp. 129–130.

33. *The Competitive Advantage of Nations*, p. 373.

34. Ibid., p. 377.

35. *A Dynamic Theory of Personality*. New York: McGraw Hill, 1935.

36. *Riding the Waves of Culture*, Alfons Trompenaars (London: Economist Books, 1993), pp. 73–74.

37. *Germany and the Germans*, p. 189.

38. Ibid., p. 110.

39. Ibid., p. 343.

40. Ibid., p. 138.

CHAPTER 10   Sweden's Social Individualism: Between Raging Horses

1. *Sweden: The Middle Way*, Marquis Childs. New Haven: Yale Univ. Press, 1936.

2. "Managing International Business: A Swedish Model," Gunnar Hedlund, in *Sweden at the Edge*, Michael Maccoby, ed. Philadelphia: Univ. of Pennsylvania Press, 1991.

3. Ibid.

4. "Sweden: A History," by Torsten Hendriksson, in *World Book Encyclopedia*. Chicago: World Books, 1978.

5. New York: Simon and Schuster, 1956.

6. *Ett drömspel* (Dream Play), quoted in *A History of Swedish Literature*, Ingemar Algulin. Stockholm: The Swedish Institute, 1989.

7. See "Modernism and Proletarian Realism" in *A History of Swedish Literature*, pp. 174–254.

8. Lund: Utbildingshuset Studentlitteratur, 1981.

9. Ibid., p. 9.

10. *Moments of Truth*. New York: Harper & Row, 1986, pp. 32–34.

11. See "Production Philosophy at Volvo," by Berth Jonsson, and "Volvo Components: From Sweatshop to Playground," by Jan Forslin, in *Sweden at the Edge*, pp. 78–144.

12. *The Competitive Advantage of Nations*. (New York Free Press, 1990), pp. 651–652.

13. "The Year of the Ideas: How BAHCO Turned Around," C. M. Hampden-Turner, in *Creating Corporate Culture*. Reading: Addison-Wesley, 1992, p. 132.

14. See "Lessons for American Managers" in *Sweden at the Edge*, pp. 297–301.

15. "French with a Swedish Accent" in *Creating Corporate Culture*.

16. See "Business and Union Leaders Respond" in *Sweden at the Edge*, p. 37.

17. "French with a Swedish Accent," p. 160.

18. "The Year of the Ideas: How BAHCO Turned Around," pp. 136–137.

19. "The Volvo Truck Company," by Lars Agren and Jan Forslin, in *Sweden at the Edge*, pp. 241–242.

20. "Volvo Components: From Sweatshop to Playground," pp. 121–143.

21. "French with a Swedish Accent," pp. 166–167.

22. Personal communication with Goran Carstedt.

23. "French with a Swedish Accent," p. 121.

24. Ibid., p. 76.

25. *Sweden at the Edge*, pp. 5–7.

26. *Cultures and Organisations*, Geert Hofstede. pp. 79–99. The term *feminine* is perhaps unfortunate, including as it does "stress on equality," "modesty," "negotiated resolution to conflict," "importance of people," and "men are allowed to be tender."

27. "Managing International Business: The Swedish Model" in *Sweden at the Edge*, pp. 201–220.

28. Ibid., pp. 213–215; see also "Action in Heterarchies: New Approaches to Managing the MNC" (with D. Rolander), in *Managing the Global Firm*, G. Hedlund, C. Bartlett, and Y. Doz, eds. London: Routledge, 1990.

29. *Many Dimensional Man*, New York: Oxford University Press, 1977.

30. "Managing International Business," p. 213.

31. Ibid., p. 209.

32. "Small Business in Sweden" in *Sweden at the Edge*, pp. 302–318.

32. Ibid.

CHAPTER 11   Self-Constructed Lands: The Dutch as God's Apprentices

1. *The Netherlands in Perspective*, William Z. Shetter. Leiden: Martinus Nijhoff, 1987, pp. 31–32.

2. *Of Dutch Ways*, Helen Colijn. New York: Harper & Row, 1984, pp. 40–41.

3. *Social and Cultural Report*. The Hague: Government Publishing Office, 1992; see also *The Netherlands in Perspective*, pp. 97–104.

4. A well-known Shell story.

5. *The Netherlands in Perspective*, p. 142.

6. Ibid., pp. 188–201.

7. *Managing Across Borders*, Christopher A. Bartlett and Sumantra Ghoshal. Boston: Harvard Business School Press, 1991, pp. 106–107.

8. Amsterdam: Becht, 1983, pp. 117–118; quoted in *The Netherlands in Perspective*, p. 124.

9. *Cultures and Organisations*, New York: McGraw-Hill, 1991, pp. 79–108.

10. *The Destruction of the Dutch Jews*. New York: Dutton, 1969; see also *The Netherlands in Perspective*, pp. 227–229.

11. *The Duality of Human Existence*, David Bakan. Boston: Beacon, 1967, p. 164.

12. *West European Party Systems*, H. Daalder and P. Mair. London: Sage, 1983.

13. *The Netherlands in Perspective*, op. cit. pp. 178–187.

14. Quoted in Ibid., p. 275.

15. Ibid., pp. 121–122.

16. Ibid., p. 282.

17. *The Competitive Advantage of Nations*, Michael E. Porter. (New York: Free Press, 1990), p. 671.

18. Boston: Beacon, 1970.

19. *The Netherlands in Perspective*, p. 263.

20. See "Scenarios: Uncharted Waters Ahead," Pierre Wack, in *Harvard Business Review*, September/October 1985.

21. March/April 1988.

22. *The Dutch Puzzle*, Duke de Baena. The Hague: Boucher, 1966, p. 8.

23. A Dutch business professor who years ago stressed the role of dilemma and paradox was Fritz Haselhoff; see *Ondernemingsstrategie, een dilemma: de moderne ondernemingsorganisatie in het spanningsveld van doelmatigheid, overleving en zingeving*. Alphen aan de Rijn: Samson, 1977.

24. Quoted in *The Netherlands in Perspective*, p. 271.

CHAPTER 12   Britannia Rules the Airwaves

1. For the inverse relationship between M.B.A.s and national economic performance, see *What Went Wrong*, D. L. Bartlett and James B. Steele. (Kansas City: Andrews and McMeel, 1992), p. 100.

2. *Gentlemen and Tradesmen*, Charles M. Hampden-Turner. London: Routledge and Kegan Paul, 1983, pp. 53–55.

3. Quoted in *The Times*, 9 December 1992.

4. *Gentlemen and Tradesmen*, p. 3.

5. Quoted in *The Rise of the Plutocrats*, Jamie Camplin (London: Constable, 1978) p. 46.

6. *The New Anatomy of Britain*, Anthony Sampson. London: Hodder and Stoughton, 1971.

7. See "Greed in the Boardroom," *Sunday Times*, 2 June 1991, Section 4, p. 3; see also "Scandal: Twelve Months That Rocked the City," Andrew Davidson, in *Sunday Times*, 29 December 1991.

8. Lester Thurow points out the mutual admiration society between the British and American business press during the Thatcher-Reagan era. The vast majority of "foreign" news in each country turned out to be about the other; see *Head to Head*, p. 29.

9. *Gentlemen and Tradesmen*, p. 37.

10. Quoted in *The Neophiliacs*, Christopher Booker (London: Fontana, 1970), p. 131.

11. New York: Basic Books/Harper Colophon, 1978, pp. xi–xxix.

12. *Too Few Producers*, Robert Bacon and Walter Eltis. London: Macmillan, 1978.

13. *The Times*, 7 November 1992, p. 2.

14. *The Rise and Fall of the British Manager*, Alistair Mant (London: Macmillan, 1971), p. 19.

15. *The Competitive Advantage of Nations*, New York: Free Press, 1990, p. 566.

16. Ibid., p. 565.

17. For a more rosy view of the Financial Control conglomerate company, see *Strategic Styles*, Michael Goold and Andrew Campbell (Oxford: Basil Blackwell, 1988).

18. "The Hanson File," Channel 4 Television, January 1991; see also "Time Up for Hanson?" *The Sunday Times*, 2 February 1992.

19. *Strategic Styles*.

20. "The Economic Possibilities for our Grandchildren," *Essays in Persuasion*. Cambridge Univ. Press, 1930.

21. *The Unprincipled Society: New Demands, Old Politics*. London: Fontana, 1986, pp. 225–226.

22. *The Rise and Decline of Nations*, Mancur Olson. New Haven: Yale Univ. Press, 1982.

23. "The UK's Manufacturing Performance Has Been Dismal," John Wells, in the *Independent*, 15 March 1992.

24. *The Unprincipled Society*, p. 243.

25. *Gentlemen and Tradesmen*, pp. 182–200.

26. New York: Vintage, 1964.

27. "Runaway World: Reith Lecture." London, BBC, 1968; see also *The Two Cultures* (Cambridge: Cambridge Univ. Press, 1961).

28. "Executive Career Patterns," in *Manufacturing and Management*, Michael Fores and Ian Glover, eds. London: HMSO, 1978.

29. *The Two Cultures*, p. 15.

30. The concept is from *The Pragmatics of Human Communication*, Paul Watzlawick, H. H. Beavin, and Don Jackson (New York: Norton, 1967).

31. *The Sunday Times*, 18 October 1992.

32. "Pandora's Box," BBC 2, 14 November 1992.

33. *Keynes' Economics and the Theory of Value and Distribution*, John Eatwell and Murray Milgate, eds. London: Macmillan, 1978; quoted in *Whatever Happened to Britain?* John Eatwell (London: BBC/Gerald Duckworth, 1982), p. 29.

34. "Pandora's Box."

CHAPTER 13　Crisis and Contradiction: Exceptional France

1. See *Management in France*, Jean Louis Barsoux and Peter Lawrence (London: Cassell, 1990); also "The Business Culture of France," Colin Gordon, in *Business Cultures of Europe*, Collin Randlesome, ed. pp. 58–106.

2. *General Industrial Management*. London: Pitman, 1949, p. 26; see also *Organisation Theory*, D. S. Pugh, ed. (London: Penguin Books, 1983), pp. 101–123.

3. *Suicide: A Study in Sociology*. Glencoe, NY: Free Press, 1951.

4. *The Bureaucratic Phenomenon*. Chicago: Univ. of Chicago Press, 1964.

5. *Durée et Simultanéité*. Paris: Alcan, 1922.

6. *Freedom and Coordination: Lectures in Business Organization*. New York: Garland, 1987, p. 32.

7. *The Phenomenology of Perception*. New York: Humanities Press, 1962.

8. Quoted in *Euroquake*, Daniel Burstein (New York: Simon & Schuster, 1991), p. 37.

9. Quoted in *In Search of France*, Stanley Hoffmann (Cambridge, Mass: Harvard Univ. Press, 1963), p. 231.

10. *General Industrial Management*, p. 20.

11. See *France*, Marshall Davidson. New York: American Heritage Publishing, 1971, p. 196

12. "France: Ideological Divisions and Global Reality," Janice McCormick, in *Ideology and National Competitiveness*, George C. Lodge and Ezra F. Vogel (Boston: Harvard Business School Press, 1981), pp. 58–60.

13. *Pascal's Pensees, or Thoughts on Religion*. Mount Vernon, N.Y.: Peter Pauper Press, 1946, p. 35; quoted by Rollo May in *Freedom and Destiny* (New York: Norton, 1981), p. 103.

14. *Harvard Business Review*, "The Making of a French Manager," July–August 1991, pp. 58–61.

15. *The Rebel*. New York: Vintage, 1956.

16. *Sain Genet*, John Paul Sartre (New York: George Braziller, 1963).

17. *No Exit and Three Other Plays*. New York: Vintage, 1955.

18. "Organizational Development and Change," *American Review of Psychology* 33 (1982), pp. 343–367.

19. See *L'anesthésie socials dans l'enterprise*, L. Loue. Paris: Payot, 1974.

20. *Actors and Systems*, Michel Crozier and E. Friedberg. Chicago: Univ. of Chicago Press, 1980.

21. "Organization Development and Change," p. 358.

22. "The Cultural Diversity of Western Conceptions of Management," *International Studies of Management and Organization* 13 (1–2) 1983, p. 83.

23. See "Managerial Views of Organization Structure in France and the U.S.A.," George Izzerelli and André Laurent, in *International Studies of Management and Organization* (San Francisco: Jossey-Bass, 1986), pp. 75–96.

24. See "Rebuilding Rome in France," Carl Gardner, in *The Independent*, 9 January 1991, p. 17.

25. "Cross-Cultural Management for Pan European Companies" in *Europe 1992 and Beyond*, Spyros Makridakis, ed. San Francisco: Jossey-Bass, 1990.

26. London: Macmillan, 1964.

27. "The Cross-Cultural Puzzle of International Human Resource Management" in *Human Resource Management* 25 (1) 1986, p. 95.

28. *The French*, Theodore Zeldin. London: William Collins, p. 390–392.

29. *Annual Report on International Competitiveness*, Geneva: IMD, 1990.

30. *Europe 1992 and Beyond*.

31. *Cultures of France and Germany*. New York: Intercultural Press, 1987, p. 148.

32. Ibid., p. 151.

33. Paris: Edition de Seuil, 1991.

34. "Jacques The Lad," Nigel Dudley, February 1991, pp. 20–28.

35. Ibid., p. 20–21.

36. Ibid., p. 22.

37. Ibid., p. 23.

38. "Cultural Diversity of Western Conceptions of Management," *International Studies of Mgt. and Organization*.

Index

PIATKUS BUSINESS BOOKS

Piatkus Business Books have been created for people who need expert knowledge readily available in a clear and easy-to-follow format. All the books are written by specialists in their field. They will help you improve your skills quickly and effortlessly in the workplace and on a personal level. Titles include:

General Management and Business Skills

Beware the Naked Man Who Offers You His Shirt Harvey Mackay

Be Your Own PR Expert: the complete guide to publicity and public relations Bill Penn

Brain Power: the 12-week mental training programme Marilyn vos Savant and Leonore Fleischer

Complete Conference Organiser's Handbook, The Robin O'Connor

Complete Time Management System, The Christian H Godefroy and John Clark

Confident Decision Making J Edward Russo and Paul J H Schoemaker

Creating Abundance Andrew Ferguson

Creative Thinking Michael LeBoeuf

Dealing with Difficult People Roberta Cava

Energy Factor, The: how to motivate your workforce Art McNeil

Firing On All Cylinders: the quality management system for high-powered corporate performance Jim Clemmer with Barry Sheehy

Great Boom Ahead, The Harry Dent

How to Implement Corporate Change John Spencer and Adrian Pruss

Influential Manager, The: how to develop a powerful management style Lee Bryce

Leadership Skills for Every Manager Jim Clemmer and Art McNeil

Lure the Tiger Out of the Mountains: timeless tactics from the East for today's successful manager Gao Yuan

Managing Your Team John Spencer and Adrian Pruss

Perfectly Legal Tax Loopholes Stephen Courtney

Play to Your Strengths Donald O Clifton and Paula Nelson

Problem Employees: how to improve their behaviour and their performance Peter Wylie and Mardy Grothe

Problem Solving Techniques That Really Work Malcolm Bird

Profit Through the Post: How to set up and run a successful mail order business Alison Cork

Quantum Learning: unleash the genius within you Bobbi DePorter with Mike Hernacki

Right Brain Manager, The: how to use the power of your mind to achieve personal and professional success Dr Harry Alder

Smart Questions for Successful Managers Dorothy Leeds

Strategy of Meetings, The George David Kieffer

Sales and Customer Services

Art of the Hard Sell, The Robert L Shook

Creating Customers David H Bangs

Guerrilla Marketing Excellence Jay Conrad Levinson

How to Close Every Sale Joe Girard

How to Collect the Money You Are Owed Malcolm Bird

How to Succeed in Network Marketing Len Hawkins

How to Win Customers and Keep Them for Life Michael LeBoeuf
Making Profits: a six-month plan for the small business Malcolm Bird
Sales Power: the Silva mind method for sales professionals José Silva and Ed
    Bernd Jr
Selling Edge, The Patrick Forsyth
Telephone Selling Techniques That Really Work Bill Good
Winning New Business: a practical guide to successful sales presentations Dr
    David Lewis

Presentation and Communication
Better Business Writing Maryann V Piotrowski
Complete Book of Business Etiquette, The Lynne Brennan and David Block
Confident Conversation Dr Lillian Glass
Confident Speaking: how to communicate effectively using the Power Talk System
    Christian H Godefroy and Stephanie Barrat
He Says, She Says: closing the communication gap between the sexes Dr Lillian
    Glass
Marketing Yourself: how to sell yourself and get the jobs you've always wanted
    Dorothy Leeds
Networking and Mentoring: a woman's guide Dr Lily M Segerman-Peck
Outstanding Negotiator, The Christian H Godefroy and Luis Robert
Personal Power Philippa Davies
Powerspeak: the complete guide to public speaking and presentation Dorothy
    Leeds
Presenting Yourself: a personal image guide for men Mary Spillane
Presenting Yourself: a personal image guide for women Mary Spillane
Say What You Mean and Get What You Want George R. Walther
Your Total Image Philippa Davies

For a free brochure with further information on our complete range of business
    titles, please write to:

Piatkus Books
Freepost 7 (WD 4505)
London W1E 4EZ

PIATKUS

Charles Hampden-Turner is permanent
visitor at the Cambridge University Judge
Institute of Management and visiting
professor at Erasmus University in the
Netherlands. **Fons Trompenaars** is
managing director of the Centre for
International Business Studies in the
Netherlands. They are well-known
international consultants on cross-cultural
management whose clients have included
Motorola, Apple Computer, Advanced
Micro Devices, Clorox, Analog Devices,
British Petroleum, TRW, Eastman Kodak
and Royal Dutch/Shell.